Democracy in America

Democracy
IN AMERICA

By *ALEXIS DE TOCQUEVILLE*

THE HENRY REEVE TEXT
AS REVISED BY FRANCIS BOWEN
NOW FURTHER CORRECTED AND EDITED
WITH A HISTORICAL ESSAY, EDITORIAL
NOTES, AND BIBLIOGRAPHIES BY
PHILLIPS BRADLEY

Volume II

VINTAGE BOOKS
A Division of Random House

NEW YORK

THE ATTENTION OF THE READER is called to the extensive historical essay by the editor which begins on page 389 of the present edition, and which discusses in detail Tocqueville and his work.

VINTAGE BOOKS

are published by ALFRED A. KNOPF, INC.

and RANDOM HOUSE, INC.

Distributed in Canada by Random House of Canada Limited, Toronto. Manufactured in the United States of America.

E98765432

Author's Preface

TO THE SECOND PART

THE AMERICANS have a democratic state of society, which has naturally suggested to them certain laws and certain political manners. It has also created in their minds many feelings and opinions which were unknown in the old aristocratic societies of Europe. It has destroyed or modified the old relations of men to one another and has established new ones. The aspect of civil society has been as much altered as the face of the political world.

I have treated of the former subject in the work which I published, five years ago, on American Democracy; the latter is the object of the present book. These two Parts complete each other and form but a single work.

But I must warn the reader immediately against an error that would be very prejudicial to me. Because I attribute so many different effects to the principle of equality, it might be inferred that I consider this principle as the only cause of everything that takes place in our day. This would be attributing to me a very narrow view of things.

A multitude of the opinions, sentiments, and instincts that belong to our times owe their origin to circumstances that have nothing to do with the principle of equality or are even hostile to it. Thus, taking the United States for example, I could easily prove that the nature of the country, the origin of its inhabitants, the religion of the early settlers, their acquired knowledge, their previous habits, have exercised, and still do exercise, independently of democracy, an immense influence upon their modes of thought and feeling. Other causes, equally independent of the principle of equality, would be found in Europe and would explain much of what is passing there.

I recognize the existence and the efficiency of all these various causes; but my subject does not lead me to speak of them. I have not undertaken to point out the origin and nature of all our inclinations and all our ideas; I have only endeavored to show how far both of them are affected by the equality of men's conditions.

As I am firmly convinced that the democratic revolution which we are now beholding is an irresistible fact, against which it would be neither desirable nor prudent to contend, some persons perhaps may be surprised that, in the course of this book, I have often applied language of strong censure to the democratic communities which this revolution has created. The simple reason is, that precisely because I was not an opponent of democracy I wished to speak of it with all sincerity. Men will not receive the truth from their enemies, and it is very seldom offered to them by their friends; on this very account I have frankly uttered it. I believed that many persons would take it upon themselves to inform men of the benefits which they might hope to receive from the establishment of equality, while very few would venture to point out from afar the dangers with which it would be attended. It is principally towards these dangers, therefore, that I directed my gaze; and, believing that I had clearly discerned what they are, it would have been cowardice to say nothing about them.

I hope the same impartiality will be found in this second work which people seemed to observe in its predecessor. Placed between the conflicting opinions that divide my countrymen, I have endeavored for the time to stifle in my own bosom the sympathy or the aversion that I felt for either. If the readers of my book find in it a single phrase intended to flatter either of the great parties that have agitated our country, or any one of the petty factions that in our day harass and weaken it, let them raise their voices and accuse me.

The subject that I wished to cover by my investigations is immense, for it includes most of the feelings and opinions produced by the new condition of the world's affairs. Such a subject certainly exceeds my strength, and in the treatment of it I have not been able to satisfy myself. But even if I could not attain the goal towards which I strove, my readers will at least do me this justice, that I conceived and pursued my enterprise in a spirit which could make me worthy of succeeding.

Contents of VOLUME II

First Book

INFLUENCE OF DEMOCRACY ON THE ACTION OF INTELLECT IN THE UNITED STATES

Second Book

INFLUENCE OF DEMOCRACY ON THE FEELINGS OF THE AMERICANS

Third Book

INFLUENCE OF DEMOCRACY ON MANNERS PROPERLY SO CALLED

Fourth Book

INFLUENCE OF DEMOCRATIC IDEAS AND FEELINGS ON POLITICAL SOCIETY

Democracy in America

SECOND PART

FIRST BOOK

INFLUENCE OF DEMOCRACY ON THE ACTION OF INTELLECT IN THE UNITED STATES

Chapter I

PHILOSOPHICAL METHOD OF THE AMERICANS

I THINK that in no country in the civilized world is less attention paid to philosophy than in the United States. The Americans have no philosophical school of their own, and they care but little for all the schools into which Europe is divided, the very names of which are scarcely known to them.

Yet it is easy to perceive that almost all the inhabitants of the United States use their minds in the same manner, and direct them according to the same rules; that is to say, without ever having taken the trouble to define the rules, they have a philosophical method common to the whole people.

To evade the bondage of system and habit, of family maxims, class opinions, and, in some degree, of national prejudices; to accept tradition only as a means of information, and existing facts only as a lesson to be used in doing otherwise and doing better; to seek the reason of things for oneself, and in oneself alone; to tend to results without being bound to means, and to strike through the form to the substance—such are the principal characteristics of what I shall call the philosophical method of the Americans.

But if I go further and seek among these characteristics the principal one, which includes almost all the rest, I discover that in most of the operations of the mind each American appeals only to the individual effort of his own understanding.

America is therefore one of the countries where the precepts of Descartes are least studied and are best applied. Nor is this surprising. The Americans do not read the works of Descartes, because their social condition deters them from speculative studies; but they follow his maxims, because this same social condition naturally disposes their minds to adopt them.

In the midst of the continual movement that agitates a democratic community, the tie that unites one generation to another is relaxed or broken; every man there readily loses all trace of the ideas of his forefathers or takes no care about them.

Men living in this state of society cannot derive their belief from the opinions of the class to which they belong; for, so to speak, there are no longer any classes, or those which still exist are composed of such mobile elements that the body can never exercise any real control over its members.

As to the influence which the intellect of one man may have on that of another, it must necessarily be very limited in a country where the citizens, placed on an equal footing, are all closely seen by one another; and where, as no signs of incontestable greatness or superiority are perceived in any one of them, they are constantly brought back to their own reason as the most obvious and proximate source of truth. It is not only confidence in this or that man which is destroyed, but the disposition to trust the authority of any man whatsoever. Everyone shuts himself up tightly within himself and insists upon judging the world from there.

The practice of Americans leads their minds to other habits, to fixing the standard of their judgment in themselves alone. As they perceive that they succeed in resolving without assistance all the little difficulties which their practical life presents, they readily conclude that everything in the world may be explained, and that nothing in it transcends the limits of the understanding. Thus they fall to denying what they cannot comprehend; which leaves them but little faith for whatever is extraordinary and an almost insurmountable distaste for whatever is supernatural. As it is on their own testimony that they are accustomed to rely, they like to discern the object which engages their attention with extreme clearness; they therefore strip off as much as possible all that covers it; they rid themselves of whatever separates them from it, they remove whatever conceals it from sight, in order to view it more closely and in the broad light of day. This disposition of mind soon leads them to condemn forms, which they regard as useless and inconvenient veils placed between them and the truth.

The Americans, then, have found no need of drawing philosophical method out of books; they have found it in themselves. The same thing may be remarked in what has taken place in Europe. This same method has only been established and made popular in Europe in proportion as the condition of society has become more equal and men have grown more like one another. Let us consider for a moment the connection of the periods in which this change may be traced.

In the sixteenth century reformers subjected some of the dogmas of the ancient faith to the scrutiny of private judgment; but they still withheld it from the discussion of all the rest. In the seventeenth century Bacon in the natural sciences and Descartes in philosophy properly so called abolished received formulas, destroyed the empire of tradition, and overthrew the authority of the schools. The philosophers of the eighteenth century, generalizing at length on the same principle, undertook to submit to the private judgment of each man all the objects of his belief.

Who does not perceive that Luther, Descartes, and Voltaire employed the same method, and that they differed only in the greater or less use which they professed should be made of it? Why did the reformers confine themselves so closely within the circle of religious ideas? Why did Descartes, choosing to apply his method only to certain matters, though he had made it fit to be applied to all, declare that men might judge for themselves in matters philosophical, but not in matters political? How did it happen that in the eighteenth century those general applications were all at once drawn from this same method, which Descartes and his predecessors either had not perceived or had rejected? To what, lastly, is the fact to be attributed that at this period the method we are speaking of suddenly emerged from the schools, to penetrate into society and become the common standard of intelligence; and that after it had become popular among the French, it was ostensibly adopted or secretly followed by all the nations of Europe?

The philosophical method here designated may have been born in the sixteenth century; it may have been more accurately defined and more extensively applied in the seventeenth; but neither in the one nor in the other could it be commonly adopted. Political laws, the condition of society, and the habits of mind that are derived from these causes were as yet opposed to it.

It was discovered at a time when men were beginning to equalize and assimilate their conditions. It could be generally followed only in ages when those conditions had at length become nearly equal and men nearly alike.

The philosophical method of the eighteenth century, then, is not only French, but democratic; and this explains why it was so readily admitted throughout Europe, where it has contributed so powerfully to change the face of society. It is not because the French have changed their former opinions and altered their former manners that they have convulsed the world, but because they were the first to generalize and bring to light a philosophical method by the aid of which it became easy to attack all that was old and to open a path to all that was new.

If it be asked why at the present day this same method is more rigorously followed and more frequently applied by the French than by the Americans, although the principle of equality is no less complete and of more ancient date among the latter people, the fact may be attributed to two circumstances, which it is first essential to have clearly understood.

It must never be forgotten that religion gave birth to Anglo-American society. In the United States, religion is therefore mingled with all the habits of the nation and all the feelings of patriotism, whence it derives a peculiar force. To this reason another of no less power may be added: in America religion has, as it were, laid down its own limits. Religious institutions have remained wholly distinct from political institutions, so that former laws have been easily changed while former belief has remained unshaken. Christianity has therefore retained a strong hold on the public mind in America; and I would more particularly remark that its sway is not only that of a philosophical doctrine which has been adopted upon inquiry, but of a religion which is believed without discussion. In the United States, Christian sects are infinitely diversified and perpetually modified; but Christianity itself is an established and irresistible fact, which no one undertakes either to attack or to defend. The Americans, having admitted the principal doctrines of the Christian religion without inquiry, are obliged to accept in like manner a great number of moral truths originating in it and connected with it. Hence the activity of individual analysis is restrained within narrow limits, and many of the most important of human opinions are removed from its influence.

The second circumstance to which I have alluded is that the social condition and the Constitution of the Americans are democratic, but they have not had a democratic revolution. They arrived on the soil they occupy in nearly the condition in which we see them at the present day; and this is of considerable importance.

There are no revolutions that do not shake existing belief, enervate authority, and throw doubts over commonly received ideas. Every revolution has more or less the effect of releasing men to their own conduct and of opening before the mind of each one of them an almost limitless perspective. When equality of conditions succeeds a protracted conflict between the different classes of which the elder society was composed, envy, hatred, and uncharitableness, pride and exaggerated self-confidence seize upon the human heart, and plant their sway in it for a time. This, independently of equality itself, tends powerfully to divide men, to lead them to mistrust the judgment of one another, and to seek the light of truth nowhere but in themselves. Everyone then attempts to be his own sufficient guide and makes it his boast to form his own opinions on all subjects. Men are no longer bound together by ideas, but by interests; and it would seem as if human opinions were reduced to a sort of intellectual dust, scattered on every side, unable to collect, unable to cohere.

Thus that independence of mind which equality supposes to exist is never so great, never appears so excessive, as at the time when equality is beginning to establish itself and in the course of that painful labor by which it is established. That sort of intellectual freedom which equality may give ought, therefore, to be very carefully distinguished from the anarchy which revolution brings. Each of these two things must be separately considered in order not to conceive exaggerated hopes or fears of the future.

I believe that the men who will live under the new forms of society will make frequent use of their private judgment, but I am far from thinking that they will often abuse it. This is attributable to a cause which is more generally applicable to democratic countries, and which, in the long run, must restrain, within fixed and sometimes narrow limits, individual freedom of thought.

I shall proceed to point out this cause in the next chapter.

Chapter II

OF THE PRINCIPAL SOURCE OF BELIEF AMONG DEMOCRATIC NATIONS

AT DIFFERENT periods dogmatic belief is more or less common. It arises in different ways, and it may change its object and its form; but under no circumstances will dogmatic belief cease to exist, or, in other words, men will never cease to entertain some opinions on trust and without discussion. If everyone undertook to form all his own opinions and to seek for truth by isolated paths struck out by himself alone, it would follow that no considerable number of men would ever unite in any common belief.

But obviously without such common belief no society can prosper; say, rather, no society can exist; for without ideas held in common there is no common action, and without common action there may still be men, but there is no social body. In order that society should exist and, *a fortiori,* that a society should prosper, it is necessary that the minds of all the citizens should be rallied and held together by certain predominant ideas; and this cannot be the case unless each of them sometimes draws his opinions from the common source and consents to accept certain matters of belief already formed.

If I now consider man in his isolated capacity, I find that dogmatic belief is not less indispensable to him in order to live alone than it is to enable him to co-operate with his fellows. If man were forced to demonstrate for himself all the truths of which he makes daily use, his task would never end. He would exhaust his strength in preparatory demonstrations without ever advancing beyond them. As, from the shortness of his lite, he has not the time, nor, from the limits of his intelligence, the capacity, to act in this way, he is reduced to take on trust a host of facts and opinions which he has not had either the time or the power to verify for himself, but which men of greater ability have found out, or which the crowd adopts. On this groundwork he raises for himself the structure of his own thoughts; he is not led to proceed in this manner by choice, but is constrained by the inflexible law of his condition. There is no philosopher in the world so great but that he believes a million things on the faith of other people and accepts a great many more truths than he demonstrates.

This is not only necessary but desirable. A man who should undertake to inquire into everything for himself could devote to each thing but little time and attention. His task would keep his mind in perpetual unrest, which would prevent him from penetrating to the depth of any truth or of making his mind adhere firmly to any conviction. His intellect would be at once independent and powerless. He must therefore make his choice from among the various objects of human belief and adopt many opinions without discussion in order to search the better into that smaller number which he sets apart for investigation. It is true that whoever receives an opinion on the word of another does so far enslave his mind, but it is a salutary servitude, which allows him to make a good use of freedom.

A principle of authority must then always occur, under all circumstances, in some part or other of the moral and intellectual world. Its place is variable, but a place it necessarily has. The independence of individual minds may be greater or it may be less; it cannot be unbounded. Thus the question is, not to know whether any intellectual authority exists in an age of democracy, but simply where it resides and by what standard it is to be measured.

I have shown in the preceeding chapter how equality of conditions leads men to entertain a sort of instinctive incredulity of the supernatural and a very lofty and often exaggerated opinion of human understanding. The men who live at a period of social equality are not therefore easily led to place that intellectual authority to which they bow either beyond or above humanity. They commonly seek for the sources of truth in themselves or in those who are like themselves. This would be enough to prove that at such periods no new religion could be established, and that all schemes for such a purpose would be not only impious, but absurd and irrational. It may be foreseen that a democratic people will not easily give credence to divine missions; that they will laugh at modern prophets; and that they will seek to discover the chief arbiter of their belief within, and not beyond, the limits of their kind.

When the ranks of society are unequal, and men unlike one another in condition, there are some individuals wielding the power of superior intelligence, learning, and enlightenment, while the multitude are sunk in ignorance and prejudice. Men living at these aristocratic periods are therefore naturally induced to shape their opinions by the standard of a superior person, or a superior class of persons, while they are averse to recognizing the infallibility of the mass of the people.

The contrary takes place in ages of equality. The nearer the people are drawn to the common level of an equal and similar condition, the less prone does each man become to place implicit faith in a certain man or a certain class of men. But his readiness to believe the multitude increases, and opinion is more than ever mistress of the world. Not only is common opinion the only guide which private judgment retains among a democratic people, but among such a people it possesses a power infinitely beyond what it has elsewhere. At periods of equality men have no faith in one another, by reason of their common resemblance; but this very resemblance gives them almost unbounded confidence in the judgment of the public; for it would seem probable that, as they are all endowed with equal means of judging, the greater truth should go with the greater number.

When the inhabitant of a democratic country compares himself individually with all those about him, he feels with pride that he is the equal of any one of them; but when he comes to survey the totality of his fellows and to place himself in contrast with so huge a body, he is instantly overwhelmed by the sense of his own insignificance and weakness. The same equality that renders him independent of each of his fellow citizens, taken severally, exposes him alone and unprotected to the influence of the greater number. The public, therefore, among a democratic people, has a singular power, which aristocratic nations cannot conceive; for it does not persuade others to its beliefs, but it imposes them and makes them permeate the thinking of everyone by a sort of enormous pressure of the mind of all upon the individual intelligence.

In the United States the majority undertakes to supply a

multitude of ready-made opinions for the use of individuals, who are thus relieved from the necessity of forming opinions of their own. Everybody there adopts great numbers of theories, on philosophy, morals, and politics, without inquiry, upon public trust; and if we examine it very closely, it will be perceived that religion itself holds sway there much less as a doctrine of revelation than as a commonly received opinion.

The fact that the political laws of the Americans are such that the majority rules the community with sovereign sway materially increases the power which that majority naturally exercises over the mind. For nothing is more customary in man than to recognize superior wisdom in the person of his oppressor. This political omnipotence of the majority in the United States doubtless augments the influence that public opinion would obtain without it over the minds of each member of the community; but the foundations of that influence do not rest upon it. They must be sought for in the principle of equality itself, not in the more or less popular institutions which men living under that condition may give themselves. The intellectual dominion of the greater number would probably be less absolute among a democratic people governed by a king than in the sphere of a pure democracy, but it will always be extremely absolute; and by whatever political laws men are governed in the ages of equality, it may be foreseen that faith in public opinion will become for them a species of religion, and the majority its ministering prophet.

Thus intellectual authority will be different, but it will not be diminished; and far from thinking that it will disappear, I augur that it may readily acquire too much preponderance and confine the action of private judgment within narrower limits than are suited to either the greatness or the happiness of the human race. In the principle of equality I very clearly discern two tendencies; one leading the mind of every man to untried thoughts, the other prohibiting him from thinking at all. And I perceive how, under the dominion of certain laws, democracy would extinguish that liberty of the mind to which a democratic social condition is favorable; so that, after having broken all the bondage once imposed on it by ranks or by men, the human mind would be closely fettered to the general will of the greatest number.

If the absolute power of a majority were to be substituted by democratic nations for all the different powers that checked or retarded overmuch the energy of individual minds, the evil would only have changed character. Men would not have found the means of independent life; they would simply have discovered (no easy task) a new physiognomy of servitude. There is, and I cannot repeat it too often, there is here matter for profound reflection to those who look on freedom of thought as a holy thing and who hate not only the despot, but despotism. For myself, when I feel the hand of power lie heavy on my brow, I care but little to know who oppresses me; and I am not the more disposed to pass beneath the yoke because it is held out to me by the arms of a million men.

Chapter III

WHY THE AMERICANS SHOW MORE APTITUDE AND TASTE FOR GENERAL IDEAS THAN THEIR FOREFATHERS, THE ENGLISH

THE DEITY does not regard the human race collectively. He surveys at one glance and severally all the beings of whom mankind is composed; and he discerns in each man the resemblances that assimilate him to all his fellows, and the differences that distinguish him from them. God, therefore, stands in no need of general ideas; that is to say, he never feels the necessity of collecting a considerable number of analogous objects under the same form for greater convenience in thinking.

Such, however, is not the case with man. If the human mind were to attempt to examine and pass a judgment on all the individual cases before it, the immensity of detail would soon lead it astray and it would no longer see anything. In this strait, man has recourse to an imperfect but necessary expedient, which at the same time assists and demonstrates his weakness.

Having superficially considered a certain number of objects and noticed their resemblance, he assigns to them a common name, sets them apart, and proceeds onwards.

General ideas are no proof of the strength, but rather of the insufficiency of the human intellect; for there are in nature no beings exactly alike, no things precisely identical, no rules indiscriminately and alike applicable to several objects at once. The chief merit of general ideas is that they enable the human mind to pass a rapid judgment on a great many objects at once; but, on the other hand, the notions they convey are never other than incomplete, and they always cause the mind to lose as much in accuracy as it gains in comprehensiveness.

As social bodies advance in civilization, they acquire the knowledge of new facts and they daily lay hold almost unconsciously of some particular truths. The more truths of this kind a man apprehends, the more general ideas he is naturally led to conceive. A multitude of particular facts cannot be seen separately without at last discovering the common tie that connects them. Several individuals lead to the notion of the species, several species to that of the genus. Hence the habit and the taste for general ideas will always be greatest among a people of ancient culture and extensive knowledge.

But there are other reasons which impel men to generalize their ideas or which restrain them from doing so.

The Americans are much more addicted to the use of general ideas than the English and entertain a much greater relish for them. This appears very singular at first, when it is remembered that the two nations have the same origin, that they lived for centuries under the same laws, and that they still incessantly interchange their opinions and their manners. This contrast becomes much more striking still if we fix our eyes on our own part of the world and compare together the two most enlightened nations that inhabit it. It would seem as if the mind of the English could tear itself only reluctantly and painfully away from the observation of particular facts, to rise from them to their causes, and that it only generalizes in spite of itself. Among the French, on the contrary, the taste for general ideas would seem to have grown to so ardent a passion that it must be satisfied on every occasion. I am informed every morning when I wake that some general and eternal law has just been discovered which I never heard mentioned before. There is not a mediocre scribbler who does not try his hand at discovering truths applicable to a great kingdom and who is not very ill pleased with himself if he does not succeed in compressing the human race into the compass of an article.

So great a dissimilarity between two very enlightened nations surprises me. If I again turn my attention to England and observe the events which have occurred there in the last half-century, I think I may affirm that a taste for general ideas increases in that country in proportion as its ancient constitution is weakened.

The state of civilization is therefore insufficient by itself to explain what suggests to the human mind the love of general ideas or diverts it from them.

When the conditions of men are very unequal and the inequalities are permanent, individual men gradually become so dissimilar that each class assumes the aspect of a distinct race. Only one of these classes is ever in view at the same instant; and, losing sight of that general tie which binds them all within the vast bosom of mankind, the observation invariably rests, not on man, but on certain men. Those who live in this aristocratic state of society never, therefore, conceive very general ideas respecting themselves; and that is enough to imbue them with a habitual distrust of such ideas and an instinctive aversion for them.

He, on the contrary, who inhabits a democratic country sees around him on every hand men differing but little from one another; he cannot turn his mind to any one portion of mankind without expanding and dilating his thought till it embraces the whole. All the truths that are applicable to himself appear to him equally and similarly applicable to each of his fellow citizens and fellow men. Having contracted the habit of generalizing his ideas in the study which engages him most and interests him most, he transfers the same habit to all his pursuits; and thus it is that the craving to discover general laws in everything, to include a great number of objects under the same formula, and to explain a mass of facts by a single cause becomes an ardent and sometimes an undiscerning passion in the human mind.

Nothing shows the truth of this proposition more clearly than the opinions of the ancients respecting their slaves. The most profound and capacious minds of Rome and Greece were never able to reach the idea, at once so general and so simple, of the common likeness of men and of the common birthright of each to freedom; they tried to prove that slavery was in the order of nature and that it would always exist. Nay, more, everything shows that those of the ancients who had been slaves before they became free, many of whom have left us excellent writings, themselves regarded servitude in no other light.

All the great writers of antiquity belonged to the aristocracy of masters, or at least they saw that aristocracy established and uncontested before their eyes. Their mind, after it had expanded itself in several directions, was barred from further progress in this one; and the advent of Jesus Christ upon earth was required to teach that all the members of the human race are by nature equal and alike.

In the ages of equality all men are independent of each other, isolated, and weak. The movements of the multitude are not permanently guided by the will of any individuals; at such times humanity seems always to advance of itself. In order, therefore, to explain what is passing in the world, man is driven to seek for some great causes, which, acting in the same manner on all our fellow creatures, thus induce them all voluntarily to pursue the same track. This again naturally leads the human mind to conceive general ideas and superinduces a taste for them.

I have already shown in what way the equality of conditions leads every man to investigate truth for himself. It may readily be perceived that a method of this kind must insensibly beget a tendency to general ideas in the human mind. When I repudiate the traditions of rank, professions, and birth, when I escape from the authority of example to seek out, by the single effort of my reason, the path to be followed, I am inclined to derive the motives of my opinions from human nature itself, and this leads me necessarily, and almost unconsciously, to adopt a great number of very general notions.

All that I have here said explains why the English display much less aptitude and taste for the generalization of ideas than their American progeny, and still less again than their neighbors the French; and likewise why the English of the present day display more than their forefathers did.

The English have long been a very enlightened and a very aristocratic nation; their enlightened condition urged them constantly to generalize, and their aristocratic habits confined them to the particular. Hence arose that philosophy, at once bold and timid, broad and narrow, which has hitherto prevailed in England and which still obstructs and stagnates so many minds in that country.

Independently of the causes I have pointed out in what goes before, others may be discerned less apparent, but no less efficacious, which produce among almost every democratic people a taste, and frequently a passion, for general ideas. A distinction must be made between ideas of this kind. Some of them are the result of slow, minute, and conscientious labor of the mind, and these extend the sphere of human knowledge; others spring up at once from the first rapid exercise of the wits and beget none but very superficial and uncertain notions.

Men who live in ages of equality have a great deal of curiosity and little leisure; their life is so practical, so confused, so excited, so active, that but little time remains to them for thought. Such men are prone to general ideas because they are thereby spared the trouble of studying particulars; they contain, if I may so speak, a great deal in a little compass, and give, in a little time, a great return. If, then, on a brief and inattentive investigation, they think they discern a common relation between certain objects, inquiry is not pushed any further; and without examining in detail how far these several objects agree or differ, they are hastily arranged under one formula, in order to pass to another subject.

One of the distinguishing characteristics of a democratic period is the taste that all men then have for easy success and present enjoyment. This occurs in the pursuits of the intellect as well as in all others. Most of those who live in a time of equality are full of an ambition equally alert and indolent: they want to obtain great success immediately, but they would prefer to avoid great effort. These conflicting tendencies lead straight to the search for general ideas, by the aid of which they flatter themselves that they can delineate vast objects with little pains and draw the attention of the public without much trouble.

And I do not know that they are wrong in thinking so. For their readers are as much averse to investigating anything to the bottom as they are; and what is generally sought in the productions of mind is easy pleasure and information without labor.

If aristocratic nations do not make sufficient use of general ideas, and frequently treat them with inconsiderate disdain, it is true, on the other hand, that a democratic people is always ready to carry ideas of this kind to excess and to espouse them with injudicious warmth.

Chapter IV

WHY THE AMERICANS HAVE NEVER BEEN SO EAGER AS THE FRENCH FOR GENERAL IDEAS IN POLITICAL AFFAIRS

I HAVE observed that the Americans show a less decided taste for general ideas than the French. This is especially true in politics.

Although the Americans infuse into their legislation far more general ideas than the English, and although they strive more than the latter to adjust the practice of affairs to theory, no political bodies in the United States have ever shown so much love for general ideas as the Constituent Assembly and the Convention in France. At no time has the American people laid hold on ideas of this kind with the passionate energy of the French people in the eighteenth century, or displayed the same blind confidence in the value and absolute truth of any theory.

This difference between the Americans and the French originates in several causes, but principally in the following one. The Americans are a democratic people who have always directed public affairs themselves. The French are a democratic people who for a long time could only speculate on the best manner of conducting them. The social condition of the French led them to conceive very general ideas on the subject of government, while their political constitution prevented them from correcting those ideas by experiment and from gradually detecting their insufficiency; whereas in America the two things constantly balance and correct each other.

It may seem at first sight that this is very much opposed to what I have said before, that democratic nations derive their love of theory from the very excitement of their active life. A more attentive examination will show that there is nothing contradictory in the proposition.

Men living in democratic countries eagerly lay hold of general ideas because they have but little leisure and because these ideas spare them the trouble of studying particulars. This is true, but it is only to be understood of those matters which are not the necessary and habitual subjects of their thoughts. Mercantile men will take up very eagerly, and without any close scrutiny, all the general ideas on philosophy, politics, science, or the arts which may be presented to them; but for such as relate to commerce, they will not receive them without inquiry or adopt them without reserve. The same thing applies to statesmen with regard to general ideas in politics.

If, then, there is a subject upon which a democratic people is peculiarly liable to abandon itself, blindly and extravagantly, to general ideas, the best corrective that can be used will be to make that subject a part of their daily practical occupation. They will then be compelled to enter into details, and the details will teach them the weak points of the theory. This remedy may frequently be a painful one, but its effect is certain.

Thus it happens that the democratic institutions which compel every citizen to take a practical part in the government moderate that excessive taste for general theories in politics which the principle of equality suggests.

Chapter V

HOW RELIGION IN THE UNITED STATES AVAILS ITSELF OF DEMOCRATIC TENDENCIES

I HAVE shown in a preceding chapter that men cannot do without dogmatic belief, and even that it is much to be desired that such belief should exist among them. I now add that, of all the kinds of dogmatic belief, the most desirable appears to me to be dogmatic belief in matters of religion; and this is a clear inference, even from no higher consideration than the interests of this world.

There is hardly any human action, however particular it may be, that does not originate in some very general idea men have conceived of the Deity, of his relation to mankind, of the nature of their own souls, and of their duties to their fellow creatures. Nor can anything prevent these ideas from being the common spring from which all the rest emanates.

Men are therefore immeasurably interested in acquiring fixed ideas of God, of the soul, and of their general duties to their Creator and their fellow men; for doubt on these first principles would abandon all their actions to chance and would condemn them in some way to disorder and impotence.

This, then, is the subject on which it is most important for each of us to have fixed ideas; and unhappily it is also the subject on which it is most difficult for each of us, left to himself, to settle his opinions by the sole force of his reason. None but minds singularly free from the ordinary cares of life, minds at once penetrating, subtle, and trained by thinking, can, even with much time and care, sound the depths of these truths that are so necessary. And, indeed, we see that philosophers are themselves almost always surrounded with uncertainties; that at every step the natural light which illuminates their path grows dimmer and less secure; and that, in spite of all their efforts, they have discovered as yet only a few conflicting notions, on which the mind of man has been tossed about for thousands of years without ever firmly grasping the truth or finding novelty even in its errors. Studies of this nature are far above the average capacity of men; and, even if the majority of mankind were capable of such pursuits, it is evident that leisure to cultivate them would still be wanting.

Fixed ideas about God and human nature are indispensable to the daily practice of men's lives; but the practice of their lives prevents them from acquiring such ideas.

The difficulty appears to be without a parallel. Among the sciences there are some that are useful to the mass of mankind and are within its reach; others can be approached only by the few and are not cultivated by the many, who require nothing beyond their more remote applications: but the daily practice of the science I speak of is indispensable to all, although the study of it is inaccessible to the greater number.

General ideas respecting God and human nature are therefore the ideas above all others which it is most suitable to withdraw from the habitual action of private judgment and in which there is most to gain and least to lose by recognizing a principle of authority.

The first object and one of the principal advantages of religion is to furnish to each of these fundamental questions a solution that is at once clear, precise, intelligible, and lasting, to the mass of mankind. There are religions that are false and very absurd, but it may be affirmed that any religion which remains within the circle I have just traced, without pretending to go beyond it (as many religions have attempted to do, for the purpose of restraining on every side the free movement of the human mind), imposes a salutary restraint on the intellect; and it must be admitted that, if it does not save men in another world, it is at least very conducive to their happiness and their greatness in this.

This is especially true of men living in free countries. When the religion of a people is destroyed, doubt gets hold of the higher powers of the intellect and half paralyzes all the others. Every man accustoms himself to having only confused and changing notions on the subjects most interesting to his fellow creatures and himself. His opinions are ill-defended and easily abandoned; and, in despair of ever solving by himself the hard problems respecting the destiny of man, he ignobly submits to think no more about them.

Such a condition cannot but enervate the soul, relax the springs of the will, and prepare a people for servitude. Not only does it happen in such a case that they allow their freedom to be taken from them; they frequently surrender it themselves. When there is no longer any principle of authority in religion any more than in politics, men are speedily frightened at the aspect of this unbounded independence. The constant agitation of all surrounding things alarms and exhausts them. As everything is at sea in the sphere of the mind, they determine at least that the mechanism of society shall be firm and fixed; and as they cannot resume their ancient belief, they assume a master.

For my own part, I doubt whether man can ever support at the same time complete religious independence and entire political freedom. And I am inclined to think that if faith be wanting in him, he must be subject; and if he be free, he must believe.

Perhaps, however, this great utility of religions is still more obvious among nations where equality of conditions prevails than among others. It must be acknowledged that equality, which brings great benefits into the world, nevertheless suggests to men (as will be shown hereafter) some very dangerous propensities. It tends to isolate them from one another, to concentrate every man's attention upon himself; and it lays open the soul to an inordinate love of material gratification.

The greatest advantage of religion is to inspire diametrically contrary principles. There is no religion that does not place the object of man's desires above and beyond the treasures of earth and that does not naturally raise his soul to regions far above those of the senses. Nor is there any which does not impose on man some duties towards his kind and thus draw him at times from the contemplation of himself. This is found in the most false and dangerous religions.

Religious nations are therefore naturally strong on the very point on which democratic nations are weak; this shows of what importance it is for men to preserve their religion as their conditions become more equal.

I have neither the right nor the intention of examining the supernatural means that God employs to infuse religious belief into the heart of man. I am at this moment considering religions in a purely human point of view; my object is to inquire by what means they may most easily retain their sway in the democratic ages upon which we are entering.

It has been shown that at times of general culture and equality the human mind consents only with reluctance to adopt dogmatic opinions and feels their necessity acutely only in spiritual matters. This proves, in the first place, that at such times religions ought more cautiously than at any other to confine themselves within their own precincts; for in seeking to extend their power beyond religious matters, they incur a risk of not being believed at all. The circle within which they seek to restrict the human intellect ought therefore to be carefully traced, and beyond its verge the mind should be left entirely free to its own guidance.

Mohammed professed to derive from Heaven, and has inserted in the Koran, not only religious doctrines, but political maxims, civil and criminal laws, and theories of science. The Gospel, on the contrary, speaks only of the general relations of men to God and to each other, beyond which it inculcates and imposes no point of faith. This alone, besides a thousand other reasons, would suffice to prove that the former of these religions will never long predominate in a cultivated and democratic age, while the latter is destined to retain its sway at these as at all other periods.

In continuation of this same inquiry I find that for religions to maintain their authority, humanly speaking, in democratic ages, not only must they confine themselves strictly within the circle of spiritual matters, but their power also will depend very much on the nature of the belief they inculcate, on the external forms they assume, and on the obligations they impose.

The preceding observation, that equality leads men to very general and very vast ideas, is principally to be understood in respect to religion. Men who are similar and equal in the world readily conceive the idea of the one God, governing every man by the same laws and granting to every man future happiness on the same conditions. The idea of the unity of mankind constantly leads them back to the idea of the unity of the Creator; while on the contrary in a state of society where men are broken up into very unequal ranks, they are apt to devise as many deities as there are nations, castes, classes, or families, and to trace a thousand private roads to heaven.

It cannot be denied that Christianity itself has felt, to some extent, the influence that social and political conditions exercise on religious opinions.

When the Christian religion first appeared upon earth, Providence, by whom the world was doubtless prepared for its coming, had gathered a large portion of the human race, like an immense flock, under the scepter of the Cæsars. The men of whom this multitude was composed were distinguished by numerous differences, but they had this much in common: that they all obeyed the same laws, and that every subject was so weak and insignificant in respect to the Emperor that all appeared equal when their condition was contrasted with his. This novel and peculiar state of mankind necessarily predisposed men to listen to the general truths that Christianity teaches, and may serve to explain the facility and rapidity with which they then penetrated into the human mind.

The counterpart of this state of things was exhibited after the destruction of the Empire. The Roman world being then, as it were, shattered into a thousand fragments, each nation resumed its former individuality. A scale of ranks soon grew up in the bosom of these nations; the different races were more sharply defined, and each nation was divided by castes into several peoples. In the midst of this common effort, which seemed to be dividing human society into as many fragments as possible, Christianity did not lose sight of the leading general ideas that it had brought into the world. But it appeared, nevertheless, to lend itself as much as possible to the new tendencies created by this distribution of mankind into fractions. Men continue to worship one God, the Creator and Preserver of all things; but every people, every city, and, so to speak, every man thought to obtain some distinct privilege and win the favor of an especial protector near the throne of grace. Unable to subdivide the Deity, they multiplied and unduly enhanced the importance of his agents. The homage due to saints and angels became an almost idolatrous worship for most Christians; and it might be feared for a moment that the religion of Christ would retrograde towards the superstitions which it had overcome.

It seems evident that the more the barriers are removed

which separate one nation from another and one citizen from another, the stronger is the bent of the human mind, as if by its own impulse, towards the idea of a single and all-powerful Being, dispensing equal laws in the same manner to every man. In democratic ages, then, it is particularly important not to allow the homage paid to secondary agents to be confused with the worship due to the Creator alone.

Another truth is no less clear, that religions ought to have fewer external observances in democratic periods than at any others.

In speaking of philosophical method among the Americans I have shown that nothing is more repugnant to the human mind in an age of equality than the idea of subjection to forms. Men living at such times are impatient of figures; to their eyes, symbols appear to be puerile artifices used to conceal or to set off truths that should more naturally be bared to the light of day; they are unmoved by ceremonial observances and are disposed to attach only a secondary importance to the details of public worship.

Those who have to regulate the external forms of religion in a democratic age should pay a close attention to these natural propensities of the human mind in order not to run counter to them unnecessarily.

I firmly believe in the necessity of forms, which fix the human mind in the contemplation of abstract truths and aid it in embracing them warmly and holding them with firmness. Nor do I suppose that it is possible to maintain a religion without external observances; but, on the other hand, I am persuaded that in the ages upon which we are entering it would be peculiarly dangerous to multiply them beyond measure, and that they ought rather to be limited to as much as is absolutely necessary to perpetuate the doctrine itself, which is the substance of religion, of which the ritual is only the form.[1] A religion which became more insistent in details, more inflexible, and more burdened with small observances during the time that men became more equal would soon find itself limited to a band of fanatic zealots in the midst of a skeptical multitude.

[1] In all religions there are some ceremonies that are inherent in the substance of the faith itself, and in these nothing should on any account be changed. This is especially the case with Roman Catholicism, in which the doctrine and the form are frequently so closely united as to form but one point of belief.

I anticipate the objection that, as all religions have general and eternal truths for their object, they cannot thus shape themselves to the shifting inclinations of every age without forfeiting their claim to certainty in the eyes of mankind. To this I reply again that the principal opinions which constitute a creed, and which theologians call articles of faith, must be very carefully distinguished from the accessories connected with them. Religions are obliged to hold fast to the former, whatever be the peculiar spirit of the age; but they should take good care not to bind themselves in the same manner to the latter at a time when everything is in transition and when the mind, accustomed to the moving pageant of human affairs, reluctantly allows itself to be fixed on any point. The permanence of external and secondary things seems to me to have a chance of enduring only when civil society is itself static; under any other circumstances I am inclined to regard it as dangerous.

We shall see that of all the passions which originate in or are fostered by equality, there is one which it renders peculiarly intense, and which it also infuses into the heart of every man; I mean the love of well-being. The taste for well-being is the prominent and indelible feature of democratic times.

It may be believed that a religion which should undertake to destroy so deep-seated a passion would in the end be destroyed by it; and if it attempted to wean men entirely from the contemplation of the good things of this world in order to devote their faculties exclusively to the thought of another, it may be foreseen that the minds of men would at length escape its grasp, to plunge into the exclusive enjoyment of present and material pleasures.

The chief concern of religion is to purify, to regulate, and to restrain the excessive and exclusive taste for well-being that men feel in periods of equality; but it would be an error to attempt to overcome it completely or to eradicate it. Men cannot be cured of the love of riches, but they may be persuaded to enrich themselves by none but honest means.

This brings me to a final consideration, which comprises, as it were, all the others. The more the conditions of men are equalized and assimilated to each other, the more important is it for religion, while it carefully abstains from the daily turmoil of secular affairs, not needlessly to run counter to the ideas that generally prevail or to the permanent interests that exist in the mass of the people. For as public opinion grows to be more and more the first and most irresistible of existing powers, the religious principle has no external support strong enough to enable it long to resist its attacks. This is not less true of a democratic people ruled by a despot than of a republic. In ages of equality kings may often command obedience, but the majority always commands belief; to the majority, therefore, deference is to be paid in whatever is not contrary to the faith.

I showed in the first Part of this work how the American clergy stand aloof from secular affairs. This is the most obvious but not the only example of their self-restraint. In America religion is a distinct sphere, in which the priest is sovereign, but out of which he takes care never to go. Within its limits he is master of the mind; beyond them he leaves men to themselves and surrenders them to the independence and instability that belong to their nature and their age. I have seen no country in which Christianity is clothed with fewer forms, figures, and observances than in the United States, or where it presents more distinct, simple, and general notions to the mind. Although the Christians of America are divided into a multitude of sects, they all look upon their religion in the same light. This applies to Roman Catholicism as well as to the other forms of belief. There are no Roman Catholic priests who show less taste for the minute individual observances, for extraordinary or peculiar means of salvation, or who cling more to the spirit and less to the letter of the law than the Roman Catholic priests of the United States. Nowhere is that doctrine of the church which prohibits the worship reserved to God alone from being offered to the saints more clearly inculcated or more generally followed. Yet the Roman Catholics of America are very submissive and very sincere.

Another remark is applicable to the clergy of every communion. The American ministers of the Gospel do not attempt to draw or to fix all the thoughts of man upon the life to come; they are willing to surrender a portion of his heart to the cares of the present, seeming to consider the goods of this world as important, though secondary, objects. If they take no part themselves in productive labor, they are at least interested in its progress and they applaud its results;

and while they never cease to point to the other world as the great object of the hopes and fears of the believer, they do not forbid him honestly to court prosperity in this. Far from attempting to show that these things are distinct and contrary to one another, they study rather to find out on what point they are most nearly and closely connected.

All the American clergy know and respect the intellectual supremacy exercised by the majority; they never sustain any but necessary conflicts with it. They take no share in the altercations of parties, but they readily adopt the general opinions of their country and their age, and they allow themselves to be borne away without opposition in the current of feeling and opinion by which everything around them is carried along. They endeavor to amend their contemporaries, but they do not quit fellowship with them. Public opinion is therefore never hostile to them; it rather supports and protects them, and their belief owes its authority at the same time to the strength which is its own and to that which it borrows from the opinions of the majority.

Thus it is that by respecting all democratic tendencies not absolutely contrary to herself and by making use of several of them for her own purposes, religion sustains a successful struggle with that spirit of individual independence which is her most dangerous opponent.

Chapter VI

THE PROGRESS OF ROMAN CATHOLICISM IN THE UNITED STATES

AMERICA is the most democratic country in the world, and it is at the same time (according to reports worthy of belief) the country in which the Roman Catholic religion makes most progress. At first sight this is surprising.

Two things must here be accurately distinguished: quality makes men want to form their own opinions; but, on the other hand, it imbues them with the taste and the idea of unity, simplicity, and impartiality in the power that governs society. Men living in democratic times are therefore very prone to shake off all religious authority; but if they consent to subject themselves to any authority of this kind, they choose at least that it should be single and uniform. Religious powers not radiating from a common center are naturally repugnant to their minds; and they almost as readily conceive that there should be no religion as that there should be several.

At the present time, more than in any preceding age, Roman Catholics are seen to lapse into infidelity, and Protestants to be converted to Roman Catholicism. If you consider Catholicism within its own organization, it seems to be losing; if you consider it from outside, it seems to be gaining. Nor is this difficult to explain. The men of our days are naturally little disposed to believe; but as soon as they have any religion, they immediately find in themselves a latent instinct that urges them unconsciously towards Catholicism. Many of the doctrines and practices of the Roman Catholic Church astonish them, but they feel a secret admiration for its discipline, and its great unity attracts them. If Catholicism could at length withdraw itself from the political animosities to which it has given rise, I have hardly any doubt but that the same spirit of the age which appears to be so opposed to it would become so favorable as to admit of its great and sudden advancement.

One of the most ordinary weaknesses of the human intellect is to seek to reconcile contrary principles and to purchase peace at the expense of logic. Thus there have ever been and will ever be men who, after having submitted some portion of their religious belief to the principle of authority, will seek to exempt several other parts of their faith from it and to keep their minds floating at random between liberty and obedience. But I am inclined to believe that the number of these thinkers will be less in democratic than in other ages, and that our posterity will tend more and more to a division into only two parts, some relinquishing Christianity entirely and others returning to the Church of Rome.

Chapter VII

WHAT CAUSES DEMOCRATIC NATIONS TO INCLINE TOWARDS PANTHEISM

I SHALL show hereafter how the preponderant taste of a democratic people for very general ideas manifests itself in politics, but I wish to point out at present its principal effect on philosophy.

It cannot be denied that pantheism has made great progress in our age. The writings of a part of Europe bear visible marks of it: the Germans introduce it into philosophy, and the French into literature. Most of the works of imagination published in France contain some opinions or some tinge caught from pantheistic doctrines or they disclose some tendency to such doctrines in their authors. This appears to me not to proceed only from an accidental, but from a permanent cause.

When the conditions of society are becoming more equal and each individual man becomes more like all the rest, more weak and insignificant, a habit grows up of ceasing to notice the citizens and considering only the people, of overlooking individuals to think only of their kind. At such times the human mind seeks to embrace a multitude of different objects at once, and it constantly strives to connect a variety of consequences with a single cause. The idea of unity so possesses man and is sought by him so generally that if he thinks he has found it, he readily yields himself to repose in that belief. Not content with the discovery that there is nothing in the world but a creation and a Creator, he is still embarrassed by this primary division of things and seeks to expand and simplify his conception by including God and the universe in one great whole.

If there is a philosophical system which teaches that all things material and immaterial, visible and invisible, which the world contains are to be considered only as the several parts of an immense Being, who alone remains eternal amidst the continual change and ceaseless transformation of all that constitutes him, we may readily infer that such a system, although it destroy the individuality of man, or rather because it destroys that individuality, will have secret charms for men living in democracies. All their habits of thought prepare them to conceive it and predispose them to adopt it. It naturally attracts and fixes their imagination; it fosters the pride while it soothes the indolence of their minds.

Among the different systems by whose aid philosophy endeavors to explain the universe I believe pantheism to be one of those most fitted to seduce the human mind in democratic times. Against it all who abide in their attachment to the true greatness of man should combine and struggle.

Chapter VIII

HOW EQUALITY SUGGESTS TO THE AMERICANS THE IDEA OF THE INDEFINITE PERFECTIBILITY OF MAN

EQUALITY suggests to the human mind several ideas that would not have originated from any other source, and it modifies almost all those previously entertained. I take as an example the idea of human perfectibility, because it is one of the principal notions that the intellect can conceive and because it constitutes of itself a great philosophical theory, which is everywhere to be traced by its consequences in the conduct of human affairs.

Although man has many points of resemblance with the brutes, one trait is peculiar to himself: he improves; they are incapable of improvement. Mankind could not fail to discover this difference from the beginning. The idea of perfectibility is therefore as old as the world; equality did not give birth to it, but has imparted to it a new character.

When the citizens of a community are classed according to rank, profession, or birth and when all men are forced to follow the career which chance has opened before them, everyone thinks that the utmost limits of human power are to be discerned in proximity to himself, and no one seeks any longer to resist the inevitable law of his destiny. Not, indeed, that an aristocratic people absolutely deny man's faculty of self-improvement, but they do not hold it to be indefinite; they can conceive amelioration, but not change: they imagine that the future condition of society may be better, but not essentially different; and, while they admit that humanity has made progress and may still have some to make, they assign to it beforehand certain impassable limits.

Thus they do not presume that they have arrived at the supreme good or at absolute truth (what people or what man was ever wild enough to imagine it?), but they cherish an opinion that they have pretty nearly reached that degree of greatness and knowledge which our imperfect nature admits of; and as nothing moves about them, they are willing to fancy that everything is in its fit place. Then it is that the legislator affects to lay down eternal laws; that kings and nations will raise none but imperishable monuments; and that the present generation undertakes to spare generations to come the care of regulating their destinies.

In proportion as castes disappear and the classes of society draw together, as manners, customs, and laws vary, because of the tumultuous intercourse of men, as new facts arise, as new truths are brought to light, as ancient opinions are dissipated and others take their place, the image of an ideal but always fugitive perfection presents itself to the human mind. Continual changes are then every instant occurring under the observation of every man; the position of some is rendered worse, and he learns but too well that no people and no individual, however enlightened they may be, can lay claim to infallibility; the condition of others is improved, whence he infers that man is endowed with an indefinite faculty for improvement. His reverses teach him that none have discovered absolute good; his success stimulates him to the never ending pursuit of it. Thus, forever seeking, forever falling to rise again, often disappointed, but not discouraged, he tends unceasingly towards that unmeasured greatness so indistinctly visible at the end of the long track which humanity has yet to tread.

It can hardly be believed how many facts naturally flow from the philosophical theory of the indefinite perfectibility of man or how strong an influence it exercises even on those who, living entirely for the purposes of action and not of thought, seem to conform their actions to it without knowing anything about it.

I accost an American sailor and inquire why the ships of his country are built so as to last for only a short time; he answers without hesitation that the art of navigation is every day making such rapid progress that the finest vessel would become almost useless if it lasted beyond a few years. In these words, which fell accidentally, and on a particular subject, from an uninstructed man, I recognize the general and systematic idea upon which a great people direct all their concerns.

Aristocratic nations are naturally too liable to narrow the scope of human perfectibility; democratic nations, to expand it beyond reason.

Chapter IX

THE EXAMPLE OF THE AMERICANS DOES NOT PROVE THAT A DEMOCRATIC PEOPLE CAN HAVE NO APTITUDE AND NO TASTE FOR SCIENCE, LITERATURE, OR ART

IT MUST be acknowledged that in few of the civilized nations of our time have the higher sciences made less progress than in the United States; and in few have great artists, distinguished poets, or celebrated writers been more rare. Many Europeans, struck by this fact, have looked upon it as a natural and inevitable result of equality; and they have thought that if a democratic state of society and democratic institutions were ever to prevail over the whole earth, the human mind would gradually find its beacon lights grow dim, and men would relapse into a period of darkness.

To reason thus is, I think, to confound several ideas that it is important to divide and examine separately; it is to mingle, unintentionally, what is democratic with what is only American.

The religion professed by the first immigrants and bequeathed by them to their descendants, simple in its forms, austere and almost harsh in its principles, and hostile to external symbols and to ceremonial pomp, is naturally unfavorable to the fine arts and yields only reluctantly to the pleasures of literature. The Americans are a very old and a very enlightened people, who have fallen upon a new and unbounded country, where they may extend themselves at pleasure and which they may fertilize without difficulty. This state of things is without a parallel in the history of the world. In America everyone finds facilities unknown elsewhere for making or increasing his fortune. The spirit of gain is always eager, and the human mind, constantly diverted from the pleasures of imagination and the labors of the intellect, is there swayed by no impulse but the pursuit of wealth. Not only are manufacturing and commercial classes to be found in the United States, as they are in all other countries, but, what never occurred elsewhere, the whole community is simultaneously engaged in productive industry and commerce.

I am convinced, however, that if the Americans had been alone in the world, with the freedom and the knowledge acquired by their forefathers and the passions which are their own, they would not have been slow to discover that progress cannot long be made in the application of the sciences without cultivating the theory of them; that all the arts are perfected by one another: and, however absorbed they might have been by the pursuit of the principal object of their desires, they would speedily have admitted that it is necessary to turn aside from it occasionally in order the better to attain it in the end.

The taste for the pleasures of mind, moreover, is so natural to the heart of civilized man that among the highly civilized nations, which are least disposed to give themselves up to these pursuits, a certain number of persons is always to be found who take part in them. This intellectual craving, once felt, would very soon have been satisfied.

But at the very time when the Americans were naturally inclined to require nothing of science but its special applications to the useful arts and the means of rendering life comfortable, learned and literary Europe was engaged in exploring the common sources of truth and in improving at the same time all that can minister to the pleasures or satisfy the wants of man.

At the head of the enlightened nations of the Old World the inhabitants of the United States more particularly identified one to which they were closely united by a common origin and by kindred habits. Among this people they found distinguished men of science, able artists, writers of eminence; and they were enabled to enjoy the treasures of the intellect without laboring to amass them. In spite of the ocean that intervenes, I cannot consent to separate America from Europe. I consider the people of the United States as that portion of the English people who are commissioned to explore the forests of the New World, while the rest of the nation, enjoying more leisure and less harassed by the drudgery of life, may devote their energies to thought and enlarge in all directions the empire of mind.

The position of the Americans is therefore quite exceptional, and it may be believed that no democratic people will ever be placed in a similar one. Their strictly Puritanical origin, their exclusively commercial habits, even the country they inhabit, which seems to divert their minds from the pursuit of science, literature, and the arts, the proximity of Europe, which allows them to neglect these pursuits without relapsing into barbarism, a thousand special causes, of which I have only been able to point out the most important, have singularly concurred to fix the mind of the American upon purely practical objects. His passions, his wants, his education, and everything about him seem to unite in drawing the native of the United States earthward; his religion alone bids him turn, from time to time, a transient and distracted glance to heaven. Let us cease, then, to view all democratic nations under the example of the American people, and attempt to survey them at length with their own features.

It is possible to conceive a people not subdivided into any castes or scale of ranks, among whom the law, recognizing no privileges, should divide inherited property into equal shares, but which at the same time should be without knowledge and without freedom. Nor is this an empty hypothesis: a despot may find that it is his interest to render his subjects equal and to leave them ignorant, in order more easily to keep them slaves. Not only would a democratic people of this kind show neither aptitude nor taste for science, literature, or art, but it would probably never arrive at the possession of them. The law of descent would of itself provide for the destruction of large fortunes at each succeeding generation, and no new fortunes would be acquired. The poor man, without either knowledge or freedom, would not so much as conceive the idea of raising himself to wealth; and the rich man would allow himself to be degraded to poverty, without a notion of self-defense. Between these two members of the community complete and invincible equality would soon be established. No one would then have time or taste to devote himself to the pursuits or pleasures of the intellect, but all men would remain paralyzed in a state of common ignorance and equal servitude.

When I conceive a democratic society of this kind, I

fancy myself in one of those low, close, and gloomy abodes where the light which breaks in from without soon faints and fades away. A sudden heaviness overpowers me, and I grope through the surrounding darkness to find an opening that will restore me to the air and the light of day. But all this is not applicable to men already enlightened who retain their freedom after having abolished those peculiar and hereditary rights which perpetuated the tenure of property in the hands of certain individuals or certain classes.

When men living in a democratic state of society are enlightened, they readily discover that they are not confined and fixed by any limits which force them to accept their present fortune. They all, therefore, conceive the idea of increasing it. If they are free, they all attempt it, but all do not succeed in the same manner. The legislature, it is true, no longer grants privileges, but nature grants them. As natural inequality is very great, fortunes become unequal as soon as every man exerts all his faculties to get rich.

The law of descent prevents the establishment of wealthy families, but it does not prevent the existence of wealthy individuals. It constantly brings back the members of the community to a common level, from which they as constantly escape; and the inequality of fortunes augments in proportion as their knowledge is diffused and their liberty increased.

A sect which arose in our time and was celebrated for its talents and its extravagance proposed to concentrate all property in the hands of a central power, whose function it should afterwards be to parcel it out to individuals according to their merits. This would have been a method of escaping from that complete and eternal equality which seems to threaten democratic society. But it would be a simpler and less dangerous remedy to grant no privilege to any, giving to all equal cultivation and equal independence and leaving everyone to determine his own position. Natural inequality will soon make way for itself, and wealth will spontaneously pass into the hands of the most capable.

Free and democratic communities, then, will always contain a multitude of people enjoying opulence or a competency. The wealthy will not be so closely linked to one another as the members of the former aristocratic class of society; their inclinations will be different, and they will scarcely ever enjoy leisure as secure or complete; but they will be far more numerous than those who belonged to that class of society could ever be. These persons will not be strictly confined to the cares of practical life, and they will still be able, though in different degrees, to indulge in the pursuits and pleasures of the intellect. In those pleasures they will indulge, for if it is true that the human mind leans on one side to the limited, the material, and the useful, it naturally rises on the other to the infinite, the spiritual, and the beautiful. Physical wants confine it to the earth, but as soon as the tie is loosened, it will rise of itself.

Not only will the number of those who can take an interest in the productions of mind be greater, but the taste for intellectual enjoyment will descend step by step even to those who in aristocratic societies seem to have neither time nor ability to indulge in them. When hereditary wealth, the privileges of rank, and the prerogatives of birth have ceased to be and when every man derives his strength from himself alone, it becomes evident that the chief cause of disparity between the fortunes of men is the mind. Whatever tends to invigorate, to extend, or to adorn the mind rises instantly to a high value. The utility of knowledge becomes singularly conspicuous even to the eyes of the multitude; those who have no taste for its charms set store upon its results and make some efforts to acquire it.

In free and enlightened democratic times there is nothing to separate men from one another or to retain them in their place; they rise or sink with extreme rapidity. All classes mingle together because they live so close together. They communicate and intermingle every day; they imitate and emulate one another. This suggests to the people many ideas, notions, and desires that they would never have entertained if the distinctions of rank had been fixed and society at rest. In such nations the servant never considers himself as an entire stranger to the pleasures and toils of his master, nor the poor man to those of the rich; the farmer tries to resemble the townsman, and the provinces to take after the metropolis. No one easily allows himself to be reduced to the mere material cares of life; and the humblest artisan casts at times an eager and a furtive glance into the higher regions of the intellect. People do not read with the same notions or in the same manner as they do in aristocratic communities, but the circle of readers is unceasingly expanded, till it includes all the people.

As soon as the multitude begins to take an interest in the labors of the mind, it finds out that to excel in some of them is a powerful means of acquiring fame, power, or wealth. The restless ambition that equality begets instantly takes this direction, as it does all others. The number of those who cultivate science, letters, and the arts, becomes immense. The intellectual world starts into prodigious activity; everyone endeavors to open for himself a path there and to draw the eyes of the public after him. Something analogous occurs to what happens in society in the United States politically considered. What is done is often imperfect, but the attempts are innumerable; and although the results of individual effort are commonly very small, the total amount is always very large.

It is therefore not true to assert that men living in democratic times are naturally indifferent to science, literature and the arts; only it must be acknowledged that they cultivate them after their own fashion and bring to the task their own peculiar qualifications and deficiencies.

Chapter X

WHY THE AMERICANS ARE MORE ADDICTED TO PRACTICAL THAN TO THEORETICAL SCIENCE

If a democratic state of society and democratic institutions do not retard the onward course of the human mind, they incontestably guide it in one direction in preference to another. Their efforts, thus circumscribed, are still exceedingly great, and I may be pardoned if I pause for a moment to contemplate them.

I had occasion, in speaking of the philosophical method of the American people, to make several remarks that it is necessary to make use of here.

Equality begets in man the desire of judging of everything for himself; it gives him in all things a taste for the tangible and the real, a contempt for tradition and for forms. These general tendencies are principally discernible in the peculiar subject of this chapter.

Those who cultivate the sciences among a democratic people are always afraid of losing their way in visionary speculation. They mistrust systems; they adhere closely to facts and study facts with their own senses. As they do not easily defer to the mere name of any fellow man, they are never inclined to rest upon any man's authority; but, on the contrary, they are unremitting in their efforts to find out the weaker points of their neighbor's doctrine. Scientific precedents have little weight with them; they are never long detained by the subtlety of the schools nor ready to accept big words for sterling coin; they penetrate, as far as they can, into the principal parts of the subject that occupies them, and they like to expound them in the popular language. Scientific pursuits then follow a freer and safer course, but a less lofty one.

The mind, it appears to me, may divide science into three parts.

The first comprises the most theoretical principles and

those more abstract notions whose application is either unknown or very remote.

The second is composed of those general truths that still belong to pure theory, but lead nevertheless by a straight and short road to practical results.

Methods of application and means of execution make up the third.

Each of these different portions of science may be separately cultivated, although reason and experience prove that no one of them can prosper long if it is absolutely cut off from the two others.

In America the purely practical part of science is admirably understood, and careful attention is paid to the theoretical portion which is immediately requisite to application. On this head the Americans always display a clear, free, original, and inventive power of mind. But hardly anyone in the United States devotes himself to the essentially theoretical and abstract portion of human knowledge. In this respect the Americans carry to excess a tendency that is, I think, discernible, though in a less degree, among all democratic nations.

Nothing is more necessary to the culture of the higher sciences or of the more elevated departments of science than meditation; and nothing is less suited to meditation than the structure of democratic society. We do not find there, as among an aristocratic people, one class that keeps quiet because it is well off; and another that does not venture to stir because it despairs of improving its condition. Everyone is in motion, some in quest of power, others of gain. In the midst of this universal tumult, this incessant conflict of jarring interests, this continual striving of men after fortune, where is that calm to be found which is necessary for the deeper combinations of the intellect? How can the mind dwell upon any single point when everything whirls around it, and man himself is swept and beaten onwards by the heady current that rolls all things in its course?

You must make the distinction between the sort of permanent agitation that is characteristic of a peaceful democracy and the tumultuous and revolutionary movements that almost always attend the birth and growth of democratic society. When a violent revolution occurs among a highly civilized people, it cannot fail to give a sudden impulse to their feelings and ideas. This is more particularly true of democratic revolutions, which stir up at once all the classes of which a people is composed and beget at the same time inordinate ambition in the breast of every member of the community. The French made surprising advances in the exact sciences at the very time at which they were finishing the destruction of the remains of their former feudal society; yet this sudden fecundity is not to be attributed to democracy, but to the unexampled revolution that attended its growth. What happened at that period was a special incident, and it would be unwise to regard it as the test of a general principle.

Great revolutions are not more common among democratic than among other nations; I am even inclined to believe that they are less so. But there prevails among those populations a small, distressing motion, a sort of incessant jostling of men, which annoys and disturbs the mind without exciting or elevating it.

Men who live in democratic communities not only seldom indulge in meditation, but they naturally entertain very little esteem for it. A democratic state of society and democratic institutions keep the greater part of men in constant activity; and the habits of mind that are suited to an active life are not always suited to a contemplative one. The man of action is frequently obliged to content himself with the best he can get because he would never accomplish his purpose if he chose to carry every detail to perfection. He has occasion perpetually to rely on ideas that he has not had leisure to search to the bottom; for he is much more frequently aided by the seasonableness of an idea than by its strict accuracy; and in the long run he risks less in making use of some false principles than in spending his time in establishing all his principles on the basis of truth. The world is not led by long or learned demonstrations; a rapid glance at particular incidents, the daily study of the fleeting passions of the multitude, the accidents of the moment, and the art of turning them to account decide all its affairs.

In the ages in which active life is the condition of almost everyone, men are generally led to attach an excessive value to the rapid bursts and superficial conceptions of the intellect, and on the other hand to undervalue unduly its slower and deeper labors. This opinion of the public influences the judgment of the men who cultivate the sciences; they are persuaded that they may succeed in those pursuits without meditation, or are deterred from such pursuits as demand it.

There are several methods of studying the sciences. Among a multitude of men you will find a selfish, mercantile, and trading taste for the discoveries of the mind, which must not be confounded with that disinterested passion which is kindled in the heart of a few. A desire to utilize knowledge is one thing; the pure desire to know is another. I do not doubt that in a few minds and at long intervals an ardent, inexhaustible love of truth springs up, self-supported and living in ceaseless fruition, without ever attaining full satisfaction. It is this ardent love, this proud, disinterested love of what is true, that raises men to the abstract sources of truth, to draw their mother knowledge thence.

If Pascal had had nothing in view but some large gain, or even if he had been stimulated by the love of fame alone, I cannot conceive that he would ever have been able to rally all the powers of his mind, as he did, for the better discovery of the most hidden things of the Creator. When I see him, as it were, tear his soul from all the cares of life to devote it wholly to these researches and, prematurely snapping the links that bind the body to life, die of old age before forty, I stand amazed and perceive that no ordinary cause is at work to produce efforts so extraordinary.

The future will prove whether these passions, at once so rare and so productive, come into being and into growth as easily in the midst of democratic as in aristocratic communities. For myself, I confess that I am slow to believe it.

In aristocratic societies the class that gives the tone to opinion and has the guidance of affairs, being permanently and hereditarily placed above the multitude, naturally conceives a lofty idea of itself and of man. It loves to invent for him noble pleasures, to carve out splendid objects for his ambition. Aristocracies often commit very tyrannical and inhuman actions, but they rarely entertain groveling thoughts; and they show a kind of haughty contempt of little pleasures, even while they indulge in them. The effect is to raise greatly the general pitch of society. In aristocratic ages vast ideas are commonly entertained of the dignity, the power, and the greatness of man. These opinions exert their influence on those who cultivate the sciences as well as on the rest of the community. They facilitate the natural impulse of the mind to the highest regions of thought, and they naturally prepare it to conceive a sublime, almost a divine love of truth.

Men of science at such periods are consequently carried away towards theory; and it even happens that they frequently conceive an inconsiderate contempt for practice. "Archimedes," says Plutarch, "was of so lofty a spirit that he never condescended to write any treatise on the manner of constructing all these engines of war. And as he held this science of inventing and putting together engines, and all arts generally speaking which tended to any useful end in practice, to be vile, low, and mercenary, he spent his talents and his studious hours in writing only of those things whose beauty and subtlety had in them no admixture of necessity." Such is the aristocratic aim of science; it cannot be the same in democratic nations.

The greater part of the men who constitute these nations are extremely eager in the pursuit of actual and physical gratification. As they are always dissatisfied with the position that they occupy and are always free to leave it, they think of nothing but the means of changing their fortune or increasing it. To minds thus predisposed, every new method that leads by a shorter road to wealth, every machine that spares labor, every instrument that diminishes the cost of production, every discovery that facilitates pleasures or augments them, seems to be the grandest effort of the human intellect. It is chiefly from these motives that a democratic people addicts itself to scientific pursuits, that it understands and respects them. In aristocratic ages science is more particularly called upon to furnish gratification to the mind; in democracies, to the body.

You may be sure that the more democratic, enlightened, and free a nation is, the greater will be the number of these interested promoters of scientific genius and the more will discoveries immediately applicable to productive industry confer on their authors gain, fame, and even power. For in democracies the working class take a part in public affairs; and public honors as well as pecuniary remuneration may be awarded to those who deserve them.

In a community thus organized, it may easily be conceived that the human mind may be led insensibly to the neglect of theory; and that it is urged, on the contrary, with unparalleled energy, to the applications of science, or at least to that portion of theoretical science which is necessary to those who make such applications. In vain will some instinctive inclination raise the mind towards the loftier spheres of the intellect; interest draws it down to the middle zone. There it may develop all its energy and restless activity and bring forth wonders. These very Americans who have not discovered one of the general laws of mechanics have introduced into navigation an instrument that changes the aspect of the world.

Assuredly I do not contend that the democratic nations of our time are destined to witness the extinction of the great luminaries of man's intelligence, or even that they will never bring new lights into existence. At the age at which the world has now arrived, and among so many cultivated nations perpetually excited by the fever of productive industry, the bonds that connect the different parts of science cannot fail to strike the observer; and the taste for practical science itself, if it is enlightened, ought to lead men not to neglect theory. In the midst of so many attempted applications of so many experiments repeated every day, it is almost impossible that general laws should not frequently be brought to light; so that great discoveries would be frequent, though great inventors may be few.

I believe, moreover, in high scientific vocations. If the democratic principle does not, on the one hand, induce men to cultivate science for its own sake, on the other it enormously increases the number of those who do cultivate it. Nor is it credible that among so great a multitude a speculative genius should not from time to time arise inflamed by the love of truth alone. Such a one, we may be sure, would dive into the deepest mysteries of nature, whatever the spirit of his country and his age. He requires no assistance in his course; it is enough that he is not checked in it. All that I mean to say is this: permanent inequality of conditions leads men to confine themselves to the arrogant and sterile research for abstract truths, while the social condition and the institutions of democracy prepare them to seek the immediate and useful practical results of the sciences. This tendency is natural and inevitable; it is curious to be acquainted with it, and it may be necessary to point it out.

If those who are called upon to guide the nations of our time clearly discerned from afar off these new tendencies, which will soon be irresistible, they would understand that, possessing education and freedom, men living in democratic ages cannot fail to improve the industrial part of science, and that henceforward all the efforts of the constituted authorities ought to be directed to support the highest branches of learning and to foster the nobler passion for science itself. In the present age the human mind must be coerced into theoretical studies; it runs of its own accord to practical applications; and, instead of perpetually referring it to the minute examination of secondary effects, it is well to divert it from them sometimes, in order to raise it up to the contemplation of primary causes.

Because the civilization of ancient Rome perished in consequence of the invasion of the Barbarians, we are perhaps too apt to think that civilization cannot perish in any other manner. If the light by which we are guided is ever extinguished, it will dwindle by degrees and expire of itself. By dint of close adherence to mere applications, principles would be lost sight of; and when the principles were wholly forgotten, the methods derived from them would be ill pursued. New methods could no longer be invented, and men would continue, without intelligence and without art, to apply scientific processes no longer understood.

When Europeans first arrived in China, three hundred years ago, they found that almost all the arts had reached a certain degree of perfection there, and they were surprised that a people which had attained this point should not have gone beyond it. At a later period they discovered traces of some higher branches of science that had been lost. The nation was absorbed in productive industry; the greater part of its scientific processes had been preserved, but science itself no longer existed there. This served to explain the strange immobility in which they found the minds of this people. The Chinese, in following the track of their forefathers, had forgotten the reasons by which the latter had been guided. They still used the formula without asking for its meaning; they retained the instrument, but they no longer possessed the art of altering or renewing it. The Chinese, then, had lost the power of change; for them improvement was impossible. They were compelled at all times and in all points to imitate their predecessors lest they should stray into utter darkness by deviating for an instant from the path already laid down for them. The source of human knowledge was all but dry; and though the stream still ran on, it could neither swell its waters nor alter its course.

Notwithstanding this, China had existed peaceably for centuries. The invaders who had conquered the country assumed the manners of the inhabitants, and order prevailed there. A sort of physical prosperity was everywhere discernible; revolutions were rare, and war was, so to speak, unknown.

It is then a fallacy to flatter ourselves with the reflection that the barbarians are still far from us; for if there are some nations that allow civilization to be torn from their grasp, there are others who themselves trample it underfoot.

Chapter XI

IN WHAT SPIRIT THE AMERICANS CULTIVATE THE ARTS

IT WOULD BE to waste the time of my readers and my own if I strove to demonstrate how the general mediocrity of fortunes, the absence of superfluous wealth, the universal desire for comfort, and the constant efforts by which everyone attempts to procure it make the taste for the useful predominate over the love of the beautiful in the heart of man. Democratic nations, among whom all these things exist, will therefore cultivate the arts that serve to render life easy in preference to those whose object is to adorn it. They will habitually prefer the useful to the beautiful, and they will require that the beautiful should be useful.

But I propose to go further, and, after having pointed out this first feature, to sketch several others.

It commonly happens that in the ages of privilege the practice of almost all the arts becomes a privilege, and that every profession is a separate sphere of action, into which it is not allowable for everyone to enter. Even when productive industry is free, the fixed character that belongs to aristocratic nations gradually segregates all the persons who practice the same art till they form a distinct class, always composed of the same families, whose members are all known to each other and among whom a public opinion of their own and a species of corporate pride soon spring up. In a class or guild of this kind each artisan has not only his fortune to make, but his reputation to preserve. He is not exclusively swayed by his own interest or even by that of his customer, but by that of the body to which he belongs; and the interest of that body is that each artisan should produce the best possible workmanship. In aristocratic ages the object of the arts is therefore to manufacture as well as possible, not with the greatest speed or at the lowest cost.

When, on the contrary, every profession is open to all,

when a multitude of persons are constantly embracing and abandoning it, and when its several members are strangers, indifferent to and because of their numbers hardly seen by each other, the social tie is destroyed, and each workman, standing alone, endeavors simply to gain the most money at the least cost. The will of the customer is then his only limit. But at the same time a corresponding change takes place in the customer also. In countries in which riches as well as power are concentrated and retained in the hands of a few, the use of the greater part of this world's goods belongs to a small number of individuals, who are always the same. Necessity, public opinion, or moderate desires exclude all others from the enjoyment of them. As this aristocratic class remains fixed at the pinnacle of greatness on which it stands, without diminution or increase, it is always acted upon by the same wants and affected by them in the same manner. The men of whom it is composed naturally derive from their superior and hereditary position a taste for what is extremely well made and lasting. This affects the general way of thinking of the nation in relation to the arts. It often occurs among such a people that even the peasant will rather go without the objects he covets than procure them in a state of imperfection. In aristocracies, then, the handicraftsmen work for only a limited number of fastidious customers; the profit they hope to make depends principally on the perfection of their workmanship.

Such is no longer the case when, all privileges being abolished, ranks are intermingled and men are forever rising or sinking in the social scale. Among a democratic people a number of citizens always exists whose patrimony is divided and decreasing. They have contracted, under more prosperous circumstances, certain wants, which remain after the means of satisfying such wants are gone; and they are anxiously looking out for some surreptitious method of providing for them. On the other hand, there is always in democracies a large number of men whose fortune is on the increase, but whose desires grow much faster than their fortunes, and who gloat upon the gifts of wealth in anticipation, long before they have means to obtain them. Such men are eager to find some short cut to these gratifications, already almost within their reach. From the combination of these two causes the result is that in democracies there is always a multitude of persons whose wants are above their means and who are very willing to take up with imperfect satisfaction rather than abandon the object of their desires altogether.

The artisan readily understands these passions, for he himself partakes in them. In an aristocracy he would seek to sell his workmanship at a high price to the few; he now conceives that the more expeditious way of getting rich is to sell them at a low price to all. But there are only two ways of lowering the price of commodities. The first is to discover some better, shorter, and more ingenious method of producing them; the second is to manufacture a larger quantity of goods, nearly similar, but of less value. Among a democratic population all the intellectual faculties of the workman are directed to these two objects: he strives to invent methods that may enable him not only to work better, but more quickly and more cheaply; or if he cannot succeed in that, to diminish the intrinsic quality of the thing he makes, without rendering it wholly unfit for the use for which it is intended. When none but the wealthy had watches, they were almost all very good ones; few are now made that are worth much, but everybody has one in his pocket. Thus the democratic principle not only tends to direct the human mind to the useful arts, but it induces the artisan to produce with great rapidity many imperfect commodities, and the consumer to content himself with these commodities.

Not that in democracies the arts are incapable, in case of need, of producing wonders. This may occasionally be so if customers appear who are ready to pay for time and trouble. In this rivalry of every kind of industry, in the midst of this immense competition and these countless experiments, some excellent workmen are formed who reach the utmost limits of their craft. But they rarely have an opportunity of showing what they can do; they are scrupulously sparing of their powers; they remain in a state of accomplished mediocrity, which judges itself, and, though well able to shoot beyond the mark before it, aims only at what it hits. In aristocracies, on the contrary, workmen always do all they can; and when they stop, it is because they have reached the limit of their art.

When I arrive in a country where I find some of the finest productions of the arts, I learn from this fact nothing of the social condition or of the political constitution of the country. But if I perceive that the productions of the arts are generally of an inferior quality, very abundant, and very cheap, I am convinced that among the people where this occurs privilege is on the decline and that ranks are beginning to intermingle and will soon become one.

The handicraftsmen of democratic ages not only endeavor to bring their useful productions within the reach of the whole community, but strive to give to all their commodities attractive qualities that they do not in reality possess. In the confusion of all ranks everyone hopes to appear what he is not, and makes great exertions to succeed in this object. This sentiment, indeed, which is only too natural to the heart of man, does not originate in the democratic principle; but that principle applies it to material objects. The hypocrisy of virtue is of every age, but the hypocrisy of luxury belongs more particularly to the ages of democracy.

To satisfy these new cravings of human vanity the arts have recourse to every species of imposture; and these devices sometimes go so far as to defeat their own purpose. Imitation diamonds are now made which may be easily mistaken for real ones; as soon as the art of fabricating false diamonds becomes so perfect that they cannot be distinguished from real ones, it is probable that both will be abandoned and become mere pebbles again.

This leads me to speak of those arts which are called, by way of distinction, the fine arts. I do not believe that it is a necessary effect of a democratic social condition and of democratic institutions to diminish the number of those who cultivate the fine arts, but these causes exert a powerful influence on the manner in which these arts are cultivated. Many of those who had already contracted a taste for the fine arts are impoverished; on the other hand, many of those who are not yet rich begin to conceive that taste, at least by imitation; the number of consumers increases, but opulent and fastidious consumers become more scarce. Something analogous to what I have already pointed out in the useful arts then takes place in the fine arts; the productions of artists are more numerous, but the merit of each production is diminished. No longer able to soar to what is great, they cultivate what is pretty and elegant, and appearance is more attended to than reality.

In aristocracies a few great pictures are produced; in democratic countries a vast number of insignificant ones. In the former statues are raised of bronze; in the latter, they are modeled in plaster.

When I arrived for the first time at New York, by that part of the Atlantic Ocean which is called the East River, I was surprised to perceive along the shore, at some distance from the city, a number of little palaces of white marble, several of which were of classic architecture. When I went the next day to inspect more closely one which had particularly attracted my notice, I found that its walls were of whitewashed brick, and its columns of painted wood. All the edifices that I had admired the night before were of the same kind.

The social condition and the institutions of democracy impart, moreover, certain peculiar tendencies to all the imitative arts, which it is easy to point out. They frequently withdraw them from the delineation of the soul to fix them exclusively on that of the body, and they substitute the representation of motion and sensation for that of sentiment and thought; in a word, they put the real in the place of the ideal.

I doubt whether Raphael studied the minute intricacies of the mechanism of the human body as thoroughly as the draftsmen of our own time. He did not attach the same importance as they do to rigorous accuracy on this point because he aspired to surpass nature. He sought to make of man something which should be superior to man and to embellish beauty itself. David and his pupils, on the contrary, were as good anatomists as they were painters. They wonderfully depicted the models that they had before their eyes, but they rarely imagined anything beyond them; they followed nature with fidelity, while Raphael sought for something better than nature. They have left us an exact portraiture of man, but he discloses in his works a glimpse of Divinity.

This remark as to the manner of treating a subject is no less applicable to its choice. The painters of the Renaissance generally sought far above themselves, and away from their own time, for mighty subjects which left to their imagination an unbounded range. Our painters often employ their talents in the exact imitation of the details of private life, which they have always before their eyes; and they are forever copying trivial objects, the originals of which are only too abundant in nature.

Chapter XII

WHY THE AMERICANS RAISE SOME INSIGNIFICANT MONUMENTS AND OTHERS THAT ARE VERY GRAND

I HAVE just observed that in democratic ages monuments of the arts tend to become more numerous and less important. I now hasten to point out the exception to this rule.

In a democratic community individuals are very weak, but the state, which represents them all and contains them all in its grasp, is very powerful. Nowhere do citizens appear so insignificant as in a democratic nation; nowhere does the nation itself appear greater or does the mind more easily take in a wide survey of it. In democratic communities the imagination is compressed when men consider themselves; it expands indefinitely when they think of the state. Hence it is that the same men who live on a small scale in cramped dwellings frequently aspire to gigantic splendor in the erection of their public monuments.

The Americans have traced out the circuit of an immense city on the site which they intend to make their capital, but which up to the present time is hardly more densely peopled than Pontoise, though, according to them, it will one day contain a million inhabitants. They have already rooted up trees for ten miles around lest they should interfere with the future citizens of this imaginary metropolis. They have erected a magnificent palace for Congress in the center of the city and have given it the pompous name of the Capitol.

The several states of the Union are every day planning and erecting for themselves prodigious undertakings which would astonish the engineers of the great European nations.

Thus democracy not only leads men to a vast number of inconsiderable productions; it also leads them to raise some monuments on the largest scale; but between these two extremes there is a blank. A few scattered specimens of enormous buildings can therefore teach us nothing of the social condition and the institutions of the people by whom they were raised. I may add, though the remark is outside my subject, that they do not make us better acquainted with its greatness, its civilization, and its real prosperity. Whenever a power of any kind is able to make a whole people co-operate in a single undertaking, that power, with a little knowledge and a great deal of time, will succeed in obtaining something enormous from efforts so multiplied. But this does not lead to the conclusion that the people are very happy, very enlightened, or even very strong.

The Spaniards found the city of Mexico full of magnificent temples and vast palaces, but that did not prevent Cortes from conquering the Mexican Empire with six hundred foot-soldiers and sixteen horses.

If the Romans had been better acquainted with the laws of hydraulics, they would not have constructed all the aqueducts that surround the ruins of their cities; they would have made a better use of their power and their wealth. If they had invented the steam-engine, perhaps they would not have extended to the extremities of their empire those long artificial ways which are called Roman roads. These things are the splendid memorials at the same time of their ignorance and of their greatness.

A people that left no other vestige than a few leaden pipes in the earth and a few iron rods on its surface might have been more the master of nature than the Romans.

Chapter XIII

LITERARY CHARACTERISTICS OF DEMOCRATIC TIMES

WHEN a traveler goes into a bookseller's shop in the United States and examines the American books on the shelves, the number of works appears very great, while that of known authors seems, on the contrary, extremely small. He will first find a multitude of elementary treatises, destined to teach the rudiments of human knowledge. Most of these books were written in Europe; the Americans reprint them, adapting them to their own use. Next comes an enormous quantity of religious works, Bibles, sermons, edifying anecdotes, controversial divinity, and reports of charitable societies; lastly appears the long catalogue of political pamphlets. In America parties do not write books to combat each other's opinions, but pamphlets, which are circulated for a day with incredible rapidity and then expire.

In the midst of all these obscure productions of the human brain appear the more remarkable works of a small number of authors whose names are, or ought to be, known to Europeans.

Although America is perhaps in our days the civilized country in which literature is least attended to, still a large number of persons there take an interest in the productions of the mind and make them, if not the study of their lives, at least the charm of their leisure hours. But England supplies these readers with most of the books that they require. Almost all important English books are republished in the United States. The literary genius of Great Britain still darts its rays into the recesses of the forests of the New World. There is hardly a pioneer's hut that does not contain a few odd volumes of Shakespeare. I remember that I read the feudal drama of *Henry V* for the first time in a log cabin.

Not only do the Americans constantly draw upon the treasures of English literature, but it may be said with truth that they find the literature of England growing on their own soil. The larger part of that small number of men in the United States who are engaged in the composition of literary works are English in substance and still more so in form. Thus they transport into the midst of democracy the ideas and literary fashions that are current among the aristocratic nation they have taken for their model. They paint with colors borrowed from foreign manners; and as they hardly ever represent the country they were born in as it really is, they are seldom popular there.

The citizens of the United States are themselves so convinced that it is not for them that books are published, that before they can make up their minds upon the merit of one of their authors, they generally wait till his fame has been ratified in England; just as in pictures the author of an original is held entitled to judge of the merit of a copy.

The inhabitants of the United States have, then, at present, properly speaking, no literature. The only authors whom I acknowledge as American are the journalists. They indeed are not great writers, but they speak the language of their country and make themselves heard. Other authors are aliens; they are to the Americans what the imitators of the Greeks and Romans were to us at the revival of learning, an object of curiosity, not of general sympathy. They amuse the mind, but they do not act upon the manners of the people.

I have already said that this state of things is far from originating in democracy alone, and that the causes of it must be sought for in several peculiar circumstances independent of the democratic principle. If the Americans, retaining the same laws and social condition, had had a different origin and had been transported into another country, I do not question that they would have had a literature. Even as they are, I am convinced that they will ultimately have one; but its character will be different from that which marks the American literary productions of our time, and that character will be peculiarly its own. Nor is it impossible to trace this character beforehand.

In an aristocratic people, among whom letters are cultivated, I suppose that intellectual occupations, as well as the affairs of government, are concentrated in a ruling class. The literary as well as the political career is almost entirely confined to this class, or to those nearest to it in rank. These premises suffice for a key to all the rest.

When a small number of the same men are engaged at the same time upon the same objects, they easily concert with one another and agree upon certain leading rules that are to govern them each and all. If the object that attracts the attention of these men is literature, the productions of the mind will soon be subjected by them to precise canons, from which it will no longer be allowable to depart. If these men occupy a hereditary position in the country, they will be naturally inclined, not only to adopt a certain number of fixed rules for themselves, but to follow those which their forefathers laid down for their own guidance; their code will be at once strict and traditional. As they are not necessarily engrossed by the cares of daily life, as they have never been so, any more than their fathers were before them, they have learned to take an interest, for several generations back, in the labors of mind. They have learned to understand literature as an art, to love it in the end for its own sake, and to feel a scholar-like satisfaction in seeing men conform to its rules. Nor is this all: the men of whom I speak began and will end their lives in easy or affluent circumstances; hence they have naturally conceived a taste for carefully chosen gratifications and a love of refined and delicate pleasures. Moreover, a kind of softness of mind and heart, which they frequently contract in the midst of this long and peaceful enjoyment of so much welfare, leads them to put aside, even from their pleasures, whatever might be too startling or too acute. They had rather be amused than intensely excited; they wish to be interested, but not to be carried away.

Now let us fancy a great number of literary performances executed by the men, or for the men, whom I have just described, and we shall readily conceive a style of literature in which everything will be regular and prearranged. The slightest work will be carefully wrought in its least details; art and labor will be conspicuous in everything; each kind of writing will have rules of its own, from which it will not be allowed to swerve and which distinguish it from all others. Style will be thought of almost as much importance as thought, and the form will be no less considered than the matter; the diction will be polished, measured and uniform. The tone of the mind will be always dignified, seldom very animated, and writers will care more to perfect what they produce than to multiply their productions. It will sometimes happen that the members of the literary class, always living among themselves and writing for themselves alone, will entirely lose sight of the rest of the world, which will infect them with a false and labored style; they will lay down minute literary rules for their exclusive use, which will insensibly lead them to deviate from common sense and finally to transgress the bounds of nature. By dint of striving after a mode of parlance different from the popular, they will arrive at a sort of aristocratic jargon which is hardly less remote from pure language than is the coarse dialect of the people. Such are the natural perils of literature among aristocracies. Every aristocracy that keeps itself entirely aloof from the people becomes impotent, a fact which is as true in literature as it is in politics.[1]

Let us now turn the picture and consider the other side of it: let us transport ourselves into the midst of a democracy not unprepared by ancient traditions and present culture to partake in the pleasures of mind. Ranks are there intermingled and identified; knowledge and power are both infinitely subdivided and, if I may use the expression, scattered on every side. Here, then, is a motley multitude whose intellectual wants are to be supplied. These new votaries of the pleasures of mind have not all received the same education; they do not resemble their fathers; nay, they perpetually differ from themselves, for they live in a state of incessant change of place, feelings, and fortunes. The mind of each is therefore unattached to that of his fellows by tradition or common habits; and they have never had the power, the inclination, or the time to act together. It is from the bosom of this heterogeneous and agitated mass, however, that au-

[1] All this is especially true of the aristocratic countries that have been long and peacefully subject to a monarchical government. When liberty prevails in an aristocracy, the higher ranks are constantly obliged to make use of the lower classes; and when they use, they approach them. This frequently introduces something of a democratic spirit into an aristocratic community. There springs up, moreover, in a governing privileged body an energy and habitually bold policy, a taste for stir and excitement, which must infallibly affect all literary performances.

thors spring; and from the same source their profits and their fame are distributed.

I can without difficulty understand that under these circumstances I must expect to meet in the literature of such a people with but few of those strict conventional rules which are admitted by readers and writers in aristocratic times. If it should happen that the men of some one period were agreed upon any such rules, that would prove nothing for the following period; for among democratic nations each new generation is a new people. Among such nations, then, literature will not easily be subjected to strict rules, and it is impossible that any such rules should ever be permanent.

In democracies it is by no means the case that all who cultivate literature have received a literary education; and most of those who have some tinge of belles-lettres are engaged either in politics or in a profession that only allows them to taste occasionally and by stealth the pleasures of mind. These pleasures, therefore, do not constitute the principal charm of their lives, but they are considered as a transient and necessary recreation amid the serious labors of life. Such men can never acquire a sufficiently intimate knowledge of the art of literature to appreciate its more delicate beauties; and the minor shades of expression must escape them. As the time they can devote to letters is very short, they seek to make the best use of the whole of it. They prefer books which may be easily procured, quickly read, and which require no learned researches to be understood. They ask for beauties self-proffered and easily enjoyed; above all, they must have what is unexpected and new. Accustomed to the struggle, the crosses, and the monotony of practical life, they require strong and rapid emotions, startling passages, truths or errors brilliant enough to rouse them up and to plunge them at once, as if by violence, into the midst of the subject.

Why should I say more, or who does not understand what is about to follow before I have expressed it? Taken as a whole, literature in democratic ages can never present, as it does in the periods of aristocracy, an aspect of order, regularity, science, and art; its form, on the contrary, will ordinarily be slighted, sometimes despised. Style will frequently be fantastic, incorrect, overburdened, and loose, almost always vehement and bold. Authors will aim at rapidity of execution more than at perfection of detail. Small productions will be more common than bulky books; there will be more wit than erudition, more imagination than profundity; and literary performances will bear marks of an untutored and rude vigor of thought, frequently of great variety and singular fecundity. The object of authors will be to astonish rather than to please, and to stir the passions more than to charm the taste.

Here and there, indeed, writers will doubtless occur who will choose a different track and who, if they are gifted with superior abilities, will succeed in finding readers in spite of their defects or their better qualities; but these exceptions will be rare, and even the authors who so depart from the received practice in the main subject of their works will always relapse into it in some lesser details.

I have just depicted two extreme conditions, but nations never leap from the first to the second; they reach it only by stages and through infinite gradation. In the progress that an educated people makes from the one to the other, there is almost always a moment when the literary genius of democratic nations coinciding with that of aristocratic nations, both seek to establish their sway jointly over the human mind. Such epochs are transient, but very brilliant; they are fertile without exuberance, and animated without confusion. The French literature of the eighteenth century may serve as an example.

I should say more than I mean if I were to assert that the literature of a nation is always subordinate to its social state and its political constitution. I am aware that, independently of these causes, there are several others which confer certain characteristics on literary productions; but these appear to me to be the chief. The relations that exist between the social and political condition of a people and the genius of its authors are always numerous; whoever knows the one is never completely ignorant of the other.

Chapter XIV

THE TRADE OF LITERATURE

DEMOCRACY not only infuses a taste for letters among the trading classes. but introduces a trading spirit into literature.

In aristocracies readers are fastidious and few in number; in democracies they are far more numerous and far less difficult to please. The consequence is that among aristocratic nations no one can hope to succeed without great exertion, and this exertion may earn great fame, but can never procure much money; while among democratic nations a writer may flatter himself that he will obtain at a cheap rate a moderate reputation and a large fortune. For this purpose he need not be admired; it is enough that he is liked.

The ever increasing crowd of readers and their continual craving for something new ensure the sale of books that nobody much esteems.

In democratic times the public frequently treat authors as kings do their courtiers; they enrich and despise them. What more is needed by the venal souls who are born in courts or are worthy to live there?

Democratic literature is always infested with a tribe of writers who look upon letters as a mere trade; and for some few great authors who adorn it, you may reckon thousands of idea-mongers.

Chapter XV

THE STUDY OF GREEK AND LATIN LITERATURE IS PECULIARLY USEFUL IN DEMOCRATIC COMMUNITIES

WHAT was called the People in the most democratic republics of antiquity was very unlike what we designate by that term. In Athens all the citizens took part in public affairs; but there were only twenty thousand citizens to more than three hundred and fifty thousand inhabitants. All the rest were slaves, and discharged the greater part of those duties which belong at the present day to the lower or even to the middle classes. Athens, then, with her universal suffrage, was, after all, merely an aristocratic republic, in which all the nobles had an equal right to the government.

The struggle between the patricians and plebeians of Rome must be considered in the same light: it was simply an internal feud between the elder and younger branches of the same family. All belonged to the aristocracy and all had the aristocratic spirit.

It is to be remarked, moreover, that, among the ancients books were always scarce and dear, and that very great difficulties impeded their publication and circulation. These circumstances concentrated literary tastes and habits among a small number of men, who formed a small literary aristocracy out of the choicer spirits of the great political aristocracy. Accordingly, nothing goes to prove that literature was ever treated as a trade among the Greeks and Romans.

These communities, which were not only aristocracies, but very polished and free nations, of course imparted to their literary productions the special defects and merits that characterize the literature of aristocratic times. And indeed a very superficial survey of the works of ancient authors will suffice to convince us that if those writers were sometimes deficient in variety and fertility in their subjects, or in boldness, vivacity, and power of generalization in their thoughts, they always displayed exquisite care and skill in their details. Nothing in their works seems to be done hastily or at random; every line is written for the eye of the connoisseur and is shaped after some conception of ideal beauty. No literature places those fine qualities in which the writers of democracies are naturally deficient in bolder relief than that of the ancients; no literature, therefore, ought to be more studied in democratic times. This study is better suited than any other to combat the literary defects inherent in those times; as for their natural literary qualities, these will spring up of their own accord without its being necessary to learn to acquire them.

It is important that this point should be clearly understood. A particular study may be useful to the literature of a people without being appropriate to its social and political wants. If men were to persist in teaching nothing but the literature of the dead languages in a community where everyone is habitually led to make vehement exertions to augment or to maintain his fortune, the result would be a very polished, but a very dangerous set of citizens. For as their social and political condition would give them every day a sense of wants, which their education would never teach them to supply, they would perturb the state, in the name of the Greeks and Romans, instead of enriching it by their productive industry.

It is evident that in democratic communities the interest of individuals as well as the security of the commonwealth demands that the education of the greater number should be scientific, commercial, and industrial rather than literary. Greek and Latin should not be taught in all the schools; but it is important that those who, by their natural disposition or their fortune, are destined to cultivate letters or prepared to relish them should find schools where a complete knowledge of ancient literature may be acquired and where the true scholar may be formed. A few excellent universities would do more towards the attainment of this object than a multitude of bad grammar-schools, where superfluous matters, badly learned, stand in the way of sound instruction in necessary studies.

All who aspire to literary excellence in democratic nations ought frequently to refresh themselves at the springs of ancient literature; there is no more wholesome medicine for the mind. Not that I hold the literary productions of the ancients to be irreproachable, but I think that they have some special merits, admirably calculated to counterbalance our peculiar defects. They are a prop on the side on which we are in most danger of falling.

Chapter XVI

HOW AMERICAN DEMOCRACY HAS MODIFIED THE ENGLISH LANGUAGE

IF the reader has rightly understood what I have already said on the subject of literature in general, he will have no difficulty in understanding that species of influence which a democratic social condition and democratic institutions may exercise over language itself, which is the chief instrument of thought.

American authors may truly be said to live rather in England than in their own country, since they constantly study the English writers and take them every day for their models. But it is not so with the bulk of the population, which is more immediately subjected to the peculiar causes acting upon the United States. It is not, then, to the written, but to the spoken language that attention must be paid if we would detect the changes which the idiom of an aristocratic people may undergo when it becomes the language of a democracy.

Englishmen of education, and more competent judges than I can be of the nicer shades of expression, have frequently assured me that the language of the educated classes in the United States is notably different from that of the educated classes in Great Britain. They complain, not only that the Americans have brought into use a number of new words (the difference and the distance between the two countries might suffice to explain that much), but that these new words are more especially taken from the jargon of parties, the mechanical arts, or the language of trade. In addition to this, they assert that old English words are often used by the Americans in new acceptations; and lastly, that the inhabitants of the United States frequently intermingle phraseology in the strangest manner, and sometimes place words together which are always kept apart in the language of the mother country. These remarks, which were made to me at various times by persons who appeared to be worthy of credit, led me to reflect upon the subject; and my reflections brought me, by theoretical reasoning, to the same point at which my informants had arrived by practical observation.

In aristocracies language must naturally partake of that state of repose in which everything remains. Few new words are coined because few new things are made; and even if new things were made, they would be designated by known words, whose meaning had been determined by tradition. If it happens that the human mind bestirs itself at length or is aroused by light breaking in from without, the novel expressions that are introduced have a learned, intellectual, and philosophical character, showing that they do not originate in a democracy. After the fall of Constantinople had turned the tide of science and letters towards the west, the French language was almost immediately invaded by a multitude of new words, which all had Greek and Latin roots. An erudite neologism then sprang up in France, which was confined to the educated classes, and which produced no sensible effect, or at least a very gradual one, upon the people.

All the nations of Europe successively exhibited the same change. Milton alone introduced more than six hundred words into the English language, almost all derived from the Latin, the Greek, or the Hebrew. The constant agitation that prevails in a democratic community tends unceasingly, on the contrary, to change the character of the language, as it does the aspect of affairs. In the midst of this general stir and competition of minds, many new ideas are formed, old ideas are lost, or reappear, or are subdivided into an infinite variety of minor shades. The consequence is that many words must fall into desuetude, and others must be brought into use.

Besides, democratic nations love change for its own sake, and this is seen in their language as much as in their politics. Even when they have no need to change words, they sometimes have the desire.

The genius of a democratic people is not only shown by the great number of words they bring into use, but also by the nature of the ideas these new words represent. Among such a people the majority lays down the law in language as well as in everything else; its prevailing spirit is as manifest in this as in other respects. But the majority is more engaged in business than in study, in political and commercial interests than in philosophical speculation or literary pursuits. Most of the words coined or adopted for its use will bear the mark of these habits; they will mainly serve to express the wants of business, the passions of party, or the details of the public administration. In these departments the language will constantly grow, while it will gradually lose ground in metaphysics and theology.

As to the source from which democratic nations are accustomed to derive their new expressions and the manner in which they coin them, both may easily be described. Men living in democratic countries know but little of the language that was spoken at Athens or at Rome, and they do not care to dive into the lore of antiquity to find the expression that they want. If they sometimes have recourse to learned etymologies, vanity will induce them to search for roots from the dead languages; but erudition does not naturally furnish them its resources. The most ignorant, it sometimes happens, will use them most. The eminently democratic desire to get above their own sphere will often lead them to seek to dignify a vulgar profession by a Greek or Latin name. The lower the calling is and the more remote from learning, the more pompous and erudite is its appelation. Thus the French rope-dancers have transformed themselves into *acrobates* and *funambules.*

Having little knowledge of the dead languages, democratic nations are apt to borrow words from living tongues, for they have constant mutual intercourse, and the inhabitants of different countries imitate each other the more readily as they grow more like each other every day.

But it is principally upon their own languages that democratic nations attempt to make innovations. From time to time they resume and restore to use forgotten expressions in their vocabulary, or they borrow from some particular class of the community a term peculiar to it, which they introduce with a figurative meaning into the language of daily life. Many expressions which originally belonged to the technical language of a profession or a party are thus drawn into general circulation.

The most common expedient employed by democratic nations to make an innovation in language consists in giving an unwonted meaning to an expression already in use. This method is very simple, prompt, and convenient; no learning is required to use it correctly and ignorance itself rather facilitates the practice; but that practice is most dangerous to the language. When a democratic people double the meaning of a word in this way, they sometimes render the meaning which it retains as ambiguous as that which it acquires. An author begins by a slight deflection of a known expression from its primitive meaning, and he adapts it, thus modified, as well as he can to his subject. A second writer twists the sense of the expression in another way; a third takes possession of it for another purpose; and as there is no common appeal to the sentence of a permanent tribunal that may definitively settle the meaning of the word, it remains in an unsettled condition. The consequence is that writers hardly ever appear to dwell upon a single thought, but they always seem to aim at a group of ideas, leaving the reader to judge which of them has been hit.

This is a deplorable consequence of democracy. I had rather that the language should be made hideous with words imported from the Chinese, the Tatars, or the Hurons than that the meaning of a word in our own language should become indeterminate. Harmony and uniformity are only secondary beauties in composition: many of these things are conventional, and, strictly speaking, it is possible to do without them; but without clear phraseology there is no good language.

The principle of equality necessarily introduces several other changes into language.

In aristocratic ages, when each nation tends to stand aloof from all others and likes to have a physiognomy of its own, it often happens that several communities which have a common origin become nevertheless strangers to each other; so that, without ceasing to understand the same language, they no longer all speak it in the same manner. In these ages each nation is divided into a certain number of classes, which see but little of each other and do not intermingle. Each of these classes contracts and invariably retains habits of mind peculiar to itself and adopts by choice certain terms which afterwards pass from generation to generation, like their estates. The same idiom then comprises a language of the poor and a language of the rich, a language of the commoner and a language of the nobility, a learned language and a colloquial one. The deeper the divisions and the more impassable the barriers of society become, the more must this be the case. I would lay a wager that among the castes of India there are amazing variations of language, and that there is almost as much difference between the language of a pariah and that of a Brahmin as there is in their dress.

When, on the contrary, men, being no longer restrained by ranks, meet on terms of constant intercourse, when castes are destroyed and the classes of society are recruited from and intermixed with each other, all the words of a language are mingled. Those which are unsuitable to the greater number perish; the remainder form a common store, whence everyone chooses pretty nearly at random. Almost all the different dialects that divided the idioms of European nations are manifestly declining; there is no patois in the New World, and it is disappearing every day from the old countries.

The influence of this revolution in social condition is as much felt in style as it is in language. Not only does everyone use the same words, but a habit springs up of using them without discrimination. The rules which style had set up are almost abolished: the line ceases to be drawn between expressions which seem by their very nature vulgar and others which appear to be refined. Persons springing from different ranks of society carry with them the terms and expressions they are accustomed to use into whatever circumstances they may enter; thus the origin of words is lost like the origin of individuals, and there is as much confusion in language as there is in society.

I am aware that in the classification of words there are rules which do not belong to one form of society any more than to another, but which are derived from the nature of things. Some expressions and phrases are vulgar because the ideas they are meant to express are low in themselves; others are of a higher character because the objects they are intended to designate are naturally lofty. No intermixture of ranks will ever efface these differences. But the principle of equality cannot fail to root out whatever is merely conventional and arbitrary in the forms of thought. Perhaps the necessary classification that I have just pointed out will always be less respected by a democratic people than by any other, because among such a people there are no men who are permanently disposed, by education, culture, and leisure, to study the natural laws of language and who cause those laws to be respected by their own observance of them.

I shall not leave this topic without touching on a feature of democratic languages that is, perhaps, more characteristic of them than any other. It has already been shown that democratic nations have a taste and sometimes a passion for general ideas, and that this arises from their peculiar merits and defects. This liking for general ideas is displayed in democratic languages by the continual use of generic terms or abstract expressions and by the manner in which they are employed. This is the great merit and the great imperfection of these languages.

Democratic nations are passionately addicted to generic terms and abstract expressions because these modes of speech enlarge thought and assist the operations of the mind by enabling it to include many objects in a small compass. A democratic writer will be apt to speak of *capacities* in the abstract for men of capacity and without specifying the objects to which their capacity is applied; he will talk about *actualities* to designate in one word the things passing before his eyes at the moment; and, in French, he will comprehend under the term *éventualités* whatever may happen in the universe, dating from the moment at which he speaks. Democratic writers are perpetually coining abstract words of this kind, in which they sublimate into further abstraction the abstract terms of the language. Moreover, to render their mode of speech more succinct, they personify the object of these abstract terms and make it act like a real person. Thus they would say in French: *La force des choses veut que les capacités gouvernent.*

I cannot better illustrate what I mean than by my own example. I have frequently used the word *equality* in an absolute sense; nay, I have personified equality in several places; thus I have said that equality does such and such things or refrains from doing others. It may be affirmed that the writers of the age of Louis XIV would not have spoken in this manner; they would never have thought of using the word *equality* without applying it to some particular thing; and they would rather have renounced the term altogether than have consented to make it a living personage.

These abstract terms which abound in democratic languages, and which are used on every occasion without attaching them to any particular fact, enlarge and obscure the thoughts they are intended to convey; they render the mode of speech more succinct and the idea contained in it less clear. But with regard to language, democratic nations prefer obscurity to labor.

I do not know, indeed, whether this loose style has not some secret charm for those who speak and write among these nations. As the men who live there are frequently left to the efforts of their individual powers of mind, they are almost always a prey to doubt; and as their situation in life is forever changing, they are never held fast to any of their opinions by the immobility of their fortunes. Men living in democratic countries, then, are apt to entertain unsettled ideas, and they require loose expressions to convey them. As they never know whether the idea they express today will be appropriate to the new position they may occupy tomorrow, they naturally acquire a liking for abstract terms. An abstract term is like a box with a false bottom; you may put in it what ideas you please, and take them out again without being observed.

Among all nations generic and abstract terms form the basis of language. I do not, therefore, pretend that these terms are found only in democratic languages; I say only that men have a special tendency in the ages of democracy to multiply words of this kind, to take them always by themselves in their most abstract acceptation, and to use them on all occasions, even when the nature of the discourse does not require them.

Chapter XVII

OF SOME SOURCES OF POETRY AMONG DEMOCRATIC NATIONS

MANY different meanings have been given to the word *poetry*. It would weary my readers if I were to discuss which of these definitions ought to be selected; I prefer telling them at once that which I have chosen. In my opinion, Poetry is the search after, and the delineation of, the Ideal.

The Poet is he who, by suppressing a part of what exists, by adding some imaginary touches to the picture, and by combining certain real circumstances that do not in fact happen together, completes and extends the work of nature. Thus the object of poetry is not to represent what is true, but to adorn it and to present to the mind some loftier image. Verse, regarded as the ideal beauty of language, may be eminently poetical; but verse does not of itself constitute poetry.

I now proceed to inquire whether among the actions, the sentiments, and the opinions of democratic nations there are any which lead to a conception of the ideal, and which may for this reason be considered as natural sources of poetry.

It must, in the first place, be acknowledged that the taste for ideal beauty, and the pleasure derived from the expression of it, are never so intense or so diffused among a democratic as among an aristocratic people. In aristocratic nations it sometimes happens that the body acts as it were spontaneously, while the higher faculties are bound and burdened by repose. Among these nations the people will often display poetic tastes, and their fancy sometimes ranges beyond and above what surrounds them.

But in democracies the love of physical gratification, the notion of bettering one's condition, the excitement of competition, the charm of anticipated success, are so many spurs to urge men onward in the active professions they have embraced, without allowing them to deviate for an instant from the track. The main stress of the faculties is to this point.

The imagination is not extinct, but its chief function is to devise what may be useful and to represent what is real. The principle of equality not only diverts men from the description of ideal beauty; it also diminishes the number of objects to be described.

Aristocracy, by maintaining society in a fixed position, is favorable to the solidity and duration of positive religions as well as to the stability of political institutions. Not only does it keep the human mind within a certain sphere of belief, but it predisposes the mind to adopt one faith rather than another. An aristocratic people will always be prone to place intermediate powers between God and man. In this respect it may be said that the aristocratic element is favorable to poetry. When the universe is peopled with supernatural beings, not palpable to sense, but discovered by the mind, the imagination ranges freely; and poets, finding a thousand subjects to delineate, also find a countless audience to take an interest in their productions.

In democratic ages it sometimes happens, on the contrary, that men are as much afloat in matters of faith as they are in their laws. Skepticism then draws the imagination of poets back to earth and confines them to the real and visible world. Even when the principle of equality does not disturb religious conviction, it tends to simplify it and to divert attention from secondary agents, to fix it principally on the Supreme Power.

Aristocracy naturally leads the human mind to the contemplation of the past and fixes it there. Democracy, on the contrary, gives men a sort of instinctive distaste for what is ancient. In this respect aristocracy is far more favorable to poetry; for things commonly grow larger and more obscure as they are more remote, and for this twofold reason they are better suited to the delineation of the ideal.

After having deprived poetry of the past, the principle of equality robs it in part of the present. Among aristocratic nations there is a certain number of privileged personages whose situation is, as it were, without and above the condition of man; to these, power, wealth, fame, wit, refinement, and distinction in all things appear peculiarly to belong. The crowd never sees them very closely or does not watch them in minute details, and little is needed to make the description of such men poetical. On the other hand, among the same people you will meet with classes so ignorant, low, and enslaved that they are no less fit objects for poetry, from the excess of their rudeness and wretchedness, than the former are from their greatness and refinement. Besides, as the different classes of which an aristocratic community is composed are widely separated and imperfectly acquainted with each other, the imagination may always represent them with some addition to, or some subtraction from, what they really are.

In democratic communities, where men are all insignificant and very much alike, each man instantly sees all his fellows when he surveys himself. The poets of democratic ages, therefore, can never take any man in particular as the subject of a piece; for an object of slender importance, which is distinctly seen on all sides, will never lend itself to an ideal conception.

Thus the principle of equality, in proportion as it has established itself in the world, has dried up most of the old springs of poetry. Let us now attempt to see what new ones it may disclose.

When skepticism had depopulated heaven, and the progress of equality had reduced each individual to smaller and better-known proportions, the poets, not yet aware of what they could substitute for the great themes that were departing together with the aristocracy, turned their eyes to inanimate nature. As they lost sight of gods and heroes, they set themselves to describe streams and mountains. Thence originated, in the last century, that kind of poetry which has been called, by way of distinction, *descriptive*. Some have thought that this embellished delineation of all the physical and inanimate objects which cover the earth was the kind of poetry peculiar to democratic ages; but I believe this to be an error, and that it belongs only to a period of transition.

I am persuaded that in the end democracy diverts the imagination from all that is external to man and fixes it on man alone. Democratic nations may amuse themselves for a while with considering the productions of nature, but they are excited in reality only by a survey of themselves. Here, and here alone, the true sources of poetry among such nations are to be found; and it may be believed that the poets who neglect to draw their inspirations hence will lose all sway over the minds which they would enchant, and will be left in the end with none but unimpassioned spectators of their transports.

I have shown how the ideas of progress and of the indefinite perfectibility of the human race belong to democratic ages. Democratic nations care but little for what has been, but they are haunted by visions of what will be; in this direction their unbounded imagination grows and dilates beyond all measure. Here, then, is the widest range open to the genius of poets, which allows them to remove their performances to a sufficient distance from the eye. Democracy, which shuts the past against the poet, opens the future before him.

As all the citizens who compose a democratic community are nearly equal and alike, the poet cannot dwell upon any one of them; but the nation itself invites the exercise of his powers. The general similitude of individuals, which renders any one of them taken separately an improper subject of poetry, allows poets to include them all in the same imagery and to take a general survey of the people itself. Democratic nations have a clearer perception than any others of their own aspect; and an aspect so imposing is admirably fitted to the delineation of the ideal.

I readily admit that the Americans have no poets; I cannot allow that they have no poetic ideas. In Europe people talk a great deal of the wilds of America, but the Americans themselves never think about them; they are insensible to the wonders of inanimate nature and they may be said not to perceive the mighty forests that surround them till they fall beneath the hatchet. Their eyes are fixed upon another sight: the American people views its own march across these wilds, draining swamps, turning the course of rivers, peopling solitudes, and subduing nature. This magnificent image of themselves does not meet the gaze of the Americans at intervals only; it may be said to haunt every one of them in his least as well as in his most important actions and to be always flitting before his mind.

Nothing conceivable is so petty, so insipid, so crowded with paltry interests—in one word, so anti-poetic—as the life of a man in the United States. But among the thoughts which it suggests, there is always one that is full of poetry, and this is the hidden nerve which gives vigor to the whole frame.

In aristocratic ages each people as well as each individual is prone to stand separate and aloof from all others. In democratic ages the extreme fluctations of men and the impatience of their desires keep them perpetually on the move, so that the inhabitants of different countries intermingle, see, listen to, and borrow from each other. It is not only the members of the same community, then, who grow more alike; communities themselves are assimilated to one another, and the whole assemblage presents to the eye of the spectator one vast democracy, each citizen of which is a nation. This displays the aspect of mankind for the first time in the broadest light. All that belongs to the existence of the human race taken as a whole, to its vicissitudes and its future, becomes an abundant mine of poetry.

The poets who lived in aristocratic ages have been eminently successful in their delineations of certain incidents in the life of a people or a man; but none of them ever ventured to include within his performances the destinies of mankind, a task which poets writing in democratic ages may attempt.

At that same time at which every man, raising his eyes above his country, begins at length to discern mankind at large, the Deity is more and more manifest to the human mind in full and entire majesty. If in democratic ages faith in positive religion be often shaken and the belief in intermediate agents, by whatever name they are called, be overcast, on the other hand men are disposed to conceive a far broader idea of Providence itself, and its interference in human affairs assumes a new and more imposing appearance to their eyes. Looking at the human race as one great whole, they easily conceive that its destinies are regulated by the same design; and in the actions of every individual they are led to acknowledge a trace of that universal and eternal plan by which God rules our race. This consideration may be taken as another prolific source of poetry which is opened in democratic times.

Democratic poets will always appear trivial and frigid if they seek to invest gods, demons, or angels with corporeal forms and if they attempt to draw them down from heaven to dispute the supremacy of earth. But if they strive to connect the great events they commemorate with the general providential designs that govern the universe and, without showing the finger of the Supreme Governor, reveal the thoughts of the Supreme Mind, their works will be admired and understood, for the imagination of their contemporaries takes this direction of its own accord.

It may be foreseen in like manner that poets living in democratic times will prefer the delineation of passions and ideas to that of persons and achievements. The language, the dress, and the daily actions of men in democracies are repugnant to conceptions of the ideal. These things are not poetical in themselves; and if it were otherwise, they would cease to be so, because they are too familiar to all those to whom the poet would speak of them. This forces the poet constantly to search below the external surface which is palpable to the senses, in order to read the inner soul; and nothing lends itself more to the delineation of the ideal than the scrutiny of the hidden depths in the immaterial nature of man. I need not traverse earth and sky to discover a wondrous object woven of contrasts, of infinite greatness and littleness, of intense gloom and amazing brightness, capable at once of exciting pity, admiration, terror, contempt. I have only to look at myself. Man springs out of nothing, crosses time, and disappears forever in the bosom of God; he is seen but for a moment, wandering on the verge of the two abysses, and there he is lost.

If man were wholly ignorant of himself, he would have no poetry in him; for it is impossible to describe what the mind does not conceive. If man clearly discerned his own nature, his imagination would remain idle and would have nothing to add to the picture. But the nature of man is sufficiently disclosed for him to know something of himself, and sufficiently obscure for all the rest to be plunged in thick darkness, in which he gropes forever, and forever in vain, to lay hold on some completer notion of his being.

Among a democratic people poetry will not be fed with legends or the memorials of old traditions. The poet will not attempt to people the universe with supernatural beings, in whom his readers and his own fancy have ceased to believe; nor will he coldly personify virtues and vices, which are better received under their own features. All these resources fail him; but Man remains, and the poet needs no more. The destinies of mankind, man himself taken aloof from his country and his age and standing in the presence of Nature and of God, with his passions, his doubts, his rare prosperities and inconceivable wretchedness, will become the chief, if not the sole, theme of poetry among these nations.

Experience may confirm this assertion if we consider the productions of the greatest poets who have appeared since the world has been turned to democracy. The authors of our age who have so admirably delineated the features of Faust, Childe Harold, René, and Jocelyn did not seek to record the actions of an individual, but to enlarge and to throw light on some of the obscurer recesses of the human heart.

Such are the poems of democracy. The principle of equality does not, then, destroy all the subjects of poetry: it renders them less numerous, but more vast.

Chapter XVIII

WHY AMERICAN WRITERS AND ORATORS OFTEN USE AN INFLATED STYLE

I HAVE frequently noticed that the Americans, who generally treat of business in clear, plain language, devoid of all ornament and so extremely simple as to be often coarse, are apt to become inflated as soon as they attempt a more poetical diction. They then vent their pomposity from one end of a harangue to the other; and to hear them lavish imagery on every occasion, one might fancy that they never spoke of anything with simplicity.

The English less frequently commit a similar fault. The cause of this may be pointed out without much difficulty. In democratic communities, each citizen is habitually engaged in the contemplation of a very puny object: namely, himself. If he ever raises his looks higher, he perceives only the immense form of society at large or the still more imposing aspect of mankind. His ideas are all either extremely minute and clear or extremely general and vague; what lies between is a void. When he has been drawn out of his own sphere, therefore, he always expects that some amazing object will be offered to his attention; and it is on these terms alone that he consents to tear himself for a moment from the petty, complicated cares that form the charm and the excitement of his life.

This appears to me sufficiently to explain why men in democracies, whose concerns are in general so paltry, call upon their poets for conceptions so vast and descriptions so unlimited.

The authors, on their part, do not fail to obey a propensity of which they themselves partake; they perpetually inflate their imaginations, and, expanding them beyond all bounds, they not infrequently abandon the great in order to reach the gigantic. By these means they hope to attract the observation of the multitude and to fix it easily upon themselves; nor are their hopes disappointed, for as the multitude seeks for nothing in poetry but objects of vast dimensions, it has neither the time to measure with accuracy the proportions of all the objects set before it nor a taste sufficiently correct to perceive at once in what respect they are out of proportion. The author and the public at once vitiate one another.

We have also seen that among democratic nations the sources of poetry are grand, but not abundant. They are soon exhausted; and poets, not finding the elements of the ideal in what is real and true, abandon them entirely and create monsters. I do not fear that the poetry of democratic nations will prove insipid or that it will fly too near the ground; I rather apprehend that it will be forever losing itself in the clouds and that it will range at last to purely imaginary regions. I fear that the productions of democratic poets may often be surcharged with immense and incoherent imagery, with exaggerated descriptions and strange creations; and that the fantastic beings of their brain may sometimes make us regret the world of reality.

Chapter XIX

SOME OBSERVATIONS ON THE DRAMA AMONG DEMOCRATIC NATIONS

WHEN the revolution that has changed the social and political state of an aristocratic people begins to penetrate into literature, it generally first manifests itself in the drama, and it always remains conspicuous there.

The spectator of a dramatic piece is, to a certain extent, taken by surprise by the impression it conveys. He has no time to refer to his memory or to consult those more able to judge than himself. It does not occur to him to resist the new literary tendencies that begin to be felt by him; he yields to them before he knows what they are.

Authors are very prompt in discovering which way the taste of the public is thus secretly inclined. They shape their productions accordingly; and the literature of the stage, after having served to indicate the approaching literary revolution, speedily completes it altogether. If you would judge beforehand of the literature of a people that is lapsing into democracy, study its dramatic productions.

The literature of the stage, moreover, even among aristocratic nations, constitutes the most democratic part of their literature. No kind of literary gratification is so much within the reach of the multitude as that which is derived from theatrical representations. Neither preparation nor study is required to enjoy them; they lay hold on you in the midst of your prejudices and your ignorance. When the yet untutored love of the pleasures of mind begins to affect a class of the community, it immediately draws them to the stage. The theaters of aristocratic nations have always been filled with spectators not belonging to the aristocracy. At the theater alone, the higher ranks mix with the middle and the lower classes; there alone do the former consent to listen to the opinion of the latter, or at least to allow them to give an opinion at all. At the theater men of cultivation and of literary attainments have always had more difficulty than elsewhere in making their taste prevail over that of the people and in preventing themselves from being carried away by the latter. The pit has frequently made laws for the boxes.

If it be difficult for an aristocracy to prevent the people from getting the upper hand in the theater, it will readily be understood that the people will be supreme there when democratic principles have crept into the laws and customs, when ranks are intermixed, when minds as well as fortunes are brought more nearly together, and when the upper class has lost, with its hereditary wealth, its power, its traditions, and its leisure. The tastes and propensities natural to democratic nations in respect to literature will therefore first be discernible in the drama, and it may be foreseen that they will break out there with vehemence. In written productions the literary canons of aristocracy will be gently, gradually, and, so to speak, legally modified; at the theater they will be riotously overthrown.

The drama brings out most of the good qualities and almost all the defects inherent in democratic literature. Democratic communities hold erudition very cheap and care but little for what occurred at Rome and Athens; they want to hear something that concerns themselves, and the delineation of the present age is what they demand. When the heroes and the manners of antiquity are frequently brought upon the stage and dramatic authors faithfully observe the rules of antiquated precedent, that is enough to warrant a conclusion that the democratic classes have not yet got the upper hand in the theaters.

Racine makes a very humble apology in the preface to the *Britannicus* for having disposed of Junia among the Vestals, who, according to Aulus Gellius, he says, "admitted no one below six years of age, nor above ten." We may be sure that he would neither have accused nor defended himself for such an offense if he had written for our contemporaries.

A fact of this kind illustrates not only the state of literature at the time when it occurred, but also that of society itself. A democratic stage does not prove that the nation is in a state of democracy, for, as we have just seen, it may happen even in aristocracies that democratic tastes affect the drama; but when the spirit of aristocracy reigns exclusively on the stage, the fact irrefragably demonstrates that the whole of society is aristocratic; and it may be boldly inferred that the same lettered and learned class that sways the dramatic writers commands the people and governs the country.

The refined tastes and the arrogant bearing of an aristocracy, when it manages the stage, will rarely fail to lead it to make a kind of selection in human nature. Some of the conditions of society claim its chief interest, and the scenes that delineate their manners are preferred upon the stage. Certain virtues, and even certain vices, are thought more particularly to deserve to figure there; and they are applauded while all others are excluded. On the stage, as well as elsewhere, an aristocratic audience wishes to meet only persons of quality and to be moved only by the misfortunes of kings. The same remark applies to style: an aristocracy is apt to impose upon dramatic authors certain modes of expression that give the key in which everything is to be delivered. By these means the stage frequently comes to delineate only one side of man, or sometimes even to represent what is not to be met with in human nature at all, to rise above nature and to go beyond it.

In democratic communities the spectators have no such preferences, and they rarely display any such antipathies: they like to see on the stage that medley of conditions, feelings, and opinions that occurs before their eyes. The drama becomes more striking, more vulgar, and more true. Sometimes, however, those who write for the stage in democracies also transgress the bounds of human nature; but it is on a different side from their predecessors. By seeking to represent in minute detail the little singularities of the present moment and the peculiar characteristics of certain personages, they forget to portray the general features of the race.

When the democratic classes rule the stage, they introduce as much license in the manner of treating subjects as in the choice of them. As the love of the drama is, of all literary tastes, that which is most natural to democratic nations, the number of authors and of spectators, as well as of theatrical representations, is constantly increasing among these communities. Such a multitude, composed of elements so different and scattered in so many different places, cannot acknowledge the same rules or submit to the same laws. No agreement is possible among judges so numerous, who do not know when they may meet again, and therefore each pronounces his own separate opinion on the piece. If the effect of democracy is generally to question the authority of all literary rules and conventions, on the stage it abolishes them altogether and puts in their place nothing but the caprice of each author and each public.

The drama also displays in a special manner the truth of what I have before said in speaking more generally of style and art in democratic literature. In reading the criticisms that were occasioned by the dramatic productions of the age of Louis XIV one is surprised to notice the great stress which the public laid on the probability of the plot, and the importance that was attached to the perfect consistency of the characters and to their doing nothing that could not be easily explained and understood. The value which was set upon the forms of language at that period, and the paltry strife about words with which dramatic authors were assailed, are no less surprising. It would seem that the men of the age of Louis XIV attached very exaggerated importance to those details which may be perceived in the study, but which escape attention on the stage; for, after all, the principal object of a dramatic piece is to be performed, and its chief merit is to affect the audience. But the audience and the readers in that age were the same: on leaving the theater they called up the author for judgment at their own firesides.

In democracies dramatic pieces are listened to, but not read. Most of those who frequent the amusements of the stage do not go there to seek the pleasures of mind, but the keen emotions of the heart. They do not expect to hear a fine literary work, but to see a play; and provided the author writes the language of his country correctly enough to be understood, and his characters excite curiosity and awaken sympathy, the audience are satisfied. They ask no more of fiction and immediately return to real life. Accuracy of style is therefore less required, because the attentive observance of its rules is less perceptible on the stage.

As for the probability of the plot, it is incompatible with perpetual novelty, surprise, and rapidity of invention. It is therefore neglected, and the public excuses the neglect. You may be sure that if you succeed in bringing your audience into the presence of something that affects them, they will not care by what road you brought them there, and they will never reproach you for having excited their emotions in spite of dramatic rules.

The Americans, when they go to the theater, very broadly display all the different propensities that I have here described; but it must be acknowledged that as yet very few of them go to the theater at all. Although playgoers and plays have prodigiously increased in the United States in the last forty years, the population indulge in this kind of amusement only with the greatest reserve. This is attributable to peculiar causes, which the reader is already acquainted with and of which a few words will suffice to remind him.

The Puritans who founded the American republics not only were enemies to amusements, but they professed an especial abhorrence for the stage. They considered it as an abominable pastime; and as long as their principles prevailed with undivided sway, scenic performances were wholly unknown among them. These opinions of the first fathers of the colonies have left very deep traces on the minds of their descendants.

The extreme regularity of habits and the great strictness of morals that are observable in the United States have as yet little favored the growth of dramatic art. There are no dramatic subjects in a country which has witnessed no great political catastrophes and in which love invariably leads by a straight and easy road to matrimony. People who spend every day in the week in making money, and Sunday in going to church, have nothing to invite the Muse of Comedy.

A single fact suffices to show that the stage is not very popular in the United States. The Americans, whose laws allow of the utmost freedom, and even license of language in all other respects, have nevertheless subjected their dramatic authors to a sort of censorship. Theatrical performances can take place only by permission of the municipal authorities. This may serve to show how much communities are like individuals; they surrender themselves unscrupulously to their ruling passions and afterwards take the greatest care not to yield too much to the vehemence of tastes that they do not possess.

No portion of literature is connected by closer or more numerous ties with the present condition of society than the drama. The drama of one period can never be suited to the following age if in the interval an important revolution has affected the manners and laws of the nation.

The great authors of a preceding age may be read, but pieces written for a different public will not attract an audience. The dramatic authors of the past live only in books. The traditional taste of certain individuals, vanity, fashion, or the genius of an actor may sustain or resuscitate for a time the aristocratic drama among a democracy; but it will speedily fall away of itself, not overthrown, but abandoned.

Chapter XX

SOME CHARACTERISTICS OF HISTORIANS IN DEMOCRATIC TIMES

HISTORIANS who write in aristocratic ages are inclined to refer all occurrences to the particular will and character of certain individuals; and they are apt to attribute the most important revolutions to slight accidents. They trace out the smallest causes with sagacity, and frequently leave the greatest unperceived.

Historians who live in democratic ages exhibit precisely opposite characteristics. Most of them attribute hardly any influence to the individual over the destiny of the race, or to citizens over the fate of a people; but, on the other hand, they assign great general causes to all petty incidents. These contrary tendencies explain each other.

When the historian of aristocratic ages surveys the theater of the world, he at once perceives a very small number of prominent actors who manage the whole piece. These great personages, who occupy the front of the stage, arrest attention and fix it on themselves; and while the historian is bent on penetrating the secret motives which make these persons speak and act, the others escape his memory. The importance of the things that some men are seen to do gives him an exaggerated estimate of the influence that one man may possess, and naturally leads him to think that in order to explain the impulses of the multitude, it is necessary to refer them to the particular influence of some one individual.

When, on the contrary, all the citizens are independent of one another, and each of them is individually weak, no one is seen to exert a great or still less a lasting power over the community. At first sight individuals appear to be absolutely devoid of any influence over it, and society would seem to advance alone by the free and voluntary action of all the men who compose it. This naturally prompts the mind to search for that general reason which operates upon so many men's faculties at once and turns them simultaneously in the same direction.

I am very well convinced that even among democratic nations the genius, the vices, or the virtues of certain individuals retard or accelerate the natural current of a people's history; but causes of this secondary and fortuitous nature are infinitely more various, more concealed, more complex, less powerful, and consequently less easy to trace, in periods of equality than in ages of aristocracy, when the task of the historian is simply to detach from the mass of general events the particular influence of one man or of a few men. In the former case the historian is soon wearied by the toil, his mind loses itself in this labyrinth, and, in his inability clearly to discern or conspicuously to point out the influence of individuals, he denies that they have any. He prefers talking about the characteristics of race, the physical conformation of the country, or the genius of civilization, and thus abridges his own labors and satisfies his reader better at less cost.

M. de Lafayette says somewhere in his *Memoirs* that the exaggerated system of general causes affords surprising consolations to second-rate statesmen. I will add that its effects are not less consolatory to second-rate historians; it can always furnish a few mighty reasons to extricate them from the most difficult part of their work, and it indulges the indolence or incapacity of their minds while it confers upon them the honors of deep thinking.

For myself, I am of the opinion that, at all times, one great portion of the events of this world are attributable to very general facts and another to special influences. These two kinds of cause are always in operation; only their proportion varies. General facts serve to explain more things in democratic than in aristocratic ages, and fewer things are then assignable to individual influences. During periods of aristocracy the reverse takes place: special influences are stronger, general causes weaker; unless, indeed, we consider as a general cause the fact itself of the inequality of condition, which allows some individuals to baffle the natural tendencies of all the rest.

The historians who seek to describe what occurs in democratic societies are right, therefore, in assigning much to general causes and in devoting their chief attention to discover them; but they are wrong in wholly denying the special influence of individuals because they cannot easily trace or follow it.

The historians who live in democratic ages not only are prone to assign a great cause to every incident, but are also given to connect incidents together so as to deduce a system from them. In aristocratic ages, as the attention of historians is constantly drawn to individuals, the connection of events escapes them; or rather they do not believe in any such connection. To them, the thread of history seems constantly to be broken by the course of one man's life. In democratic ages, on the contrary, as the historian sees much more of actions than of actors, he may easily establish some kind of sequence and methodical order among the former.

Ancient literature, which is so rich in fine historical compositions, does not contain a single great historical system, while the poorest of modern literatures abound with them. It would appear that the ancient historians did not make sufficient use of those general theories which our historical writers are ever ready to carry to excess.

Those who write in democratic ages have another more dangerous tendency. When the traces of individual action upon nations are lost, it often happens that you see the world move without the impelling force being evident. As it becomes extremely difficult to discern and analyze the reasons that, acting separately on the will of each member of the community, concur in the end to produce movement in the whole mass, men are led to believe that this movement is involuntary and that societies unconsciously obey some superior force ruling over them. But even when the general fact that governs the private volition of all individuals is supposed to be discovered upon the earth, the principle of human free-will is not made certain. A cause sufficiently extensive to affect millions of men at once and sufficiently strong to bend them all together in the same direction may well seem irresistible, having seen that mankind do yield to it, the mind is close upon the inference that mankind cannot resist it.

Historians who live in democratic ages, then, not only deny that the few have any power of acting upon the destiny of a people, but deprive the people themselves of the power of modifying their own condition, and they subject them either to an inflexible Providence or to some blind necessity. According to them, each nation is indissolubly bound by its position, its origin, its antecedents, and its character to a certain lot that no efforts can ever change. They involve generation in generation, and thus, going back from age to age, and from necessity to necessity, up to the origin of the world, they forge a close and enormous chain, which girds and binds the human race. To their minds it is not enough to show what events have occurred: they wish to show that events could not have occurred otherwise. They take a nation arrived at a certain stage of its history and affirm that it could not but follow the track that brought it thither. It is easier to make such an assertion than to show how the nation might have adopted a better course.

In reading the historians of aristocratic ages, and especially those of antiquity, it would seem that, to be master of his lot and to govern his fellow creatures, man requires only to be master of himself. In perusing the historical volumes which our age has produced, it would seem that man is utterly powerless over himself and over all around him. The historians of antiquity taught how to command; those of our time teach only how to obey; in their writings the author often appears great, but humanity is always diminutive.

If this doctrine of necessity, which is so attractive to those who write history in democratic ages, passes from authors to their readers till it infects the whole mass of the community and gets possession of the public mind, it will soon paralyze the activity of modern society and reduce Christians to the level of the Turks.

Moreover, I would observe that such doctrines are peculiarly dangerous at the period at which we have arrived. Our contemporaries are only too prone to doubt of human free-will, because each of them feels himself confined on every side by his own weakness; but they are still willing to acknowledge the strength and independence of men united in society. Do not let this principle be lost sight of, for the great object in our time is to raise the faculties of men, not to complete their prostration.

Chapter XXI

OF PARLIAMENTARY ELOQUENCE IN THE UNITED STATES

AMONG aristocratic nations all the members of the community are connected with and dependent upon each other; the graduated scale of different ranks acts as a tie which keeps everyone in his proper place and the whole body in subordination. Something of the same kind always occurs in the political assemblies of these nations. Parties naturally range themselves under certain leaders, whom they obey by a sort of instinct, which is only the result of habits contracted elsewhere. They carry the manners of general society into the lesser assemblage.

In democratic countries it often happens that a great number of citizens are tending to the same point; but each one moves thither, or at least flatters himself that he moves, only of his own accord. Accustomed to regulate his doings by personal impulse alone, he does not willingly submit to dictation from without. This taste and habit of independence accompany him into the councils of the nation. If he consents to connect himself with other men in the prosecution of the same purpose, at least he chooses to remain free to contribute to the common success after his own fashion. Hence it is that in democratic countries parties are so impatient of control and are never manageable except in moments of great public danger. Even then the authority of leaders, which under such circumstances may be able to make men act or speak, hardly ever reaches the extent of making them keep silence.

Among aristocratic nations the members of political assemblies are at the same time members of the aristocracy. Each of them enjoys high established rank in his own right, and the position that he occupies in the assembly is often less important in his eyes than that which he fills in the country. This consoles him for playing no part in the discussion of public affairs and restrains him from too eagerly attempting to play an insignificant one.

In America it generally happens that a representative becomes somebody only from his position in the assembly. He is therefore perpetually haunted by a craving to acquire importance there, and he feels a petulant desire to be constantly obtruding his opinions upon his fellow members. His own vanity is not the only stimulant which urges him on in this course, but also that of his constituents and the continual necessity of propitiating them. Among aristocratic nations a member of the legislature is rarely in strict dependence upon his constituents: he is frequently to them a sort of unavoidable representative; sometimes they are themselves strictly dependent upon him, and if, at length, they reject him, he may easily get elected elsewhere or, retiring from public life, he may still enjoy the pleasures of splendid idleness. In a democratic country, like the United States, a representative has hardly ever a lasting hold on the minds of his constituents. However small an electoral body may be, the fluctuations of democracy are constantly changing its aspect; it must therefore be courted unceasingly. A representative is never sure of his supporters, and, if they forsake him, he is left without a resource; for his natural position is not sufficiently elevated for him to be easily known to those not close to him; and, with the complete state of independence prevailing among the people, he cannot hope that his friends or the government will send him down to be returned by an electoral body unacquainted with him. The seeds of his fortune, therefore, are sown in his own neighborhood; from that nook of earth he must start, to raise himself to command the people and to influence the destinies of the world. Thus it is natural that in democratic countries the members of political assemblies should think more of their constituents than of their party, while in aristocracies they think more of their party than of their constituents.

But what ought to be said to gratify constituents is not always what ought to be said in order to serve the party to which representatives profess to belong. The general interest of a party frequently demands that members belonging to it should not speak on great questions which they understand imperfectly; that they should speak but little on those minor questions which impede the great ones; lastly, and for the most part, that they should not speak at all. To keep silence is the most useful service that an indifferent spokesman can render to the commonwealth.

Constituents, however, do not think so. The population of a district send a representative to take a part in the government of a country because they entertain a very high notion of his merits. As men appear greater in proportion to the littleness of the objects by which they are surrounded, it may be assumed that the opinion entertained of the delegate will be so much the higher as talents are more rare among his constituents. It will therefore frequently happen that the less constituents ought to expect from their representative, the more they anticipate from him; and however incompetent he may be, they will not fail to call upon him for signal exertions, corresponding to the rank they have conferred upon him.

Independently of his position as a legislator of the state, electors also regard their representative as the natural patron of the constituency in the legislature; they almost consider him as the proxy of each of his supporters, and they flatter themselves that he will not be less zealous in defense of their private interests than of those of the country. Thus electors are well assured beforehand that the representative of their choice will be an orator, that he will speak often if he can, and that, in case he is forced to refrain, he will strive at any rate to compress into his less frequent orations an inquiry into all the great questions of state, combined with a statement of all the petty grievances they have themselves to complain of; so that, even though he is not able to come forward frequently, he should on each occasion prove what he is capable of doing; and that, instead of perpetually lavishing his powers, he should occasionally condense them in a small compass, so as to furnish a sort of complete and brilliant epitome of his constituents and of himself. On these terms they will vote for him at the next election.

These conditions drive worthy men of humble abilities to despair; who, knowing their own powers, would never voluntarily have come forward. But thus urged on, the representative begins to speak, to the great alarm of his friends; and rushing imprudently into the midst of the most celebrated orators, he perplexes the debate and wearies the House.

All laws that tend to make the representative more dependent on the elector affect not only the conduct of the legislators, as I have remarked elsewhere, but also their language. They exercise a simultaneous influence on affairs themselves and on the manner in which affairs are discussed.

There is hardly a member of Congress who can make up his mind to go home without having dispatched at least one speech to his constituents, or who will endure any interruption until he has introduced into his harangue whatever useful suggestions may be made touching the four-and-twenty states of which the Union is composed, and especially the district that he represents. He therefore presents to the mind of his auditors a succession of great general truths (which he himself comprehends and expresses only confusedly) and of petty minutiæ, which he is but too able to discover and to point out. The consequence is that the debates of that great assembly are frequently vague and perplexed and that they seem to drag their slow length along rather than to advance towards a distinct object. Some such state of things will, I believe, always arise in the public assemblies of democracies.

Propitious circumstances and good laws might succeed in drawing to the legislature of a democratic people men very superior to those who are returned by the Americans to Congress; but nothing will ever prevent the men of slender abilities who sit there from obtruding themselves with complacency, and in all ways, upon the public. The evil does not appear to me to be susceptible of entire cure, because it originates not only in the tactics of that assembly, but in its constitution and in that of the country. The inhabitants of the United States seem themselves to consider the matter in this light; and they show their long experience of parliamentary life, not by abstaining from making bad speeches, but by courageously submitting to hear them made. They are resigned to it as to an evil that they know to be inevitable.

I have shown the petty side of political debates in democratic assemblies; let me now exhibit the imposing one. The proceedings within the Parliament of England for the last one hundred and fifty years have never occasioned any great sensation outside that country; the opinions and feelings expressed by the speakers have never awakened much sympathy even among the nations placed nearest to the great arena of British liberty; whereas Europe was excited by the very first debates that took place in the small colonial assemblies of America at the time of the Revolution.

This was attributable not only to particular and fortuitous circumstances, but to general and lasting causes. I can conceive nothing more admirable or more powerful than a great orator debating great questions of state in a democratic assembly. As no particular class is ever represented there by men commissioned to defend its own interests, it is always to the whole nation, and in the name of the whole nation, that the orator speaks. This expands his thoughts and heightens his power of language. As precedents have there but little weight, as there are no longer any privileges attached to certain property, nor any rights inherent in certain individuals, the mind must have recourse to general truths derived from human nature to solve the particular question under discussion. Hence the political debates of a democratic people, however small it may be, have a degree of breadth that frequently renders them attractive to mankind. All men are interested by them because they treat of *man*, who is everywhere the same.

Among the greatest aristocratic nations, on the contrary, the most general questions are almost always argued on some special grounds derived from the practice of a particular time or the rights of a particular class, which interest that class alone, or at most the people among whom that class happens to exist.

It is owing to this as much as to the greatness of the French people and the favorable disposition of the nations who listen to them that the great effect which the French political debates sometimes produce in the world must be attributed. The orators of France frequently speak to mankind even when they are addressing their countrymen only.

SECOND BOOK

INFLUENCE OF DEMOCRACY ON THE FEELINGS OF THE AMERICANS

Chapter I

WHY DEMOCRATIC NATIONS SHOW A MORE ARDENT AND ENDURING LOVE OF EQUALITY THAN OF LIBERTY

THE FIRST and most intense passion that is produced by equality of condition is, I need hardly say, the love of that equality. My readers will therefore not be surprised that I speak of this feeling before all others.

Everybody has remarked that in our time, and especially in France, this passion for equality is every day gaining ground in the human heart. It has been said a hundred times that our contemporaries are far more ardently and tenaciously attached to equality than to freedom; but as I do not find that the causes of the fact have been sufficiently analyzed, I shall endeavor to point them out.

It is possible to imagine an extreme point at which freedom and equality would meet and blend. Let us suppose that all the people take a part in the government, and that each one of them has an equal right to take part in it. As no one is different from his fellows, none can exercise a tyrannical power; men will be perfectly free because they are all entirely equal; and they will all be perfectly equal because they are entirely free. To this ideal state democratic nations tend. This is the only complete form that equality can assume upon earth; but there are a thousand others which, without being equally perfect, are not less cherished by those nations.

The principle of equality may be established in civil society without prevailing in the political world. There may be equal rights of indulging in the same pleasures, of entering the same professions, of frequenting the same places; in a word, of living in the same manner and seeking wealth by the same means, although all men do not take an equal share in the government. A kind of equality may even be established in the political world though there should be no political freedom there. A man may be the equal of all his countrymen save one, who is the master of all without distinction and who selects equally from among them all the agents of his power. Several other combinations might be easily imagined by which very great equality would be united to institutions more or less free or even to institutions wholly without freedom.

Although men cannot become absolutely equal unless they are entirely free, and consequently equality, pushed to its furthest extent, may be confounded with freedom, yet there is good reason for distinguishing the one from the other. The taste which men have for liberty and that which they feel for equality are, in fact, two different things; and I am not afraid to add that among democratic nations they are two unequal things.

Upon close inspection it will be seen that there is in every age some peculiar and preponderant fact with which all others are connected; this fact almost always gives birth to some pregnant idea or some ruling passion, which attracts to itself and bears away in its course all the feelings and opinions of the time; it is like a great stream towards which each of the neighboring rivulets seems to flow.

Freedom has appeared in the world at different times and under various forms; it has not been exclusively bound to any social condition, and it is not confined to democracies. Freedom cannot, therefore, form the distinguishing characteristic of democratic ages. The peculiar and preponderant fact that marks those ages as its own is the equality of condition; the ruling passion of men in those periods is the love of this equality. Do not ask what singular charm the men of democratic ages find in being equal, or what special reasons they may have for clinging so tenaciously to equality rather than to the other advantages that society holds out to them: equality is the distinguishing characteristic of the age they live in; that of itself is enough to explain that they prefer it to all the rest.

But independently of this reason there are several others which will at all times habitually lead men to prefer equality to freedom.

If a people could ever succeed in destroying, or even in diminishing the equality that prevails in its own body, they could do so only by long and laborious efforts. Their social condition must be modified, their laws abolished, their opinions superseded, their habits changed, their manners corrupted. But political liberty is more easily lost; to neglect to hold it fast is to allow it to escape. Therefore not only do men cling to equality because it is dear to them; they also adhere to it because they think it will last forever.

That political freedom in its excesses may compromise the tranquillity, the property, the lives of individuals is obvious even to narrow and unthinking minds. On the contrary, none but attentive and clear-sighted men perceive the perils with which equality threatens us, and they commonly avoid pointing them out. They know that the calamities they apprehend are remote and flatter themselves that they will only fall upon future generations, for which the present generation takes but little thought. The evils that freedom sometimes brings with it are immediate; they are apparent to all, and all are more or less affected by them. The evils that extreme equality may produce are slowly disclosed; they creep gradually into the social frame; they are seen only at intervals; and at the moment at which they become most violent, habit already causes them to be no longer felt.

The advantages that freedom brings are shown only by the lapse of time, and it is always easy to mistake the cause in which they originate. The advantages of equality are immediate, and they may always be traced from their source.

Political liberty bestows exalted pleasures from time to time upon a certain number of citizens. Equality every day confers a number of small enjoyments on every man. The charms of equality are every instant felt and are within the reach of all; the noblest hearts are not insensible to them, and the most vulgar souls exult in them. The passion that equality creates must therefore be at once strong and general. Men cannot enjoy political liberty unpurchased by some sacrifices, and they never obtain it without great exertions. But the pleasures of equality are self-proffered; each of the petty incidents of life seems to occasion them, and in order to taste them, nothing is required but to live.

Democratic nations are at all times fond of equality, but there are certain epochs at which the passion they entertain for it swells to the height of fury. This occurs at the moment when the old social system, long menaced, is overthrown after a severe internal struggle, and the barriers of rank are at length thrown down. At such times men pounce upon equality as their booty, and they cling to it as to some precious treasure which they fear to lose. The passion for equality penetrates on every side into men's hearts, expands there, and fills them entirely. Tell them not that by this blind surrender of themselves to an exclusive passion they risk their dearest interests; they are deaf. Show them not freedom escaping from their grasp while they are looking another way; they are blind, or rather they can discern but one object to be desired in the universe.

What I have said is applicable to all democratic nations; what I am about to say concerns the French alone. Among most modern nations, and especially among all those of the continent of Europe, the taste and the idea of freedom began to exist and to be developed only at the time when social conditions were tending to equality and as a consequence of that very equality. Absolute kings were the most efficient levelers of ranks among their subjects. Among these nations equality preceded freedom; equality was therefore a fact of some standing when freedom was still a novelty; the one had already created customs, opinions, and laws belonging to it when the other, alone and for the first time, came into actual existence. Thus the latter was still only an affair of opinion and of taste while the former had already crept into the habits of the people, possessed itself of their manners, and given a particular turn to the smallest actions in their lives. Can it be wondered at that the men of our own time prefer the one to the other?

I think that democratic communities have a natural taste for freedom; left to themselves, they will seek it, cherish it, and view any privation of it with regret. But for equality their passion is ardent, insatiable, incessant, invincible; they call for equality in freedom; and if they cannot obtain that, they still call for equality in slavery. They will endure poverty, servitude, barbarism, but they will not endure aristocracy.

This is true at all times, and especially in our own day. All men and all powers seeking to cope with this irresistible passion will be overthrown and destroyed by it. In our age freedom cannot be established without it, and despotism itself cannot reign without its support.

Chapter II

OF INDIVIDUALISM IN DEMOCRATIC COUNTRIES

I HAVE shown how it is that in ages of equality every man seeks for his opinions within himself; I am now to show how it is that in the same ages all his feelings are turned towards himself alone. *Individualism* is a novel expression, to which a novel idea has given birth. Our fathers were only acquainted with *égoïsme* (selfishness). Selfishness is a passionate and exaggerated love of self, which leads a man to connect everything with himself and to prefer himself to everything in the world. Individualism is a mature and calm feeling, which disposes each member of the community to sever himself from the mass of his fellows and to draw apart with his family and his friends, so that after he has thus formed a little circle of his own, he willingly leaves society at large to itself. Selfishness originates in blind instinct; individualism proceeds from erroneous judgment more than from depraved feelings; it originates as much in deficiencies of mind as in perversity of heart.

Selfishness blights the germ of all virtue; individualism, at first, only saps the virtues of public life; but in the long run it attacks and destroys all others and is at length absorbed in downright selfishness. Selfishness is a vice as old as the world, which does not belong to one form of society more than to another; individualism is of democratic origin, and it threatens to spread in the same ratio as the equality of condition.

Among aristocratic nations, as families remain for centuries in the same condition, often on the same spot, all generations become, as it were, contemporaneous. A man almost always knows his forefathers and respects them; he thinks he already sees his remote descendants and he loves them. He willingly imposes duties on himself towards the former and the latter, and he will frequently sacrifice his personal gratifications to those who went before and to those who will come after him. Aristocratic institutions, moreover, have the effect of closely binding every man to several of his fellow citizens. As the classes of an aristocratic people are strongly marked and permanent, each of them is regarded by its own members as a sort of lesser country, more tangible and more cherished than the country at large. As in aristocratic communities all the citizens occupy fixed positions, one above another, the result is that each of them always sees a man above himself whose patronage is necessary to him, and below himself another man whose co-operation he may claim. Men living in aristocratic ages are therefore almost always closely attached to something placed out of their own sphere, and they are often disposed to forget themselves. It is true that in these ages the notion of human fellowship is faint and that men seldom think of sacrificing themselves for mankind; but they often sacrifice themselves for other men. In democratic times, on the contrary, when the duties of each individual to the race are much more clear, devoted service to any one man becomes more rare; the bond of human affection is extended, but it is relaxed.

Among democratic nations new families are constantly springing up, others are constantly falling away, and all that remain change their condition; the woof of time is every instant broken and the track of generations effaced. Those who went before are soon forgotten; of those who will come after, no one has any idea: the interest of man is confined to those in close propinquity to himself. As each class gradually approaches others and mingles with them, its members become undifferentiated and lose their class identity for each other. Aristocracy had made a chain of all the members of the community, from the peasant to the king; democracy breaks that chain and severs every link of it.

As social conditions become more equal, the number of persons increases who, although they are neither rich nor powerful enough to exercise any great influence over their fellows, have nevertheless acquired or retained sufficient education and fortune to satisfy their own wants. They owe nothing to any man, they expect nothing from any man; they acquire the habit of always considering themselves as standing alone, and they are apt to imagine that their whole destiny is in their own hands.

Thus not only does democracy make every man forget his ancestors, but it hides his descendants and separates his contemporaries from him; it throws him back forever upon himself alone and threatens in the end to confine him entirely within the solitude of his own heart.

Chapter III

INDIVIDUALISM STRONGER AT THE CLOSE OF A DEMOCRATIC REVOLUTION THAN AT OTHER PERIODS

THE PERIOD when the construction of democratic society upon the ruins of an aristocracy has just been completed is especially that at which this isolation of men from one another and the selfishness resulting from it most forcibly strike the observer. Democratic communities not only contain a large number of independent citizens, but are constantly filled with men who, having entered but yesterday upon their independent condition, are intoxicated with their new power. They entertain a presumptuous confidence in their own strength, and as they do not suppose that they can henceforward ever have occasion to claim the assistance of their fellow creatures, they do not scruple to show that they care for nobody but themselves.

An aristocracy seldom yields without a protracted struggle, in the course of which implacable animosities are kindled between the different classes of society. These passions survive the victory, and traces of them may be observed in the midst of the democratic confusion that ensues. Those members of the community who were at the top of the late gradations of rank cannot immediately forget their former greatness; they will long regard themselves as aliens in the midst of the newly composed society. They look upon all those whom this state of society has made their equals as oppressors, whose destiny can excite no sympathy; they have lost sight of their former equals and feel no longer bound to their fate by a common interest; each of them, standing aloof, thinks that he is reduced to care for himself alone. Those, on the contrary, who were formerly at the foot of the social scale and who have been brought up to the common level by a sudden revolution cannot enjoy their newly acquired independence without secret uneasiness; and if they meet with some of their former superiors on the same footing as themselves, they stand aloof from them with an expression of triumph and fear.

It is, then, commonly at the outset of democratic society that citizens are most disposed to live apart. Democracy leads men not to draw near to their fellow creatures; but democratic revolutions lead them to shun each other and perpetuate in a state of equality the animosities that the state of inequality created.

The great advantage of the Americans is that they have arrived at a state of democracy without having to endure a democratic revolution, and that they are born equal instead of becoming so.

Chapter IV

THAT THE AMERICANS COMBAT THE EFFECTS OF INDIVIDUALISM BY FREE INSTITUTIONS

DESPOTISM, which by its nature is suspicious, sees in the separation among men the surest guarantee of its continuance, and it usually makes every effort to keep them separate. No vice of the human heart is so acceptable to it as selfishness: a despot easily forgives his subjects for not loving him, provided they do not love one another. He does not ask them to assist him in governing the state; it is enough that they do not aspire to govern it themselves. He stigmatizes as turbulent and unruly spirits those who would combine their exertions to promote the prosperity of the community; and, perverting the natural meaning of words, he applauds as good citizens those who have no sympathy for any but themselves.

Thus the vices which despotism produces are precisely those which equality fosters. These two things perniciously complete and assist each other. Equality places men side by side, unconnected by any common tie; despotism raises barriers to keep them asunder; the former predisposes them not to consider their fellow creatures, the latter makes general indifference a sort of public virtue.

Despotism, then, which is at all times dangerous, is more particularly to be feared in democratic ages. It is easy to see that in those same ages men stand most in need of freedom. When the members of a community are forced to attend to public affairs, they are necessarily drawn from the circle of their own interests and snatched at times from self-observation. As soon as a man begins to treat of public affairs in public, he begins to perceive that he is not so independent of his fellow men as he had at first imagined, and that in order to obtain their support he must often lend them his co-operation.

When the public govern, there is no man who does not

feel the value of public goodwill or who does not endeavor to court it by drawing to himself the esteem and affection of those among whom he is to live. Many of the passions which congeal and keep asunder human hearts are then obliged to retire and hide below the surface. Pride must be dissembled; disdain dares not break out; selfishness fears its own self. Under a free government, as most public offices are elective, the men whose elevated minds or aspiring hopes are too closely circumscribed in private life constantly feel that they cannot do without the people who surround them. Men learn at such times to think of their fellow men from ambitious motives; and they frequently find it, in a manner, their interest to forget themselves.

I may here be met by an objection derived from electioneering intrigues, the meanness of candidates, and the calumnies of their opponents. These are occasions of enmity which occur the oftener the more frequent elections become. Such evils are doubtless great, but they are transient; whereas the benefits that attend them remain. The desire of being elected may lead some men for a time to violent hostility; but this same desire leads all men in the long run to support each other; and if it happens that an election accidentally severs two friends, the electoral system brings a multitude of citizens permanently together who would otherwise always have remained unknown to one another. Freedom produces private animosities, but despotism gives birth to general indifference.

The Americans have combated by free institutions the tendency of equality to keep men asunder, and they have subdued it. The legislators of America did not suppose that a general representation of the whole nation would suffice to ward off a disorder at once so natural to the frame of democratic society and so fatal; they also thought that it would be well to infuse political life into each portion of the territory in order to multiply to an infinite extent opportunities of acting in concert for all the members of the community and to make them constantly feel their mutual dependence. The plan was a wise one. The general affairs of a country engage the attention only of leading politicians, who assemble from time to time in the same places; and as they often lose sight of each other afterwards, no lasting ties are established between them. But if the object be to have the local affairs of a district conducted by the men who reside there, the same persons are always in contact, and they are, in a manner, forced to be acquainted and to adapt themselves to one another.

It is difficult to draw a man out of his own circle to interest him in the destiny of the state, because he does not clearly understand what influence the destiny of the state can have upon his own lot. But if it is proposed to make a road cross the end of his estate, he will see at a glance that there is a connection between this small public affair and his greatest private affairs; and he will discover, without its being shown to him, the close tie that unites private to general interest. Thus far more may be done by entrusting to the citizens the administration of minor affairs than by surrendering to them in the control of important ones, towards interesting them in the public welfare and convincing them that they constantly stand in need of one another in order to provide for it. A brilliant achievement may win for you the favor of a people at one stroke; but to earn the love and respect of the population that surrounds you, a long succession of little services rendered and of obscure good deeds, a constant habit of kindness, and an established reputation for disinterestedness will be required. Local freedom, then, which leads a great number of citizens to value the affection of their neighbors and of their kindred, perpetually brings men together and forces them to help one another in spite of the propensities that sever them.

In the United States the more opulent citizens take great care not to stand aloof from the people; on the contrary, they constantly keep on easy terms with the lower classes: they listen to them, they speak to them every day. They know that the rich in democracies always stand in need of the poor, and that in democratic times you attach a poor man to you more by your manner than by benefits conferred. The magnitude of such benefits, which sets off the difference of condition, causes a secret irritation to those who reap advantage from them, but the charm of simplicity of manners is almost irresistible; affability carries men away, and even want of polish is not always displeasing. This truth does not take root at once in the minds of the rich. They generally resist it as long as the democratic revolution lasts, and they do not acknowledge it immediately after that revolution is accomplished. They are very ready to do good to the people, but they still choose to keep them at arm's length; they think that is sufficient, but they are mistaken. They might spend fortunes thus without warming the hearts of the population around them; that population does not ask them for the sacrifice of their money, but of their pride.

It would seem as if every imagination in the United States were upon the stretch to invent means of increasing the wealth and satisfying the wants of the public. The best-informed inhabitants of each district constantly use their information to discover new truths that may augment the general prosperity; and if they have made any such discoveries, they eagerly surrender them to the mass of the people.

When the vices and weaknesses frequently exhibited by those who govern in America are closely examined, the prosperity of the people occasions, but improperly occasions, surprise. Elected magistrates do not make the American democracy flourish; it flourishes because the magistrates are elective.

It would be unjust to suppose that the patriotism and the zeal that every American displays for the welfare of his fellow citizens are wholly insincere. Although private interest directs the greater part of human actions in the United States as well as elsewhere, it does not regulate them all. I must say that I have often seen Americans make great and real sacrifices to the public welfare; and I have noticed a hundred instances in which they hardly ever failed to lend faithful support to one another. The free institutions which the inhabitants of the United States possess, and the political rights of which they make so much use, remind every citizen, and in a thousand ways, that he lives in society. They every instant impress upon his mind the notion that it is the duty as well as the interest of men to make themselves useful to their fellow creatures; and as he sees no particular ground of animosity to them, since he is never either their master or their slave, his heart readily leans to the side of kindness. Men attend to the interests of the public, first by necessity, afterwards by choice; what was intentional becomes an instinct, and by dint of working for the good of one's fellow citizens, the habit and the taste for serving them are at length acquired.

Many people in France consider equality of condition as

one evil and political freedom as a second. When they are obliged to yield to the former, they strive at least to escape from the latter. But I contend that in order to combat the evils which equality may produce, there is only one effectual remedy: namely, political freedom.

Chapter V

OF THE USE WHICH THE AMERICANS MAKE OF PUBLIC ASSOCIATIONS IN CIVIL LIFE

I DO not propose to speak of those political associations by the aid of which men endeavor to defend themselves against the despotic action of a majority or against the aggressions of regal power. That subject I have already treated. If each citizen did not learn, in proportion as he individually becomes more feeble and consequently more incapable of preserving his freedom single-handed, to combine with his fellow citizens for the purpose of defending it, it is clear that tyranny would unavoidably increase together with equality.

Only those associations that are formed in civil life without reference to political objects are here referred to. The political associations that exist in the United States are only a single feature in the midst of the immense assemblage of associations in that country. Americans of all ages, all conditions, and all dispositions constantly form associations. They have not only commercial and manufacturing companies, in which all take part, but associations of a thousand other kinds, religious, moral, serious, futile, general or restricted, enormous or diminutive. The Americans make associations to give entertainments, to found seminaries, to build inns, to construct churches, to diffuse books, to send missionaries to the antipodes; in this manner they found hospitals, prisons, and schools. If it is proposed to inculcate some truth or to foster some feeling by the encouragement of a great example, they form a society. Wherever at the head of some new undertaking you see the government in France, or a man of rank in England, in the United States you will be sure to find an association.

I met with several kinds of associations in America of which I confess I had no previous notion; and I have often admired the extreme skill with which the inhabitants of the

United States succeed in proposing a common object for the exertions of a great many men and inducing them voluntarily to pursue it.

I have since traveled over England, from which the Americans have taken some of their laws and many of their customs; and it seemed to me that the principle of association was by no means so constantly or adroitly used in that country. The English often perform great things singly, whereas the Americans form associations for the smallest undertakings. It is evident that the former people consider association as a powerful means of action, but the latter seem to regard it as the only means they have of acting.

Thus the most democratic country on the face of the earth is that in which men have, in our time, carried to the highest perfection the art of pursuing in common the object of their common desires and have applied this new science to the greatest number of purposes. Is this the result of accident, or is there in reality any necessary connection between the principle of association and that of equality?

Aristocratic communities always contain, among a multitude of persons who by themselves are powerless, a small number of powerful and wealthy citizens, each of whom can achieve great undertakings single-handed. In aristocratic societies men do not need to combine in order to act, because they are strongly held together. Every wealthy and powerful citizen constitutes the head of a permanent and compulsory association, composed of all those who are dependent upon him or whom he makes subservient to the execution of his designs.

Among democratic nations, on the contrary, all the citizens are independent and feeble; they can do hardly anything by themselves, and none of them can oblige his fellow men to lend him their assistance. They all, therefore, become powerless if they do not learn voluntarily to help one another. If men living in democratic countries had no right and no inclination to associate for political purposes, their independence would be in great jeopardy, but they might long preserve their wealth and their cultivation: whereas if they never acquired the habit of forming associations in ordinary life, civilization itself would be endangered. A people among whom individuals lost the power of achieving great things single-handed, without acquiring the means of producing them by united exertions, would soon relapse into barbarism.

Unhappily, the same social condition that renders associations so necessary to democratic nations renders their formation more difficult among those nations than among all others. When several members of an aristocracy agree to combine, they easily succeed in doing so; as each of them brings great strength to the partnership, the number of its members may be very limited; and when the members of an assocation are limited in number, they may easily become mutually acquainted, understand each other, and establish fixed regulations. The same opportunities do not occur among democratic nations, where the associated members must always be very numerous for their association to have any power.

I am aware that many of my countrymen are not in the least embarrassed by this difficulty. They contend that the more enfeebled and incompetent the citizens become, the more able and active the government ought to be rendered in order that society at large may execute what individuals can no longer accomplish. They believe this answers the whole difficulty, but I think they are mistaken.

A government might perform the part of some of the largest American companies, and several states, members of the Union, have already attempted it; but what political power could ever carry on the vast multitude of lesser undertakings which the American citizens perform every day, with the assistance of the principle of association? It is easy to foresee that the time is drawing near when man will be less and less able to produce, by himself alone, the commonest necessaries of life. The task of the governing power will therefore perpetually increase, and its very efforts will extend it every day. The more it stands in the place of associations, the more will individuals, losing the notion of combining together, require its assistance: these are causes and effects that unceasingly create each other. Will the administration of the country ultimately assume the management of all the manufactures which no single citizen is able to carry on? And if a time at length arrives when, in consequence of the extreme subdivision of landed property, the soil is split into an infinite number of parcels, so that it can be cultivated only by companies of tillers, will it be necessary that the head of the government should leave the helm of state to follow the plow? The morals and the intelligence of a democratic people would be as much endangered as its business and manufactures if the government ever wholly usurped the place of private companies.

Feelings and opinions are recruited, the heart is enlarged, and the human mind is developed only by the reciprocal influence of men upon one another. I have shown that these influences are almost null in democratic countries; they must therefore be artificially created, and this can only be accomplished by associations.

When the members of an aristocratic community adopt a new opinion or conceive a new sentiment, they give it a station, as it were, beside themselves, upon the lofty platform where they stand; and opinions or sentiments so conspicuous to the eyes of the multitude are easily introduced into the minds or hearts of all around. In democratic countries the governing power alone is naturally in a condition to act in this manner, but it is easy to see that its action is always inadequate, and often dangerous. A government can no more be competent to keep alive and to renew the circulation of opinions and feelings among a great people than to manage all the speculations of productive industry. No sooner does a government attempt to go beyond its political sphere and to enter upon this new track than it exercises, even unintentionally, an insupportable tyranny; for a government can only dictate strict rules, the opinions which it favors are rigidly enforced, and it is never easy to discriminate between its advice and its commands. Worse still will be the case if the government really believes itself interested in preventing all circulation of ideas; it will then stand motionless and oppressed by the heaviness of voluntary torpor. Governments, therefore, should not be the only active powers; associations ought, in democratic nations, to stand in lieu of those powerful private individuals whom the equality of conditions has swept away.

As soon as several of the inhabitants of the United States have taken up an opinion or a feeling which they wish to promote in the world, they look out for mutual assistance; and as soon as they have found one another out, they combine. From that moment they are no longer isolated men, but a power seen from afar, whose actions serve for an example and whose language is listened to. The first time I heard in the United States that a hundred thousand men had bound themselves publicly to abstain from spirituous liquors, it appeared to me more like a joke than a serious engagement, and I did not at once perceive why these temperate citizens could not content themselves with drinking water by their own firesides. I at last understood that these hundred thousand Americans, alarmed by the progress of drunkenness around them, had made up their minds to patronize temperance. They acted in just the same way as a man of high rank who should dress very plainly in order to inspire the humbler orders with a contempt of luxury. It is probable that if these hundred thousand men had lived in France, each of them would singly have memorialized the government to watch the public houses all over the kingdom.

Nothing, in my opinion, is more deserving of our attention than the intellectual and moral associations of America. The political and industrial associations of that country strike us forcibly; but the others elude our observation, or if we discover them, we understand them imperfectly because we have hardly ever seen anything of the kind. It must be acknowledged, however, that they are as necessary to the American people as the former, and perhaps more so. In democratic countries the science of association is the mother of science; the progress of all the rest depends upon the progress it has made.

Among the laws that rule human societies there is one which seems to be more precise and clear than all others. If men are to remain civilized or to become so, the art of associating together must grow and improve in the same ratio in which the equality of conditions is increased.

Chapter VI

OF THE RELATION BETWEEN PUBLIC ASSOCIATIONS AND THE NEWSPAPERS

WHEN men are no longer united among themselves by firm and lasting ties, it is impossible to obtain the co-operation of any great number of them unless you can persuade every man whose help you require that his private interest obliges him voluntarily to unite his exertions to the exertions of all the others. This can be habitually and conveniently effected only by means of a newspaper; nothing but a newspaper can drop the same thought into a thousand minds at the same moment. A newspaper is an adviser that does not require to be sought, but that comes of its own accord and talks to you briefly every day of the common weal, without distracting you from your private affairs.

Newspapers therefore become more necessary in proportion as men become more equal and individualism more to be feared. To suppose that they only serve to protect freedom would be to diminish their importance: they maintain civilization. I shall not deny that in democratic countries newspapers frequently lead the citizens to launch together into very ill-digested schemes; but if there were no newspapers there would be no common activity. The evil which they produce is therefore much less than that which they cure.

The effect of a newspaper is not only to suggest the same purpose to a great number of persons, but to furnish means for executing in common the designs which they may have singly conceived. The principal citizens who inhabit an aristocratic country discern each other from afar; and if they wish to unite their forces, they move towards each other, drawing a multitude of men after them. In democratic countries, on the contrary, it frequently happens that a great number of men who wish or who want to combine cannot accomplish it because as they are very insignificant and lost amid the crowd, they cannot see and do not know where to find one another. A newspaper then takes up the notion or the feeling that had occurred simultaneously, but singly, to each of them. All are then immediately guided towards this beacon; and these wandering minds, which had long sought each other in darkness, at length meet and unite. The newspaper brought them together, and the newspaper is still necessary to keep them united.

In order that an association among a democratic people should have any power, it must be a numerous body. The persons of whom it is composed are therefore scattered over a wide extent, and each of them is detained in the place of his domicile by the narrowness of his income or by the small unremitting exertions by which he earns it. Means must then be found to converse every day without seeing one another, and to take steps in common without having met. Thus hardly any democratic association can do without newspapers.

Consequently, there is a necessary connection between public associations and newspapers: newspapers make associations, and associations make newspapers; and if it has been correctly advanced that associations will increase in number as the conditions of men become more equal, it is not less certain that the number of newspapers increases in proportion to that of associations. Thus it is in America that we find at the same time the greatest number of associations and of newspapers.

This connection between the number of newspapers and that of associations leads us to the discovery of a further connection between the state of the periodical press and the form of the administration in a country, and shows that the number of newspapers must diminish or increase among a democratic people in proportion as its administration is more or less centralized. For among democratic nations the exercise of local powers cannot be entrusted to the principal members of the community as in aristocracies. Those powers must be either abolished or placed in the hands of very large numbers of men, who then in fact constitute an association permanently established by law for the purpose of administering the affairs of a certain extent of territory; and they require a journal to bring to them every day, in the midst of their own minor concerns, some intelligence of the state of their public weal. The more numerous local powers are, the greater is the number of men in whom they are vested by law; and as this want is hourly felt, the more profusely do newspapers abound.

The extraordinary subdivision of administrative power has much more to do with the enormous number of American newspapers than the great political freedom of the country and the absolute liberty of the press. If all the inhabitants of the Union had the suffrage, but a suffrage which should extend only to the choice of their legislators in Congress, they would require but few newspapers, because they would have to act together only on very important, but very rare, occasions. But within the great national association lesser associations have been established by law in every county, every city, and indeed in every village, for the purposes of local administration. The laws of the country thus compel every American to co-operate every day of his life with some of his fellow citizens for a common purpose, and each one of them requires a newspaper to inform him what all the others are doing.

I am of the opinion that a democratic people[1] without any national representative assemblies but with a great number of small local powers would have in the end more newspapers than another people governed by a centralized administration and an elective legislature. What best explains to me the enormous circulation of the daily press in the United States is that among the Americans I find the utmost national freedom combined with local freedom of every kind.

There is a prevailing opinion in France and England that the circulation of newspapers would be indefinitely increased by removing the taxes which have been laid upon the press. This is a very exaggerated estimate of the effects of such a reform. Newspapers increase in numbers, not according to their cheapness, but according to the more or less frequent want which a great number of men may feel for intercommunication and combination.

In like manner I should attribute the increasing influence

[1] I say a *democratic people:* the administration of an aristocratic people may be very decentralized and yet the want of newspapers be little felt, because local powers are then vested in the hands of a very small number of men, who either act apart or know each other and can easily meet and come to an understanding.

of the daily press to causes more general than those by which it is commonly explained. A newspaper can survive only on the condition of publishing sentiments or principles common to a large number of men. A newspaper, therefore, always represents an association that is composed of its habitual readers. This association may be more or less defined, more or less restricted, more or less numerous; but the fact that the newspaper keeps alive is a proof that at least the germ of such an association exists in the minds of its readers.

This leads me to a last reflection, with which I shall conclude this chapter. The more equal the conditions of men become and the less strong men individually are, the more easily they give way to the current of the multitude and the more difficult it is for them to adhere by themselves to an opinion which the multitude discard. A newspaper represents an association; it may be said to address each of its readers in the name of all the others and to exert its influence over them in proportion to their individual weakness. The power of the newspaper press must therefore increase as the social conditions of men become more equal.

Chapter VII

RELATION OF CIVIL TO POLITICAL ASSOCIATIONS

THERE is only one country on the face of the earth where the citizens enjoy unlimited freedom of association for political purposes. This same country is the only one in the world where the continual exercise of the right of association has been introduced into civil life and where all the advantages which civilization can confer are procured by means of it.

In all the countries where political associations are prohibited, civil associations are rare. It is hardly probable that this is the result of accident, but the inference should rather be that there is a natural and perhaps a necessary connection between these two kinds of associations.

Certain men happen to have a common interest in some concern; either a commercial undertaking is to be managed, or some speculation in manufactures to be tried: they meet, they combine, and thus, by degrees, they become familiar with the principle of association. The greater the multiplicity of small affairs, the more do men, even without knowing it, acquire facility in prosecuting great undertakings in common.

Civil associations, therefore, facilitate political association; but, on the other hand, political association singularly strengthens and improves associations for civil purposes. In civil life every man may, strictly speaking, fancy that he can provide for his own wants; in politics he can fancy no such thing. When a people, then, have any knowledge of public life, the notion of associations and the wish to coalesce present themselves every day to the minds of the whole community; whatever natural repugnance may restrain men from acting in concert, they will always be ready to combine for the sake of a party. Thus political life makes the love and practice of association more general; it imparts a desire of union and teaches the means of combination to numbers of men who otherwise would have always lived apart.

Politics give birth not only to numerous associations, but to associations of great extent. In civil life it seldom happens that any one interest draws a very large number of men to act in concert; much skill is required to bring such an interest into existence; but in politics opportunities present themselves every day. Now, it is solely in great associations that the general value of the principle of association is displayed. Citizens who are individually powerless do not very clearly anticipate the strength that they may acquire by uniting together; it must be shown to them in order to be understood. Hence it is often easier to collect a multitude for a public purpose than a few persons; a thousand citizens do not see what interest they have in combining together; ten thousand will be perfectly aware of it. In politics men combine for great undertakings, and the use they make of the principle of association in important affairs practically teaches them that it is their interest to help one another in those of less moment. A political association draws a number of individuals at the same time out of their own circle; however they may be naturally kept asunder by age, mind, and fortune, it places them nearer together and brings them into contact. Once met, they can always meet again.

Men can embark in few civil partnerships without risking a portion of their possessions; this is the case with all manufacturing and trading companies. When men are as yet but little versed in the art of association and are acquainted with its principal rules, they are afraid, when first they combine in this manner, of buying their experience dear. They therefore prefer depriving themselves of a powerful instrument of success to running the risks that attend the use of it. They are less reluctant, however, to join political associations, which appear to them to be without danger because they risk no money in them. But they cannot belong to these associations for any length of time without finding out how order is maintained among a large number of men and by what contrivance they are made to advance, harmoniously and methodically, to the same object. Thus they learn to surrender their own will to that of all the rest and to make their own exertions subordinate to the common impulse, things which it is not less necessary to know in civil than in political associations. Political associations may therefore be considered as large free schools, where all the members of the community go to learn the general theory of association.

But even if political association did not directly contribute to the progress of civil association, to destroy the former would be to impair the latter. When citizens can meet in public only for certain purposes, they regard such meetings as a strange proceeding of rare occurrence, and they rarely think at all about it. When they are allowed to meet freely for all purposes, they ultimately look upon public association as the universal, or in a manner the sole, means that men can employ to accomplish the different purposes they may have in view. Every new want instantly revives the notion. The art of association then becomes, as I have said before, the mother of action, studied and applied by all.

When some kinds of associations are prohibited and others allowed, it is difficult to distinguish the former from the latter beforehand. In this state of doubt men abstain from them altogether, and a sort of public opinion passes current which tends to cause any association whatsoever to be regarded as a bold and almost an illicit enterprise.[1]

It is therefore chimerical to suppose that the spirit of association, when it is repressed on some one point, will nevertheless display the same vigor on all others; and that

[1] This is more especially true when the executive government has a discretionary power of allowing or prohibiting associations. When certain associations are simply prohibited by law, and the courts of justice have to punish infringements of that law, the evil is far less considerable. Then every citizen knows beforehand pretty nearly what he has to expect. He judges himself before he is judged by the law, and, abstaining from prohibited associations, he embarks on those which are legally sanctioned. It is by these restrictions that all free nations have always admitted that the right of association might be limited. But if the legislature should invest a man with a power of ascertaining beforehand which associations are dangerous and which are useful and should authorize him to destroy all associations in the bud or to allow them to be formed, as nobody would be able to foresee in what cases associations might be established and in what cases they would be put down, the spirit of association would be entirely paralyzed. The former of these laws would assail only certain associations; the latter would apply to society itself, and inflict an injury upon it. I can conceive that a government which respects the rule of law may have recourse to the former, but I do not concede that any government has the right of enacting the latter.

if men be allowed to prosecute certain undertakings in common, that is quite enough for them eagerly to set about them. When the members of a community are allowed and accustomed to combine for all purposes, they will combine as readily for the lesser as for the more important ones; but if they are allowed to combine only for small affairs, they will be neither inclined nor able to effect it. It is in vain that you will leave them entirely free to prosecute their business on joint-stock account; they will hardly care to avail themselves of the rights you have granted to them; and after having exhausted your strength in vain efforts to put down prohibited associations, you will be surprised that you cannot persuade men to form the associations you encourage.

I do not say that there can be no civil associations in a country where political association is prohibited, for men can never live in society without embarking in some common undertakings; but I maintain that in such a country civil associations will always be few in number, feebly planned, unskillfully managed, that they will never form any vast designs, or that they will fail in the execution of them.

This naturally leads me to think that freedom of association in political matters is not so dangerous to public tranquillity as is supposed, and that possibly, after having agitated society for some time, it may strengthen the state in the end. In democratic countries political associations are, so to speak, the only powerful persons who aspire to rule the state. Accordingly, the governments of our time look upon associations of this kind just as sovereigns in the Middle Ages regarded the great vassals of the crown: they entertain a sort of instinctive abhorrence of them and combat them on all occasions. They bear a natural goodwill to civil associations, on the contrary, because they readily discover that instead of directing the minds of the community to public affairs these institutions serve to divert them from such reflections, and that, by engaging them more and more in the pursuit of objects which cannot be attained without public tranquillity, they deter them from revolutions. But these governments do not attend to the fact that political associations tend amazingly to multiply and facilitate those of a civil character, and that in avoiding a dangerous evil they deprive themselves of an efficacious remedy.

When you see the Americans freely and constantly forming associations for the purpose of promoting some political principle, of raising one man to the head of affairs, or of wresting power from another, you have some difficulty in understanding how men so independent do not constantly fall into the abuse of freedom. If, on the other hand, you survey the infinite number of trading companies in operation in the United States, and perceive that the Americans are on every side unceasingly engaged in the execution of important and difficult plans, which the slightest revolution would throw into confusion, you will readily comprehend why people so well employed are by no means tempted to perturb the state or to destroy that public tranquillity by which they all profit.

Is it enough to observe these things separately, or should we not discover the hidden tie that connects them? In their political associations the Americans, of all conditions, minds, and ages, daily acquire a general taste for association and grow accustomed to the use of it. There they meet together in large numbers, they converse, they listen to one another, and they are mutually stimulated to all sorts of undertakings. They afterwards transfer to civil life the notions they have thus acquired and make them subservient to a thousand purposes. Thus it is by the enjoyment of a dangerous freedom that the Americans learn the art of rendering the dangers of freedom less formidable.

If a certain moment in the existence of a nation is selected, it is easy to prove that political associations perturb the state and paralyze productive industry; but take the whole life of a people, and it may perhaps be easy to demonstrate that freedom of association in political matters is favorable to the prosperity and even to the tranquillity of the community.

I said in the former part of this work: "The unrestrained liberty of political association cannot be entirely assimilated to the liberty of the press. The one is at the same time less necessary and more dangerous than the other. A nation may confine it within certain limits without ceasing to be mistress of itself, and it may sometimes be obliged to do so in order to maintain its own authority." And further on I added: "It cannot be denied that the unrestrained liberty of association for political purposes is the last degree of liberty which a people is fit for. If it does not throw them into anarchy, it perpetually brings them, as it were, to the verge of it." Thus I do not think that a nation is always at liberty to invest its citizens with an absolute right of association for political purposes; and I doubt whether, in any country or in any age, it is wise to set no limits to freedom of association.

A certain nation, it is said, could not maintain tranquillity in the community, cause the laws to be respected, or establish a lasting government if the right of association were not confined within narrow limits. These blessings are doubtless invaluable, and I can imagine that to acquire or to preserve them a nation may impose upon itself severe temporary restrictions: but still it is well that the nation should know at what price these blessings are purchased. I can understand that it may be advisable to cut off a man's arm in order to save his life, but it would be ridiculous to assert that he will be as dexterous as he was before he lost it.

Chapter VIII

HOW THE AMERICANS COMBAT INDIVIDUALISM BY THE PRINCIPLE OF SELF-INTEREST RIGHTLY UNDERSTOOD

WHEN the world was managed by a few rich and powerful individuals, these persons loved to entertain a lofty idea of the duties of man. They were fond of professing that it is praiseworthy to forget oneself and that good should be done without hope of reward, as it is by the Deity himself. Such were the standard opinions of that time in morals.

I doubt whether men were more virtuous in aristocratic ages than in others, but they were incessantly talking of the beauties of virtue, and its utility was only studied in secret. But since the imagination takes less lofty flights, and every man's thoughts are centered in himself, moralists are alarmed by this idea of self-sacrifice and they no longer venture to present it to the human mind. They therefore content themselves with inquiring whether the personal advantage of each member of the community does not consist in working for the good of all; and when they have hit upon some point on which private interest and public interest meet and amalgamate, they are eager to bring it into notice. Observations of this kind are gradually mutiplied; what was only a single remark becomes a general principle, and it is held as a truth that man serves himself in serving his fellow creatures and that his private interest is to do good.

I have already shown, in several parts of this work, by what means the inhabitants of the United States almost always manage to combine their own advantage with that of their fellow citizens; my present purpose is to point out the general rule that enables them to do so. In the United States hardly anybody talks of the beauty of virtue, but they maintain that virtue is useful and prove it every day. The American moralists do not profess that men ought to sacrifice themselves for their fellow creatures *because* it is noble to make such sacrifices, but they boldly aver that such sacrifices are as necessary to him who imposes them upon himself as to him for whose sake they are made.

They have found out that, in their country and their age, man is brought home to himself by an irresistible force; and, losing all hope of stopping that force, they turn all their thoughts to the direction of it. They therefore do not deny that every man may follow his own interest, but they endeavor to prove that it is the interest of every man to be virtuous. I shall not here enter into the reasons they allege, which would divert me from my subject; suffice it to say that they have convinced their fellow countrymen.

Montaigne said long ago: "Were I not to follow the straight road for its straightness, I should follow it for having found by experience that in the end it is commonly the happiest and most useful track." The doctrine of interest rightly understood is not then new, but among the Americans of our time it finds universal acceptance; it has become popular there; you may trace it at the bottom of all their actions, you will remark it in all they say. It is as often asserted by the poor man as by the rich. In Europe the principle of interest is much grosser than it is in America, but it is also less common and especially it is less avowed; among us, men still constantly feign great abnegations which they no longer feel.

The Americans, on the other hand, are fond of explaining almost all the actions of their lives by the principle of self-interest rightly understood; they show with complacency how an enlightened regard for themselves constantly prompts them to assist one another and inclines them willingly to sacrifice a portion of their time and property to the welfare of the state. In this respect I think they frequently fail to do themselves justice; for in the United States as well as elsewhere people are sometimes seen to give way to those disinterested and spontaneous impulses that are natural to man; but the Americans seldom admit that they yield to emotions of this kind; they are more anxious to do honor to their philosophy than to themselves.

I might here pause without attempting to pass a judgment on what I have described. The extreme difficulty of the subject would be my excuse, but I shall not avail myself of it;

and I had rather that my readers, clearly perceiving my object, would refuse to follow me than that I should leave them in suspense.

The principle of self-interest rightly understood is not a lofty one, but it is clear and sure. It does not aim at mighty objects, but attains without exertion all those at which it aims. As it lies within the reach of all capacities, everyone can without difficulty learn and retain it. By its admirable conformity to human weaknesses it easily obtains great dominion; nor is that dominion percarious, since the principle checks one personal interest by another, and uses, to direct the passions, the very same instrument that excites them.

The principle of self-interest rightly understood produces no great acts of self-sacrifice, but it suggests daily small acts of self-denial. By itself it cannot suffice to make a man virtuous; but it disciplines a number of persons in habits of regularity, temperance, moderation, foresight, self-command; and if it does not lead men straight to virtue by the will, it gradually draws them in that direction by their habits. If the principle of interest rightly understood were to sway the whole moral world, extraordinary virtues would doubtless be more rare; but I think that gross depravity would then also be less common. The principle of interest rightly understood perhaps prevents men from rising far above the level of mankind, but a great number of other men, who were falling far below it, are caught and restrained by it. Observe some few individuals, they are lowered by it; survey mankind, they are raised.

I am not afraid to say that the principle of self-interest rightly understood appears to me the best suited of all philosophical theories to the wants of the men of our time, and that I regard it as their chief remaining security against themselves. Towards it, therefore, the minds of the moralists of our age should turn; even should they judge it to be incomplete, it must nevertheless be adopted as necessary.

I do not think, on the whole, that there is more selfishness among us than in America; the only difference is that there it is enlightened, here it is not. Each American knows when to sacrifice some of his private interests to save the rest; we want to save everything, and often we lose it all. Everybody I see about me seems bent on teaching his contemporaries, by precept and example, that what is useful is never wrong.

Will nobody undertake to make them understand how what is right may be useful?

No power on earth can prevent the increasing equality of conditions from inclining the human mind to seek out what is useful or from leading every member of the community to be wrapped up in himself. It must therefore be expected that personal interest will become more than ever the principal if not the sole spring of men's actions; but it remains to be seen how each man will understand his personal interest. If the members of a community, as they become more equal, become more ignorant and coarse, it is difficult to foresee to what pitch of stupid excesses their selfishness may lead them; and no one can foretell into what disgrace and wretchedness they would plunge themselves lest they should have to sacrifice something of their own well-being to the prosperity of their fellow creatures.

I do not think that the system of self-interest as it is professed in America is in all its parts self-evident, but it contains a great number of truths so evident that men, if they are only educated, cannot fail to see them. Educate, then, at any rate, for the age of implicit self-sacrifice and instinctive virtues is already flitting far away from us, and the time is fast approaching when freedom, public peace, and social order itself will not be able to exist without education.

Chapter IX

THAT THE AMERICANS APPLY THE PRINCIPLE OF SELF-INTEREST RIGHTLY UNDERSTOOD TO RELIGIOUS MATTERS

IF THE principle of self-interest rightly understood had nothing but the present world in view, it would be very insufficient, for there are many sacrifices that can find their recompense only in another; and whatever ingenuity may be put forth to demonstrate the utility of virtue, it will never be an easy task to make that man live aright who has no thought of dying.

It is therefore necessary to ascertain whether the principle of self-interest rightly understood can be easily reconciled with religious belief. The philosophers who inculcate this system of morals tell men that to be happy in this life they must watch their own passions and steadily control their excess; that lasting happiness can be secured only by renouncing a thousand transient gratifications; and that a man must perpetually triumph over himself in order to secure his own advantage. The founders of almost all religions have held to the same language. The track they point out to man is the same, only the goal is more remote; instead of placing in this world the reward of the sacrifices they impose, they transport it to another.

Nevertheless, I cannot believe that all those who practice virtue from religious motives are actuated only by the hope of a recompense. I have known zealous Christians who constantly forgot themselves to work with greater ardor for the happiness of their fellow men, and I have heard them declare that all they did was only to earn the blessings of a future state. I cannot but think that they deceive themselves; I respect them too much to believe them.

Christianity, indeed, teaches that a man must prefer his neighbor to himself in order to gain eternal life; but Christianity also teaches that men ought to benefit their fellow creatures for the love of God! A sublime expression! Man searches by his intellect into the divine conception and sees that order is the purpose of God; he freely gives his own efforts to aid in prosecuting this great design, and, while he sacrifices his personal interests to this consummate order of all created things, expects no other recompense than the pleasure of contemplating it.

I do not believe that self-interest is the sole motive of religious men, but I believe that self-interest is the principal means that religions themselves employ to govern men, and I do not question that in this way they strike the multitude and become popular. I do not see clearly why the principle of interest rightly understood should undermine the religious opinions of men; it seems to me more easy to show why it should strengthen them. Let it be supposed that in order to attain happiness in this world, a man combats his instincts on all occasions and deliberately calculates every action of his life; that instead of yielding blindly to the impetuosity of first desires, he has learned the art of resisting them, and that he has accustomed himself to sacrifice without an effort the pleasure of a moment to the lasting interest of his whole life. If such a man believes in the religion that he professes, it will cost him but little to submit to the restrictions it may impose. Reason herself counsels him to obey, and habit has prepared him to endure these limitations. If he should have conceived any doubts as to the object of his hopes, still he will not easily allow himself to be stopped by them; and he will decide that it is wise to risk some of the advantages of this world in order to preserve his rights to the great inheritance promised him in another. "To be mistaken in believing that the Christian religion is true," says Pascal, "is no great loss to anyone; but how dreadful to be mistaken in believing it to be false!"

The Americans do not affect a brutal indifference to a future state; they affect no puerile pride in despising perils that they hope to escape from. They therefore profess their religion without shame and without weakness; but even in their zeal there generally is something so indescribably tranquil, methodical, and deliberate that it would seem as if the head far more than the heart brought them to the foot of the altar.

Not only do the Americans follow their religion from interest, but they often place in this world the interest that makes them follow it. In the Middle Ages the clergy spoke of nothing but a future state; they hardly cared to prove that a sincere Christian may be a happy man here below. But the American preachers are constantly referring to the earth, and it is only with great difficulty that they can divert their attention from it. To touch their congregations, they always show them how favorable religious opinions are to freedom and public tranquillity; and it is often difficult to ascertain from their discourses whether the principal object of religion is to procure eternal felicity in the other world or prosperity in this.

Chapter X

OF THE TASTE FOR PHYSICAL WELL-BEING IN AMERICA

In America the passion for physical well-being is not always exclusive, but it is general; and if all do not feel it in the same manner, yet it is felt by all. The effort to satisfy even the least wants of the body and to provide the little conveniences of life is uppermost in every mind. Something of an analogous character is more and more apparent in Europe. Among the causes that produce these similar consequences in both hemispheres, several are so connected with my subject as to deserve notice.

When riches are hereditarily fixed in families, a great number of men enjoy the comforts of life without feeling an exclusive taste for those comforts. The heart of man is not so much caught by the undisturbed possession of anything valuable as by the desire, as yet imperfectly satisfied, of possessing it and by the incessant dread of losing it. In aristocratic communities the wealthy, never having experienced a condition different from their own, entertain no fear of changing it; the existence of such conditions hardly occurs to them. The comforts of life are not to them the end of life, but simply a way of living; they regard them as existence itself, enjoyed but scarcely thought of. As the natural and instinctive taste that all men feel for being well off is thus satisfied without trouble and without apprehension, their faculties are turned elsewhere and applied to more arduous and lofty undertakings, which excite and engross their minds.

Hence it is that in the very midst of physical gratifications the members of an aristocracy often display a haughty contempt of these very enjoyments and exhibit singular powers of endurance under the privation of them. All the revolutions which have ever shaken or destroyed aristocracies have shown how easily men accustomed to superfluous luxuries can do without the necessaries of life; whereas men who have toiled to acquire a competency can hardly live after they have lost it.

If I turn my observation from the upper to the lower classes, I find analogous effects produced by opposite causes. Among a nation where aristocracy predominates in society and keeps it stationary, the people in the end get as much accustomed to poverty as the rich to their opulence. The latter bestow no anxiety on their physical comforts because they enjoy them without an effort; the former do not think of things which they despair of obtaining and which they hardly know enough of to desire. In communities of this kind the imagination of the poor is driven to seek another world; the miseries of real life enclose it, but it escapes from their control and flies to seek its pleasures far beyond.

When, on the contrary, the distinctions of ranks are obliterated and privileges are destroyed, when hereditary property is subdivided and education and freedom are widely diffused, the desire of acquiring the comforts of the world haunts the imagination of the poor, and the dread of losing them that of the rich. Many scanty fortunes spring up; those who possess them have a sufficient share of physical gratifications to conceive a taste for these pleasures, not enough to satisfy it. They never procure them without exertion, and they never indulge in them without apprehension. They are therefore always straining to pursue or to retain gratifications so delightful, so imperfect, so fugitive.

If I were to inquire what passion is most natural to men who are stimulated and circumscribed by the obscurity of their birth or the mediocrity of their fortune, I could discover none more peculiarly appropriate to their condition than this love of physical prosperity. The passion for physical comforts is essentially a passion of the middle classes; with those classes it grows and spreads, with them it is preponderant. From them it mounts into the higher orders of society and descends into the mass of the people.

I never met in America any citizen so poor as not to cast a glance of hope and envy on the enjoyments of the rich or whose imagination did not possess itself by anticipation of those good things that fate still obstinately withheld from him.

On the other hand, I never perceived among the wealthier inhabitants of the United States that proud contempt of physical gratifications which is sometimes to be met with even in the most opulent and dissolute aristocracies. Most of these wealthy persons were once poor; they have felt the sting of want; they were long a prey to adverse fortunes; and now that the victory is won, the passions which accompanied the contest have survived it; their minds are, as it were, intoxicated by the small enjoyments which they have pursued for forty years.

Not but that in the United States, as elsewhere, there is a certain number of wealthy persons who, having come into their property by inheritance, possess without exertion an opulence they have not earned. But even these men are not less devotedly attached to the pleasures of material life. The love of well-being has now become the predominant taste of the nation; the great current of human passions runs in that channel and sweeps everything along in its course.

Chapter XI

PECULIAR EFFECTS OF THE LOVE OF PHYSICAL GRATIFICATIONS IN DEMOCRATIC TIMES

IT MAY BE supposed, from what has just been said, that the love of physical gratifications must constantly urge the Americans to irregularities in morals, disturb the peace of families, and threaten the security of society at large. But it is not so: the passion for physical gratifications produces in democracies effects very different from those which it occasions in aristocratic nations.

It sometimes happens that, wearied with public affairs and sated with opulence, amid the ruin of religious belief and the decline of the state, the heart of an aristocracy may by degrees be seduced to the pursuit of sensual enjoyments alone. At other times the power of the monarch or the weakness of the people, without stripping the nobility of their fortune, compels them to stand aloof from the administration of affairs and, while the road to mighty enterprise is closed, abandons them to the disquietude of their own desires; they then fall back heavily upon themselves and seek in the pleasures of the body oblivion of their former greatness.

When the members of an aristocratic body are thus exclusively devoted to the pursuit of physical gratifications, they commonly turn in that direction all the energy which they derive from their long experience of power. Such men are not satisfied with the pursuit of comfort; they require sumptuous depravity and splendid corruption. The worship they pay the senses is a gorgeous one, and they seem to vie with one another in the art of degrading their own natures. The stronger, the more famous, and the more free an aristocracy has been, the more depraved will it then become; and however brilliant may have been the luster of its virtues, I dare predict that they will always be surpassed by the splendor of its vices.

The taste for physical gratifications leads a democratic people into no such excesses. The love of well-being is there displayed as a tenacious, exclusive, universal passion, but its range is confined. To build enormous palaces, to conquer or to mimic nature, to ransack the world in order to gratify the passions of a man, is not thought of, but to add a few yards of land to your field, to plant an orchard, to enlarge a dwelling, to be always making life more comfortable and convenient, to avoid trouble, and to satisfy the smallest wants without effort and almost without cost. These are small objects, but the soul clings to them; it dwells upon them closely and day by day, till they at last shut out the rest of the world and sometimes intervene between itself and heaven.

This, it may be said, can be applicable only to those members of the community who are in humble circumstances; wealthier individuals will display tastes akin to those which belonged to them in aristocratic ages. I contest the proposition: in point of physical gratifications, the most opulent members of a democracy will not display tastes very different from those of the people; whether it be that, springing from the people, they really share those tastes or that they esteem it a duty to submit to them. In democratic society the sensuality of the public has taken a moderate and tranquil course, to which all are bound to conform: it is as difficult to depart from the common rule by one's vices as by one's virtues. Rich men who live amid democratic nations are therefore more intent on providing for their smallest wants than for their extraordinary enjoyments; they gratify a number of petty desires without indulging in any great irregularities of passion; thus they are more apt to become enervated than debauched.

The special taste that the men of democratic times entertain for physical enjoyments is not naturally opposed to the principles of public order; nay, it often stands in need of order that it may be gratified. Nor is it adverse to regularity of morals, for good morals contribute to public tranquillity and are favorable to industry. It may even be frequently combined with a species of religious morality; men wish to be as well off as they can in this world without forgoing their chance of another. Some physical gratifications cannot be indulged in without crime; from such they strictly abstain.

The enjoyment of others is sanctioned by religion and morality; to these the heart, the imagination, and life itself are unreservedly given up, till, in snatching at these lesser gifts, men lose sight of those more precious possessions which constitute the glory and the greatness of mankind.

The reproach I address to the principle of equality is not that it leads men away in the pursuit of forbidden enjoyments, but that it absorbs them wholly in quest of those which are allowed. By these means a kind of virtuous materialism may ultimately be established in the world, which would not corrupt, but enervate, the soul and noiselessly unbend its springs of action.

Chapter XII

WHY SOME AMERICANS MANIFEST A SORT OF FANATICAL SPIRITUALISM

ALTHOUGH the desire of acquiring the good things of this world is the prevailing passion of the American people, certain momentary outbreaks occur when their souls seem suddenly to burst the bonds of matter by which they are restrained and to soar impetuously towards heaven. In all the states of the Union, but especially in the half-peopled country of the Far West, itinerant preachers may be met with who hawk about the word of God from place to place. Whole families, old men, women, and children, cross rough passes and untrodden wilds, coming from a great distance, to join a camp-meeting, where, in listening to these discourses, they totally forget for several days and nights the cares of business and even the most urgent wants of the body.

Here and there in the midst of American society you meet with men full of a fanatical and almost wild spiritualism, which hardly exists in Europe. From time to time strange sects arise which endeavor to strike out extraordinary paths to eternal happiness. Religious insanity is very common in the United States.

Nor ought these facts to surprise us. It was not man who implanted in himself the taste for what is infinite and the love of what is immortal; these lofty instincts are not the offspring of his capricious will; their steadfast foundation is fixed in human nature, and they exist in spite of his efforts. He may cross and distort them; destroy them he cannot.

The soul has wants which must be satisfied; and whatever pains are taken to divert it from itself, it soon grows weary, restless, and disquieted amid the enjoyments of sense. If ever the faculties of the great majority of mankind were exclusively bent upon the pursuit of material objects, it might be anticipated that an amazing reaction would take place in the souls of some men. They would drift at large in the world of spirits, for fear of remaining shackled by the close bondage of the body.

It is not, then, wonderful if in the midst of a community whose thoughts tend earthward a small number of individuals are to be found who turn their looks to heaven. I should be surprised if mysticism did not soon make some advance among a people solely engaged in promoting their own worldly welfare.

It is said that the deserts of the Thebaid were peopled by the persecutions of the emperors and the massacres of the Circus; I should rather say that it was by the luxuries of Rome and the Epicurean philosophy of Greece.

If their social condition, their present circumstances, and their laws did not confine the minds of the Americans so closely to the pursuit of worldly welfare, it is probable that they would display more reserve and more experience whenever their attention is turned to things immaterial, and that they would check themselves without difficulty. But they feel imprisoned within bounds, which they will apparently never be allowed to pass. As soon as they have passed these bounds, their minds do not know where to fix themselves and they often rush unrestrained beyond the range of common sense.

Chapter XIII

WHY THE AMERICANS ARE SO RESTLESS IN THE MIDST OF THEIR PROSPERITY

In certain remote corners of the Old World you may still sometimes stumble upon a small district that seems to have been forgotten amid the general tumult, and to have remained stationary while everything around it was in motion. The inhabitants, for the most part, are extremely ignorant and poor; they take no part in the business of the country and are frequently oppressed by the government, yet their countenances are generally placid and their spirits light.

In America I saw the freest and most enlightened men placed in the happiest circumstances that the world affords; it seemed to me as if a cloud habitually hung upon their brow, and I thought them serious and almost sad, even in their pleasures.

The chief reason for this contrast is that the former do not think of the ills they endure, while the latter are forever brooding over advantages they do not possess. It is strange to see with what feverish ardor the Americans pursue their own welfare, and to watch the vague dread that constantly torments them lest they should not have chosen the shortest path which may lead to it.

A native of the United States clings to this world's goods as if he were certain never to die; and he is so hasty in grasping at all within his reach that one would suppose he was constantly afraid of not living long enough to enjoy them. He clutches everything, he holds nothing fast, but soon loosens his grasp to pursue fresh gratifications.

In the United States a man builds a house in which to spend his old age, and he sells it before the roof is on; he plants a garden and lets it just as the trees are coming into bearing; he brings a field into tillage and leaves other men to gather the crops; he embraces a profession and gives it up;

he settles in a place, which he soon afterwards leaves to carry his changeable longings elsewhere. If his private affairs leave him any leisure, he instantly plunges into the vortex of politics; and if at the end of a year of unremitting labor he finds he has a few days' vacation, his eager curiosity whirls him over the vast extent of the United States, and he will travel fifteen hundred miles in a few days to shake off his happiness. Death at length overtakes him, but it is before he is weary of his bootless chase of that complete felicity which forever escapes him.

At first sight there is something surprising in this strange unrest of so many happy men, restless in the midst of abundance. The spectacle itself, however, is as old as the world; the novelty is to see a whole people furnish an exemplification of it.

Their taste for physical gratifications must be regarded as the original source of that secret disquietude which the actions of the Americans betray and of that inconstancy of which they daily afford fresh examples. He who has set his heart exclusively upon the pursuit of worldly welfare is always in a hurry, for he has but a limited time at his disposal to reach, to grasp, and to enjoy it. The recollection of the shortness of life is a constant spur to him. Besides the good things that he possesses, he every instant fancies a thousand others that death will prevent him from trying if he does not try them soon. This thought fills him with anxiety, fear, and regret and keeps his mind in ceaseless trepidation, which leads him perpetually to change his plans and his abode.

If in addition to the taste for physical well-being a social condition be added in which neither laws nor customs retain any person in his place, there is a great additional stimulant to this restlessness of temper. Men will then be seen continually to change their track for fear of missing the shortest cut to happiness.

It may readily be conceived that if men passionately bent upon physical gratifications desire eagerly, they are also easily discouraged; as their ultimate object is to enjoy, the means to reach that object must be prompt and easy or the trouble of acquiring the gratification would be greater than the gratification itself. Their prevailing frame of mind, then, is at once ardent and relaxed, violent and enervated. Death is often less dreaded by them than perseverance in continuous efforts to one end.

The equality of conditions leads by a still straighter road to several of the effects that I have here described. When all the privileges of birth and fortune are abolished, when all professions are accessible to all, and a man's own energies may place him at the top of any one of them, an easy and unbounded career seems open to his ambition and he will readily persuade himself that he is born to no common destinies. But this is an erroneous notion, which is corrected by daily experience. The same equality that allows every citizen to conceive these lofty hopes renders all the citizens less able to realize them; it circumscribes their powers on every side, while it gives freer scope to their desires. Not only are they themselves powerless, but they are met at every step by immense obstacles, which they did not at first perceive. They have swept away the privileges of some of their fellow creatures which stood in their way, but they have opened the door to universal competition; the barrier has changed its shape rather than its position. When men are nearly alike and all follow the same track, it is very difficult for any one individual to walk quickly and cleave a way through the dense throng that surrounds and presses on him. This constant strife between the inclination springing from the equality of condition and the means it supplies to satisfy them harasses and wearies the mind.

It is possible to conceive of men arrived at a degree of freedom that should completely content them; they would then enjoy their independence without anxiety and without impatience. But men will never establish any equality with which they can be contented. Whatever efforts a people may make, they will never succeed in reducing all the conditions of society to a perfect level; and even if they unhappily attained that absolute and complete equality of position, the inequality of minds would still remain, which, coming directly from the hand of God, will forever escape the laws of man. However democratic, then, the social state and the political constitution of a people may be, it is certain that every member of the community will always find out several points about him which overlook his own position; and we may foresee that his looks will be doggedly fixed in that direction. When inequality of conditions is the common law of society, the most marked inequalities do not strike the eye; when everything is nearly on the same level, the slightest are marked enough to hurt it. Hence the desire of equality always becomes more insatiable in proportion as equality is more complete.

Among democratic nations, men easily attain a certain equality of condition, but they can never attain as much as they desire. It perpetually retires from before them, yet without hiding itself from their sight, and in retiring draws them on. At every moment they think they are about to grasp it; it escapes at every moment from their hold. They are near enough to see its charms, but too far off to enjoy them; and before they have fully tasted its delights, they die.

To these causes must be attributed that strange melancholy which often haunts the inhabitants of democratic countries in the midst of their abundance, and that disgust at life which sometimes seizes upon them in the midst of calm and easy circumstances. Complaints are made in France that the number of suicides increases; in America suicide is rare, but insanity is said to be more common there than anywhere else. These are all different symptoms of the same disease. The Americans do not put an end to their lives, however disquieted they may be, because their religion forbids it; and among them materialism may be said hardly to exist, notwithstanding the general passion for physical gratification. The will resists, but reason frequently gives way.

In democratic times enjoyments are more intense than in the ages of aristocracy, and the number of those who partake in them is vastly larger: but, on the other hand, it must be admitted that man's hopes and desires are oftener blasted, the soul is more stricken and perturbed, and care itself more keen.

Chapter XIV

HOW THE TASTE FOR PHYSICAL GRATIFICATIONS IS UNITED IN AMERICA TO LOVE OF FREEDOM AND ATTENTION TO PUBLIC AFFAIRS

When a democratic state turns to absolute monarchy, the activity that was before directed to public and to private affairs is all at once centered on the latter. The immediate consequence is, for some time, great physical prosperity, but this impulse soon slackens and the amount of productive industry is checked. I do not know if a single trading or manufacturing people can be cited, from the Tyrians down to the Florentines and the English, who were not a free people also. There is therefore a close bond and necessary relation between these two elements, freedom and productive industry.

This proposition is generally true of all nations, but especially of democratic nations. I have already shown that men who live in ages of equality have a continual need of forming associations in order to procure the things they desire; and, on the other hand, I have shown how great political freedom improves and diffuses the art of association. Freedom in these ages is therefore especially favorable to the production of wealth; nor is it difficult to perceive that despotism is especially adverse to the same result.

The nature of despotic power in democratic ages is not to be fierce or cruel, but minute and meddling. Despotism of this kind, though it does not trample on humanity, is directly opposed to the genius of commerce and the pursuits of industry.

Thus the men of democratic times require to be free in order to procure more readily those physical enjoyments for which they are always longing. It sometimes happens, however, that the excessive taste they conceive for these same enjoyments makes them surrender to the first master who appears. The passion for worldly welfare then defeats itself and, without their perceiving it, throws the object of their desires to a greater distance.

There is, indeed, a most dangerous passage in the history of a democratic people. When the taste for physical gratifications among them has grown more rapidly than their education and their experience of free institutions, the time will come when men are carried away and lose all self-restraint at the sight of the new possessions they are about to obtain. In their intense and exclusive anxiety to make a fortune they lose sight of the close connection that exists between the private fortune of each and the prosperity of all. It is not necessary to do violence to such a people in order to strip them of the rights they enjoy; they themselves willingly loosen their hold. The discharge of political duties appears to them to be a troublesome impediment which diverts them from their occupations and business. If they are required to elect representatives, to support the government by personal service, to meet on public business, they think they have no time, they cannot waste their precious hours in useless engagements; such idle amusements are unsuited to serious men who are engaged with the more important interests of life. These people think they are following the principle of self-interest, but the idea they entertain of that principle is a very crude one; and the better to look after what they call their own business, they neglect their chief business, which is to remain their own masters.

As the citizens who labor do not care to attend to public affairs, and as the class which might devote its leisure to these duties has ceased to exist, the place of the government is, as it were, unfilled. If at that critical moment some able and ambitious man grasps the supreme power, he will find the road to every kind of usurpation open before him. If he attends for some time only to the material prosperity of the country, no more will be demanded of him. Above all, he must ensure public tranquillity: men who are possessed by the passion for physical gratification generally find out that the turmoil of freedom disturbs their welfare before they discover how freedom itself serves to promote it. If the slightest rumor of public commotion intrudes into the petty pleasures of private life, they are aroused and alarmed by it. The fear of anarchy perpetually haunts them, and they are always ready to fling away their freedom at the first disturbance.

I readily admit that public tranquillity is a great good, but at the same time I cannot forget that all nations have been enslaved by being kept in good order. Certainly it is not to be inferred that nations ought to despise public tranquillity, but that state ought not to content them. A nation that asks nothing of its government but the maintenance of order is already a slave at heart, the slave of its own well-being, awaiting only the hand that will bind it.

By such a nation the despotism of faction is not less to be dreaded than the despotism of an individual. When the bulk of the community are engrossed by private concerns, the smallest parties need not despair of getting the upper hand in public affairs. At such times it is not rare to see on the great stage of the world, as we see in our theaters, a multitude represented by a few players, who alone speak in the name of an absent or inattentive crowd: they alone are in action, while all others are stationary; they regulate everything by their own caprice; they change the laws and tyrannize at will over the manners of the country; and then men wonder to see into how small a number of weak and worthless hands a great people may fall.

Hitherto the Americans have fortunately escaped all the perils that I have just pointed out, and in this respect they are really deserving of admiration. Perhaps there is no country in the world where fewer idle men are to be *met* with than in America, or where all who work are more eager to promote their own welfare. But if the passion of the Americans for physical gratifications is vehement, at least it is not indiscriminate; and reason, though unable to restrain it, still directs its course.

An American attends to his private concerns as if he were alone in the world, and the next minute he gives himself up to the common welfare as if he had forgotten them. At one time he seems animated by the most selfish cupidity; at another, by the most lively patriotism. The human heart cannot be thus divided. The inhabitants of the United States alternately display so strong and so similar a passion for their own welfare and for their freedom that it may be supposed that these passions are united and mingled in some part of their character. And indeed the Americans believe their freedom to be the best instrument and surest safeguard of their welfare; they are attached to the one by the other. They by no means think that they are not called upon to take a part in public affairs; they believe, on the contrary, that their chief business is to secure for themselves a government which will allow them to acquire the things they covet and which will not debar them from the peaceful enjoyment of those possessions which they have already acquired.

Chapter XV

HOW RELIGIOUS BELIEF SOMETIMES TURNS THE THOUGHTS OF AMERICANS TO IMMATERIAL PLEASURES

IN THE United States on the seventh day of every week the trading and working life of the nation seems suspended; all noises cease; a deep tranquillity, say rather the solemn calm of meditation, succeeds the turmoil of the week, and the soul resumes possession and contemplation of itself. On this day the marts of traffic are deserted; every member of the community, accompanied by his children, goes to church, where he listens to strange language which would seem unsuited to his ear. He is told of the countless evils caused by pride and covetousness; he is reminded of the necessity of checking his desires, of the finer pleasures that belong to virtue alone, and of the true happiness that attends it. On his return home he does not turn to the ledgers of his business, but he opens the book of Holy Scripture; there he meets with sublime and affecting descriptions of the greatness and goodness of the Creator, of the infinite magnificence of the handiwork of God, and of the lofty destinies of man, his duties, and his immortal privileges.

Thus it is that the American at times steals an hour from himself, and, laying aside for a while the petty passions which agitate his life, and the ephemeral interests which engross it, he strays at once into an ideal world, where all is great, eternal, and pure.

I have endeavored to point out, in another part of this work, the causes to which the maintenance of the political institutions of the Americans is attributable, and religion appeared to be one of the most prominent among them. I am now treating of the Americans in an individual capacity, and I again observe that religion is not less useful to each citizen than to the whole state. The Americans show by their practice that they feel the high necessity of imparting morality to democratic communities by means of religion. What they think of themselves in this respect is a truth of which every democratic nation ought to be thoroughly persuaded.

I do not doubt that the social and political constitution of a people predisposes them to adopt certain doctrines and tastes, which afterwards flourish without difficulty among them; while the same causes may divert them from certain other opinions and propensities without any voluntary effort and, as it were, without any distinct consciousness on their part. The whole art of the legislator is correctly to discern beforehand these natural inclinations of communities of men, in order to know whether they should be fostered or whether it may not be necessary to check them. For the duties incumbent on the legislator differ at different times; only the goal towards which the human race ought ever to be tending is stationary; the means of reaching it are perpetually varied.

If I had been born in an aristocratic age, in the midst of a nation where the hereditary wealth of some and the irremediable penury of others equally diverted men from the idea of bettering their condition and held the soul, as it were, in a state of torpor, fixed on the contemplation of another world, I should then wish that it were possible for me to rouse that people to a sense of their wants; I should seek to discover more rapid and easy means for satisfying the fresh desires that I might have awakened; and, directing the most strenuous efforts of the citizens to physical pursuits, I should endeavor to stimulate them to promote their own well-being. If it happened that some men were thus immoderately incited to the pursuit of riches and caused to display an excessive liking for physical gratifications, I should not be alarmed; these peculiar cases would soon disappear in the general aspect of the whole community.

The attention of the legislators of democracies is called to other cares. Give democratic nations education and freedom and leave them alone. They will soon learn to draw from this world all the benefits that it can afford; they will improve each of the useful arts and will day by day render life more comfortable, more convenient, and more easy. Their social condition naturally urges them in this direction; I do not fear that they will slacken their course.

But while man takes delight in this honest and lawful pursuit of his own well-being, it is to be apprehended that in the end he may lose the use of his sublimest faculties, and that while he is busied in improving all around him, he may at length degrade himself. Here, and here only, does the peril lie. It should therefore be the unceasing object of the legislators of democracies and of all the virtuous and enlightened men who live there to raise the souls of their fellow citizens and keep them lifted up towards heaven. It is necessary that all who feel an interest in the future destinies of democratic society should unite, and that all should make joint and continual efforts to diffuse the love of the infinite, lofty aspirations, and a love of pleasures not of earth. If among the opinions of democratic people any of those pernicious theories exist which tend to inculcate that all perishes with the body, let men by whom such theories are professed be marked as the natural foes of the whole people.

The materialists are offensive to me in many respects; their doctrines I hold to be pernicious, and I am disgusted at their arrogance. If their system could be of any utility to man, it would seem to be by giving him a modest opinion of himself; but these reasoners show that it is not so; and when they think they have said enough to prove that they are brutes, they appear as proud as if they had demonstrated that they are gods.

Materialism, among all nations, is a dangerous disease of the human mind; but it is more especially to be dreaded among a democratic people because it readily amalgamates with that vice which is most familiar to the heart under such circumstances. Democracy encourages a taste for physical gratification; this taste, if it become excessive, soon disposes men to believe that all is matter only; and materialism, in its turn, hurries them on with mad impatience to these same delights; such is the fatal circle within which democratic nations are driven round. It were well that they should see the danger and hold back.

Most religions are only general, simple, and practical means of teaching men the doctrine of the immortality of the soul. That is the greatest benefit which a democratic people derives from its belief, and hence belief is more necessary to such a people than to all others. When, therefore, any religion has struck its roots deep into a democracy, beware that you do not disturb it; but rather watch it carefully, as the most precious bequest of aristocratic ages. Do not seek to supersede the old religious opinions of men by new ones, lest in the passage from one faith to another, the soul being left for a while stripped of all belief, the love of physical gratifications should grow upon it and fill it wholly.

The doctrine of metempsychosis is assuredly not more rational than that of materialism; nevertheless, if it were absolutely necessary that a democracy should choose one of the two, I should not hesitate to decide that the community would run less risk of being brutalized by believing that the soul of man will pass into the carcass of a hog than by believing that the soul of man is nothing at all. The belief in a supersensual and immortal principle, united for a time to matter, is so indispensable to man's greatness that its effects are striking even when it is not united to the doctrine of future reward and punishment, or even when it teaches no more than that after death the divine principle contained in man is absorbed in the Deity or transferred to animate the frame of some other creature. Men holding so imperfect a belief will still consider the body as the secondary and inferior portion of their nature, and will despise it even while they yield to its influence; whereas they have a natural esteem and secret admiration for the immaterial part of man, even though they sometimes refuse to submit to its authority. That is enough to give a lofty cast to their opinions and their tastes, and to bid them tend, with no interested motive, and as it were by impulse, to pure feelings and elevated thoughts.

It is not certain that Socrates and his followers had any fixed opinions as to what would befall man hereafter; but the sole point of belief which they did firmly maintain, that the soul has nothing in common with the body and survives it, was enough to give the Platonic philosophy that sublime aspiration by which it is distinguished.

It is clear from the works of Plato that many philosophical writers, his predecessors or contemporaries, professed materialism. These writers have not reached us or have reached us in mere fragments. The same thing has happened in almost all ages; the greater part of the most famous minds in literature adhere to the doctrines of a spiritual philosophy. The instinct and the taste of the human race maintain those doctrines; they save them often in spite of men themselves and raise the names of their defenders above the tide of time. It must not, then, be supposed that at any period or under any political condition the passion for physical gratifications and the opinions which are superinduced by that passion can ever content a whole people. The heart of man is of a larger mold; it can at once comprise a taste for the possessions of earth and the love of those of heaven; at times it may seem to cling devotedly to the one, but it will never be long without thinking of the other.

If it be easy to see that it is more particularly important in democratic ages that spiritual opinions should prevail, it is not easy to say by what means those who govern democratic nations may make them predominate. I am no believer in the prosperity any more than in the durability of official philosophies; and as to state religions, I have always held that if they be sometimes of momentary service to the interests of political power, they always sooner or later become fatal to the church. Nor do I agree with those who think that, to raise religion in the eyes of the people and to make them do honor to her spiritual doctrines, it is desirable indirectly to give her ministers a political influence which the laws deny them. I am so much alive to the almost inevitable dangers which beset religious belief whenever the clergy take part in public affairs, and I am so convinced that Christianity must be maintained at any cost in the bosom of modern democracies, that I had rather shut up the priesthood within the sanctuary than allow them to step beyond it.

What means then remain in the hands of constituted authorities to bring men back to spiritual opinions or to hold them fast to the religion by which those opinions are suggested?

My answer will do me harm in the eyes of politicians. I believe that the sole effectual means which governments can employ in order to have the doctrine of the immortality of the soul duly respected is always to act as if they believed in it themselves; and I think that it is only by scrupulous conformity to religious morality in great affairs that they can hope to teach the community at large to know, to love, and to observe it in the lesser concerns of life.

Chapter XVI

HOW EXCESSIVE CARE FOR WORLDLY WELFARE MAY IMPAIR THAT WELFARE

THERE is a closer tie than is commonly supposed between the improvement of the soul and the amelioration of what belongs to the body. Man may leave these two things apart and consider each of them alternately, but he cannot sever them entirely without at last losing sight of both.

The beasts have the same senses as ourselves, and very nearly the same appetites. We have no sensual passions which are not common to our race and theirs and which are not to be found, at least in the germ, in a dog as well as in a man. Whence is it, then, that the animals can provide only for their first and lowest wants, whereas we can infinitely vary and endlessly increase our enjoyments?

We are superior to the beasts in this, that we use our souls to find out those material benefits to which they are only led by instinct. In man the angel teaches the brute the art of satisfying its desires. It is because man is capable of rising above the things of the body, and of scorning life itself, of which the beasts have not the least notion, that he can multiply these same goods of the body to a degree of which the inferior races cannot conceive.

Whatever elevates, enlarges, and expands the soul renders it more capable of succeeding in those very undertakings which do not concern it. Whatever, on the other hand, enervates or lowers it weakens it for all purposes, the chief as well as the least, and threatens to render it almost equally impotent for both. Hence the soul must remain great and strong, though it were only to devote its strength and greatness from time to time to the service of the body. If men were ever to content themselves with material objects, it is probable that they would lose by degrees the art of producing them; and they would enjoy them in the end, like the brutes, without discernment and without improvement.

Chapter XVII

HOW, WHEN CONDITIONS ARE EQUAL AND SKEPTICISM IS RIFE, IT IS IMPORTANT TO DIRECT HUMAN ACTIONS TO DISTANT OBJECTS

In ages of faith the final aim of life is placed beyond life. The men of those ages, therefore, naturally almost involuntarily accustom themselves to fix their gaze for many years on some immovable object towards which they are constantly tending, and they learn by insensible degrees to repress a multitude of petty passing desires in order to be the better able to content that great and lasting desire which possesses them. When these same men engage in the affairs of this world, the same habits may be traced in their conduct. They are apt to set up some general and certain aim and end to their actions here below, towards which all their efforts are directed; they do not turn from day to day to chase some novel object of desire, but they have settled designs which they are never weary of pursuing.

This explains why religious nations have so often achieved such lasting results; for while they were thinking only of the other world, they had found out the great secret of success in this. Religions give men a general habit of conducting themselves with a view to eternity; in this respect they are not less useful to happiness in this life than to felicity hereafter, and this is one of their chief political characteristics.

But in proportion as the light of faith grows dim, the range of man's sight is circumscribed, as if the end and aim of human actions appeared every day to be more within his reach. When men have once allowed themselves to think no more of what is to befall them after life, they readily lapse into that complete and brutal indifference to futurity which is but too conformable to some propensities of mankind. As soon as they have lost the habit of placing their chief hopes upon remote events, they naturally seek to gratify without delay their smallest desires; and no sooner do they despair of living forever, than they are disposed to act as if they were to exist but for a single day. In skeptical ages it is always to be feared, therefore, that men may perpetually give way to their daily casual desires, and that, wholly renouncing whatever cannot be acquired without protracted effort, they may establish nothing great, permanent, and calm.

If the social condition of a people, under these circumstances, becomes democratic, the danger which I here point out is thereby increased. When everyone is constantly striving to change his position, when an immense field for competition is thrown open to all, when wealth is amassed or dissipated in the shortest possible space of time amid the turmoil of democracy, visions of sudden and easy fortunes, of great possessions easily won and lost, of chance under all its forms haunt the mind. The instability of society itself fosters the natural instability of man's desires. In the midst of these perpetual fluctuations of his lot, the present looms large upon his mind; it hides the future, which becomes indistinct, and men seek only to think about tomorrow.

In those countries in which, unhappily, irreligion and democracy coexist, philosophers and those in power ought to be always striving to place the objects of human actions far beyond man's immediate range. Adapting himself to the spirit of his country and his age, the moralist must learn to vindicate his principles in that position. He must constantly endeavor to show his contemporaries that even in the midst of the perpetual commotion around them it is easier than they think to conceive and to execute protracted undertakings. He must teach them that although the aspect of mankind may have changed, the methods by which men may provide for their prosperity in this world are still the same; and that among democratic nations as well as elsewhere it is only by resisting a thousand petty selfish passions of the hour that the general and unquenchable passion for happiness can be satisfied.

The task of those in power is not less clearly marked out. At all times it is important that those who govern nations should act with a view to the future: but this is even more necessary in democratic and skeptical ages than in any others. By acting thus the leading men of democracies not only make public affairs prosperous, but also teach private individuals, by their example, the art of managing their private concerns.

Above all, they must strive as much as possible to banish chance from the sphere of politics. The sudden and undeserved promotion of a courtier produces only a transient impression in an aristocratic country, because the aggregate institutions and opinions of the nation habitually compel men to advance slowly in tracks which they cannot get out of. But nothing is more pernicious than similar instances of favor exhibited to a democratic people; they give the last impulse to the public mind in a direction where everything hurries it onwards. At times of skepticism and equality more especially, the favor of the people or of the prince, which chance may confer or chance withhold, ought never to stand in lieu of attainments or services. It is desirable that every advancement should there appear to be the result of some effort, so that no greatness should be of too easy acquirement and that ambition should be obliged to fix its gaze long upon an object before it is gratified.

Governments must apply themselves to restore to men that love of the future with which religion and the state of society no longer inspire them; and, without saying so, they must practically teach the community day by day that wealth, fame, and power are the rewards of labor, that great success stands at the utmost range of long desires, and that there is nothing lasting but what is obtained by toil.

When men have accustomed themselves to foresee from afar what is likely to befall them in the world and to feed upon hopes, they can hardly confine their minds within the precise limits of life, and they are ready to break the boundary and cast their looks beyond. I do not doubt that, by training the members of a community to think of their future condition in this world, they would be gradually and unconsciously brought nearer to religious convictions. Thus the means that allow men, up to a certain point, to go without religion are perhaps, after all, the only means we still possess for bringing mankind back, by a long and roundabout path, to a state of faith.

Chapter XVIII

WHY AMONG THE AMERICANS ALL HONEST CALLINGS ARE CONSIDERED HONORABLE

Among a democratic people, where there is no hereditary wealth, every man works to earn a living, or has worked, or is born of parents who have worked. The notion of labor is therefore presented to the mind, on every side, as the necessary, natural, and honest condition of human existence. Not only is labor not dishonorable among such a people, but it is held in honor; the prejudice is not against it, but in its favor. In the United States a wealthy man thinks that he owes it to public opinion to devote his leisure to some kind of industrial or commercial pursuit or to public business. He would think himself in bad repute if he employed his life solely in living. It is for the purpose of escaping this obligation to work that so many rich Americans come to Europe, where they find some scattered remains of aristocratic society, among whom idleness is still held in honor.

Equality of conditions not only ennobles the notion of labor, but raises the notion of labor as a source of profit.

In aristocracies it is not exactly labor that is despised, but labor with a view to profit. Labor is honorable in itself when it is undertaken at the bidding of ambition or virtue. Yet in aristocratic society it constantly happens that he who works for honor is not insensible to the attractions of profit. But these two desires intermingle only in the depths of his soul; he carefully hides from every eye the point at which they join; he would gladly conceal it from himself. In aristocratic countries there are few public officers who do not affect to serve their country without interested motives. Their salary is an incident of which they think but little and of which they always affect not to think at all. Thus the notion of profit is kept distinct from that of labor; however they may be united in point of fact, they are not thought of together.

In democratic communities these two notions are, on the

contrary, always palpably united. As the desire of well-being is universal, as fortunes are slender or fluctuating, as everyone wants either to increase his own resources or to provide fresh ones for his progeny, men clearly see that it is profit that, if not wholly, at least partially leads them to work. Even those who are principally actuated by the love of fame are necessarily made familiar with the thought that they are not exclusively actuated by that motive; and they discover that the desire of getting a living is mingled in their minds with the desire of making life illustrious.

As soon as, on the one hand, labor is held by the whole community to be an honorable necessity of man's condition, and, on the other, as soon as labor is always ostensibly performed, wholly or in part, for the purpose of earning remuneration, the immense interval that separated different callings in aristocratic societies disappears. If all are not alike, all at least have one feature in common. No profession exists in which men do not work for money; and the remuneration that is common to them all gives them all an air of resemblance.

This serves to explain the opinions that the Americans entertain with respect to different callings. In America no one is degraded because he works, for everyone about him works also; nor is anyone humiliated by the notion of receiving pay, for the President of the United States also works for pay. He is paid for commanding, other men for obeying orders. In the United States professions are more or less laborious, more or less profitable; but they are never either high or low: every honest calling is honorable.

Chapter XIX

WHAT CAUSES ALMOST ALL AMERICANS TO FOLLOW INDUSTRIAL CALLINGS

AGRICULTURE is perhaps, of all the useful arts, that which improves most slowly among democratic nations. Frequently, indeed, it would seem to be stationary, because other arts are making rapid strides towards perfection. On the other hand, almost all the tastes and habits that the equality of condition produces naturally lead men to commercial and industrial occupations.

Suppose an active, enlightened, and free man, enjoying a competency, but full of desires; he is too poor to live in idleness, he is rich enough to feel himself protected from the immediate fear of want, and he thinks how he can better his condition. This man has conceived a taste for physical gratifications, which thousands of his fellow men around him indulge in; he has himself begun to enjoy these pleasures, and he is eager to increase his means of satisfying these tastes more completely. But life is slipping away, time is urgent; to what is he to turn? The cultivation of the ground promises an almost certain result to his exertions, but a slow one; men are not enriched by it without patience and toil. Agriculture is therefore only suited to those who already have great superfluous wealth or to those whose penury bids them seek only a bare subsistence. The choice of such a man as we have supposed is soon made; he sells his plot of ground, leaves his dwelling, and embarks on some hazardous but lucrative calling.

Democratic communities abound in men of this kind; and in proportion as the equality of conditions becomes greater, their multitude increases. Thus, democracy not only swells the number of working-men, but leads men to prefer one kind of labor to another; and while it diverts them from agriculture, it encourages their tastes for commerce and manufactures.[1]

This spirit may be observed even among the richest members of the community. In democratic countries, however opulent a man is supposed to be, he is almost always discontented with his fortune because he finds that he is less rich than his father was, and he fears that his sons will be less rich than himself. Most rich men in democracies are therefore constantly haunted by the desire of obtaining wealth, and they naturally turn their attention to trade and manufactures, which appear to offer the readiest and most efficient means of success. In this respect they share the instincts of the poor without feeling the same necessities; say, rather, they feel the most imperious of all necessities, that of not sinking in the world.

In aristocracies the rich are at the same time the governing power. The attention that they unceasingly devote to important public affairs diverts them from the lesser cares that trade and manufactures demand. But if an individual happens to turn his attention to business, the will of the body to which he belongs will immediately prevent him from pursuing it; for, however men may declaim against the rule of numbers, they cannot wholly escape it; and even among those aristocratic bodies that most obstinately refuse to acknowledge the rights of the national majority, a private majority is formed which governs the rest.[2]

In democratic countries, where money does not lead those who possess it to political power, but often removes them

[1] It has often been remarked that manufacturers and merchants are inordinately addicted to physical gratifications, and this has been attributed to commerce and manufactures; but that, I apprehend, is to take the effect for the cause. The taste for physical gratifications is not imparted to men by commerce or manufactures, but it is rather this taste that leads men to engage in commerce and manufactures, as a means by which they hope to satisfy themselves more promptly and more completely. If commerce and manufactures increase the desire of well-being, it is because every passion gathers strength in proportion as it is cultivated, and is increased by all the efforts made to satiate it. All the causes that make the love of worldly welfare predominate in the heart of man are favorable to the growth of commerce and manufactures. Equality of conditions is one of those causes; it encourages trade, not directly, by giving men a taste for business, but indirectly, by strengthening and expanding in their minds a taste for well-being.

[2] See Appendix T.

from it, the rich do not know how to spend their leisure. They are driven into active life by the disquietude and the greatness of their desires, by the extent of their resources, and by the taste for what is extraordinary, which is almost always felt by those who rise, by whatever means, above the crowd. Trade is the only road open to them. In democracies nothing is greater or more brilliant than commerce; it attracts the attention of the public and fills the imagination of the multitude; all energetic passions are directed towards it. Neither their own prejudices nor those of anybody else can prevent the rich from devoting themselves to it. The wealthy members of democracies never form a body which has manners and regulations of its own; the opinions peculiar to their class do not restrain them, and the common opinions of their country urge them on. Moreover, as all the large fortunes that are found in a democratic community are of commercial growth, many generations must succeed one another before their possessors can have entirely laid aside their habits of business.

Circumscribed within the narrow space that politics leaves them, rich men in democracies eagerly embark in commercial enterprise; there they can extend and employ their natural advantages, and, indeed, it is even by the boldness and the magnitude of their industrial speculations that we may measure the slight esteem in which productive industry would have been held by them if they had been born in an aristocracy.

A similar observation is likewise applicable to all men living in democracies, whether they are poor or rich. Those who live in the midst of democratic fluctuations have always before their eyes the image of chance; and they end by liking all undertakings in which chance plays a part. They are therefore all led to engage in commerce, not only for the sake of the profit it holds out to them, but for the love of the constant excitement occasioned by that pursuit.

The United States of America has only been emancipated for half a century from the state of colonial dependence in which it stood to Great Britain; the number of large fortunes there is small and capital is still scarce. Yet no people in the world have made such rapid progress in trade and manufactures as the Americans; they constitute at the present day the second maritime nation in the world, and although their manufactures have to struggle with almost insurmountable natural impediments, they are not prevented from making great and daily advances.

In the United States the greatest undertakings and speculations are executed without difficulty, because the whole population are engaged in productive industry, and because the poorest as well as the most opulent members of the commonwealth are ready to combine their efforts for these purposes. The consequences is that a stranger is constantly amazed by the immense public works executed by a nation which contains, so to speak, no rich men. The Americans arrived but as yesterday on the territory which they inhabit, and they have already changed the whole order of nature for their own advantage. They have joined the Hudson to the Mississippi and made the Atlantic Ocean communicate with the Gulf of Mexico, across a continent of more than five hundred leagues in extent which separates the two seas. The longest railroads that have been constructed up to the present time are in America.

But what most astonishes me in the United States is not so much the marvelous grandeur of some undertakings as the innumerable multitude of small ones. Almost all the farmers of the United States combine some trade with agriculture; most of them make agriculture itself a trade. It seldom happens that an American farmer settles for good upon the land which he occupies; especially in the districts of the Far West, he brings land into tillage in order to sell it again, and not to farm it; he builds a farmhouse on the speculation that, as the state of the country will soon be changed by the increase of population, a good price may be obtained for it.

Every year a swarm of people from the North arrive in the Southern states and settle in the parts where the cotton plant and the sugar-cane grow. These men cultivate the soil in order to make it produce in a few years enough to enrich them; and they already look forward to the time when they may return home to enjoy the competency thus acquired. Thus the Americans carry their businesslike qualities into agriculture, and their trading passions are displayed in that as in their other pursuits.

The Americans make immense progress in productive industry, because they all devote themselves to it at once; and for this same reason they are exposed to unexpected and formidable embarrassments. As they are all engaged in commerce, their commercial affairs are affected by such various and complex causes that it is impossible to foresee what difficulties may arise. As they are all more or less engaged in productive industry, at the least shock given to business all private fortunes are put in jeopardy at the same time, and the state is shaken. I believe that the return of these commercial panics is an endemic disease of the democratic nations of our age. It may be rendered less dangerous, but it cannot be cured, because it does not originate in accidental circumstances, but in the temperament of these nations.

Chapter XX

HOW AN ARISTOCRACY MAY BE CREATED BY MANUFACTURES

I HAVE shown how democracy favors the growth of manufactures and increases without limit the numbers of the manufacturing classes; we shall now see by what side-road manufacturers may possibly, in their turn, bring men back to aristocracy.

It is acknowledged that when a workman is engaged every day upon the same details, the whole commodity is produced with greater ease, speed, and economy. It is likewise acknowledged that the cost of production of manufactured goods is diminished by the extent of the establishment in which they are made and by the amount of capital employed or of credit. These truths had long been imperfectly discerned, but in our time they have been demonstrated. They have been already applied to many very important kinds of manufactures, and the humblest will gradually be governed by them. I know of nothing in politics that deserves to fix the attention of the legislator more closely than these two new axioms of the science of manufactures.

When a workman is unceasingly and exclusively engaged in the fabrication of one thing, he ultimately does his work with singular dexterity; but at the same time he loses the general faculty of applying his mind to the direction of the work. He every day becomes more adroit and less industrious; so that it may be said of him that in proportion as the workman improves, the man is degraded. What can be expected of a man who has spent twenty years of his life in making heads for pins? And to what can that mighty human intelligence which has so often stirred the world be applied in him except it be to investigate the best method of making pins' heads? When a workman has spent a considerable portion of his existence in this manner, his thoughts are forever set upon the object of his daily toil; his body has contracted certain fixed habits, which it can never shake off; in a word, he no longer belongs to himself, but to the calling that he has chosen. It is in vain that laws and manners have been at pains to level all the barriers round such a man and to open to him on every side a thousand different paths to fortune; a theory of manufactures more powerful than customs and laws binds him to a craft, and frequently to a spot, which he cannot leave; it assigns to him a certain place in society, beyond which he cannot go; in the midst of universal movement it has rendered him stationary.

In proportion as the principle of the division of labor is more extensively applied, the workman becomes more weak, more narrow-minded, and more dependent. The art advances, the artisan recedes. On the other hand, in proportion as it becomes more manifest that the productions of manufactures are by so much the cheaper and better as the manufacture is larger and the amount of capital employed more considerable, wealthy and educated men come forward to embark in manufactures, which were heretofore abandoned to poor or ignorant handicraftsmen. The magnitude of the efforts required and the importance of the results to be obtained attract them. Thus at the very time at which the science of manufactures lowers the class of workmen, it raises the class of masters.

While the workman concentrates his faculties more and more upon the study of a single detail, the master surveys an extensive whole, and the mind of the latter is enlarged in proportion as that of the former is narrowed. In a short time the one will require nothing but physical strength without intelligence; the other stands in need of science, and almost of genius, to ensure success. This man resembles more and more the administrator of a vast empire; that man, a brute.

The master and the workman have then here no similarity, and their differences increase every day. They are connected only like the two rings at the extremities of a long chain. Each of them fills the station which is made for him, and which he does not leave; the one is continually, closely, and necessarily dependent upon the other and seems as much born to obey as that other is to command. What is this but aristocracy?

As the conditions of men constituting the nation become more and more equal, the demand for manufactured commodities becomes more general and extensive, and the cheapness that places these objects within the reach of slender fortunes becomes a great element of success. Hence there are every day more men of great opulence and education who devote their wealth and knowledge to manufactures and who seek, by opening large establishments and by a strict division of labor, to meet the fresh demands which are made on all sides. Thus, in proportion as the mass of the nation turns to democracy, that particular class which is engaged in manufactures becomes more aristocratic. Men grow more alike in the one, more different in the other; and inequality increases in the less numerous class in the same ratio in which it decreases in the community. Hence it would appear, on searching to the bottom, that aristocracy should naturally spring out of the bosom of democracy.

But this kind of aristocracy by no means resembles those kinds which preceded it. It will be observed at once that, as it applies exclusively to manufactures and to some manufacturing callings, it is a monstrous exception in the general aspect of society. The small aristocratic societies that are formed by some manufacturers in the midst of the immense democracy of our age contain, like the great aristocratic societies of former ages, some men who are very opulent and a multitude who are wretchedly poor. The poor have few means of escaping from their condition and becoming rich, but the rich are constantly becoming poor, or they give up business when they have realized a fortune. Thus the elements of which the class of the poor is composed are fixed, but the elements of which the class of the rich is composed are not so. To tell the truth, though there are rich men, the class of rich men does not exist; for these rich individuals have no feelings or purposes, no traditions or hopes, in common; there are individuals, therefore, but no definite class.

Not only are the rich not compactly united among themselves, but there is no real bond between them and the poor. Their relative position is not a permanent one; they are constantly drawn together or separated by their interests. The workman is generally dependent on the master, but not on any particular master; these two men meet in the factory, but do not know each other elsewhere; and while they come into contact on one point, they stand very far apart on all others. The manufacturer asks nothing of the workman but his labor; the workman expects nothing from him but his wages. The one contracts no obligation to protect nor the other to defend, and they are not permanently connected either by habit or by duty. The aristocracy created by business rarely settles in the midst of the manufacturing population which it directs; the object is not to govern that population, but to use it. An aristocracy thus constituted can have no great hold upon those whom it employs, and even if it succeeds in retaining them at one moment, they escape the next; it knows not how to will, and it cannot act.

The territorial aristocracy of former ages was either bound by law, or thought itself bound by usage, to come to the relief of its serving-men and to relieve their distresses. But the manufacturing aristocracy of our age first impoverishes and debases the men who serve it and then abandons them to be supported by the charity of the public. This is a natural consequence of what has been said before. Between the workman and the master there are frequent relations, but no real association.

I am of the opinion, on the whole, that the manufacturing aristocracy which is growing up under our eyes is one of the harshest that ever existed in the world; but at the same time it is one of the most confined and least dangerous. Nevertheless, the friends of democracy should keep their eyes anxiously fixed in this direction; for if ever a permanent inequality of conditions and aristocracy again penetrates into the world, it may be predicted that this is the gate by which they will enter.

THIRD BOOK

INFLUENCE OF DEMOCRACY ON MANNERS PROPERLY SO CALLED

Chapter I

HOW CUSTOMS ARE SOFTENED AS SOCIAL CONDITIONS BECOME MORE EQUAL

We perceive that for several centuries social conditions have tended to equality, and we discover that at the same time the customs of society have been softened. Are these two things merely contemporaneous or does any secret link exist between them so that the one cannot advance without the other? Several causes may concur to render the customs of a people less rude, but of all these causes the most powerful appears to me to be the equality of conditions. Equality of conditions and greater mildness in customs are, then, in my eyes, not only contemporaneous occurrences, but correlative facts.

When the fabulists seek to interest us in the actions of beasts, they invest them with human notions and passions; the poets who sing of spirits and angels do the same; there is no wretchedness so deep nor any happiness so pure as to fill the human mind and touch the heart unless we are ourselves held up to our own eyes under other features.

This is strictly applicable to our present subject. When all men are irrevocably marshaled in an aristocratic community according to their professions, their property, and their birth, the members of each class, considering themselves as children of the same family, cherish a constant and lively sympathy towards one another, which can never be felt in an equal degree by the citizens of a democracy. But the same feeling does not exist between the several classes towards each other.

Among an aristocratic people each caste has its own opinions, feelings, rights, customs, and modes of living. Thus the men who compose it do not resemble the mass of their fellow citizens; they do not think or feel in the same manner, and they scarcely believe that they belong to the same race. They cannot, therefore, thoroughly understand what others feel nor judge of others by themselves. Yet they are sometimes eager to lend one another aid; but this is not contrary to my previous observation.

These aristocratic institutions, which made the beings of one and the same race so different, nevertheless bound them to one another by close political ties. Although the serf had no natural interest in the fate of the nobles, he did not the less think himself obliged to devote his person to the service of that noble who happened to be his lord; and although the noble held himself to be a different nature from that of his serfs, he nevertheless held that his duty and his honor required him to defend, at the risk of his own life, those who dwelt upon his domains.

It is evident that these mutual obligations did not originate in the law of nature, but in the law of society; and that the claim of social duty was more stringent than that of mere humanity. These services were not supposed to be due from man to man, but to the vassal or to the lord. Feudal institutions awakened a lively sympathy for the sufferings of certain men, but none at all for the miseries of mankind. They infused generosity rather than mildness into the customs of the time; and although they prompted men to great acts of self-devotion, they created no real sympathies, for real sympathies can exist only between those who are alike, and in aristocratic ages men acknowledge none but the members of their own caste to be like themselves.

When the chroniclers of the Middle Ages, who all belonged to the aristocracy by birth or education, relate the tragic end of a noble, their grief flows apace; whereas they tell you at a breath and without wincing of massacres and tortures inflicted on the common sort of people. Not that these writers felt habitual hatred or systematic disdain for the people; war between the several classes of the community was not yet declared. They were impelled by an instinct rather than by a passion; as they had formed no clear notion of a poor man's sufferings, they cared but little for his fate.

The same feelings animated the lower orders whenever the feudal tie was broken. The same ages that witnessed so many heroic acts of self-devotion on the part of vassals for their lords were stained with atrocious barbarities practiced from time to time by the lower classes on the higher.

It must not be supposed that this mutual insensibility arose solely from the absence of public order and education, for traces of it are to be found in the following centuries, which became tranquil and enlightened while they remained aristocratic.

In 1675 the lower classes in Brittany revolted at the imposition of a new tax. These disturbances were put down with unexampled severity. Observe the language in which Madame de Sévigné, a witness of these horrors, relates them to her daughter:

> Aux Rochers, October 30, 1675
>
> Your letter from Aix, my daughter, is droll enough. At least, read your letters over again before sending them; allow yourself to be surprised by the pretty things that you have put into them and console yourself by this pleasure for the trouble you have had in writing so many. Then you have kissed all of Provence, have you? There would be no satisfaction in kissing all Brittany, unless one liked to smell of wine. . . . Do you wish to hear the news from Rennes? A tax of a hundred thousand crowns has been imposed upon the citizens; and if this sum is not produced within four-and-twenty hours, it is to be doubled, and collected by the soldiers. They have cleared the houses and sent away the occupants of one of the great streets and forbidden anybody to receive them on pain of death; so that the poor wretches (old men, women near their confinement, and children included) may be seen wandering around and crying on their departure from this city, without knowing where to go, and without food or a place to lie in. Day before yesterday a fiddler was broken on the wheel for getting up a dance and stealing some stamped paper. He was quartered after death,

and his limbs exposed at the four corners of the city. Sixty citizens have been thrown into prison, and the business of punishing them is to begin tomorrow. This province sets a fine example to the others, teaching them above all that of respecting the governors and their wives, and of never throwing stones into their garden.[1]

Yesterday, a delightful day, Madame de Tarente visited these wilds; there is no question about preparing a chamber or a collation; she comes by the gate, and returns the same way. . . .

In another letter she adds:

You talk very pleasantly about our miseries, but we are no longer so jaded with capital punishments; only one a week now, just to keep up appearances. It is true that hanging now seems to me quite a cooling entertainment. I have got a wholly new idea of justice since I have been in this region. Your galley-slaves seem to me a society of good people who have retired from the world in order to lead a quiet life.

It would be a mistake to suppose that Madame de Sévigné, who wrote these lines, was a selfish or cruel person; she was passionately attached to her children and very ready to sympathize in the sorrows of her friends; nay, her letters show that she treated her vassals and servants with kindness and indulgence. But Madame de Sévigné had no clear notion of suffering in anyone who was not a person of quality.

In our time the harshest man, writing to the most insensible person of his acquaintance, would not venture to indulge in the cruel jocularity that I have quoted; and even if his own manners allowed him to do so, the manners of society at large would forbid it. Whence does this arise? Have we more sensibility than our fathers? I do not know that we have, but I am sure that our sensibility is extended to many more objects.

When all the ranks of a community are nearly equal, as all men think and feel in nearly the same manner, each of them may judge in a moment of the sensations of all the

[1] To understand this last pleasantry, it should be recalled that Madame de Grignan was the wife of the Governor of Provence.

others; he casts a rapid glance upon himself, and that is enough. There is no wretchedness into which he cannot readily enter, and a secret instinct reveals to him its extent. It signifies not that strangers or foes are the sufferers; imagination puts him in their place; something like a personal feeling is mingled with his pity and makes himself suffer while the body of his fellow creature is in torture.

In democratic ages men rarely sacrifice themselves for one another, but they display general compassion for the members of the human race. They inflict no useless ills, and they are happy to relieve the griefs of others when they can do so without much hurting themselves; they are not disinterested, but they are humane.

Although the Americans have in a manner reduced selfishness to a social and philosophical theory, they are nevertheless extremely open to compassion. In no country is criminal justice administered with more mildness than in the United States. While the English seem disposed carefully to retain the bloody traces of the Middle Ages in their penal legislation, the Americans have almost expunged capital punishment from their codes. North America is, I think, the only country upon earth in which the life of no one citizen has been taken for a political offense in the course of the last fifty years.

The circumstance which conclusively shows that this singular mildness of the Americans arises chiefly from their social condition is the manner in which they treat their slaves. Perhaps there is not, on the whole, a single European colony in the New World in which the physical condition of the blacks is less severe than in the United States; yet the slaves still endure frightful misery there and are constantly exposed to very cruel punishments. It is easy to perceive that the lot of these unhappy beings inspires their masters with but little compassion and that they look upon slavery not only as an institution which is profitable to them, but as an evil which does not affect them. Thus the same man who is full of humanity towards his fellow creatures when they are at the same time his equals becomes insensible to their afflictions as soon as that equality ceases. His mildness should therefore be attributed to the equality of conditions rather than to civilization and education.

What I have here remarked of individuals is to a certain

extent applicable to nations. When each nation has its distinct opinions, belief, laws, and customs, it looks upon itself as the whole of mankind and is moved by no sorrows but its own. Should war break out between two nations animated by this feeling, it is sure to be waged with great cruelty.

At the time of their highest culture the Romans slaughtered the generals of their enemies, after having dragged them in triumph behind a car; and they flung their prisoners to the beasts of the Circus for the amusement of the people. Cicero, who declaimed so vehemently at the notion of crucifying a Roman citizen, had not a word to say against these horrible abuses of victory. It is evident that, in his eyes, a barbarian did not belong to the same human race as a Roman.

On the contrary, in proportion as nations become more like each other, they become reciprocally more compassionate, and the law of nations is mitigated.

Chapter II

HOW DEMOCRACY RENDERS THE HABITUAL INTERCOURSE OF THE AMERICANS SIMPLE AND EASY

DEMOCRACY does not attach men strongly to one another, but it places their habitual intercourse on an easier footing.

If two Englishmen chance to meet at the antipodes, where they are surrounded by strangers whose language and manners are almost unknown to them, they will first stare at each other with much curiosity and a kind of secret uneasiness; they will then turn away, or if one accosts the other, they will take care to converse only with a constrained and absent air, upon very unimportant subjects. Yet there is no enmity between these men; they have never seen each other before, and each believes the other to be a respectable person. Why, then, should they stand so cautiously apart? We must go back to England to learn the reason.

When it is birth alone, independent of wealth, that classes men in society, everyone knows exactly what his own position is in the social scale; he does not seek to rise, he does not fear to sink. In a community thus organized men of different castes communicate very little with one another; but if accident brings them together, they are ready to converse without hoping or fearing to lose their own position. Their intercourse is not on a footing of equality, but it is not constrained.

When a moneyed aristocracy succeeds to an aristocracy of birth, the case is altered. The privileges of some are still extremely great, but the possibility of acquiring those privileges is open to all; whence it follows that those who possess them are constantly haunted by the apprehension of losing them or of other men's sharing them; those who do not yet enjoy them long to possess them at any cost or, if they fail, to appear at least to possess them, this being not impossible. As the social importance of men is no longer ostensibly and permanently fixed by blood and is infinitely varied by wealth, ranks still exist, but it is not easy clearly to distinguish at a glance those who respectively belong to them. Secret hostilities then arise in the community; one set of men endeavor by innumerable artifices to penetrate, or to appear to penetrate, among those who are above them; another set are constantly in arms against these usurpers of their rights; or, rather, the same individual does both at once, and while he seeks to raise himself into a higher circle, he is always on the defensive against the intrusion of those below him.

Such is the condition of England at the present time, and I am of the opinion that the peculiarity just adverted to must be attributed principally to this cause. As aristocratic pride is still extremely great among the English, and as the limits of aristocracy are ill-defined, everybody lives in constant dread lest advantage should be taken of his familiarity. Unable to judge at once of the social position of those he meets, an Englishman prudently avoids all contact with them. Men are afraid lest some slight service rendered should draw them into an unsuitable acquaintance; they dread civilities, and they avoid the obtrusive gratitude of a stranger quite as much as his hatred.

Many people attribute these singular antisocial propensities and the reserved and taciturn bearing of the English to purely physical causes. I may admit that there is something of it in their race, but much more of it is attributable to their social condition, as is proved by the contrast of the Americans.

In America, where the privileges of birth never existed and where riches confer no peculiar rights on their possessors, men unacquainted with one another are very ready to frequent the same places and find neither peril nor advantage in the free interchange of their thoughts. If they meet by accident, they neither seek nor avoid intercourse; their manner is therefore natural, frank, and open; it is easy to see that they hardly expect or learn anything from one another, and that they do not care to display any more than to conceal their position in the world. If their demeanor is often cold and serious, it is never haughty or constrained; and if they do not converse, it is because they are not in a humor to talk, not because they think it their interest to be silent.

In a foreign country two Americans are at once friends simply because they are Americans. They are repulsed by no prejudice; they are attracted by their common country. For two Englishmen the same blood is not enough; they must be brought together by the same rank. The Americans notice this unsociable mood of the English as much as the French do and are not less astonished by it. Yet Americans are connected with England by their origin, their religion, their language, and partially by their customs; they differ only in their social condition. It may therefore be inferred that the reserve of the English proceeds from the constitution of their country much more than from that of its inhabitants.

Chapter III

WHY THE AMERICANS SHOW SO LITTLE SENSITIVENESS IN THEIR OWN COUNTRY AND ARE SO SENSITIVE IN EUROPE

THE TEMPER of the Americans is vindictive, like that of all serious and reflecting nations. They hardly ever forget an offense, but it is not easy to offend them, and their resentment is as slow to kindle as it is to abate.

In aristocratic communities, where a small number of persons manage everything, the outward intercourse of men is subject to settled conventional rules. Everyone then thinks he knows exactly what marks of respect or of condescension he ought to display, and none are presumed to be ignorant of the science of etiquette. These usages of the first class in society afterwards serve as a model to all the others; besides this, each of the latter lays down a code of its own, to which all its members are bound to conform. Thus the rules of politeness form a complex system of legislation, which it is difficult to be perfectly master of, but from which it is dangerous for anyone to deviate; so that men are constantly exposed involuntarily to inflict or to receive bitter affronts.

But as the distinctions of rank are obliterated, as men differing in education and in birth meet and mingle in the same places of resort, it is almost impossible to agree upon the rules of good breeding. As its laws are uncertain, to disobey them is not a crime, even in the eyes of those who know what they are; men attach more importance to intentions than to forms, and they grow less civil, but at the same time less quarrelsome.

There are many little attentions that an American does not care about; he thinks they are not due to him, or he presumes that they are not known to be due. He therefore either does not perceive a rudeness or he forgives it; his manners become less courteous, and his character more plain and masculine.

The mutual indulgence that the Americans display and the manly confidence with which they treat one another also result from another deeper and more general cause, which I have already referred to in the preceding chapter. In the United States the distinctions of rank in civil society are slight, in political society they are nil; an American, therefore, does not think himself bound to pay particular attentions to any of his fellow citizens, nor does he require such attentions from them towards himself. As he does not see that it is his interest eagerly to seek the company of any of his countrymen, he is slow to fancy that his own company is declined. Despising no one on account of his station, he does not imagine that anyone can despise him for that cause, and until he has clearly perceived an insult, he does not suppose that an affront was intended. The social condition of the Americans naturally accustoms them not to take offense in small matters, and, on the other hand, the democratic freedom which they enjoy transfuses this same mildness of temper into the character of the nation.

The political institutions of the United States constantly bring citizens of all ranks into contact and compel them to pursue great undertakings in concert. People thus engaged have scarcely time to attend to the details of etiquette, and they are besides too strongly interested in living harmoniously for them to stick at such things. They therefore soon acquire a habit of considering the feelings and opinions of those whom they meet more than their manners, and they do not allow themselves to be annoyed by trifles.

I have often noticed in the United States that it is not easy to make a man understand that his presence may be dispensed with; hints will not always suffice to shake him off. I contradict an American at every word he says, to show him that his conversation bores me; he instantly labors with fresh pertinacity to convince me; I preserve a dogged silence, and he thinks I am meditating deeply on the truths that he is uttering; at last I rush from his company, and he supposes that some urgent business hurries me elsewhere. This man will never understand that he wearies me to death unless I tell him so, and the only way to get rid of him is to make him my enemy for life.

At first sight it appears surprising that the same man, transported to Europe, suddenly becomes so sensitive and captious that I often find it as difficult to avoid offending him here as it was there to put him out of countenance. These two opposite effects proceed from the same cause. Democratic institutions generally give men a lofty notion of their country and of themselves. An American leaves his coun ry with a heart swollen with pride; on arriving in Europe, he at once finds out that we are not so engrossed by the United States and the great people who inhabit it as he had supposed, and this begins to annoy him. He has been informed that the conditions of society are not equal in our part of the globe, and he observes that among the nations of Europe the traces of rank are not wholly obliterated, that wealth and birth still retain some indeterminate privileges, which force themselves upon his notice while they elude definition. He is therefore profoundly ignorant of the place that he ought to occupy in this half-ruined scale of classes, which are sufficiently distinct to hate and despise each other, yet sufficiently alike for him to be always confounding them. He is afraid of ranking himself too high; still more is he afraid of being ranked too low. This twofold peril keeps his mind constantly on the stretch and embarrasses all he says and does.

He learns from tradition that in Europe ceremonial observances were infinitely varied according to different ranks; this recollection of former times completes his perplexity, and he is the more afraid of not obtaining those marks of respect which are due to him, as he does not exactly know in what they consist. He is like a man surrounded by traps: society is not a recreation for him, but a serious toil: he weighs your least actions, interrogates your looks, and scrutinizes all you say lest there should be some hidden allusion to affront him. I doubt whether there was ever a provincial man of quality so punctilious in breeding as he is: he endeavors to attend to the slightest rules of etiquette and does not allow one of them to be waived towards himself; he is full of scruples and at the same time of pretensions; he wishes to do enough, but fears to do too much, and as he does not very well know the limits of the one or of the other, he keeps up a haughty and embarrassed air of reserve.

But this is not all: here is yet another queer twist of the human heart. An American is forever talking of the admirable equality that prevails in the United States; aloud he makes it the boast of his country, but in secret he deplores it for himself, and he aspires to show that, for his part, he is an exception to the general state of things which he vaunts. There is hardly an American to be met with who does not claim some remote kindred with the first founders of the colonies; and as for the scions of the noble families of England, America seemed to me to be covered with them. When an opulent American arrives in Europe, his first care is to surround himself with all the luxuries of wealth; he is so afraid of being taken for the plain citizen of a democracy that he adopts a hundred distorted ways of bringing some new instance of his wealth before you every day. His house will be in the most fashionable part of the town; he will always be surrounded by a host of servants. I have heard an American complain that in the best houses of Paris the society was rather mixed; the taste which prevails there was not pure enough for him, and he ventured to hint that, in his opinion, there was a want of elegance of manner; he could not accustom himself to see wit concealed under such unpretending forms.

These contrasts ought not to surprise us. If the vestiges of former aristocratic distinctions were not so completely effaced in the United States, the Americans would be less simple and less tolerant in their own country; they would require less, and be less fond of borrowed manners, in ours.

Chapter IV

CONSEQUENCES OF THE THREE PRECEDING CHAPTERS

When men feel a natural compassion for the sufferings of one another, when they are brought together by easy and frequent intercourse, and no sensitive feelings keep them asunder, it may readily be supposed that they will lend assistance to one another whenever it is needed. When an American asks for the co-operation of his fellow citizens, it is seldom refused; and I have often seen it afforded spontaneously, and with great goodwill. If an accident happens on the highway, everybody hastens to help the sufferer; if some great and sudden calamity befalls a family, the purses of a thousand strangers are at once willingly opened and small but numerous donations pour in to relieve their distress.

It often happens, among the most civilized nations of the globe, that a poor wretch is as friendless in the midst of a crowd as the savage in his wilds; this is hardly ever the case in the United States. The Americans, who are always cold and often coarse in their manners, seldom show insensibility; and if they do not proffer services eagerly, yet they do not refuse to render them.

All this is not in contradiction to what I have said before on the subject of individualism. The two things are so far from combating each other that I can see how they agree. Equality of condition, while it makes men feel their independence, shows them their own weakness: they are free, but exposed to a thousand accidents; and experience soon teaches them that although they do not habitually require the assistance of others, a time almost always comes when they cannot do without it.

In Europe we constantly see that men of the same profession are always ready to assist one another; they are all exposed to the same ills, and that is enough to teach them to seek mutual preservation, however hard-hearted and selfish they may otherwise be. When one of them falls into danger from which the others may save him by a slight transient sacrifice or a sudden effort, they do not fail to make the attempt. Not that they are deeply interested in his fate, for if, by chance, their exertions are unavailing, they immediately forget the object of them and return to their own business; but a sort of tacit and almost involuntary agreement has been passed between them, by which each one owes to the others a temporary support, which he may claim for himself in turn.

Extend to a people the remark here applied to a class and you will understand my meaning. A similar covenant exists, in fact, between all the citizens of a democracy: they all feel themselves subject to the same weakness and the same dangers; and their interest, as well as their sympathy, makes it a rule with them to lend one another assistance when required. The more equal social conditions become, the more do men display this reciprocal disposition to oblige each other. In democracies no great benefits are conferred, but good offices are constantly rendered; a man seldom displays self-devotion, but all men are ready to be of service to one another.

Chapter V

HOW DEMOCRACY AFFECTS THE RELATIONS OF MASTERS AND SERVANTS

AN AMERICAN who had traveled for a long time in Europe once said to me: "The English treat their servants with a stiffness and imperiousness of manner which surprise us; but, on the other hand, the French sometimes treat their attendants with a degree of familiarity or of politeness which we cannot understand. It looks as if they were afraid to give orders; the relative position of the superior and the inferior is poorly maintained." The remark was a just one, and I have often made it myself. I have always considered England as the country of all the world where in our time the bond of domestic service is drawn most tightly, and France as the country where it is most relaxed. Nowhere have I seen masters stand so high or so low as in these two countries. Between these two extremes the Americans are to be placed. Such is the fact as it appears upon the surface of things; to discover the causes of that fact, it is necessary to search the matter thoroughly.

No communities have ever yet existed in which social conditions have been so equal that there were neither rich nor poor, and, consequently, neither masters nor servants. Democracy does not prevent the existence of these two classes, but it changes their dispositions and modifies their mutual relations.

Among aristocratic nations servants form a distinct class, not more variously composed than that of their masters. A settled order is soon established; in the former as well as in the latter class a scale is formed, with numerous distinctions or marked gradations of rank, and generations succeed one another thus, without any change of position. These two communities are superposed one above the other, always distinct, but regulated by analogous principles. This aristocratic constitution does not exert a less powerful influence on the notions and manners of servants than on those of masters; and although the effects are different, the same cause may easily be traced.

Both classes constitute small communities in the heart of the nation, and certain permanent notions of right and wrong are ultimately established among them. The different acts of human life are viewed by one peculiar and unchanging light. In the society of servants, as in that of masters, men exercise a great influence over one another: they acknowledge settled rules, and in the absence of law they are guided by a sort of public opinion; their habits are settled, and their conduct is placed under a certain control.

These men, whose destiny it is to obey, certainly do not understand fame, virtue, honesty, and honor in the same manner as their masters; but they have a pride, a virtue, and an honesty pertaining to their condition; and they have a notion, if I may use the expression, of a sort of servile honor.[1] Because a class is mean, it must not be supposed that all who belong to it are mean-hearted; to think so would be a great mistake. However lowly it may be, he who is foremost there and who has no notion of quitting it occupies an aristocratic position which inspires him with lofty feelings, pride, and self-respect, that fit him for the higher virtues and for actions above the common.

Among aristocratic nations it was by no means rare to find men of noble and vigorous minds in the service of the great, who did not feel the servitude they bore and who submitted to the will of their masters without any fear of their displeasure.

But this was hardly ever the case among the inferior ranks of domestic servants. It may be imagined that he who occupies the lowest stage of the order of menials stands very low indeed. The French created a word on purpose to designate the servants of the aristocracy; they called them "lackeys." This word *lackey* served as the strongest expression, when all others were exhausted, to designate human meanness.

[1] If the principal opinions by which men are guided are examined closely and in detail, the analogy appears still more striking, and one is surprised to find among them, just as much as among the haughtiest scions of a feudal race, pride of birth, respect of their ancestry and their descendants, disdain of their inferiors, a dread of contact, and a taste for etiquette, precedents and antiquity.

Under the old French monarchy to denote by a single expression a low-spirited, contemptible fellow it was usual to say that he had the *soul of a lackey;* the term was enough to convey all that was intended.

The permanent inequality of conditions not only gives servants certain peculiar virtues and vices, but places them in a peculiar relation with respect to their masters. Among aristocratic nations the poor man is familiarized from his childhood with the notion of being commanded; to whichever side he turns his eyes, the graduated structure of society and the aspect of obedience meet his view. Hence in those countries the master readily obtains prompt, complete, respectful, and easy obedience from his servants, because they revere in him not only their master, but the class of masters. He weighs down their will by the whole weight of the aristocracy. He orders their actions; to a certain extent, he even directs their thoughts. In aristocracies the master often exercises, even without being aware of it, an amazing sway over the opinions, the habits, and the manners of those who obey him, and his influence extends even further than his authority.

In aristocratic communities not only are there hereditary families of servants as well as of masters, but the same families of servants adhere for several generations to the same families of masters (like two parallel lines, which neither meet nor separate); and this considerably modifies the mutual relations of these two classes of persons. Thus although in aristocratic society the master and servant have no natural resemblance, although, on the contrary, they are placed at an immense distance on the scale of human beings by their fortune, education, and opinions, yet time ultimately binds them together. They are connected by a long series of common reminiscences, and however different they may be, they grow alike; while in democracies, where they are naturally almost alike, they always remain strangers to one another. Among an aristocratic people the master gets to look upon his servants as an inferior and secondary part of himself, and he often takes an interest in their lot by a last stretch of selfishness.

Servants, on their part, are not averse to regarding themselves in the same light; and they sometimes identify themselves with the person of the master, so that they become an appendage to him in their own eyes as well as in his. In aristocracies a servant fills a subordinate position which he cannot get out of; above him is another man, holding a superior rank, which he cannot lose. On one side are obscurity, poverty, obedience for life; on the other, and also foı life, fame, wealth, and command. The two conditions are always distinct and always in propinquity; the tie that connects them is as lasting as they are themselves.

In this predicament the servant ultimately detaches his notion of interest from his own person; he deserts himself as it were, or rather he transports himself into the character of his master and thus assumes an imaginary personality. He complacently invests himself with the wealth of those who command him; he shares their fame, exalts himself by their rank, and feeds his mind with borrowed greatness, to which he attaches more importance than those who fully and really possess it. There is something touching and at the same time ridiculous in this strange confusion of two different states of being. These passions of masters, when they pass into the souls of menials, assume the natural dimensions of the place they occupy; they are contracted and lowered. What was pride in the former becomes puerile vanity and paltry ostentation in the latter. The servants of a great man are commonly most punctilious as to the marks of respect due to him, and they attach more importance to his slightest privileges than he does himself. In France a few of these old servants of the aristocracy are still to be met with here and there; they have survived their race, which will soon disappear with them altogether.

In the United States I never saw anyone at all like them. The Americans are not only unacquainted with the kind of man, but it is hardly possible to make them understand that such ever existed. It is scarcely less difficult for them to conceive it than for us to form a correct notion of what a slave was among the Romans or a serf in the Middle Ages. All these men were, in fact, though in different degrees, results of the same cause: they are all retiring from our sight and disappearing in the obscurity of the past, together with the social condition to which they owed their origin.

Equality of conditions turns servants and masters into new beings, and places them in new relative positions. When social conditions are nearly equal, men are constantly changing their situations in life; there is still a class of menials and a class of masters, but these classes are not always composed of the same individuals, still less of the same families; and those who command are not more secure of perpetuity than those who obey. As servants do not form a separate class, they have no habits, prejudices, or manners peculiar to themselves; they are not remarkable for any particular turn of mind or moods of feeling. They know no vices or virtues of their condition, but they partake of the education, the opinions, the feelings, the virtues, and the vices of their contemporaries; and they are honest men or scoundrels in the same way as their masters are.

The conditions of servants are not less equal than those of masters. As no marked ranks or fixed subordination are to be found among them, they will not display either the meanness or the greatness that characterize the aristocracy of menials, as well as all other aristocracies. I never saw a man in the United States who reminded me of that class of confidential servants of which we still retain a reminiscence in Europe; neither did I ever meet with such a thing as a *lackey:* all traces of the one and the other have disappeared.

In democracies servants are not only equal among themselves, but it may be said that they are, in some sort, the equals of their masters. This requires explanation in order to be rightly understood. At any moment a servant may become a master, and he aspires to rise to that condition; the servant is therefore not a different man from the master. Why, then, has the former a right to command, and what compels the latter to obey except the free and temporary consent of both their wills? Neither of them is by nature inferior to the other; they only become so for a time, by covenant. Within the terms of this covenant the one is a servant, the other a master; beyond it they are two citizens of the commonwealth, two men.

I beg the reader particularly to observe that this is not only the notion which servants themselves entertain of their own condition; domestic service is looked upon by masters in the same light, and the precise limits of authority and obedience are as clearly settled in the mind of the one as in that of the other.

When the greater part of the community have long attained a condition nearly alike and when equality is an old and acknowledged fact, the public mind, which is never affected by exceptions, assigns certain general limits to the value of man, above or below which no man can long remain placed. It is in vain that wealth and poverty, authority and obedience, accidentally interpose great distances between two men; public opinion, founded upon the usual order of things, draws them to a common level and creates a species of imaginary equality between them, in spite of the real inequality of their conditions. This all-powerful opinion penetrates at length even into the hearts of those whose interest might arm them to resist it; it affects their judgment while it subdues their will.

In their inmost convictions the master and the servant no longer perceive any deep-seated difference between them, and they neither hope nor fear to meet with either at any time. They are therefore subject neither to disdain nor to anger, and they discern in each other neither humility nor pride. The master holds the contract of service to be the only source of his power, and the servant regards it as the only cause of his obedience. They do not quarrel about their reciprocal situations, but each knows his own and keeps it.

In the French army the common soldier is taken from nearly the same class as the officer and may hold the same commissions; out of the ranks he considers himself entirely equal to his military superiors, and in point of fact he is so; but when under arms, he does not hesitate to obey, and his obedience is not the less prompt, precise, and ready, for being voluntary and defined. This example may give a notion of what takes place between masters and servants in democratic communities.

It would be preposterous to suppose that those warm and deep-seated affections which are sometimes kindled in the domestic service of aristocracy will ever spring up between these two men, or that they will exhibit strong instances of self-sacrifice. In aristocracies masters and servants live apart, and frequently their only intercourse is through a third person; yet they commonly stand firmly by one another. In democratic countries the master and the servant are close together: they are in daily personal contact, but their minds do not intermingle; they have common occupations, hardly ever common interests.

Among such a people the servant always considers himself as a sojourner in the dwelling of his masters. He knew nothing of their forefathers; he will see nothing of their descendants; he has nothing lasting to expect from them. Why, then, should he identify his life with theirs, and whence should so strange a surrender of himself proceed? The reciprocal position of the two men is changed; their mutual relations must be so, too.

In all that precedes I wish that I could depend upon the example of the Americans as a whole; but I cannot do this without drawing careful distinctions regarding persons and places. In the South of the Union slavery exists; all that I have just said is consequently inapplicable there. In the North the majority of servants are either freedmen or the children of freedmen; these persons occupy an uncertain position in the public estimation; by the laws they are brought up to the level of their masters; by the manners of the country they are firmly kept below it. They do not themselves clearly know their proper place and are almost always either insolent or craven.

But in the Northern states, especially in New England, there are a certain number of whites who agree, for wages, to yield a temporary obedience to the will of their fellow citizens. I have heard that these servants commonly perform the duties of their situations with punctuality and intelligence and that, without thinking themselves naturally inferior to the person who orders them, they submit without reluctance to obey him. They appeared to me to carry into service some of those manly habits which independence and equality create. Having once selected a hard way of life, they do not seek to escape from it by indirect means; and they have sufficient respect for themselves not to refuse to their masters that obedience which they have freely promised. On their part, masters require nothing of their servants but the faithful and rigorous performance of the covenant: they do not ask for marks of respect, they do not claim their love or devoted attachment; it is enough that, as servants, they are exact and honest.

It would not, then, be true to assert that in democratic society the relation of servants and masters is disorganized; it is organized on another footing; the rule is different, but there is a rule.

It is not my purpose to inquire whether the new state of

things that I have just described is inferior to that which preceded it or simply different. Enough for me that it is fixed and determined; for what is most important to meet with among men is not any given ordering, but order.

But what shall I say of those sad and troubled times at which equality is established in the midst of the tumult of revolution, when democracy, after having been introduced into the state of society, still struggles with difficulty against the prejudices and manners of the country? The laws, and partially public opinion, already declare that no natural or permanent inferiority exists between the servant and the master. But this new belief has not yet reached the innermost convictions of the latter, or rather his heart rejects it; in the secret persuasion of his mind the master thinks that he belongs to a peculiar and superior race; he dares not say so, but he shudders at allowing himself to be dragged to the same level. His authority over his servants becomes timid and at the same time harsh; he has already ceased to entertain for them the feelings of patronizing kindness which long uncontested power always produces, and he is surprised that, being changed himself, his servant changes also. He wants his attendants to form regular and permanent habits, in a condition of domestic service that is only temporary; he requires that they should appear contented with and proud of a servile condition, which they will one day shake off, that they should sacrifice themselves to a man who can neither protect nor ruin them, and, in short, that they should contract an indissoluble engagement to a being like themselves and one who will last no longer than they will.

Among aristocratic nations it often happens that the condition of domestic service does not degrade the character of those who enter upon it, because they neither know nor imagine any other; and the amazing inequality that is manifest between them and their master appears to be the necessary and unavoidable consequence of some hidden law of Providence.

In democracies the condition of domestic service does not degrade the character of those who enter upon it, because it is freely chosen and adopted for a time only, because it is not stigmatized by public opinion and creates no permanent inequality between the servant and the master.

But while the transition from one social condition to another is going on, there is almost always a time when men's minds fluctuate between the aristocratic notion of subjection and the democratic notion of obedience. Obedience then loses its moral importance in the eyes of him who obeys; he no longer considers it as a species of divine obligation, and he does not yet view it under its purely human aspect; it has to him no character of sanctity or of justice, and he submits to it as to a degrading but profitable condition.

At that period a confused and imperfect phantom of equality haunts the minds of servants; they do not at once perceive whether the equality to which they are entitled is to be found within or without the pale of domestic service, and they rebel in their hearts against a subordination to which they have subjected themselves and from which they derive actual profit. They consent to serve and they blush to obey; they like the advantages of service, but not the master; or, rather, they are not sure that they ought not themselves to be masters, and they are inclined to consider him who orders them as an unjust usurper of their own rights.

Then it is that the dwelling of every citizen offers a spectacle somewhat analogous to the gloomy aspect of political society. A secret and internal warfare is going on there between powers ever rivals and suspicious of one another: the master is ill-natured and weak, the servant ill-natured and intractable; the one constantly attempts to evade by unfair restrictions his obligation to protect and to remunerate, the other his obligation to obey. The reins of domestic government dangle between them, to be snatched at by one or the other. The lines that divide authority from oppression, liberty from license, and right from might are to their eyes so jumbled together and confused that no one knows exactly what he is or what he may be or what he ought to be. Such a condition is not democracy, but revolution.

Chapter VI

HOW DEMOCRATIC INSTITUTIONS AND MANNERS TEND TO RAISE RENTS AND SHORTEN THE TERMS OF LEASES

WHAT has been said of servants and masters is applicable to a certain extent to landowners and farming tenants, but this subject deserves to be considered by itself.

In America there are, properly speaking, no farming tenants; every man owns the ground he tills. It must be admitted that democratic laws tend greatly to increase the number of landowners and to diminish that of farming tenants. Yet what takes place in the United States is much less attributable to the institutions of the country than to the country itself. In America land is cheap and anyone may easily become a landowner; its returns are small and its produce cannot well be divided between a landowner and a farmer. America therefore stands alone in this respect, as well as in many others, and it would be a mistake to take it as an example.

I believe that in democratic as well as in aristocratic countries there will be landowners and tenants, but the connection existing between them will be of a different kind. In aristocracies the hire of a farm is paid to the landlord, not only in rent, but in respect, regard, and duty; in democracies the whole is paid in cash. When estates are divided and passed from hand to hand, and the permanent connection that existed between families and the soil is dissolved, the landowner and the tenant are only casually brought into contact. They meet for a moment to settle the conditions of the agreement and then lose sight of each other; they are two strangers brought together by a common interest, who keenly talk over a matter of business, the sole object of which is to make money.

In proportion as property is subdivided and wealth distributed over the country, the community is filled with people whose former opulence is declining, and with others whose fortunes are of recent growth and whose wants increase more rapidly than their resources. For all such persons the smallest pecuniary profit is a matter of importance, and none of them feel disposed to waive any of their claims or to lose any portion of their income.

As ranks are intermingled, and as very large as well as very scanty fortunes become more rare, every day brings the social condition of the landowner nearer to that of the farmer: the one has not naturally any uncontested superiority over the other; between two men who are equal and not at ease in their circumstances, the contract of hire is exclusively an affair of money.

A man whose estate extends over a whole district and who owns a hundred farms is well aware of the importance of gaining at the same time the affections of some thousands of men. This object appears to call for his exertions, and to attain it he will readily make considerable sacrifices. But he who owns a hundred acres is insensible to similar considerations, and cares but little to win the private regard of his tenant.

An aristocracy does not expire, like a man, in a single day; the aristocratic principle is slowly undermined in men's opinion before it is attacked in their laws. Long before open war is declared against it, the tie that had hitherto united the higher classes to the lower may be seen to be gradually relaxed. Indifference and contempt are betrayed by one class, jealousy and hatred by the others. The intercourse between rich and poor becomes less frequent and less kind, and rents are raised. This is not the consequence of a democratic revolution, but its certain harbinger; for an aristocracy that has lost the affections of the people once and forever is like a tree dead at the root, which is the more easily torn up by the winds the higher its branches have spread.

In the course of the last fifty years the rents of farms have amazingly increased, not only in France, but throughout the greater part of Europe. The remarkable improvements that have taken place in agriculture and manufactures within the same period do not suffice, in my opinion, to explain this fact; recourse must be had to another cause, more powerful and more concealed. I believe that cause is to be found in the democratic institutions which several European nations have adopted and in the democratic passions which more or less agitate all the rest.

I have frequently heard great English landowners congratulate themselves that at the present day they derive a much larger income from their estates than their fathers did. They have perhaps good reason to be glad, but most assuredly they do not know what they are glad of. They think they are making a clear gain when it is in reality only an exchange; their influence is what they are parting with for cash, and what they gain in money will before long be lost in power.

There is yet another sign by which it is easy to know that a great democratic revolution is going on or approaching. In the Middle Ages almost all lands were leased for lives or for very long terms; the domestic economy of that period shows that leases for ninety-nine years were more frequent then than leases for twelve years are now. Men then believed that families were immortal; men's conditions seemed settled forever, and the whole of society appeared to be so fixed that it was not supposed anything would ever be stirred or shaken in its structure. In ages of equality the human mind takes a different bent: the prevailing notion is that nothing abides, and man is haunted by the thought of mutability. Under this impression the landowner and the tenant himself are instinctively averse to protracted terms of obligation; they are afraid of being tied up tomorrow by the contract that benefits them today. They do not trust themselves; they are afraid that, their standards changing, they may have trouble in ridding themselves of the thing which had been the object of their longing. And they are right to fear this, for in democratic times what is most unstable, in the midst of the instability of everything, is the heart of man.

Chapter VII

INFLUENCE OF DEMOCRACY ON WAGES

Most of the remarks that I have already made in speaking of masters and servants may be applied to masters and workmen. As the gradations of the social scale come to be less observed, while the great sink and the humble rise and poverty as well as opulence ceases to be hereditary, the distance, both in reality and in opinion, which heretofore separated the workman from the master is lessened every day. The workman conceives a more lofty opinion of his rights, of his future, of himself; he is filled with new ambition and new desires, he is harassed by new wants. Every instant he views with longing eyes the profits of his employer; and in order to share them he strives to dispose of his labor at a higher rate, and he generally succeeds at length in the attempt.

In democratic countries as well as elsewhere most of the branches of productive industry are carried on at a small cost by men little removed by their wealth or education above the level of those whom they employ. These manufacturing speculators are extremely numerous; their interests differ; they cannot therefore easily concert or combine their exertions. On the other hand, the workmen have always some sure resources which enable them to refuse to work when they cannot get what they conceive to be the fair price of their labor. In the constant struggle for wages that is going on between these two classes, their strength is divided and success alternates from one to the other.

It is even probable that in the end the interest of the working class will prevail, for the high wages which they have already obtained make them every day less dependent on their masters, and as they grow more independent, they have greater facilities for obtaining a further increase of wages.

I shall take for example that branch of productive industry which is still at the present day the most generally followed in France and in almost all the countries of the world, the cultivation of the soil. In France most of those who labor for hire in agriculture are themselves owners of certain plots of ground, which just enable them to subsist without working for anyone else. When these laborers come to offer their services to a neighboring landowner or farmer, if he refuses them a certain rate of wages they retire to their own small property and await another opportunity.

I think that, on the whole, it may be asserted that a slow and gradual rise of wages is one of the general laws of democratic communities. In proportion as social conditions become more equal, wages rise; and as wages are higher, social conditions become more equal.

But a great and gloomy exception occurs in our own time. I have shown, in a preceding chapter, that aristocracy, expelled from political society, has taken refuge in certain departments of productive industry and has established its sway there under another form; this powerfully affects the rate of wages.

As a large capital is required to embark in the great manufacturing speculations to which I allude, the number of persons who enter upon them is exceedingly limited; as their number is small, they can easily concert together and fix the rate of wages as they please.

Their workmen, on the contrary, are exceedingly numerous, and the number of them is always increasing; for from time to time an extraordinary run of business takes place during which wages are inordinately high, and they attract the surrounding population to the factories. But when men have once embraced that line of life, we have already seen that they cannot quit it again, because they soon contract habits of body and mind which unfit them for any other sort of toil. These men have generally but little education and industry, with but few resources; they stand, therefore, almost at the mercy of the master.

When competition or some other fortuitous circumstance lessens his profits, he can reduce the wages of his workmen almost at pleasure and make from them what he loses by the chances of business. Should the workmen strike, the master, who is a rich man, can very well wait, without being ruined, until necessity brings them back to him; but they must work day by day or they die, for their only property is in their hands. They have long been impoverished by oppression, and the poorer they become, the more easily they may be oppressed; they can never escape from this fatal circle of cause and consequence.

It is not surprising, then, that wages, after having sometimes suddenly risen, are permanently lowered in this branch of industry; whereas in other callings the price of labor, which generally increases but little, is nevertheless constantly augmented.

This state of dependence and wretchedness in which a part of the manufacturing population of our time live forms an exception to the general rule, contrary to the state of all the rest of the community; but for this very reason no circumstance is more important or more deserving of the legislator; for when the whole of society is in motion, it is difficult to keep any one class stationary, and when the greater number of men are opening new paths to fortune, it is no less difficult to make the few support in peace their wants and their desires.

Chapter VIII

INFLUENCE OF DEMOCRACY ON THE FAMILY

I HAVE just examined the changes which the equality of conditions produces in the mutual relations of the several members of the community among democratic nations, and among the Americans in particular. I would now go deeper and inquire into the closer ties of family; my object here is not to seek for new truths, but to show in what manner facts already known are connected with my subject.

It has been universally remarked that in our time the several members of a family stand upon an entirely new footing towards each other; that the distance which formerly separated a father from his sons has been lessened; and that paternal authority, if not destroyed, is at least impaired.

Something analogous to this, but even more striking, may be observed in the United States. In America the family, in the Roman and aristocratic signification of the word, does not exist. All that remains of it are a few vestiges in the first years of childhood, when the father exercises, without opposition, that absolute domestic authority which the feebleness of his children renders necessary and which their interest, as well as his own incontestable superiority, warrants. But as soon as the young American approaches manhood, the ties of filial obedience are relaxed day by day; master of his thoughts, he is soon master of his conduct. In America there is, strictly speaking, no adolescence: at the close of boyhood the man appears and begins to trace out his own path.

It would be an error to suppose that this is preceded by a domestic struggle in which the son has obtained by a sort of moral violence the liberty that his father refused him. The same habits, the same principles, which impel the one to assert his independence predispose the other to consider the use of that independence as an incontestable right. The former does not exhibit any of those rancorous or irregular passions which disturb men long after they have shaken off an established authority; the latter feels none of that bitter and angry regret which is apt to survive a bygone power. The father foresees the limits of his authority long beforehand, and when the time arrives, he surrenders it without a struggle; the son looks forward to the exact period at which he will be his own master, and he enters upon his freedom without precipitation and without effort, as a possession which is his own and which no one seeks to wrest from him.[1]

It may perhaps be useful to show how these changes which take place in family relations are closely connected with the social and political revolution that is approaching its consummation under our own eyes.

There are certain great social principles that a people either introduces everywhere or tolerates nowhere. In countries which are aristocratically constituted with all the gradations of rank, the government never makes a direct appeal to the mass of the governed; as men are united together, it is enough to lead the foremost; the rest will follow. This is applicable to the family as well as to all aristocracies that have a head. Among aristocratic nations social institutions recognize, in truth, no one in the family but the father; children are received by society at his hands; society governs

[1] The Americans, however, have not yet thought fit to strip the parent, as has been done in France, of one of the chief elements of parental authority by depriving him of the power of disposing of his property at his death. In the United States there are no restrictions on the powers of a testator.

In this respect, as in almost all others, it is easy to perceive that if the political legislation of the Americans is much more democratic than that of the French, the civil legislation of the latter is infinitely more democratic than that of the former. This may easily be accounted for. The civil legislation of France was the work of a man who saw that it was his interest to satisfy the democratic passions of his contemporaries in all that was not directly and immediately hostile to his own power. He was willing to allow some popular principles to regulate the distribution of property and the government of families, provided they were not to be introduced into the administration of public affairs. While the torrent of democracy overwhelmed the civil laws of the country, he hoped to find an easy shelter behind its political institutions. This policy was at once both adroit and selfish; but a compromise of this kind could not last, for in the end political institutions never fail to become the image and expression of civil society, and in this sense it may be said that nothing is more political in a nation than its civil legislation.

him, he governs them. Thus the parent not only has a natural right but acquires a political right to command them; he is the author and the support of his family, but he is also its constituted ruler.

In democracies, where the government picks out every individual singly from the mass to make him subservient to the general laws of the community, no such intermediate person is required; a father is there, in the eye of the law, only a member of the community, older and richer than his sons.

When most of the conditions of life are extremely unequal and the inequality of these conditions is permanent, the notion of a superior grows upon the imaginations of men; if the law invested him with no privileges, custom and public opinion would concede them. When, on the contrary, men differ but little from each other and do not always remain in dissimilar conditions of life, the general notion of a superior becomes weaker and less distinct; it is vain for legislation to strive to place him who obeys very much beneath him who commands; the manners of the time bring the two men nearer to one another and draw them daily towards the same level.

Although the legislation of an aristocratic people grants no peculiar privileges to the heads of families, I shall not be the less convinced that their power is more respected and more extensive than in a democracy; for I know that, whatever the laws may be, superiors always appear higher and inferiors lower in aristocracies than among democratic nations.

When men live more for the remembrance of what has been than for the care of what is, and when they are more given to attend to what their ancestors thought than to think themselves, the father is the natural and necessary tie between the past and the present, the link by which the ends of these two chains are connected. In aristocracies, then, the father is not only the civil head of the family, but the organ of its traditions, the expounder of its customs, the arbiter of its manners. He is listened to with deference, he is addressed with respect, and the love that is felt for him is always tempered with fear.

When the condition of society becomes democratic and men adopt as their general principle that it is good and lawful to judge of all things for oneself, using former points of belief not as a rule of faith, but simply as a means of information, the power which the opinions of a father exercise over those of his sons diminishes as well as his legal power.

Perhaps the subdivision of estates that democracy brings about contributes more than anything else to change the relations existing between a father and his children. When the property of the father of a family is scanty, his son and himself constantly live in the same place and share the same occupations; habit and necessity bring them together and force them to hold constant communication. The inevitable consequence is a sort of familiar intimacy, which renders authority less absolute and which can ill be reconciled with the external forms of respect.

Now, in democratic countries the class of those who are possessed of small fortunes is precisely that which gives strength to the notions and a particular direction to the manners of the community. That class makes its opinions preponderate as universally as its will, and even those who are most inclined to resist its commands are carried away in the end by its example. I have known eager opponents of democracy who allowed their children to address them with perfect colloquial equality.

Thus at the same time that the power of aristocracy is declining, the austere, the conventional, and the legal part of parental authority vanishes and a species of equality prevails around the domestic hearth. I do not know, on the whole, whether society loses by the change, but I am inclined to believe that man individually is a gainer by it. I think that in proportion as manners and laws become more democratic, the relation of father and son becomes more intimate and more affectionate; rules and authority are less talked of, confidence and tenderness are often increased, and it would seem that the natural bond is drawn closer in proportion as the social bond is loosened.

In a democratic family the father exercises no other power than that which is granted to the affection and the experience of age; his orders would perhaps be disobeyed, but his advice is for the most part authoritative. Though he is not hedged in with ceremonial respect, his sons at least accost him with confidence; they have no settled form of addressing him, but they speak to him constantly and are ready to consult him every day. The master and the constituted ruler have vanished; the father remains.

Nothing more is needed in order to judge of the difference between the two states of society in this respect than to peruse the family correspondence of aristocratic ages. The style is always correct, ceremonious, stiff, and so cold that the natural warmth of the heart can hardly be felt in the language. In democratic countries, on the contrary, the language addressed by a son to his father is always marked by mingled freedom, familiarity, and affection, which at once show that new relations have sprung up in the bosom of the family.

A similar revolution takes place in the mutual relations of children. In aristocratic families, as well as in aristocratic society, every place is marked out beforehand. Not only does the father occupy a separate rank, in which he enjoys extensive privileges, but even the children are not equal among themselves. The age and sex of each irrevocably determine his rank and secure to him certain privileges. Most of these distinctions are abolished or diminished by democracy.

In aristocratic families the eldest son, inheriting the greater part of the property and almost all the rights of the family, becomes the chief and to a certain extent the master of his brothers. Greatness and power are for him; for them, mediocrity and dependence. But it would be wrong to suppose that among aristocratic nations the privileges of the eldest son are advantageous to himself alone, or that they excite nothing but envy and hatred around him. The eldest son commonly endeavors to procure wealth and power for his brothers, because the general splendor of the house is reflected back on him who represents it; the younger sons seek to back the elder brother in all his undertakings, because the greatness and power of the head of the family better enable him to provide for all its branches. The different members of an aristocratic family are therefore very closely bound together; their interests are connected, their minds agree, but their hearts are seldom in harmony.

Democracy also binds brothers to each other, but by very different means. Under democratic laws all the children are perfectly equal and consequently independent; nothing brings them forcibly together, but nothing keeps them apart; and as they have the same origin, as they are trained under the same roof, as they are treated with the same care, and as no peculiar privilege distinguishes or divides them, the affectionate and frank intimacy of early years easily springs up between them. Scarcely anything can occur to break the tie thus formed at the outset of life, for brotherhood brings them daily together without embarrassing them. It is not, then, by interest, but by common associations and by the free sympathy of opinion and of taste that democracy unites brothers to each other. It divides their inheritance, but allows their hearts and minds to unite.

Such is the charm of these democratic manners that even the partisans of aristocracy are attracted by it; and after having experienced it for some time, they are by no means tempted to revert to the respectful and frigid observances of aristocratic families. They would be glad to retain the domestic habits of democracy if they might throw off its social conditions and its laws; but these elements are indissolubly united, and it is impossible to enjoy the former without enduring the latter.

The remarks I have made on filial love and fraternal affection are applicable to all the passions that emanate spontaneously from human nature itself.

If a certain mode of thought or feeling is the result of some peculiar condition of life, when that condition is altered nothing whatever remains of the thought or feeling. Thus a law may bind two members of the community very closely to each other; but that law being abolished, they stand asunder. Nothing was more strict than the tie that united the vassal to the lord under the feudal system; at the present day the two men do not know each other; the fear, the gratitude, and the affection that formerly connected them have vanished and not a vestige of the tie remains.

Such, however, is not the case with those feelings which are natural to mankind. Whenever a law attempts to tutor these feelings in any particular manner, it seldom fails to weaken them; by attempting to add to their intensity it robs them of some of their elements, for they are never stronger than when left to themselves.

Democracy, which destroys or obscures almost all the old conventional rules of society and which prevents men from readily assenting to new ones, entirely effaces most of the feelings to which these conventional rules have given rise; but it only modifies some others, and frequently imparts to them a degree of energy and sweetness unknown before.

Perhaps it is not impossible to condense into a single proposition the whole purport of this chapter, and of several others that preceded it. Democracy loosens social ties, but tightens natural ones; it brings kindred more closely together, while it throws citizens more apart.

Chapter IX

EDUCATION OF YOUNG WOMEN IN THE UNITED STATES

NO FREE communities ever existed without morals, and as I observed in the former part of this work, morals are the work of woman. Consequently, whatever affects the condition of women, their habits and their opinions, has great political importance in my eyes.

Among almost all Protestant nations young women are far more the mistresses of their own actions than they are in Catholic countries. This independence is still greater in Protestant countries like England, which have retained or acquired the right of self-government; freedom is then infused into the domestic circle by political habits and by religious opinions. In the United States the doctrines of Protestantism are combined with great political liberty and a most democratic state of society, and nowhere are young women surrendered so early or so completely to their own guidance.

Long before an American girl arrives at the marriageable age, her emancipation from maternal control begins; she has scarcely ceased to be a child when she already thinks for herself, speaks with freedom, and acts on her own impulse. The great scene of the world is constantly open to her view; far from seeking to conceal it from her, it is every day disclosed more completely and she is taught to survey it with a firm and calm gaze. Thus the vices and dangers of society are early revealed to her; as she sees them clearly, she views them without illusion and braves them without fear, for she is full of reliance on her own strength, and her confidence seems to be shared by all around her.

An American girl scarcely ever displays that virginal softness in the midst of young desires or that innocent and ingenuous grace which usually attend the European woman in the transition from girlhood to youth. It is rare that an American woman, at any age, displays childish timidity or ignorance. Like the young women of Europe she seeks to please, but she knows precisely the cost of pleasing. If she does not abandon herself to evil, at least she knows that it exists; and she is remarkable rather for purity of manners than for chastity of mind.

I have been frequently surprised and almost frightened at the singular address and happy boldness with which young women in America contrive to manage their thoughts and their language amid all the difficulties of free conversation; a philosopher would have stumbled at every step along the narrow path which they trod without accident and without effort. It is easy, indeed, to perceive that even amid the independence of early youth an American woman is always mistress of herself; she indulges in all permitted pleasures without yielding herself up to any of them, and her reason never allows the reins of self-guidance to drop, though it often seems to hold them loosely.

In France, where traditions of every age are still so strangely mingled in the opinions and tastes of the people, women commonly receive a reserved, retired, and almost conventual education, as they did in aristocratic times; and then they are suddenly abandoned without a guide and without assistance in the midst of all the irregularities inseparable from democratic society.

The Americans are more consistent. They have found out that in a democracy the independence of individuals cannot fail to be very great, youth premature, tastes ill-restrained, customs fleeting, public opinion often unsettled and powerless, paternal authority weak, and marital authority contested. Under these circumstances, believing that they had little chance of repressing in woman the most vehement passions of the human heart, they held that the surer way was to teach her the art of combating those passions for herself. As they could not prevent her virtue from being exposed to frequent danger, they determined that she should know how best to defend it, and more reliance was placed on the free vigor of her will than on safeguards which have been shaken or overthrown. Instead, then, of inculcating mistrust of herself, they constantly seek to enhance her confidence in her own strength of character. As it is neither possible nor desirable to keep a young woman in perpetual and complete ignorance, they hasten to give her a precocious knowledge on all subjects. Far from hiding the corruptions of the world from her, they prefer that she should see them at once and train herself to shun them, and they hold it of more importance to protect her conduct than to be over-scrupulous of the innocence of her thoughts.

Although the Americans are a very religious people, they do not rely on religion alone to defend the virtue of woman; they seek to arm her reason also. In this respect they have followed the same method as in several others: they first make vigorous efforts to cause individual independence to control itself, and they do not call in the aid of religion until they have reached the utmost limits of human strength.

I am aware that an education of this kind is not without danger; I am sensible that it tends to invigorate the judgment at the expense of the imagination and to make cold and virtuous women instead of affectionate wives and agreeable companions to man. Society may be more tranquil and better regulated, but domestic life has often fewer charms. These, however, are secondary evils, which may be braved for the sake of higher interests. At the stage at which we are now arrived, the choice is no longer left to us; a democratic education is indispensable to protect women from the dangers with which democratic institutions and manners surround them.

Chapter X

THE YOUNG WOMAN IN THE CHARACTER OF A WIFE

IN AMERICA the independence of woman is irrecoverably lost in the bonds of matrimony. If an unmarried woman is less constrained there than elsewhere, a wife is subjected to stricter obligations. The former makes her father's house an abode of freedom and of pleasure; the latter lives in the home of her husband as if it were a cloister. Yet these two different conditions of life are perhaps not so contrary as may be supposed, and it is natural that the American women should pass through the one to arrive at the other.

Religious communities and trading nations entertain peculiarly serious notions of marriage: the former consider the regularity of woman's life as the best pledge and most certain sign of the purity of her morals; the latter regard it as the highest security for the order and prosperity of the household. The Americans are at the same time a puritanical people and a commercial nation; their religious opinions as well as their trading habits consequently lead them to require much abnegation on the part of woman and a constant sacrifice of her pleasures to her duties, which is seldom demanded of her in Europe. Thus in the United States the inexorable opinion of the public carefully circumscribes woman within the narrow circle of domestic interests and duties and forbids her to step beyond it.

Upon her entrance into the world a young American woman finds these notions firmly established; she sees the rules that are derived from them; she is not slow to perceive that she cannot depart for an instant from the established usages of her contemporaries without putting in jeopardy her peace of mind, her honor, nay, even her social existence; and she finds the energy required for such an act of submission in the firmness of her understanding and in the virile habits which her education has given her. It may be said that she has learned by the use of her independence to surrender it without a struggle and without a murmur when the time comes for making the sacrifice.

But no American woman falls into the toils of matrimony as into a snare held out to her simplicity and ignorance. She has been taught beforehand what is expected of her and voluntarily and freely enters upon this engagement. She supports her new condition with courage because she chose it. As in America paternal discipline is very relaxed and the conjugal tie very strict, a young woman does not contract the latter without considerable circumspection and apprehension. Precocious marriages are rare. American women do not marry until their understandings are exercised and ripened, whereas in other countries most women generally begin to exercise and ripen their understandings only after marriage.

I by no means suppose, however, that the great change which takes place in all the habits of women in the United States as soon as they are married ought solely to be attributed to the constraint of public opinion; it is frequently imposed upon themselves by the sole effort of their own will. When the time for choosing a husband arrives, that cold and stern reasoning power which has been educated and invigorated by the free observation of the world teaches an American woman that a spirit of levity and independence in the bonds of marriage is a constant subject of annoyance, not of pleasure; it tells her that the amusements of the girl cannot become the recreations of the wife, and that the sources of a married woman's happiness are in the home of her husband. As she clearly discerns beforehand the only road that can lead to domestic happiness, she enters upon it at once and follows it to the end without seeking to turn back.

The same strength of purpose which the young wives of America display in bending themselves at once and without repining to the austere duties of their new condition is no less manifest in all the great trials of their lives. In no country in the world are private fortunes more precarious than in the United States. It is not uncommon for the same man in the course of his life to rise and sink again through all the grades that lead from opulence to poverty. American women support these vicissitudes with calm and unquenchable energy; it would seem that their desires contract as easily as they expand with their fortunes.

The greater part of the adventurers who migrate every year to people the Western wilds belong, as I observed in the former part of this work, to the old Anglo-American race of the Northern states. Many of these men, who rush so boldly onwards in pursuit of wealth, were already in the enjoyment of a competency in their own part of the country. They take their wives along with them and make them share the countless perils and privations that always attend the commencement of these expeditions. I have often met, even on the verge of the wilderness, with young women who, after having been brought up amid all the comforts of the large towns of New England, had passed, almost without any intermediate stage, from the wealthy abode of their parents to a comfortless hovel in a forest. Fever, solitude, and a tedious life had not broken the springs of their courage. Their features were impaired and faded, but their looks were firm; they appeared to be at once sad and resolute.[1] I do not doubt that these young American women had amassed, in the education of their early years, that inward strength which they displayed under these circumstances. The early culture of the girl may still, therefore, be traced, in the United States, under the aspect of marriage; her part is changed, her habits are different, but her character is the same.

[1] See Appendix U.

Chapter XI

HOW EQUALITY OF CONDITION CONTRIBUTES TO MAINTAIN GOOD MORALS IN AMERICA[1]

SOME philosophers and historians have said or hinted that the strictness of female morality was increased or diminished simply by the distance of a country from the equator. This solution of the difficulty was an easy one, and nothing was required but a globe and a pair of compasses to settle in an instant one of the most difficult problems in the condition of mankind. But I am not sure that this principle of the materialists is supported by facts. The same nations have been chaste or dissolute at different periods of their history; the strictness or the laxity of their morals depended, therefore, on some variable cause and not alone on the natural qualities of their country, which were invariable. I do not deny that in certain climates the passions which are occasioned by the mutual attraction of the sexes are peculiarly intense, but I believe that this natural intensity may always be excited or restrained by the condition of society and by political institutions.

Although the travelers who have visited North America differ on many points, they all agree in remarking that morals are far more strict there than elsewhere. It is evident that on this point the Americans are very superior to their progenitors, the English. A superficial glance at the two nations will establish the fact.

In England, as in all other countries of Europe, public malice is constantly attacking the frailties of women. Philosophers and statesmen are heard to deplore that morals are not sufficiently strict, and the literary productions of the country constantly lead one to suppose so. In America all books, novels not excepted, suppose women to be chaste, and no one thinks of relating affairs of gallantry.

[1] See Appendix V.

No doubt this great regularity of American morals is due in part to qualities of country, race, and religion, but all these causes, which operate elsewhere, do not suffice to account for it; recourse must be had to some special reason. This reason appears to me to be the principle of equality and the institutions derived from it. Equality of condition does not of itself produce regularity of morals, but it unquestionably facilitates and increases it.

Among aristocratic nations birth and fortune frequently make two such different beings of man and woman that they can never be united to each other. Their passions draw them together, but the condition of society and the notions suggested by it prevent them from contracting a permanent and ostensible tie. The necessary consequence is a great number of transient and clandestine connections. Nature secretly avenges herself for the constraint imposed upon her by the laws of man.

This is not so much the case when the equality of conditions has swept away all the imaginary or the real barriers that separated man from woman. No girl then believes that she cannot become the wife of the man who loves her, and this renders all breaches of morality before marriage very uncommon; for, whatever be the credulity of the passions, a woman will hardly be able to persuade herself that she is beloved when her lover is perfectly free to marry her and does not.

The same cause operates, though more indirectly, on married life. Nothing better serves to justify an illicit passion, either to the minds of those who have conceived it or to the world which looks on, than marriages made by compulsion or chance.[2]

[2] The literature of Europe sufficiently corroborates this remark. When a European author wishes to depict in a work of fiction any of those great catastrophes in matrimony which so frequently occur among us, he assures himself, in advance, of the compassion of the reader by bringing before him ill-assorted or compulsory marriages. Although habitual tolerance has long since relaxed our morals, an author could hardly succeed in interesting us in the misfortunes of his characters if he did not first excuse their faults. This artifice seldom fails; the daily scenes we witness prepare us beforehand to be indulgent. But American writers could never render these excuses credible to their readers; their customs and laws are opposed to it; and as they despair of rendering levity of conduct pleasing, they cease to depict it. This is one of the causes to

In a country in which a woman is always free to exercise her choice and where education has prepared her to choose rightly, public opinion is inexorable to her faults. The rigor of the Americans arises in part from this cause. They consider marriage as a covenant which is often onerous, but every condition of which the parties are strictly bound to fulfill because they knew all those conditions beforehand and were perfectly free not to have contracted them.

The very circumstances that render matrimonial fidelity more obligatory also render it more easy.

In aristocratic countries the object of marriage is rather to unite property than persons; hence the husband is sometimes at school and the wife at nurse when they are betrothed. It cannot be wondered at if the conjugal tie which unites the fortunes of the pair allows their hearts to rove; this is the result of the nature of the contract. When, on the contrary, a man always chooses a wife for himself without any external coercion or even guidance, it is generally a conformity of tastes and opinions that brings a man and a woman together, and this same conformity keeps and fixes them in close habits of intimacy.

Our forefathers had conceived a strange opinion on the subject of marriage; as they had noticed that the small number of love-matches which occurred in their time almost always turned out badly, they resolutely inferred that it was dangerous to listen to the dictates of the heart on the subject. Accident appeared to them a better guide than choice.

Yet it was not difficult to perceive that the examples that they witnessed in fact proved nothing at all. For, in the first place, if democratic nations leave a woman at liberty to choose her husband, they take care to give her mind sufficient knowledge and her will sufficient strength to make so important a choice, whereas the young women who among aristocratic nations furtively elope from the authority of their parents to throw themselves of their own accord into the arms of men whom they have had neither time to know nor ability to judge of are totally without those securities. It is not surprising that they make a bad use of their freedom of action the first time they avail themselves of it, or that they fall into such cruel mistakes when, not having

---

which must be attributed the small number of novels published in the United States.

received a democratic education, they choose to marry in conformity to democratic customs. But this is not all. When a man and woman are bent upon marriage in spite of the differences of an aristocratic state of society, the difficulties to be overcome are enormous. Having broken or relaxed the bonds of filial obedience, they have then to emancipate themselves by a final effort from the sway of custom and the tyranny of opinion; and when at length they have succeeded in this arduous task, they stand estranged from their natural friends and kinsmen. The prejudice they have crossed separates them from all and places them in a situation that soon breaks their courage and sours their hearts.

If, then, a couple married in this manner are first unhappy and afterwards criminal, it ought not to be attributed to the freedom of their choice, but rather to their living in a community in which this freedom of choice is not admitted.

Moreover, it should not be forgotten that the same effort which makes a man violently shake off a prevailing error commonly impels him beyond the bounds of reason; that to dare to declare war, in however just a cause, against the opinion of one's age and country, a violent and adventurous spirit is required, and that men of this character seldom arrive at happiness or virtue, whatever be the path they follow. And this, it may be observed by the way, is the reason why, in the most necessary and righteous revolutions, it is so rare to meet with virtuous or moderate revolutionary characters. There is, then, no just ground for surprise if a man who in an age of aristocracy chooses to consult nothing but his own opinion and his own taste in the choice of a wife soon finds that infractions of morality and domestic wretchedness invade his household; but when this same line of action is in the natural and ordinary course of things, when it is sanctioned by parental authority and backed by public opinion, it cannot be doubted that the internal peace of families will be increased by it and conjugal fidelity more rigidly observed.

Almost all men in democracies are engaged in public or professional life; and on the other hand the limited income obliges a wife to confine herself to the house in order to watch in person, and very closely, over the details of domestic economy. All these distinct and compulsory occupations are so many natural barriers, which by keeping the two sexes asunder render the solicitations of the one less frequent and less ardent, the resistance of the other more easy.

The equality of conditions cannot, it is true, ever succeed in making men chaste, but it may impart a less dangerous character to their breaches of morality. As no one has then either sufficient time or opportunity to assail a virtue armed in self-defense, there will be at the same time a great number of courtesans and a great number of virtuous women. This state of things causes lamentable cases of individual hardship, but it does not prevent the body of society from being strong and alert; it does not destroy family ties or enervate the morals of the nation. Society is endangered, not by the great profligacy of a few, but by laxity of morals among all. In the eyes of a legislator prostitution is less to be dreaded than intrigue.

The tumultuous and constantly harassed life that equality makes men lead not only distracts them from the passion of love by denying them time to indulge it, but diverts them from it by another more secret but more certain road. All men who live in democratic times more or less contract the ways of thinking of the manufacturing and trading classes; their minds take a serious, deliberate, and positive turn; they are apt to relinquish the ideal in order to pursue some visible and proximate object which appears to be the natural and necessary aim of their desires. Thus the principle of equality does not destroy the imagination, but lowers its flight to the level of the earth.

No men are less addicted to reverie than the citizens of a democracy, and few of them are ever known to give way to those idle and solitary meditations which commonly precede and produce the great emotions of the heart. It is true they attach great importance to procuring for themselves that sort of deep, regular, and quiet affection which constitutes the charm and safeguard of life, but they are not apt to run after those violent and capricious sources of excitement which disturb and abridge it.

I am aware that all this is applicable in its full extent only to America and cannot at present be extended to Europe. In the course of the last half-century, while laws and customs have impelled several European nations with unexampled force towards democracy, we have not had occasion to observe that the relations of man and woman have become more orderly or more chaste. In some places the very reverse may be detected: some classes are more strict; the general morality of the people appears to be more lax. I do not hesitate to make the remark, for I am as little disposed to flatter my contemporaries as to malign them.

This fact must distress, but it ought not to surprise us. The propitious influence that a democratic state of society may exercise upon orderly habits is one of those tendencies which can be discovered only after a time. If equality of condition is favorable to purity of morals, the social commotion by which conditions are rendered equal is adverse to it. In the last fifty years, during which France has been undergoing this transformation, it has rarely had freedom, always disturbance. Amid this universal confusion of notions and this general stir of opinions, amid this incoherent mixture of the just and the unjust, of truth and falsehood, of right and might, public virtue has become doubtful and private morality wavering. But all revolutions, whatever may have been their object or their agents, have at first produced similar consequences; even those which have in the end drawn tighter the bonds of morality began by loosening them. The violations of morality which the French frequently witness do not appear to me to have a permanent character, and this is already betokened by some curious signs of the times.

Nothing is more wretchedly corrupt than aristocracy which retains its wealth when it has lost its power and which still enjoys a vast amount of leisure after it is reduced to mere vulgar pastimes. The energetic passions and great conceptions that animated it heretofore leave it then, and nothing remains to it but a host of petty consuming vices, which cling about it like worms upon a carcass.

No one denies that the French aristocracy of the last century was extremely dissolute, yet established habits and ancient belief still preserved some respect for morality among the other classes of society. Nor will it be denied that at the present day the remnants of that same aristocracy exhibit a certain severity of morals, while laxity of morals appears to have spread among the middle and lower ranks. Thus the same families that were most profligate fifty years ago are nowadays the most exemplary, and democracy seems only to have strengthened the morality of the aristocratic classes. The French Revolution, by dividing the fortunes of the nobility, by forcing them to attend assiduously to their affairs and to their families, by making them live under the same roof with their children, and, in short, by giving a more rational and serious turn to their minds, has imparted to them, almost without their being aware of it, a reverence for religious belief, a love of order, of tranquil pleasures, of domestic endearments, and of comfort; whereas the rest of the nation, which had naturally these same tastes, was carried away into excesses by the effort that was required to overthrow the laws and political habits of the country.

The old French aristocracy has undergone the consequences of the Revolution, but it neither felt the revolutionary passions nor shared the anarchical excitement that produced it; it may easily be conceived that this aristocracy feels the salutary influence of the Revolution on its manners before those who achieved it. It may therefore be said, though at first it seems paradoxical, that at the present day the most anti-democratic classes of the nation principally exhibit the kind of morality that may reasonably be anticipated from democracy. I cannot but think that when we shall have obtained all the effects of this democratic revolution, after having got rid of the tumult it has caused, the observations which are now only applicable to the few will gradually become true of the whole community.

Chapter XII

HOW THE AMERICANS UNDERSTAND THE EQUALITY OF THE SEXES

I HAVE shown how democracy destroys or modifies the different inequalities that originate in society; but is this all, or does it not ultimately affect that great inequality of man and woman which has seemed, up to the present day, to be eternally based in human nature? I believe that the social changes that bring nearer to the same level the father and son, the master and servant, and, in general, superiors and inferiors will raise woman and make her more and more the equal of man. But here, more than ever, I feel the necessity of making myself clearly understood; for there is no subject on which the coarse and lawless fancies of our age have taken a freer range.

There are people in Europe who, confounding together the different characteristics of the sexes, would make man and woman into beings not only equal but alike. They would give to both the same functions, impose on both the same duties, and grant to both the same rights; they would mix them in all things—their occupations, their pleasures, their business. It may readily be conceived that by thus attempting to make one sex equal to the other, both are degraded, and from so preposterous a medley of the works of nature nothing could ever result but weak men and disorderly women.

It is not thus that the Americans understand that species of democratic equality which may be established between the sexes. They admit that as nature has appointed such wide differences between the physical and moral constitution of man and woman, her manifest design was to give a distinct employment to their various faculties; and they hold that improvement does not consist in making beings so dissimilar do pretty nearly the same things, but in causing each of them to fulfill their respective tasks in the best possible manner. The Americans have applied to the sexes the great principle of political economy which governs the manufacturers of our age, by carefully dividing the duties of man from those of woman in order that the great work of society may be the better carried on.

In no country has such constant care been taken as in America to trace two clearly distinct lines of action for the two sexes and to make them keep pace one with the other, but in two pathways that are always different. American women never manage the outward concerns of the family or conduct a business or take a part in political life; nor are they, on the other hand, ever compelled to perform the rough labor of the fields or to make any of those laborious efforts which demand the exertion of physical strength. No families are so poor as to form an exception to this rule. If, on the one hand, an American woman cannot escape from the quiet circle of domestic employments, she is never forced, on the other, to go beyond it. Hence it is that the women of America, who often exhibit a masculine strength of understanding and a manly energy, generally preserve great delicacy of personal appearance and always retain the manners of women although they sometimes show that they have the hearts and minds of men.

Nor have the Americans ever supposed that one consequence of democratic principles is the subversion of marital power or the confusion of the natural authorities in families. They hold that every association must have a head in order to accomplish its object, and that the natural head of the conjugal association is man. They do not therefore deny him the right of directing his partner, and they maintain that in the smaller association of husband and wife as well as in the great social community the object of democracy is to regulate and legalize the powers that are necessary, and not to subvert all power.

This opinion is not peculiar to one sex and contested by the other; I never observed that the women of America consider conjugal authority as a fortunate usurpation of their rights, or that they thought themselves degraded by submitting to it. It appeared to me, on the contrary, that they attach a sort of pride to the voluntary surrender of their own will and make it their boast to bend themselves to the yoke, not to shake it off. Such, at least, is the feeling expressed by the most virtuous of their sex; the others are silent; and in the

United States it is not the practice for a guilty wife to clamor for the rights of women while she is trampling on her own holiest duties.

It has often been remarked that in Europe a certain degree of contempt lurks even in the flattery which men lavish upon women; although a European frequently affects to be the slave of woman, it may be seen that he never sincerely thinks her his equal. In the United States men seldom compliment women, but they daily show how much they esteem them. They constantly display an entire confidence in the understanding of a wife and a profound respect for her freedom; they have decided that her mind is just as fitted as that of man to discover the plain truth, and her heart as firm to embrace it; and they have never sought to place her virtue, any more than his, under the shelter of prejudice, ignorance, and fear.

It would seem in Europe, where man so easily submits to the despotic sway of women, that they are nevertheless deprived of some of the greatest attributes of the human species and considered as seductive but imperfect beings, and (what may well provoke astonishment) women ultimately look upon themselves in the same light and almost consider it as a privilege that they are entitled to show themselves futile, feeble, and timid. The women of America claim no such privileges.

Again, it may be said that in our morals we have reserved strange immunities to man, so that there is, as it were, one virtue for his use and another for the guidance of his partner, and that, according to the opinion of the public, the very same act may be punished alternately as a crime or only as a fault. The Americans do not know this iniquitous division of duties and rights; among them the seducer is as much dishonored as his victim.

It is true that the Americans rarely lavish upon women those eager attentions which are commonly paid them in Europe, but their conduct to women always implies that they suppose them to be virtuous and refined; and such is the respect entertained for the moral freedom of the sex that in the presence of a woman the most guarded language is used lest her ear should be offended by an expression. In America a young unmarried woman may alone and without fear undertake a long journey.

The legislators of the United States, who have mitigated almost all the penalties of criminal law, still make rape a capital offense, and no crime is visited with more inexorable severity by public opinion. This may be accounted for; as the Americans can conceive nothing more precious than a woman's honor and nothing which ought so much to be respected as her independence, they hold that no punishment is too severe for the man who deprives her of them against her will. In France, where the same offense is visited with far milder penalties, it is frequently difficult to get a verdict from a jury against the prisoner. Is this a consequence of contempt of decency or contempt of women? I cannot but believe that it is a contempt of both.

Thus the Americans do not think that man and woman have either the duty or the right to perform the same offices, but they show an equal regard for both their respective parts; and though their lot is different, they consider both of them as beings of equal value. They do not give to the courage of woman the same form or the same direction as to that of man, but they never doubt her courage; and if they hold that man and his partner ought not always to exercise their intellect and understanding in the same manner, they at least believe the understanding of the one to be as sound as that of the other, and her intellect to be as clear. Thus, then, while they have allowed the social inferiority of woman to continue, they have done all they could to raise her morally and intellectually to the level of man; and in this respect they appear to me to have excellently understood the true principle of democratic improvement.

As for myself, I do not hesitate to avow that although the women of the United States are confined within the narrow circle of domestic life, and their situation is in some respects one of extreme dependence, I have nowhere seen woman occupying a loftier position; and if I were asked, now that I am drawing to the close of this work, in which I have spoken of so many important things done by the Americans, to what the singular prosperity and growing strength of that people ought mainly to be attributed, I should reply: To the superiority of their women.

Chapter XIII

HOW THE PRINCIPLE OF EQUALITY NATURALLY DIVIDES THE AMERICANS INTO A MULTITUDE OF SMALL PRIVATE CIRCLES

IT MIGHT be supposed that the final and necessary effect of democratic institutions would be to identify all the members of the community in private as well as in public life and to compel them all to live alike, but this would be to ascribe a very coarse and oppressive form to the equality which originates in democracy. No state of society or laws can render men so much alike but that education, fortune, and tastes will interpose some differences between them; and though different men may sometimes find it their interest to combine for the same purposes, they will never make it their pleasure. They will therefore always tend to evade the provisions of law, whatever they may be; and escaping in some respect from the circle in which the legislator sought to confine them, they will set up, close by the great political community, small private societies, united together by similitude of conditions, habits, and customs.

In the United States the citizens have no sort of preeminence over one another; they owe each other no mutual obedience or respect; they all meet for the administration of justice, for the government of the state, and, in general, to treat of the affairs that concern their common welfare; but I never heard that attempts have been made to bring them all to follow the same diversions or to amuse themselves promiscuously in the same places of recreation.

The Americans, who mingle so readily in their political assemblies and courts of justice, are wont carefully to separate into small distinct circles in order to indulge by themselves in the enjoyments of private life. Each of them willingly acknowledges all his fellow citizens as his equals, but will only receive a very limited number of them as his friends or his guests. This appears to me to be very natural. In proportion as the circle of public society is extended, it may be anticipated that the sphere of private intercourse will be contracted; far from supposing that the members of modern society will ultimately live in common, I am afraid they will end by forming only small coteries.

Among aristocratic nations the different classes are like vast enclosures, out of which it is impossible to get, into which it is impossible to enter. These classes have no communication with each other, but within them men necessarily live in daily contact; even though they would not naturally suit, the general conformity of a similar condition brings them near together.

But when neither law nor custom professes to establish frequent and habitual relations between certain men, their intercourse originates in the accidental similarity of opinions and tastes; hence private society is infinitely varied. In democracies, where the members of the community never differ much from each other and naturally stand so near that they may all at any time be fused in one general mass, numerous artificial and arbitrary distinctions spring up by means of which every man hopes to keep himself aloof lest he should be carried away against his will in the crowd.

This can never fail to be the case, for human institutions can be changed, but man cannot; whatever may be the general endeavor of a community to render its members equal and alike, the personal pride of individuals will always seek to rise above the line and to form somewhere an inequality to their own advantage.

In aristocracies men are separated from each other by lofty stationary barriers; in democracies they are divided by many small and almost invisible threads, which are constantly broken or moved from place to place. Thus whatever may be the progress of equality, in democratic nations a great number of small private associations will always be formed within the general pale of political society; but none of them will bear any resemblance in its manners to the higher class in aristocracies.

Chapter XIV

SOME REFLECTIONS ON AMERICAN MANNERS

NOTHING seems at first sight less important than the outward form of human actions, yet there is nothing upon which men set more store; they grow used to everything except to living in a society which has not their own manners. The influence of the social and political state of a country upon manners is therefore deserving of its serious examination.

Manners are generally the product of the very basis of character, but they are also sometimes the result of an arbitrary convention between certain men. Thus they are at once natural and acquired.

When some men perceive that they are the foremost persons in society, without contest and without effort, when they are constantly engaged on large objects, leaving the more minute details to others, and when they live in the enjoyment of wealth which they did not amass and do not fear to lose, it may be supposed that they feel a kind of haughty disdain of the petty interests and practical cares of life and that their thoughts assume a natural greatness which their language and their manners denote. In democratic countries manners are generally devoid of dignity because private life is there extremely petty in its character; and they are frequently low because the mind has few opportunities of rising above the engrossing cares of domestic interests.

True dignity in manners consists in always taking one's proper station, neither too high nor too low, and this is as much within the reach of a peasant as of a prince. In democracies all stations appear doubtful; hence it is that the manners of democracies, though often full of arrogance, are commonly wanting in dignity, and, moreover, they are never either well trained or accomplished.

The men who live in democracies are too fluctuating for a certain number of them ever to succeed in laying down a code of good breeding and in forcing people to follow it. Every man therefore behaves after his own fashion, and there is always a certain incoherence in the manners of such times, because they are molded upon the feelings and notions of each individual rather than upon an ideal model proposed for general imitation. This, however, is much more perceptible when an aristocracy has just been overthrown than after it has long been destroyed. New political institutions and new social elements then bring to the same places of resort, and frequently compel to live in common, men whose education and habits are still amazingly dissimilar, and this renders the motley composition of society peculiarly visible. The existence of a former strict code of good breeding is still remembered, but what it contained or where it is to be found is already forgotten. Men have lost the common law of manners and they have not yet made up their minds to do without it, but everyone endeavors to make to himself some sort of arbitrary and variable rule from the remnant of former usages, so that manners have neither the regularity and the dignity which they often display among aristocratic nations, nor the simplicity and freedom which they sometimes assume in democracies; they are at once constrained and without constraint.

This, however, is not the normal state of things. When the equality of conditions is long established and complete, as all men entertain nearly the same notions and do nearly the same things they do not require to agree, or to copy from one another, in order to speak or act in the same manner; their manners are constantly characterized by a number of lesser diversities, but not by any great differences. They are never perfectly alike because they do not copy from the same pattern; they are never very unlike because their social condition is the same. At first sight a traveler would say that the manners of all Americans are exactly similar; it is only upon close examination that the peculiarities in which they differ may be detected.

The English make game of the manners of the Americans, but it is singular that most of the writers who have drawn these ludicrous delineations belonged themselves to the middle classes in England, to whom the same delineations are exceedingly applicable, so that these pitiless censors furnish, for the most part, an example of the very thing they blame in the United States. They do not perceive that they are deriding themselves, to the great amusement of the aristocracy of their own country.

Nothing is more prejudicial to democracy than its outward forms of behavior; many men would willingly endure its vices who cannot support its manners. I cannot, however, admit that there is nothing commendable in the manners of a democratic people.

Among aristocratic nations, all who live within reach of the first class in society commonly strain to be like it, which gives rise to ridiculous and insipid imitations. As a democratic people do not possess any models of high breeding, at least they escape the daily necessity of seeing wretched copies of them. In democracies manners are never so refined as among aristocratic nations, but on the other hand they are never so coarse. Neither the coarse oaths of the populace nor the elegant and choice expressions of the nobility are to be heard there; the manners of such a people are often vulgar, but they are neither brutal nor mean.

I have already observed that in democracies no such thing as a regular code of good breeding can be laid down; this has some inconveniences and some advantages. In aristocracies the rules of propriety impose the same demeanor on everyone; they make all the members of the same class appear alike in spite of their private inclinations; they adorn and they conceal the natural man. Among a democratic people manners are neither so tutored nor so uniform, but they are frequently more sincere. They form, as it were, a light and loosely woven veil through which the real feelings and private opinions of each individual are easily discernible. The form and the substance of human actions, therefore, often stand there in closer relation; and if the great picture of human life is less embellished, it is more true. Thus it may be said, in one sense, that the effect of democracy is not exactly to give men any particular manners, but to prevent them from having manners at all.

The feelings, the passions, the virtues, and the vices of an aristocracy may sometimes reappear in a democracy, but not its manners; they are lost and vanish forever as soon as the democratic revolution is completed. It would seem that nothing is more lasting than the manners of an aristocratic class, for they are preserved by that class for some time after it has lost its wealth and its power; nor so fleeting, for no sooner have they disappeared than not a trace of them is to be found, and it is scarcely possible to say what they have been as soon as they have ceased to be. A change in the state of society works this miracle, and a few generations suffice to consummate it. The principal characteristics of aristocracy are handed down by history after an aristocracy is destroyed, but the light and exquisite touches of manners are effaced from men's memories almost immediately after its fall. Men can no longer conceive what these manners were when they have ceased to witness them; they are gone and their departure was unseen, unfelt, for in order to feel that refined enjoyment which is derived from choice and distinguished manners, habit and education must have prepared the heart, and the taste for them is lost almost as easily as the practice of them. Thus, not only cannot a democratic people have aristocratic manners, but they neither comprehend nor desire them; and as they never have thought of them, it is to their minds as if such things had never been. Too much importance should not be attached to this loss, but it may well be regretted.

I am aware that it has not infrequently happened that the same men have had very high-bred manners and very low-born feelings; the interior of courts has sufficiently shown what imposing externals may conceal the meanest hearts. But though the manners of aristocracy do not constitute virtue, they sometimes embellish virtue itself. It was no ordinary sight to see a numerous and powerful class of men whose every outward action seemed constantly to be dictated by a natural elevation of thought and feeling, by delicacy and regularity of taste, and by urbanity of manners. Those manners threw a pleasing illusory charm over human nature; and though the picture was often a false one, it could not be viewed without a noble satisfaction.

Chapter XV

OF THE GRAVITY OF THE AMERICANS, AND WHY IT DOES NOT PREVENT THEM FROM OFTEN DOING INCONSIDERATE THINGS

MEN who live in democratic countries do not value the simple, turbulent, or coarse diversions in which the people in aristocratic communities indulge; such diversions are thought by them to be puerile or insipid. Nor have they a greater inclination for the intellectual and refined amusements of the aristocratic classes. They want something productive and substantial in their pleasures; they want to mix actual fruition with their joy.

In aristocratic communities the people readily give themselves up to bursts of tumultuous and boisterous gaiety, which shake off at once the recollection of their privations. The inhabitants of democracies are not fond of being thus violently broken in upon, and they never lose sight of themselves without regret. Instead of these frivolous delights they prefer those more serious and silent amusements which are like business and which do not drive business wholly out of their minds.

An American, instead of going in a leisure hour to dance merrily at some place of public resort, as the fellows of his class continue to do throughout the greater part of Europe, shuts himself up at home to drink. He thus enjoys two pleasures; he can go on thinking of his business and can get drunk decently by his own fireside.

I thought that the English constituted the most serious nation on the face of the earth, but I have since seen the Americans and have changed my opinion. I do not mean to say that temperament has not a great deal to do with the character of the inhabitants of the United States, but I think that their political institutions are a still more influential cause.

I believe the seriousness of the Americans arises partly from their pride. In democratic countries even poor men entertain a lofty notion of their personal importance; they look upon themselves with complacency and are apt to suppose that others are looking at them too. With this disposition, they watch their language and their actions with care and do not lay themselves open so as to betray their deficiencies; to preserve their dignity, they think it necessary to retain their gravity.

But I detect another more deep-seated and powerful cause which instinctively produces among the Americans this astonishing gravity. Under a despotism communities give way at times to bursts of vehement joy, but they are generally gloomy and moody because they are afraid. Under absolute monarchies tempered by the customs and manners of the country, their spirits are often cheerful and even, because, as they have some freedom and a good deal of security, they are exempted from the most important cares of life; but all free nations are serious because their minds are habitually absorbed by the contemplation of some dangerous or difficult purpose. This is more especially the case among those free nations which form democratic communities. Then there is, in all classes, a large number of men constantly occupied with the serious affairs of the government; and those whose thoughts are not engaged in the matters of the commonwealth are wholly engrossed by the acquisition of a private fortune. Among such a people a serious demeanor ceases to be peculiar to certain men and becomes a habit of the nation.

We are told of small democracies in the days of antiquity in which the citizens met in the public places with garlands of roses and spent almost all their time in dancing and theatrical amusements. I do not believe in such republics any more than in that of Plato; or if the things we read of really happened, I do not hesitate to affirm that these supposed democracies were composed of very different elements from ours and that they had nothing in common with the latter except their name.

But it must not be supposed that in the midst of all their toils the people who live in democracies think themselves to be pitied; the contrary is noticed to be the case. No men are fonder of their own condition. Life would have no relish for them if they were delivered from the anxieties which harass them, and they show more attachment to their cares than aristocratic nations to their pleasures.

I am next led to inquire how it is that these same democratic nations which are so serious sometimes act in so inconsiderate a manner. The Americans, who almost always preserve a staid demeanor and a frigid air, nevertheless frequently allow themselves to be borne away, far beyond the bounds of reason, by a sudden passion or a hasty opinion and sometimes gravely commit strange absurdities.

This contrast ought not to surprise us. There is one sort of ignorance which originates in extreme publicity. In despotic states men do not know how to act because they are told nothing; in democratic nations they often act at random because nothing is to be left untold. The former do not know, the latter forget; and the chief features of each picture are lost to them in bewilderment of details.

It is astonishing what imprudent language a public man may sometimes use in free countries, and especially in democratic states, without being compromised; whereas in absolute monarchies a few words dropped by accident are enough to unmask him forever and ruin him without hope of redemption. This is explained by what goes before. When a man speaks in the midst of a great crowd, many of his words are not heard or are forthwith obliterated from the memories of those who hear them; but amid the silence of a mute and motionless throng the slightest whisper strikes the ear.

In democracies men are never stationary; a thousand chances waft them to and fro, and their life is always the sport of unforeseen or (so to speak) extemporaneous circumstances. Thus they are often obliged to do things which they have imperfectly learned, to say things which they imperfectly understand, and to devote themselves to work for which they are unprepared by long apprenticeship. In aristocracies every man has one sole object, which he unceasingly pursues; but among democratic nations the existence of man is more complex; the same mind will almost always embrace several objects at once, and these objects are frequently wholly foreign to each other. As it cannot know them all well, the mind is readily satisfied with imperfect notions of each.

When the inhabitant of a democracy is not urged by his wants, he is so at least by his desires; for of all the possessions that he sees around him, none are wholly beyond his reach. He therefore does everything in a hurry, he is always satisfied with "pretty well," and never pauses more than an instant to consider what he has been doing. His curiosity is at once insatiable and cheaply satisfied; for he cares more to know a great deal quickly than to know anything well; he has no time and but little taste to search things to the bottom.

Thus, then, a democratic people are grave because their social and political condition constantly leads them to engage in serious occupations, and they act inconsiderably because they give but little time and attention to each of these occupations. The habit of inattention must be considered as the greatest defect of the democratic character.

Chapter XVI

WHY THE NATIONAL VANITY OF THE AMERICANS IS MORE RESTLESS AND CAPTIOUS THAN THAT OF THE ENGLISH[1]

ALL FREE nations are vainglorious, but national pride is not displayed by all in the same manner. The Americans, in their intercourse with strangers, appear impatient of the smallest censure and insatiable of praise. The most slender eulogy is acceptable to them, the most exalted seldom contents them; they unceasingly harass you to extort praise, and if you resist their entreaties, they fall to praising themselves. It would seem as if, doubting their own merit, they wished to have it constantly exhibited before their eyes. Their vanity is not only greedy, but restless and jealous; it will grant nothing, while it demands everything, but is ready to beg and to quarrel at the same time.

If I say to an American that the country he lives in is a fine one, "Ay," he replies, "there is not its equal in the world." If I applaud the freedom that its inhabitants enjoy, he answers: "Freedom is a fine thing, but few nations are worthy to enjoy it." If I remark on the purity of morals that distinguishes the United States, "I can imagine," says he, "that a stranger, who has witnessed the corruption that prevails in other nations, would be astonished at the difference." At length I leave him to the contemplation of himself; but he returns to the charge and does not desist till he has got me to repeat all I had just been saying. It is impossible to conceive a more troublesome or more garrulous patriotism; it wearies even those who are disposed to respect it.

Such is not the case with the English. An Englishman calmly enjoys the real or imaginary advantages which, in his opinion, his country possesses. If he grants nothing to other nations, neither does he solicit anything for his own.

[1] See Appendix W.

The censure of foreigners does not affect him, and their praise hardly flatters him; his position with regard to the rest of the world is one of disdainful and ignorant reserve: his pride requires no sustenance; it nourishes itself. It is remarkable that two nations so recently sprung from the same stock should be so opposite to each other in their manner of feeling and conversing.

In aristocratic countries the great possess immense privileges, upon which their pride rests without seeking to rely upon the lesser advantages that accrue to them. As these privileges came to them by inheritance, they regard them in some sort as a portion of themselves, or at least as a natural right inherent in their own persons. They therefore entertain a calm sense of their own superiority; they do not dream of vaunting privileges which everyone perceives and no one contests, and these things are not sufficiently new to be made topics of conversation. They stand unmoved in their solitary greatness, well assured that they are seen by all the world without any effort to show themselves off, and that no one will attempt to drive them from that position. When an aristocracy carries on the public affairs, its national pride naturally assumes this reserved, indifferent, and haughty form, which is imitated by all the other classes of the nation.

When, on the contrary, social conditions differ but little, the slightest privileges are of some importance; as every man sees around himself a million people enjoying precisely similar or analogous advantages, his pride becomes craving and jealous, he clings to mere trifles and doggedly defends them. In democracies, as the conditions of life are very fluctuating, men have almost always recently acquired the advantages which they possess; the consequence is that they feel extreme pleasure in exhibiting them, to show others and convince themselves that they really enjoy them. As at any instant these same advantages may be lost, their possessors are constantly on the alert and make a point of showing that they still retain them. Men living in democracies love their country just as they love themselves, and they transfer the habits of their private vanity to their vanity as a nation.

The restless and insatiable vanity of a democratic people originates so entirely in the equality and precariousness of their social condition that the members of the haughtiest nobility display the very same passion in those lesser portions of their existence in which there is anything fluctuating or contested. An aristocratic class always differs greatly from the other classes of the nation, by the extent and perpetuity of its privileges; but it often happens that the only differences between the members who belong to it consist in small, transient advantages, which may any day be lost or acquired. The members of a powerful aristocracy, collected in a capital or a court, have been known to contest with virulence those frivolous privileges which depend on the caprice of fashion or the will of their master. These persons then displayed towards each other precisely the same puerile jealousies that animate the men of democracies, the same eagerness to snatch the smallest advantages which their equals contested, and the same desire to parade ostentatiously those of which they were in possession.

If national pride ever entered into the minds of courtiers, I do not question that they would display it in the same manner as the members of a democratic community.

Chapter XVII

HOW THE ASPECT OF SOCIETY IN THE UNITED STATES IS AT ONCE EXCITED AND MONOTONOUS

IT WOULD seem that nothing could be more adapted to stimulate and to feed curiosity than the aspect of the United States. Fortunes, opinions, and laws are there in ceaseless variation; it is as if immutable Nature herself were mutable, such are the changes worked upon her by the hand of man. Yet in the end the spectacle of this excited community becomes monotonous, and after having watched the moving pageant for a time, the spectator is tired of it.

Among aristocratic nations every man is pretty nearly stationary in his own sphere, but men are astonishingly unlike each other; their passions, their notions, their habits, and their tastes are essentially different: nothing changes, but everything differs. In democracies, on the contrary, all men are alike and do things pretty nearly alike. It is true that they are subject to great and frequent vicissitudes, but as the same events of good or adverse fortune are continually recurring, only the name of the actors is changed, the piece is always the same. The aspect of American society is animated because men and things are always changing, but it is monotonous because all these changes are alike.

Men living in democratic times have many passions, but most of their passions either end in the love of riches or proceed from it. The cause of this is not that their souls are narrower, but that the importance of money is really greater at such times. When all the members of a community are independent of or indifferent to each other, the co-operation of each of them can be obtained only by paying for it: this infinitely multiplies the purposes to which wealth may be applied and increases its value. When the reverence that belonged to what is old has vanished, birth, condition, and profession no longer distinguish men, or scarcely distinguish them; hardly anything but money remains to create strongly marked differences between them and to raise some of them above the common level. The distinction originating in wealth is increased by the disappearance or diminution of all other distinctions. Among aristocratic nations money reaches only to a few points on the vast circle of man's desires; in democracies it seems to lead to all.

The love of wealth is therefore to be traced, as either a principal or an accessory motive, at the bottom of all that the Americans do; this gives to all their passions a sort of family likeness and soon renders the survey of them exceedingly wearisome. This perpetual recurrence of the same passion is monotonous; the peculiar methods by which this passion seeks its own gratification are no less so.

In an orderly and peaceable democracy like the United States, where men cannot enrich themselves by war, by public office, or by political confiscation, the love of wealth mainly drives them into business and manufactures. Although these pursuits often bring about great commotions and disasters, they cannot prosper without strictly regular habits and a long routine of petty uniform acts. The stronger the passion is, the more regular are these habits and the more uniform are these acts. It may be said that it is the vehemence of their desires that makes the Americans so methodical; it perturbs their minds, but it disciplines their lives.

The remark I here apply to America may indeed be addressed to almost all our contemporaries. Variety is disappearing from the human race; the same ways of acting, thinking, and feeling are to be met with all over the world. This is not only because nations work more upon each other and copy each other more faithfully, but as the men of each country relinquish more and more the peculiar opinions and feelings of a caste, a profession, or a family, they simultaneously arrive at something nearer to the constitution of man, which is everywhere the same. Thus they become more alike, even without having imitated each other. Like travelers scattered about some large wood, intersected by paths converging to one point, if all of them keep their eyes fixed upon that point and advance towards it, they insensibly draw nearer together, though they do not seek, though they do not see and know each other; and they will be surprised at length to find themselves all collected at the same spot. All the nations which take, not any particular man, but Man himself as the object of their researches and their imitations are tending in the end to a similar state of society, like these travelers converging at the central spot of the forest.

Chapter XVIII

OF HONOR[1] IN THE UNITED STATES AND IN DEMOCRATIC COMMUNITIES

IT would seem that men employ two very distinct methods in the judgment which they pass upon the actions of their fellow men; at one time they judge them by those simple notions of right and wrong which are diffused all over the world; at another they appraise them by a few very special rules which belong exclusively to some particular age and country. It often happens that these two standards differ; they sometimes conflict, but they are never either entirely identified or entirely annulled by each other.

Honor at the periods of its greatest power sways the will more than the belief of men; and even while they yield without hesitation and without a murmur to its dictates, they feel notwithstanding, by a dim but mighty instinct, the existence of a more general, more ancient, and more holy law, which they sometimes disobey, although they do not cease to acknowledge it. Some actions have been held to be at the same time virtuous and dishonorable; a refusal to fight a duel is an instance.

I think these peculiarities may be otherwise explained than by the mere caprices of certain individuals and nations, as has hitherto been customary. Mankind is subject to general and permanent wants that have created moral laws, to the neglect of which men have ever and in all places attached the notion of censure and shame: to infringe them was *to do ill; to do well* was to conform to them.

Within this vast association of the human race lesser as-

[1] The word *honor* is not always used in the same sense either in French or in English. (1) It first signifies the esteem, glory, or reverence that a man receives from his fellow men; and in this sense a man is said *to acquire honor.* (2) Honor signifies the aggregate of those rules by the aid of which this esteem, glory, or reverence is obtained. Thus we say that *a man has always strictly obeyed the laws of honor;* or *a man has violated his honor.* In writing the present chapter I have always used the word *honor* in the latter sense.

sociations have been formed, which are called nations; and amid these nations further subdivisions have assumed the names of classes or castes. Each of these associations forms, as it were, a separate species of the human race; and though it has no essential difference from the mass of mankind, to a certain extent it stands apart and has certain wants peculiar to itself. To these special wants must be attributed the modifications which affect, in various degrees and in different countries, the mode of considering human actions and the estimate which is formed of them. It is the general and permanent interest of mankind that men should not kill each other; but it may happen to be the peculiar and temporary interest of a people or a class to justify, or even to honor, homicide.

Honor is simply that peculiar rule founded upon a peculiar state of society, by the application of which a people or a class allot praise or blame. Nothing is more unproductive to the mind than an abstract idea; I therefore hasten to call in the aid of facts and examples to illustrate my meaning.

I select the most extraordinary kind of honor which has ever been known in the world, and that which we are best acquainted with: namely, aristocratic honor springing out of feudal society. I shall explain it by means of the principle already laid down and explain the principle by means of this illustration.

I am not here led to inquire when and how the aristocracy of the Middle Ages came into existence, why it was so deeply severed from the remainder of the nation, or what founded and consolidated its power. I take its existence as an established fact, and I am endeavoring to account for the peculiar view that it took of the greater part of human actions.

The first thing that strikes me is that in the feudal world actions were not always praised or blamed with reference to their intrinsic worth, but were sometimes appreciated exclusively with reference to the person who was the actor or the object of them, which is repugnant to the general conscience of mankind. Thus some of the actions which were indifferent on the part of a man in humble life dishonored a noble; others changed their whole character according as the person aggrieved by them belonged or did not belong to the aristocracy.

When these different notions first arose, the nobility formed a distinct body amid the people, which it commanded from the inaccessible heights where it was ensconced. To maintain this peculiar position, which constituted its strength, not only did it require political privileges, but it required a standard of right and wrong for its own special use.

That some particular virtue or vice belonged to the nobility rather than to the humble classes, that certain actions were guiltless when they affected the villein which were criminal when they touched the noble, these were often arbitrary matters; but that honor or shame should be attached to a man's actions according to his condition was a result of the internal constitution of an aristocratic community. This has been actually the case in all the countries which have had an aristocracy; as long as a trace of the principle remains, these peculiarities will still exist. To debauch a woman of color scarcely injures the reputation of an American; to marry her dishonors him.

In some cases feudal honor enjoined revenge and stigmatized the forgiveness of insults; in others it imperiously commanded men to conquer their own passions and required forgetfulness of self. It did not make humanity or kindness its law, but it extolled generosity; it set more store on liberality than on benevolence; it allowed men to enrich themselves by gambling or by war, but not by labor; it preferred great crimes to small earnings; cupidity was less distasteful to it than avarice; violence it often sanctioned, but cunning and treachery it invariably reprobated as contemptible.

These fantastic notions did not proceed exclusively from the caprice of those who entertained them. A class which has succeeded in placing itself above all others, and which makes perpetual exertions to maintain this lofty position, must especially honor those virtues which are conspicuous for their dignity and splendor and which may be easily combined with pride and the love of power. Such men would not hesitate to invert the natural order of conscience in order to give these virtues precedence over all others. It may even be conceived that some of the more bold and brilliant vices would readily be set above the quiet, unpretending virtues. The very existence of such a class in society renders these things unavoidable.

The nobles of the Middle Ages placed military courage foremost among virtues and in lieu of many of them. This, again, was a peculiar opinion, which arose necessarily from the peculiar state of society. Feudal aristocracy existed by war and for war; its power had been founded by arms, and by arms that power was maintained; it therefore required nothing more than military courage, and that quality was naturally exalted above all others; whatever denoted it, even at the expense of reason and humanity, was therefore approved and frequently enjoined by the manners of the time. Such was the main principle; the caprice of man was to be traced only in minuter details. That a man should regard a tap on the cheek as an unbearable insult and should be obliged to kill in single combat the person who struck him thus lightly is an arbitrary rule; but that a noble could not tranquilly receive an insult and was dishonored if he allowed himself to take a blow without fighting were direct consequences of the fundamental principles and the wants of a military aristocracy.

Thus it was true, to a certain extent, that the laws of honor were capricious; but these caprices of honor were always confined within certain necessary limits. The peculiar rule which was called honor by our forefathers is so far from being an arbitrary law in my eyes that I would readily engage to ascribe its most incoherent and fantastic injunctions to a small number of fixed and invariable wants inherent in feudal society.

If I were to trace the notion of feudal honor into the domain of politics, I should not find it more difficult to explain its dictates. The state of society and the political institutions of the Middle Ages were such that the supreme power of the nation never governed the community directly. That power did not exist in the eyes of the people: every man looked up to a certain individual whom he was bound to obey; by that intermediate personage he was connected with all the others. Thus, in feudal society, the whole system of the commonwealth rested upon the sentiment of fidelity to the person of the lord; to destroy that sentiment was to fall into anarchy. Fidelity to a political superior was, moreover, a sentiment of which all the members of the aristocracy had constant opportunities of estimating the importance; for every one of them was a vassal as well as a lord and had to command as well as to obey. To remain faithful to the lord, to sacrifice oneself for him if called upon, to share his good or evil fortunes, to stand by him in his undertakings, whatever they might be, such were the first injunctions of feudal honor in relation to the political institutions of those times. The treachery of a vassal was branded with extraordinary severity by public opinion, and a name of peculiar infamy was invented for the offense; it was called *felony*.

On the contrary, few traces are to be found in the Middle Ages of the passion that constituted the life of the nations of antiquity; I mean patriotism. The word itself is not of very ancient date in the language.[2] Feudal institutions concealed the country at large from men's sight and rendered the love of it less necessary. The nation was forgotten in the passions that attached men to persons. Hence it was no part of the strict law of feudal honor to remain faithful to one's country. Not indeed that the love of their country did not exist in the hearts of our forefathers, but it constituted a dim and feeble instinct, which has grown more clear and strong in proportion as aristocratic classes have been abolished and the supreme power of the nation centralized.

This may be clearly seen from the contrary judgments that European nations have passed upon the various events of their histories, according to the generations by which such judgments were formed. The circumstance that most dishonored the Constable de Bourbon in the eyes of his contemporaries was that he bore arms against his King; that which most dishonors him in our eyes is that he made war against his country. We brand him as deeply as our forefathers did, but for different reasons.

I have chosen the honor of feudal times by way of illustration of my meaning because its characteristics are more distinctly marked and more familiar to us than those of any other period; but I might have taken an example elsewhere and I should have reached the same conclusion by a different road.

Although we are less perfectly acquainted with the Romans than with our own ancestors, yet we know that certain peculiar notions of glory and disgrace obtained among

[2] Even the word *patrie* was not used by French writers until the sixteenth century.

them which were not derived solely from the general principles of right and wrong. Many human actions were judged differently according as they affected a Roman citizen or a stranger, a freeman or a slave; certain vices were blazoned abroad, certain virtues were extolled above all others. "In that age," says Plutarch, in the Life of Coriolanus, "martial prowess was more honored and prized in Rome than all the other virtues, in so much that it was called *virtus,* the name of virtue itself, by applying the name of the kind to this particular species; so that *virtue* in Latin was as much as to say *valor*." Can anyone fail to recognize the peculiar want of that singular community which was formed for the conquest of the world?

Any nation would furnish us with similar grounds of observation, for, as I have already remarked, whenever men collect together as a distinct community, the notion of honor instantly grows up among them; that is to say, a system of opinions peculiar to themselves as to what is blamable or commendable; and these peculiar rules always originate in the special habits and special interests of the community.

This is applicable to a certain extent to democratic communities as well as to others, as I shall now proceed to prove by the example of the Americans.[3]

Some loose notions of the old aristocratic honor of Europe are still to be found scattered among the opinions of the Americans, but these traditional opinions are few in number, they have but little root in the country and but little power. They are like a religion which has still some temples left standing, though men have ceased to believe in it. But amid these half-obliterated notions of exotic honor some new opinions have sprung up which constitute what may be termed in our days American honor.

I have shown how the Americans are constantly driven to engage in commerce and industry. Their origin, their social condition, their political institutions, and even the region they inhabit urge them irresistibly in this direction. Their present condition, then, is that of an almost exclusively manufacturing and commercial association, placed in the midst of a new and boundless country, which their

[3] I speak here of the Americans inhabiting those states where slavery does not exist; they alone can be said to present a complete picture of democratic society.

principal object is to explore for purposes of profit. This is the characteristic that most distinguishes the American people from all others at the present time.

All those quiet virtues that tend to give a regular movement to the community and to encourage business will therefore be held in peculiar honor by that people, and to neglect those virtues will be to incur public contempt. All the more turbulent virtues, which often dazzle, but more frequently disturb society, will, on the contrary, occupy a subordinate rank in the estimation of this same people; they may be neglected without forfeiting the esteem of the community; to acquire them would perhaps be to run a risk of losing it.

The Americans make a no less arbitrary classification of men's vices. There are certain propensities which appear censurable to the general reason and the universal conscience of mankind, but which happen to agree with the peculiar and temporary wants of the American community: these propensities are lightly reproved, sometimes even encouraged; for instance, the love of wealth and the secondary propensities connected with it may be more particularly cited. To clear, to till, and to transform the vast uninhabited continent which is his domain, the American requires the daily support of an energetic passion; that passion can only be the love of wealth; the passion for wealth is therefore not reprobated in America, and, provided it does not go beyond the bounds assigned to it for public security, it is held in honor. The American lauds as a noble and praiseworthy ambition what our own forefathers in the Middle Ages stigmatized as severe cupidity, just as he treats as a blind and barbarous frenzy that ardor of conquest and martial temper which bore them to battle.

In the United States fortunes are lost and regained without difficulty; the country is boundless and its resources inexhaustible. The people have all the wants and cravings of a growing creature; and, whatever be their efforts, they are always surrounded by more than they can appropriate. It is not the ruin of a few individuals, which may be soon repaired, but the inactivity and sloth of the community at large that would be fatal to such a people. Boldness of enterprise is the foremost cause of its rapid progress, its strength, and its greatness. Commercial business is there like a vast lottery, by which a small number of men continually lose, but the state is always a gainer; such a people ought therefore to encourage and do honor to boldness in commercial speculations. But any bold speculation risks the fortune of the speculator and of all those who put their trust in him. The Americans, who make a virtue of commercial temerity, have no right in any case to brand with disgrace those who practice it. Hence arises the strange indulgence that is shown to bankrupts in the United States; their honor does not suffer by such an accident. In this respect the Americans differ, not only from the nations of Europe, but from all the commercial nations of our time; and accordingly they resemble none of them in their position or their wants.

In America all those vices that tend to impair the purity of morals and to destroy the conjugal tie are treated with a degree of severity unknown in the rest of the world. At first sight this seems strangely at variance with the tolerance shown there on other subjects, and one is surprised to meet with a morality so relaxed and also so austere among the selfsame people. But these things are less incoherent than they seem to be. Public opinion in the United States very gently represses that love of wealth which promotes the commercial greatness and the prosperity of the nation, and it especially condemns that laxity of morals which diverts the human mind from the pursuit of well-being and disturbs the internal order of domestic life which is so necessary to success in business. To earn the esteem of their countrymen, the Americans are therefore forced to adapt themselves to orderly habits; and it may be said in this sense that they make it a matter of honor to live chastely.

On one point American honor accords with the notions of honor acknowledged in Europe; it places courage as the highest virtue and treats it as the greatest of the moral necessities of man; but the notion of courage itself assumes a different aspect. In the United States martial valor is but little prized; the courage which is best known and most esteemed is that which emboldens men to brave the dangers of the ocean in order to arrive earlier in port, to support the privations of the wilderness without complaint, and solitude more cruel than privations, the courage which renders them almost insensible to the loss of a fortune laboriously acquired and instantly prompts to fresh exertions to make another. Courage of this kind is peculiarly necessary to the maintenance and prosperity of the American communities, and it is held by them in peculiar honor and estimation; to betray a want of it is to incur certain disgrace.

I have yet another characteristic point which may serve to place the idea of this chapter in stronger relief. In a democratic society like that of the United States, where fortunes are scanty and insecure, everybody works, and work opens a way to everything; this has changed the point of honor quite around and has turned it against idleness. I have sometimes met in America with young men of wealth, personally disinclined to all laborious exertion, but who had been compelled to embrace a profession. Their disposition and their fortune allowed them to remain without employment; public opinion forbade it, too imperiously to be disobeyed. In the European countries, on the contrary, where aristocracy is still struggling with the flood which overwhelms it, I have often seen men, constantly spurred on by their wants and desires, remain in idleness in order not to lose the esteem of their equals; and I have known them to submit to ennui and privations rather than to work. No one can fail to perceive that these opposite obligations are two different rules of conduct, both nevertheless originating in the notion of honor.

What our forefathers designated as honor absolutely was in reality only one of its forms; they gave a generic name to what was only a species. Honor, therefore, is to be found in democratic as well as in aristocratic ages, but it will not be difficult to show that it assumes a different aspect in the former. Not only are its injunctions different, but we shall shortly see that they are less numerous, less precise, and that its dictates are less rigorously obeyed.

The position of a caste is always much more peculiar than that of a people. Nothing is so exceptional in the world as a small community invariably composed of the same families (as was, for instance, the aristocracy of the Middle Ages) whose object is to concentrate and to retain, exclusively and hereditarily, education, wealth, and power among its own members. But the more exceptional the position of a community happens to be, the more numerous are its special wants and the more extensive are its notions of honor corresponding to those wants.

The rules of honor will therefore always be less numerous among a people not divided into castes than among any other. If ever any nations are constituted in which it may even be difficult to find any peculiar classes of society, the notion of honor will be confined to a small number of precepts, which will be more and more in accordance with the moral laws adopted by the mass of mankind.

Thus the laws of honor will be less peculiar and less multifarious among a democratic people than in an aristocracy. They will also be more obscure, and this is a necessary consequence of what goes before; for as the distinguishing marks of honor are less numerous and less peculiar, it must often be difficult to distinguish them. To this other reasons may be added. Among the aristocratic nations of the Middle Ages generation succeeded generation in vain; each family was like a never dying, ever stationary man, and the state of opinions was hardly more changeable than that of conditions. Everyone then had the same objects always before his eyes, which he contemplated from the same point; his eyes gradually detected the smallest details, and his discernment could not fail to become in the end clear and accurate. Thus not only had the men of feudal times very extraordinary opinions in matters of honor, but each of those opinions was present to their minds under a clear and precise form.

This can never be the case in America, where all men are in constant motion and where society, transformed daily by its own operations, changes its opinions together with its wants. In such a country men have glimpses of the rules of honor, but they seldom have time to fix attention upon them.

But even if society were motionless, it would still be difficult to determine the meaning that ought to be attached to the word *honor*. In the Middle Ages, as each class had its own honor, the same opinion was never received at the same time by a large number of men; and this rendered it possible to give it a determined and accurate form, which was the more easy as all those by whom it was received, having a perfectly identical and most peculiar position, were naturally disposed to agree upon the points of a law which was made for themselves alone.

Thus the code of honor became a complete and detailed

system, in which everything was anticipated and provided for beforehand, and a fixed and always palpable standard was applied to human actions. Among a democratic nation, like the Americans, in which ranks are confounded and the whole of society forms one single mass, composed of elements which are all analogous though not entirely similar, it is impossible ever to agree beforehand on what shall or shall not be allowed by the laws of honor.

Among that people, indeed, some national wants exist, which give rise to opinions common to the whole nation on points of honor: but these opinions never occur at the same time, in the same manner, or with the same intensity to the minds of the whole community; the law of honor exists, but it has no organs to promulgate it.

The confusion is far greater still in a democratic country like France, where the different classes of which the former fabric of society was composed, being brought together but not yet mingled, import day by day into each other's circles various and sometimes conflicting notions of honor, where every man, at his own will and pleasure, forsakes one portion of his forefathers' creed and retains another; so that, amid so many arbitrary measures, no common rule can ever be established, and it is almost impossible to predict which actions will be held in honor and which will be thought disgraceful. Such times are wretched, but they are of short duration.

As honor among democratic nations is imperfectly defined, its influence is of course less powerful; for it is difficult to apply with certainty and firmness a law that is not distinctly known. Public opinion, the natural and supreme interpreter of the laws of honor, not clearly discerning to which side censure or approval ought to lean, can only pronounce a hesitating judgment. Sometimes the opinion of the public may contradict itself; more frequently it does not act and lets things pass.

The weakness of the sense of honor in democracies also arises from several other causes. In aristocratic countries the same notions of honor are always entertained by only a few persons, always limited in number, often separated from the rest of their fellow citizens. Honor is easily mingled and identified in their minds with the idea of all that distinguishes their own position; it appears to them as the chief characteristic of their own rank; they apply its different rules with all the warmth of personal interest, and they feel (if I may use the expression) a passion for complying with its dictates.

This truth is extremely obvious in the old black-letter law-books on the subject of trial by battle. The nobles in their disputes were bound to use the lance and sword, whereas the villeins among themselves used only sticks, "inasmuch as," to use the words of the old books, "villeins have no honor." This did not mean, as it may be imagined at the present day, that these people were contemptible, but simply that their actions were not to be judged by the same rules that were applied to the actions of the aristocracy.

It is surprising, at first sight, that when the sense of honor is most predominant, its injunctions are usually most strange; so that the further it is removed from common reason, the better it is obeyed; whence it has sometimes been inferred that the laws of honor were strengthened by their own extravagance. The two things, indeed, originate from the same source, but the one is not derived from the other. Honor becomes fantastic in proportion to the peculiarity of the wants that it denotes and the paucity of the men by whom those wants are felt; and it is because it denotes wants of this kind that its influence is great. Thus the notion of honor is not the stronger for being fantastic, but it is fantastic and strong from the selfsame cause.

Further, among aristocratic nations each rank is different, but all ranks are fixed. Every man occupies a place in his own sphere which he cannot relinquish, and he lives there among other men who are bound by the same ties. Among these nations no man can either hope or fear to escape being seen; no man is placed so low but that he has a stage of his own, and none can avoid censure or applause by his obscurity.

In democratic states, on the contrary, where all the members of the community are mingled in the same crowd and in constant agitation, public opinion has no hold on men; they disappear at every instant and elude its power. Consequently the dictates of honor will be there less imperious and less stringent, for honor acts solely for the public eye, differing in this respect from mere virtue, which lives upon itself, contented with its own approval.

If the reader has distinctly apprehended all that goes before, he will understand that there is a close and necessary relation between the inequality of social conditions and what has here been styled honor, a relation which, if I am not mistaken, had not before been clearly pointed out. I shall therefore make one more attempt to illustrate it satisfactorily.

Suppose a nation stands apart from the rest of mankind: independently of certain general wants inherent in the human race, it will also have wants and interests peculiar to itself. Certain opinions in respect to censure or approbation forthwith arise in the community which are peculiar to itself and which are styled honor by the members of that community. Now suppose that in this same nation a caste arises which, in its turn, stands apart from all the other classes, and contracts certain peculiar wants, which give rise in their turn to special opinions. The honor of this caste, composed of a medley of the peculiar notions of the nation and the still more peculiar notions of the caste, will be as remote as it is possible to conceive from the simple and general opinions of men.

Having reached this extreme point of the argument, I now return.

When ranks are commingled and privileges abolished, the men of whom a nation is composed being once more equal and alike, their interests and wants become identical, and all the peculiar notions which each caste styled honor successively disappear. The notion of honor no longer proceeds from any other source than the wants peculiar to the nation at large, and it denotes the individual character of that nation to the world.

Lastly, if it were allowable to suppose that all the races of mankind should be commingled and that all the nations of earth should ultimately come to have the same interests, the same wants, undistinguished from each other by any characteristic peculiarities, no conventional value whatever would then be attached to men's action; they would all be regarded by all in the same light; the general necessities of mankind, revealed by conscience to every man, would become the common standard. The simple and general notions of right and wrong only would then be recognized in the world, to which, by a natural and necessary tie, the idea of censure or approbation would be attached.

Thus, to comprise all my meaning in a single proposition, the dissimilarities and inequalities of men gave rise to the notion of honor; that notion is weakened in proportion as these differences are obliterated, and with them it would disappear.

Chapter XIX

WHY SO MANY AMBITIOUS MEN AND SO LITTLE LOFTY AMBITION ARE TO BE FOUND IN THE UNITED STATES

THE FIRST thing that strikes a traveler in the United States is the innumerable multitude of those who seek to emerge from their original condition; and the second is the rarity of lofty ambition to be observed in the midst of the universally ambitious stir of society. No Americans are devoid of a yearning desire to rise, but hardly any appear to entertain hopes of great magnitude or to pursue very lofty aims. All are constantly seeking to acquire property, power, and reputation; few contemplate these things upon a great scale; and this is the more surprising as nothing is to be discerned in the manners or laws of America to limit desire or to prevent it from spreading its impulses in every direction. It seems difficult to attribute this singular state of things to the equality of social conditions, for as soon as that same equality was established in France, the flight of ambition became unbounded. Nevertheless, I think that we may find the principal cause of this fact in the social condition and democratic manners of the Americans.

All revolutions enlarge the ambition of men. This is more peculiarly true of those revolutions which overthrow an aristocracy. When the former barriers that kept back the multitude from fame and power are suddenly thrown down, a violent and universal movement takes place towards that eminence so long coveted and at length to be enjoyed. In this first burst of triumph nothing seems impossible to anyone: not only are desires boundless, but the power of satisfying them seems almost boundless too. Amid the general and sudden change of laws and customs, in this vast confusion of all men and all ordinances, the various members of the community rise and sink again with excessive rapidity, and power passes so quickly from hand to hand that none need despair of catching it in turn.

It must be recollected, moreover, that the people who destroy an aristocracy have lived under its laws; they have witnessed its splendor, and they have unconsciously imbibed the feelings and notions which it entertained. Thus, at the moment when an aristocracy is dissolved, its spirit still pervades the mass of the community, and its tendencies are retained long after it has been defeated. Ambition is therefore always extremely great as long as a democratic revolution lasts, and it will remain so for some time after the revolution is consummated.

The recollection of the extraordinary events which men have witnessed is not obliterated from their memory in a day. The passions that a revolution has roused do not disappear at its close. A sense of instability remains in the midst of re-established order; a notion of easy success survives the strange vicissitudes which gave it birth; desires still remain extremely enlarged, while the means of satisfying them are diminished day by day. The taste for large fortunes persists, though large fortunes are rare; and on every side we trace the ravages of inordinate and unsuccessful ambition kindled in hearts which it consumes in secret and in vain.

At length, however, the last vestiges of the struggle are effaced; the remains of aristocracy completely disappear; the great events by which its fall was attended are forgotten; peace succeeds to war, and the sway of order is restored in the new realm; desires are again adapted to the means by which they may be fulfilled; the wants, the opinions, and the feelings of men cohere once more; the level of the community is permanently determined, and democratic society established.

A democratic nation, arrived at this permanent and regular state of things, will present a very different spectacle from that which I have just described, and we may readily conclude that if ambition becomes great while the conditions of society are growing equal, it loses that quality when they have grown so.

As wealth is subdivided and knowledge diffused, no one is entirely destitute of education or of property; the privileges and disqualifications of caste being abolished, and men having shattered the bonds that once held them fixed, the notion of advancement suggests itself to every mind, the desire to rise swells in every heart, and all men want to mount above their station; ambition is the universal feeling.

But if the equality of conditions gives some resources to all the members of the community, it also prevents any of them from having resources of great extent, which necessarily circumscribes their desires within somewhat narrow limits. Thus, among democratic nations, ambition is ardent and continual, but its aim is not habitually lofty; and life is generally spent in eagerly coveting small objects that are within reach.

What chiefly diverts the men of democracies from lofty ambitions is not the scantiness of their fortunes, but the vehemence of the exertions they daily make to improve them. They strain their faculties to the utmost to achieve paltry results, and this cannot fail speedily to limit their range of view and to circumscribe their powers. They might be much poorer and still be greater.

The small number of opulent citizens who are to be found in a democracy do not constitute an exception to this rule. A man who raises himself by degrees to wealth and power contracts, in the course of this protracted labor, habits of prudence and restraint which he cannot afterwards shake off. A man cannot gradually enlarge his mind as he does his house.

The same observation is applicable to the sons of such a man: they are born, it is true, in a lofty position, but their parents were humble; they have grown up amid feelings and notions which they cannot afterwards easily get rid of; and it may be presumed that they will inherit the propensities of their father, as well as his wealth.

It may happen, on the contrary, that the poorest scion of a powerful aristocracy may display vast ambition, because the traditional opinions of his race and the general spirit of his order still buoy him up for some time above his fortune.

Another thing that prevents the men of democratic periods from easily indulging in the pursuit of lofty objects is the lapse of time which they foresee must take place before they can be ready to struggle for them. "It is a great advantage," says Pascal, "to be a man of quality, since it brings one man as forward at eighteen or twenty as another man would be at fifty, which is a clear gain of thirty years." Those thirty years are commonly wanting to the ambitious characters of democracies. The principle of equality, which allows every man to arrive at everything, prevents all men from rapid advancement.

In a democratic society, as well as elsewhere, there is only a certain number of great fortunes to be made; and as the paths that lead to them are indiscriminately open to all, the progress of all must necessarily be slackened. As the candidates appear to be nearly alike, and as it is difficult to make a selection without infringing the principle of equality, which is the supreme law of democratic societies, the first idea which suggests itself is to make them all advance at the same rate and submit to the same trials. Thus, in proportion as men become more alike and the principle of equality is more peaceably and deeply infused into the institutions and manners of the country, the rules for advancement become more inflexible, advancement itself slower, the difficulty of arriving quickly at a certain height far greater. From hatred of privilege and from the embarrassment of choosing, all men are at last forced, whatever may be their standard, to pass the same ordeal; all are indiscriminately subjected to a multitude of petty preliminary exercises, in which their youth is wasted and their imagination quenched, so that they despair of ever fully attaining what is held out to them; and when at length they are in a condition to perform any extraordinary acts, the taste for such things has forsaken them.

In China, where the equality of conditions is very great and very ancient, no man passes from one public office to another without undergoing a competitive trial. This probation occurs afresh at every stage of his career; and the notion is now so rooted in the manners of the people that I remember to have read a Chinese novel in which the hero, after numberless vicissitudes, succeeds at length in touching the heart of his mistress by doing well on an examination. A lofty ambition breaths with difficulty in such an atmosphere.

The remark I apply to politics extends to everything: equality everywhere produces the same effects; where the laws of a country do not regulate and retard the advancement of men by positive enactment, competition attains the same end.

In a well-established democratic community great and rapid elevation is therefore rare; it forms an exception to the common rule; and it is the singularity of such occurrences that makes men forget how rarely they happen.

Men living in democracies ultimately discover these things; they find out at last that the laws of their country open a boundless field of action before them, but that no one can hope to hasten across it. Between them and the final object of their desires they perceive a multitude of small intermediate impediments, which must be slowly surmounted; this prospect wearies and discourages their ambition at once. They therefore give up hopes so doubtful and remote, to search nearer to themselves for less lofty and more easy enjoyments. Their horizon is not bounded by the laws, but narrowed by themselves.

I have remarked that lofty ambitions are more rare in the ages of democracy than in times of aristocracy; I may add that when, in spite of these natural obstacles, they do spring into existence, their character is different. In aristocracies the career of ambition is often wide, but its boundaries are determined. In democracies ambition commonly ranges in a narrower field, but if once it gets beyond that, hardly any limits can be assigned to it. As men are individually weak, as they live asunder and in constant motion, as precedents are of little authority and laws but of short duration, resistance to novelty is languid and the fabric of society never appears perfectly erect or firmly consolidated. So that, when once an ambitious man has the power in his grasp, there is nothing he may not dare; and when it is gone from him, he meditates the overthrow of the state to regain it. This gives to great political ambition a character of revolutionary violence, which it seldom exhibits to an equal degree in aristocratic communities. The common aspect of democratic nations will present a great number of small and very rational objects of ambition, from among which a few ill-controlled desires of a larger growth will at intervals break out; but no such thing as ambition conceived and regulated on a vast scale is to be met with there.

I have shown elsewhere by what secret influence the

principle of equality makes the passion for physical gratification and the exclusive love of the present predominate in the human heart. These different propensities mingle with the sentiment of ambition and tinge it, as it were, with their hues.

I believe that ambitious men in democracies are less engrossed than any others with the interests and the judgment of posterity; the present moment alone engages and absorbs them. They are more apt to complete a number of undertakings with rapidity than to raise lasting monuments of their achievements, and they care much more for success than for fame. What they most ask of men is obedience, what they most covet is empire. Their manners, in almost all cases, have remained below their station; the consequence is that they frequently carry very low tastes into their extraordinary fortunes and that they seem to have acquired the supreme power only to minister to their coarse or paltry pleasures.

I think that in our time it is very necessary to purify, to regulate, and to proportion the feeling of ambition, but that it would be extremely dangerous to seek to impoverish and to repress it overmuch. We should attempt to lay down certain extreme limits which it should never be allowed to outstep; but its range within those established limits should not be too much checked.

I confess that I apprehend much less for democratic society from the boldness than from the mediocrity of desires. What appears to me most to be dreaded is that in the midst of the small, incessant occupations of private life, ambition should lose its vigor and its greatness; that the passions of man should abate, but at the same time be lowered; so that the march of society should every day become more tranquil and less aspiring.

I think, then, that the leaders of modern society would be wrong to seek to lull the community by a state of too uniform and too peaceful happiness, and that it is well to expose it from time to time to matters of difficulty and danger in order to raise ambition and to give it a field of action.

Moralists are constantly complaining that the ruling vice of the present time is pride. This is true in one sense, for indeed everyone thinks that he is better than his neighbor or refuses to obey his superior; but it is extremely false in another, for the same man who cannot endure subordination or equality has so contemptible an opinion of himself that he thinks he is born only to indulge in vulgar pleasures. He willingly takes up with low desires without daring to embark on lofty enterprises, of which he scarcely dreams.

Thus, far from thinking that humility ought to be preached to our contemporaries, I would have endeavors made to give them a more enlarged idea of themselves and of their kind. Humility is unwholesome to them; what they most want is, in my opinion, pride. I would willingly exchange several of our small virtues for this one vice.

Chapter XX

THE TRADE OF PLACE-HUNTING IN CERTAIN DEMOCRATIC COUNTRIES

IN THE United States, as soon as a man has acquired some education and pecuniary resources, either he endeavors to get rich by commerce or industry, or he buys land in the uncleared country and turns pioneer. All that he asks of the state is not to be disturbed in his toil and to be secure in his earnings. Among most European nations, when a man begins to feel his strength and to extend his desires, the first thing that occurs to him is to get some public employment. These opposite effects, originating in the same cause, deserve our passing notice.

When public employments are few in number, ill-paid, and precarious, while the different kinds of business are numerous and lucrative, it is to business and not to official duties that the new and eager desires created by the principle of equality turn from every side. But if, while the ranks of society are becoming more equal, the education of the people remains incomplete or their spirit the reverse of bold, if commerce and industry, checked in their growth, afford only slow and arduous means of making a fortune, the various members of the community, despairing of ameliorating their own condition, rush to the head of the state and demand its assistance. To relieve their own necessities at the cost of the public treasury appears to them the easiest and most open, if not the only way of rising above a condition which no longer contents them; place-hunting becomes the most generally followed of all trades.

This must especially be the case in those great centralized monarchies in which the number of paid offices is immense and the tenure of them tolerably secure, so that no one despairs of obtaining a place and of enjoying it as undisturbedly as a hereditary fortune.

I shall not remark that the universal and inordinate desire for place is a great social evil; that it destroys the spirit of independence in the citizen and diffuses a venal and servile humor throughout the frame of society; that it stifles the manlier virtues; nor shall I be at the pains to demonstrate that this kind of traffic creates only an unproductive activity, which agitates the country without adding to its resources. All these things are obvious. But I would observe that a government that encourages this tendency risks its own tranquillity and places its very existence in great jeopardy.

I am aware that at a time like our own, when the love and respect which formerly clung to authority are seen gradually to decline, it may appear necessary for those in power to lay a closer hold on every man by his own interest, and it may seem convenient to use his own passions to keep him in order and in silence; but this cannot long be so, and what may appear to be a source of strength for a certain time will assuredly become, in the end, a great cause of embarrassment and weakness.

Among democratic nations, as well as elsewhere, the number of official appointments has, in the end, some limits; but among those nations the number of aspirants is unlimited. It perpetually increases, with a gradual and irresistible rise, in proportion as social conditions become more equal, and is checked only by the limits of the population.

Thus, when public employments afford the only outlet for ambition, the government necessarily meets with a permanent opposition at last; for it is tasked to satisfy with limited means unlimited desires. It is very certain that, of all people in the world, the most difficult to restrain and to manage are a people of office-hunters. Whatever endeavors are made by rulers, such a people can never be contented; and it is always to be apprehended that they will ultimately overturn the constitution of the country and change the aspect of the state for the sole purpose of cleaning out the present office-holders.

The sovereigns of the present age, who strive to fix upon themselves alone all those novel desires which are aroused by equality and to satisfy them, will repent in the end, if I am not mistaken, that ever they embarked on this policy. They will one day discover that they have hazarded their own power by making it so necessary, and that the more safe and honest course would have been to teach their subjects the art of providing for themselves.

Chapter XXI

WHY GREAT REVOLUTIONS WILL BECOME MORE RARE

A PEOPLE that has existed for centuries under a system of castes and classes can arrive at a democratic state of society only by passing through a long series of more or less critical transformations, accomplished by violent efforts, and after numerous vicissitudes, in the course of which property, opinions, and power are rapidly transferred from one to another. Even after this great revolution is consummated, the revolutionary habits produced by it may long be traced, and it will be followed by deep commotion. As all this takes place at the very time when social conditions are becoming more equal, it is inferred that some concealed relation and secret tie exists between the principle of equality itself and revolution, in so much that the one cannot exist without giving rise to the other.

On this point reasoning may seem to lead to the same result as experience. Among a people whose ranks are nearly equal, no ostensible bond connects men together or keeps them settled in their station. None of them have either a permanent right or power to command, none are forced by their condition to obey; but every man, finding himself possessed of some education and some resources, may choose his own path and proceed apart from all his fellow men. The same causes that make the members of the community independent of each other continually impel them to new and restless desires and constantly spur them onwards. It therefore seems natural that in a democratic community men, things, and opinions should be forever changing their form and place, and that democratic ages should be times of rapid and incessant transformation.

But is this really the case? Does the equality of social conditions habitually and permanently lead men to revolution? Does that state of society contain some perturbing principle which prevents the community from ever subsiding into calm and disposes the citizens to alter incessantly their laws, their principles, and their manners? I do not believe it; and as the subject is important, I beg for the reader's close attention.

Almost all the revolutions that have changed the aspect of nations have been made to consolidate or to destroy social inequality. Remove the secondary causes that have produced the great convulsions of the world and you will almost always find the principle of inequality at the bottom. Either the poor have attempted to plunder the rich, or the rich to enslave the poor. If, then, a state of society can ever be founded in which every man shall have something to keep and little to take from others, much will have been done for the peace of the world.

I am aware that among a great democratic people there will always be some members of the community in great poverty and others in great opulence; but the poor, instead of forming the immense majority of the nation, as is always the case in aristocratic communities, are comparatively few in number, and the laws do not bind them together by the ties of irremediable and hereditary penury.

The wealthy, on their side, are few and powerless; they have no privileges that attract public observation; even their wealth, as it is no longer incorporated and bound up with the soil, is impalpable and, as it were, invisible. As there is no longer a race of poor men, so there is no longer a race of rich men; the latter spring up daily from the multitude and relapse into it again. Hence they do not form a distinct class which may be easily marked out and plundered; and, moreover, as they are connected with the mass of their fellow citizens by a thousand secret ties, the people cannot assail them without inflicting an injury upon themselves.

Between these two extremes of democratic communities stands an innumerable multitude of men almost alike, who, without being exactly either rich or poor, possess sufficient property to desire the maintenance of order, yet not enough to excite envy. Such men are the natural enemies of violent commotions; their lack of agitation keeps all beneath them and above them still and secures the balance of the fabric of society.

Not, indeed, that even these men are contented with what they have got or that they feel a natural abhorrence for a revolution in which they might share the spoil without sharing the calamity; on the contrary, they desire, with unexampled ardor, to get rich, but the difficulty is to know from whom riches can be taken. The same state of society that constantly prompts desires, restrains these desires within necessary limits; it gives men more liberty of changing, and less interest in change.

Not only are the men of democracies not naturally desirous of revolutions, but they are afraid of them. All revolutions more or less threaten the tenure of property; but most of those who live in democratic countries are possessed of property; not only do they possess property, but they live in the condition where men set the greatest store upon their property.

If we attentively consider each of the classes of which society is composed, it is easy to see that the passions created by property are keenest and most tenacious among the middle classes. The poor often care but little for what they possess, because they suffer much more from the want of what they have not than they enjoy the little they have. The rich have many other passions besides that of riches to satisfy; and, besides, the long and arduous enjoyment of a great fortune sometimes makes them in the end insensible to its charms. But the men who have a competency, alike removed from opulence and from penury, attach an enormous value to their possessions. As they are still almost within the reach of poverty, they see its privations near at hand and dread them; between poverty and themselves there is nothing but a scanty fortune, upon which they immediately fix their apprehensions and their hopes. Every day increases the interest they take in it, by the constant cares which it occasions; and they are the more attached to it by their continual exertions to increase the amount. The notion of surrendering the smallest part of it is insupportable to them, and they consider its total loss as the worst of misfortunes.

Now, these eager and apprehensive men of small property constitute the class that is constantly increased by the equality of conditions. Hence in democratic communities the majority of the people do not clearly see what they have to gain by a revolution, but they continually and in a thousand ways feel that they might lose by one.

I have shown, in another part of this work, that the

equality of conditions naturally urges men to embark on commercial and industrial pursuits, and that it tends to increase and to distribute real property; I have also pointed out the means by which it inspires every man with an eager and constant desire to increase his welfare. Nothing is more opposed to revolutionary passions than these things. It may happen that the final result of a revolution is favorable to commerce and manufactures; but its first consequence will almost always be the ruin of manufactures and mercantile men, because it must always change at once the general principles of consumption and temporarily upset the existing proportion between supply and demand.

I know of nothing more opposite to revolutionary attitudes than commercial ones. Commerce is naturally adverse to all the violent passions; it loves to temporize, takes delight in compromise, and studiously avoids irritation. It is patient, insinuating, flexible, and never has recourse to extreme measures until obliged by the most absolute necessity. Commerce renders men independent of one another, gives them a lofty notion of their personal importance, leads them to seek to conduct their own affairs, and teaches how to conduct them well; it therefore prepares men for freedom, but preserves them from revolutions.

In a revolution the owners of personal property have more to fear than all others; for, on the one hand, their property is often easy to seize, and, on the other, it may totally disappear at any moment—a subject of alarm to which the owners of real property are less exposed, since, although they may lose the income of their estates, they may hope to preserve the land itself through the greatest vicissitudes. Hence the former are much more alarmed at the symptoms of revolutionary commotion than the latter. Thus nations are less disposed to make revolutions in proportion as personal property is augmented and distributed among them and as the number of those possessing it is increased.

Moreover, whatever profession men may embrace and whatever species of property they may possess, one characteristic is common to them all. No one is fully contented with his present fortune; all are perpetually striving, in a thousand ways, to improve it. Consider any one of them at any period of his life and he will be found engaged with some new project for the purpose of increasing what he has.

Do not talk to him of the interests and the rights of mankind; this small domestic concern absorbs for the time all his thoughts and inclines him to defer political agitations to some other season. This not only prevents men from making revolutions, but deters men from desiring them. Violent political passions have but little hold on those who have devoted all their faculties to the pursuit of their well-being. The ardor that they display in small matters calms their zeal for momentous undertakings.

From time to time, indeed, enterprising and ambitious men will arise in democratic communities whose unbounded aspirations cannot be contented by following the beaten track. Such men like revolutions and hail their approach; but they have great difficulty in bringing them about unless extraordinary events come to their assistance. No man can struggle with advantage against the spirit of his age and country; and however powerful he may be supposed to be, he will find it difficult to make his contemporaries share in feelings and opinions that are repugnant to all their feelings and desires.

It is a mistake to believe that, when once equality of condition has become the old and uncontested state of society and has imparted its characteristics to the manners of a nation, men will easily allow themselves to be thrust into perilous risks by an imprudent leader or a bold innovator. Not indeed that they will resist him openly, by well-contrived schemes, or even by a premeditated plan of resistance. They will not struggle energetically against him, sometimes they will even applaud him; but they do not follow him. To his vehemence they secretly oppose their inertia, to his revolutionary tendencies their conservative interests, their homely tastes to his adventurous passions, their good sense to the flights of his genius, to his poetry their prose. With immense exertion he raises them for an instant, but they speedily escape from him and fall back, as it were, by their own weight. He strains himself to rouse the indifferent and distracted multitude and finds at last that he is reduced to impotence, not because he is conquered, but because he is alone.

I do not assert that men living in democratic communities are naturally stationary; I think, on the contrary, that a perpetual stir prevails in the bosom of those societies, and that rest is unknown there; but I think that men bestir themselves within certain limits, beyond which they hardly ever go. They are forever varying, altering, and restoring secondary matters; but they carefully abstain from touching what is fundamental. They love change, but they dread revolutions.

Although the Americans are constantly modifying or abrogating some of their laws, they by no means display revolutionary passions. It may be easily seen from the promptitude with which they check and calm themselves when public excitement begins to grow alarming, and at the very moment when passions seem most roused, that they dread a revolution as the worst of misfortunes and that every one of them is inwardly resolved to make great sacrifices to avoid such a catastrophe. In no country in the world is the love of property more active and more anxious than in the United States; nowhere does the majority display less inclination for those principles which threaten to alter, in whatever manner, the laws of property.

I have often remarked, that theories which are of a revolutionary nature, since they cannot be put in practice without a complete and sometimes a sudden change in the state of property and persons, are much less favorably viewed in the United States than in the great monarchical countries of Europe; if some men profess them, the bulk of the people reject them with instinctive abhorrence. I do not hesitate to say that most of the maxims commonly called democratic in France would be proscribed by the democracy of the United States. This may easily be understood: in America men have the opinions and passions of democracy; in Europe we have still the passions and opinions of revolution.

If ever America undergoes great revolutions, they will be brought about by the presence of the black race on the soil of the United States; that is to say, they will owe their origin, not to the equality, but to the inequality of condition.

When social conditions are equal, every man is apt to live apart, centered in himself and forgetful of the public. If the rules of democratic nations were either to neglect to correct this fatal tendency or to encourage it from a notion that it weans men from political passions and thus wards off revolutions, they might eventually produce the evil they seek to avoid, and a time might come when the inordinate passions of a few men. aided by the unintelligent selfishness or the pusillanimity of the greater number, would ultimately compel society to pass through strange vicissitudes. In democratic communities revolutions are seldom desired except by a minority, but a minority may sometimes effect them.

I do not assert that democratic nations are secure from revolutions; I merely say that the state of society in those nations does not lead to revolutions, but rather wards them off. A democratic people left to itself will not easily embark in great hazards; it is only led to revolutions unawares; it may sometimes undergo them, but it does not make them: and I will add that when such a people has been allowed to acquire sufficient knowledge and experience, it will not allow them to be made.

I am well aware that in this respect public institutions may themselves do much; they may encourage or repress the tendencies that originate in the state of society. I therefore do not maintain, I repeat, that a people is secure from revolutions simply because conditions are equal in the community; but I think that, whatever the institutions of such a people may be, great revolutions will always be far less frequent than is supposed, and I can easily discern a state of polity which, when combined with the principle of equality, would render society more stationary than it has ever been in our western part of the world.

The observations I have here made on events may also be applied in part to opinions. Two things are surprising in the United States: the mutability of the greater part of human actions, and the singular stability of certain principles. Men are in constant motion; the mind of man appears almost unmoved. When once an opinion has spread over the country and struck root there, it would seem that no power on earth is strong enough to eradicate it. In the United States general principles in religion, philosophy, morality, and even politics do not vary, or at least are only modified by a hidden and often an imperceptible process; even the grossest prejudices are obliterated with incredible slowness amid the continual friction of men and things.

I hear it said that it is in the nature and the habits of democracies to be constantly changing their opinions and feelings. This may be true of small democratic nations, like those of the ancient world, in which the whole community could be assembled in a public place and then excited at will by an orator. But I saw nothing of the kind among the great democratic people that dwells upon the opposite shores of the Atlantic Ocean. What struck me in the United States was the difficulty of shaking the majority in an opinion once conceived or of drawing it off from a leader once adopted. Neither speaking nor writing can accomplish it; nothing but experience will avail, and even experience must be repeated.

This is surprising at first sight, but a more attentive investigation explains the fact. I do not think that it is as easy as is supposed to uproot the prejudices of a democratic people, to change its belief, to supersede principles once established by new principles in religion, politics, and morals; in a word, to make great and frequent changes in men's minds. Not that the human mind is there at rest, it is in constant agitation; but it is engaged in infinitely varying the consequences of known principles and in seeking for new consequences rather than in seeking for new principles. Its motion is one of rapid circumvolution rather than of straightforward impulse by rapid and direct effort; it extends its orbit by small continual and hasty movements, but it does not suddenly alter its position.

Men who are equal in rights, in education, in fortune, or, to comprise all in one word, in their social condition, have necessarily wants, habits, and tastes that are hardly dissimilar. As they look at objects under the same aspect, their minds naturally tend to similar conclusions; and though each of them may deviate from his contemporaries and form opinions of his own, they will involuntarily and unconsciously concur in a certain number of received opinions. The more attentively I consider the effects of equality upon the mind, the more am I persuaded that the intellectual anarchy which we witness about us is not, as many men suppose, the natural state of democratic nations. I think it is rather to be regarded as an accident peculiar to their youth, and that it breaks out only at that period of transition when men have already snapped the former ties which bound them together, but are still amazingly different in origin, education, and manners; so that, having retained opinions, propensities, and tastes of great diversity, nothing any longer prevents men from avowing them openly. The leading opinions of men become similar in proportion as their conditions assimilate: such appears to me to be the general and permanent law; the rest is casual and transient.

I believe that it will rarely happen to any man in a democratic community suddenly to frame a system of notions very remote from that which his contemporaries have adopted; and if some such innovator appeared, I apprehend that he would have great difficulty in finding listeners, still more in finding believers. When the conditions of men are almost equal, they do not easily allow themselves to be persuaded by one another. As they all live in close intercourse, as they have learned the same things together, and as they lead the same life, they are not naturally disposed to take one of themselves for a guide and to follow him implicitly. Men seldom take the opinion of their equal or of a man like themselves upon trust.

Not only is confidence in the superior attainments of certain individuals weakened among democratic nations, as I have elsewhere remarked, but the general notion of the intellectual superiority which any man whatsoever may acquire in relation to the rest of the community is soon overshadowed. As men grow more like each other, the doctrine of the equality of the intellect gradually infuses itself into their opinions, and it becomes more difficult for any innovator to acquire or to exert much influence over the minds of a people. In such communities sudden intellectual revolutions will therefore be rare; for if we read aright the history of the world, we shall find that great and rapid changes in human opinions have been produced far less by the force of reasoning than by the authority of a name.

Observe, too, that as the men who live in democratic societies are not connected with one another by any tie, each of them must be convinced individually, while in aristocratic society it is enough to convince a few; the rest follow. If Luther had lived in an age of equality and had not had princes and potentates for his audience, he would perhaps have found it more difficult to change the aspect of Europe.

Not, indeed, that the men of democracies are naturally strongly persuaded of the certainty of their opinions or are unwavering in belief; they frequently entertain doubts that no one, in their eyes, can remove. It sometimes happens at such times that the human mind would willingly change its position, but as nothing urges or guides it forward, it oscillates to and fro without progressive motion.[1]

Even when the confidence of a democratic people has been won, it is still no easy matter to gain their attention. It is extremely difficult to obtain a hearing from men living in democracies, unless it is to speak to them of themselves. They do not attend to the things said to them, because they are always fully engrossed with the things they are doing. For, indeed, few men are idle in democratic nations; life is passed in the midst of noise and excitement, and men are so engaged in acting that little time remains to them for thinking. I would especially remark, not only that they are employed, but that they are passionately devoted to their employments. They are always in action, and each of their actions absorbs their faculties; the zeal which they display in business puts out the enthusiasm they might otherwise entertain for ideas.

I think that it is extremely difficult to excite the enthusiasm of a democratic people for any theory which has not a palpable, direct, and immediate connection with the daily occupations of life; therefore they will not easily forsake their old opinions, for it is enthusiasm that flings the minds of men out of the beaten track and effects the great revo-

[1] If I inquire what state of society is most favorable to the great revolutions of the mind, I find that it occurs somewhere between the complete equality of the whole community and the absolute separation of ranks. Under a system of castes generations succeed one another without altering men's positions; some have nothing more, others nothing better, to hope for. The imagination slumbers amid this universal silence and stillness, and the very idea of change fades from the human mind.

When ranks have been abolished and social conditions are almost equalized, all men are in ceaseless excitement, but each of them stands alone, independent and weak. This latter state of things is excessively different from the former one; yet it has one point of analogy: great revolutions of the human mind seldom occur in it.

But between these two extremes of the history of nations is an intermediate period, a period of glory as well as of ferment, when the conditions of men are not sufficiently settled for the mind to be lulled in torpor, when they are sufficiently unequal for men to exercise a vast power on the minds of one another, and when some few may modify the convictions of all. It is at such times that great reformers arise and new ideas suddenly change the face of the world.

lutions of the intellect as well as the great revolutions of the political world.

Thus democratic nations have neither time nor taste to go in search of novel opinions. Even when those they possess become doubtful, they still retain them because it would take too much time and inquiry to change them; they retain them, not as certain, but as established.

There are yet other and more cogent reasons which prevent any great change from being easily effected in the principles of a democratic people. I have already adverted to them in the nineteenth chapter.

If the influence of individuals is weak and hardly perceptible among such a people, the power exercised by the mass upon the mind of each individual is extremely great; I have already shown for what reasons. I would now observe that it is wrong to suppose that this depends solely upon the form of government and that the majority would lose its intellectual supremacy if it were to lose its political power.

In aristocracies men often have much greatness and strength of their own; when they find themselves at variance with the greater number of their fellow countrymen, they withdraw to their own circle, where they support and console themselves. Such is not the case in a democratic country; there public favor seems as necessary as the air we breathe, and to live at variance with the multitude is, as it were, not to live. The multitude require no laws to coerce those who do not think like themselves: public disapprobation is enough; a sense of their loneliness and impotence overtakes them and drives them to despair.

Whenever social conditions are equal, public opinion presses with enormous weight upon the minds of each individual; it surrounds, directs, and oppresses him; and this arises from the very constitution of society much more than from its political laws. As men grow more alike, each man feels himself weaker in regard to all the rest; as he discerns nothing by which he is considerably raised above them or distinguished from them, he mistrusts himself as soon as they assail him. Not only does he mistrust his strength, but he even doubts of his right; and he is very near acknowledging that he is in the wrong, when the greater number of his countrymen assert that he is so. The majority do not need to force him; they convince him. In whatever way the powers of a democratic community may be organized and balanced, then, it will always be extremely difficult to believe what the bulk of the people reject or to profess what they condemn.

This circumstance is extraordinarily favorable to the stability of opinions. When an opinion has taken root among a democratic people and established itself in the minds of the bulk of the community, it afterwards persists by itself and is maintained without effort, because no one attacks it. Those who at first rejected it as false ultimately receive it as the general impression, and those who still dispute it in their hearts conceal their dissent; they are careful not to engage in a dangerous and useless conflict.

It is true that when the majority of a democratic people change their opinions, they may suddenly and arbitrarily effect strange revolutions in men's minds; but their opinions do not change without much difficulty, and it is almost as difficult to show that they are changed.

Time, events, or the unaided individual action of the mind will sometimes undermine or destroy an opinion, without any outward sign of the change. It has not been openly assailed, no conspiracy has been formed to make war on it, but its followers one by one noiselessly secede; day by day a few of them abandon it, until at last it is only professed by a minority. In this state it will still continue to prevail. As its enemies remain mute or only interchange their thoughts by stealth, they are themselves unaware for a long period that a great revolution has actually been effected; and in this state of uncertainty they take no steps; they observe one another and are silent. The majority have ceased to believe what they believed before, but they still affect to believe, and this empty phantom of public opinion is strong enough to chill innovators and to keep them silent and at a respectful distance.

We live at a time that has witnessed the most rapid changes of opinion in the minds of men; nevertheless it may be that the leading opinions of society will before long be more settled than they have been for several centuries in our history; that time has not yet come, but it may perhaps be approaching. As I examine more closely the natural wants and tendencies of democratic nations, I grow persuaded that if ever social equality is generally and permanently established in the world, great intellectual and political revolutions will become more difficult and less frequent than is supposed. Because the men of democracies appear always excited, uncertain, eager, changeable in their wills and in their positions, it is imagined that they are suddenly to abrogate their laws, to adopt new opinions, and to assume new manners. But if the principle of equality predisposes men to change, it also suggests to them certain interests and tastes that cannot be satisfied without a settled order of things. Equality urges them on, but at the same time it holds them back; it spurs them, but fastens them to earth; it kindles their desires, but limits their powers.

This, however, is not perceived at first; the passions that tend to sever the citizens of a democracy are obvious enough, but the hidden force that restrains and unites them is not discernible at a glance.

Amid the ruins which surround me shall I dare to say that revolutions are not what I most fear for coming generations? If men continue to shut themselves more closely within the narrow circle of domestic interests and to live on that kind of excitement, it is to be apprehended that they may ultimately become inaccessible to those great and powerful public emotions which perturb nations, but which develop them and recruit them. When property becomes so fluctuating and the love of property so restless and so ardent, I cannot but fear that men may arrive at such a state as to regard every new theory as a peril, every innovation as an irksome toil, every social improvement as a stepping-stone to revolution, and so refuse to move altogether for fear of being moved too far. I dread, and I confess it, lest they should at last so entirely give way to a cowardly love of present enjoyment as to lose sight of the interests of their future selves and those of their descendants and prefer to glide along the easy current of life rather than to make, when it is necessary, a strong and sudden effort to a higher purpose.

It is believed by some that modern society will be always changing its aspect; for myself, I fear that it will ultimately be too invariably fixed in the same institutions, the same prejudices, the same manners, so that mankind will be stopped and circumscribed; that the mind will swing backwards and forwards forever without begetting fresh ideas; that man will waste his strength in bootless and solitary trifling, and, though in continual motion, that humanity will cease to advance.

Chapter XXII

WHY DEMOCRATIC NATIONS NATURALLY DESIRE PEACE, AND DEMOCRATIC ARMIES, WAR

THE SAME interests, the same fears, the same passions that deter democratic nations from revolutions deter them also from war; the spirit of military glory and the spirit of revolution are weakened at the same time and by the same causes. The ever increasing numbers of men of property who are lovers of peace, the growth of personal wealth which war so rapidly consumes, the mildness of manners, the gentleness of heart, those tendencies to pity which are produced by the equality of conditions, that coolness of understanding which renders men comparatively insensible to the violent and poetical excitement of arms, all these causes concur to quench the military spirit. I think it may be admitted as a general and constant rule that among civilized nations the warlike passions will become more rare and less intense in proportion as social conditions are more equal.

War is nevertheless an occurrence to which all nations are subject, democratic nations as well as others. Whatever taste they may have for peace, they must hold themselves in readiness to repel aggression, or, in other words, they must have an army. Fortune, which has conferred so many peculiar benefits upon the inhabitants of the United States, has placed them in the midst of a wilderness, where they have, so to speak, no neighbors; a few thousand soldiers are sufficient for their wants. But this is peculiar to America, not to democracy.

The equality of conditions and the manners as well as the institutions resulting from it do not exempt a democratic people from the necessity of standing armies, and their armies always exercise a powerful influence over their fate. It is therefore of singular importance to inquire what are the natural propensities of the men of whom these armies are composed.

Among aristocratic nations, especially among those in which birth is the only source of rank, the same inequality exists in the army as in the nation; the officer is noble, the soldier is a serf; the one is naturally called upon to command, the other to obey. In aristocratic armies the private soldier's ambition is therefore circumscribed within very narrow limits. Nor has the ambition of the officer an unlimited range. An aristocratic body not only forms a part of the scale of ranks in the nation, but contains a scale of ranks within itself; the members of whom it is composed are placed one above another in a particular and unvarying manner. Thus one man is born to command of a regiment, another to that of a company. When once they have reached the utmost object of their hopes, they stop of their own accord and remain contented with their lot.

There is, besides, a strong cause that in aristocracies weakens the officer's desire of promotion. Among aristocratic nations an officer, independently of his rank in the army, also occupies an elevated rank in society; the former is almost always, in his eyes, only an appendage to the latter. A nobleman who embraces the profession of arms follows it less from motives of ambition than from a sense of the duties imposed on him by his birth. He enters the army in order to find an honorable employment for the idle years of his youth and to be able to bring back to his home and his peers some honorable recollections of military life; but his principal object is not to obtain by that profession either property, distinction, or power, for he possesses these advantages in his own right and enjoys them without leaving his home.

In democratic armies all the soldiers may become officers, which makes the desire of promotion general and immeasurably extends the bounds of military ambition. The officer, on his part, sees nothing that naturally and necessarily stops him at one grade more than at another; and each grade has immense importance in his eyes because his rank in society almost always depends on his rank in the army. Among democratic nations it often happens that an officer has no property but his pay and no distinction but that of military honors; consequently, as often as his duties change, his fortune changes and he becomes, as it were, a new man. What was only an appendage to his position in aristocratic armies has thus become the main point, the basis of his whole condition.

Under the old French monarchy officers were always called by their titles of nobility; they are now always called by the title of their military rank. This little change in the forms of language suffices to show that a great revolution has taken place in the constitution of society and in that of the army.

In democratic armies the desire of advancement is almost universal: it is ardent, tenacious, perpetual; it is strengthened by all other desires and extinguished only with life itself. But it is easy to see that, of all armies in the world, those in which advancement must be slowest in time of peace are the armies of democratic countries. As the number of commissions is naturally limited while the number of competitors is almost unlimited, and as the strict law of equality is over all alike, none can make rapid progress; many can make no progress at all. Thus the desire of advancement is greater and the opportunities of advancement fewer there than elsewhere. All the ambitious spirits of a democratic army are consequently ardently desirous of war, because war makes vacancies and warrants the violation of that law of seniority which is the sole privilege natural to democracy.

We thus arrive at this singular consequence, that, of all armies, those most ardently desirous of war are democratic armies, and of all nations, those most fond of peace are democratic nations; and what makes these facts still more extraordinary is that these contrary effects are produced at the same time by the principle of equality.

All the members of the community, being alike, constantly harbor the wish and discover the possibility of changing their condition and improving their welfare; this makes them fond of peace, which is favorable to industry and allows every man to pursue his own little undertakings to their completion. On the other hand, this same equality makes soldiers dream of fields of battle, by increasing the value of military honors in the eyes of those who follow the profession of arms and by rendering those honors accessible to all. In either case the restlessness of the heart is the same, the taste for enjoyment is insatiable, the ambition of success as great; the means of gratifying it alone are different.

These opposite tendencies of the nation and the army expose democratic communities to great dangers. When a military spirit forsakes a people, the profession of arms immediately ceases to be held in honor and military men fall to the lowest rank of the public servants; they are little esteemed and no longer understood. The reverse of what takes place in aristocratic ages then occurs; the men who enter the army are no longer those of the highest, but of the lowest class. Military ambition is indulged only when no other is possible. Hence arises a circle of cause and consequence from which it is difficult to escape: the best part of the nation shuns the military profession because that profession is not honored, and the profession is not honored because the nation has ceased to follow it.

It is then no matter of surprise that democratic armies are often restless, ill-tempered, and dissatisfied with their lot, although their physical condition is commonly far better and their discipline less strict than in other countries. The soldier feels that he occupies an inferior position, and his wounded pride either stimulates his taste for hostilities that would render his services necessary or gives him a desire for revolution, during which he may hope to win by force of arms the political influence and personal importance now denied him.

The composition of democratic armies makes this last-mentioned danger much to be feared. In democratic communities almost every man has some property to preserve; but democratic armies are generally led by men without property, most of whom have little to lose in civil broils. The bulk of the nation is naturally much more afraid of revolutions than in the ages of aristocracy, but the leaders of the army much less so.

Moreover, as among democratic nations (to repeat what I have just remarked) the wealthiest, best-educated, and ablest men seldom adopt the military profession, the army, taken collectively, eventually forms a small nation by itself, where the mind is less enlarged and habits are more rude than in the nation at large. Now, this small uncivilized nation has arms in its possession and alone knows how to use them; for, indeed, the pacific temper of the community increases the danger to which a democratic people is exposed from the military and turbulent spirit of the army. Nothing is so dangerous as an army in the midst of an unwarlike nation; the excessive love of the whole community for quiet continually puts the constitution at the mercy of the soldiery.

It may therefore be asserted, generally speaking, that if democratic nations are naturally prone to peace from their interests and their propensities, they are constantly drawn to war and revolutions by their armies. Military revolutions, which are scarcely ever to be apprehended in aristocracies, are always to be dreaded among democratic nations. These perils must be reckoned among the most formidable that beset their future fate, and the attention of statesmen should be sedulously applied to find a remedy for the evil.

When a nation perceives that it is inwardly affected by the restless ambition of its army, the first thought which occurs is to give this inconvenient ambition an object by going to war. I do not wish to speak ill of war: war almost always enlarges the mind of a people and raises their character. In some cases it is the only check to the excessive growth of certain propensities that naturally spring out of the equality of conditions, and it must be considered as a necessary corrective to certain inveterate diseases to which democratic communities are liable.

War has great advantages, but we must not flatter ourselves that it can diminish the danger I have just pointed out. That peril is only suspended by it, to return more fiercely when the war is over; for armies are much more impatient of peace after having tasted military exploits. War could be a remedy only for a people who were always athirst for military glory.

I foresee that all the military rulers who may rise up in great democratic nations will find it easier to conquer with their armies than to make their armies live at peace after conquest. There are two things that a democratic people will always find very difficult, to begin a war and to end it.

Again, if war has some peculiar advantages for democratic nations, on the other hand it exposes them to certain dangers which aristocracies have no cause to dread to an equal extent. I shall point out only two of these.

Although war gratifies the army, it embarrasses and often exasperates that countless multitude of men whose minoi passions every day require peace in order to be satisfied. Thus there is some risk of its causing, under another form, the very disturbance it is intended to prevent.

No protracted war can fail to endanger the freedom of a democratic country. Not indeed that after every victory it is to be apprehended that the victorious generals will possess themselves by force of the supreme power, after the manner of Sulla and Cæsar; the danger is of another kind. War does not always give over democratic communities to military government, but it must invariably and immeasurably increase the powers of civil government; it must almost compulsorily concentrate the direction of all men and the management of all things in the hands of the administration. If it does not lead to despotism by sudden violence, it prepares men for it more gently by their habits. All those who seek to destroy the liberties of a democratic nation ought to know that war is the surest and the shortest means to accomplish it. This is the first axiom of the science.

One remedy, which appears to be obvious when the ambition of soldiers and officers becomes the subject of alarm, is to augment the number of commissions to be distributed by increasing the army. This affords temporary relief, but it plunges the country into deeper difficulties at some future period. To increase the army may produce a lasting effect in an aristocratic community, because military ambition is there confined to one class of men, and the ambition of each individual stops, as it were, at a certain limit, so that it may be possible to satisfy all who feel its influence. But nothing is gained by increasing the army among a democratic people, because the number of aspirants always rises in exactly the same ratio as the army itself. Those whose claims have been satisfied by the creation of new commissions are instantly succeeded by a fresh multitude beyond all power of satisfaction; and even those who were but now satisfied soon begin to crave more advancement, for the same excitement prevails in the ranks of the army as in the civil classes of democratic society, and what men want is, not to reach a certain grade, but to have constant promotion. Though these wants may not be very vast, they are perpetually recurring. Thus a democratic nation, by augmenting its army, allays only for a time the ambition of the military profession, which soon becomes even more formidable because the number of those who feel it is increased.

I am of the opinion that a restless and turbulent spirit is an evil inherent in the very constitution of democratic armies and beyond hope of cure. The legislators of democracies must not expect to devise any military organization capable by its influence of calming and restraining the military profession; their efforts would exhaust their powers before the object could be attained.

The remedy for the vices of the army is not to be found in the army itself, but in the country. Democratic nations are naturally afraid of disturbance and of despotism; the object is to turn these natural instincts into intelligent, deliberate, and lasting tastes. When men have at last learned to make a peaceful and profitable use of freedom and have felt its blessings, when they have conceived a manly love of order and have freely submitted themselves to discipline, these same men, if they follow the profession of arms, bring into it, unconsciously and almost against their will, these same habits and manners. The general spirit of the nation, being infused into the spirit peculiar to the army, tempers the opinions and desires engendered by military life, or represses them by the mighty force of public opinion. Teach the citizens to be educated, orderly, firm, and free and the soldiers will be disciplined and obedient.

Any law that, in repressing the turbulent spirit of the army, should tend to diminish the spirit of freedom in the nation and to overshadow the notion of law and right would defeat its object; it would do much more to favor than to defeat the establishment of military tyranny.

After all, and in spite of all precautions, a large army in the midst of a democratic people will always be a source of great danger. The most effectual means of diminishing that danger would be to reduce the army, but this is a remedy that all nations are not able to apply.

Chapter XXIII

WHICH IS THE MOST WARLIKE AND MOST REVOLUTIONARY CLASS IN DEMOCRATIC ARMIES

It is of the essence of a democratic army to be very numerous in proportion to the people to which it belongs, as I shall hereafter show. On the other hand, men living in democratic times seldom choose a military life. Democratic nations are therefore soon led to give up the system of voluntary recruiting for that of compulsory enlistment. The necessity of their social condition compels them to resort to the latter means, and it may easily be foreseen that they will all eventually adopt it.

When military service is compulsory, the burden is indiscriminately and equally borne by the whole community. This is another necessary consequence of the social condition of these nations and of their notions. The government may do almost whatever it pleases, provided it appeals to the whole community at once; it is the unequal distribution of the weight, not the weight itself, that commonly occasions resistance. But as military service is common to all the citizens, the evident consequence is that each of them remains for only a few years on active duty. Thus it is in the nature of things that the soldier in democracies only passes through the army, while among most aristocratic nations the military profession is one which the soldier adopts, or which is imposed upon him, for life.

This has important consequences. Among the soldiers of a democratic army some acquire a taste for military life; but the majority, being enlisted against their will and ever ready to go back to their homes, do not consider themselves as seriously engaged in the military profession and are always thinking of quitting it. Such men do not contract the wants and only half partake in the passions which that mode of life engenders. They adapt themselves to their military duties, but their minds are still attached to the interests and the duties that engaged them in civil life. They do not therefore imbibe the spirit of the army, or rather they infuse the spirit of the community at large into the army and retain it there. Among democratic nations the private soldiers remain most like civilians; upon them the habits of the nation have the firmest hold and public opinion has most influence. It is through the private soldiers especially that it may be possible to infuse into a democratic army the love of freedom and the respect for rights, if these principles have once been successfully inculcated in the people at large. The reverse happens among aristocratic nations, where the soldiery have eventually nothing in common with their fellow citizens and where they live among them as strangers and often as enemies.

In aristocratic armies the officers are the conservative element, because the officers alone have retained a strict connection with civil society and never forgo their purpose of resuming their place in it sooner or later. In democratic armies the private soldiers stand in this position, and from the same cause.

It often happens, on the contrary, that in these same democratic armies the officers contract tastes and wants wholly distinct from those of the nation, a fact which may be thus accounted for: Among democratic nations the man who becomes an officer severs all the ties that bound him to civil life; he leaves it forever, and no interest urges him to return to it. His true country is the army, since he owes all he has to the rank he has attained in it; he therefore follows the fortunes of the army, rises or sinks with it, and henceforward directs all his hopes to that quarter only. As the wants of an officer are distinct from those of the country, he may, perhaps, ardently desire war, or labor to bring about a revolution, at the very moment when the nation is most desirous of stability and peace.

There are, nevertheless, some causes that allay this restless and warlike spirit. Though ambition is universal and continual among democratic nations, we have seen that it is seldom great. A man who, being born in the lower classes of the community, has risen from the ranks to be an officer has already taken a prodigious step. He has gained a footing in a sphere above that which he filled in civil life, and has acquired rights which most democratic nations will always consider as inalienable.[1] He is willing to pause after so great an effort and to enjoy what he has won. The fear of risking what he has already obtained damps the desire of acquiring what he has not got. Having conquered the first and greatest impediment that opposed his advancement, he resigns himself with less impatience to the slowness of his progress. His ambition will be more and more cooled in proportion as the increasing distinction of his rank teaches him that he has more to put in jeopardy. If I am not mistaken, the least warlike and also the least revolutionary part of a democratic army will always be its chief commanders.

But the remarks I have just made on officers and soldiers are not applicable to a numerous class which, in all armies, fills the intermediate space between them; I mean the class of non-commissioned officers. This class of non-commissioned officers, which had never acted a part in history until the present century, is henceforward destined, I think, to play one of some importance. Like the officers, non-commissioned officers have broken, in their minds, all the ties which bound them to civil life; like the former, they devote themselves permanently to the service and perhaps make it even more exclusively the object of all their desires; but non-commissioned officers are men who have not yet reached a firm and lofty post at which they may pause and breathe more freely before they can attain further promotion.

By the very nature of his duties, which are invariable, a non-commissioned officer is doomed to lead an obscure, confined, comfortless, and precarious existence. As yet he sees nothing of military life but its dangers; he knows nothing but its privations and its discipline, more difficult to support than dangers; he suffers the more from his present miseries, from knowing that the constitution of society and of the army allow him to rise above them; he may, indeed, at any time obtain his commission and enter at once upon command, honors, independence, rights, and enjoyments. Not only does this object of his hopes appear to him of immense importance, but he is never sure of reaching it till

[1] The position of officers is indeed much more secure among democratic nations than elsewhere; the lower the personal standing of the man, the greater is the comparative importance of his military grade and the more just and necessary is it that the enjoyment of that rank should be secured by the laws.

it is actually his own. The grade he fills is by no means irrevocable; he is always entirely abandoned to the arbitrary pleasure of his commanding officer, for this is imperiously required by the necessity of discipline: a slight fault, a whim, may always deprive him in an instant of the fruits of many years of toil and endeavor; until he has reached the grade to which he aspires, he has accomplished nothing; not till he reaches that grade does his career seem to begin. A desperate ambition cannot fail to be kindled in a man thus incessantly goaded on by his youth, his wants, his passions, the spirit of his age, his hopes, and his fears.

Non-commissioned officers are therefore bent on war, on war always and at any cost; but if war be denied them, then they desire revolutions, to suspend the authority of established regulations and to enable them, aided by the general confusion and the political passions of the time, to get rid of their superior officers and to take their places. Nor is it impossible for them to bring about such a crisis, because their common origin and habits give them much influence over the soldiers, however different may be their passions and their desires.

It would be an error to suppose that these various characteristics of officers, non-commissioned officers, and men belong to any particular time or country; they will always occur at all times and among all democratic nations. In every democratic army the non-commissioned officers will be the worst representatives of the pacific and orderly spirit of the country, and the private soldiers will be the best. The latter will carry with them into military life the strength or weakness of the manners of the nation; they will display a faithful reflection of the community. If that community is ignorant and weak, they will allow themselves to be drawn by their leaders into disturbances, either unconsciously or against their will; if it is enlightened and energetic, the community will itself keep them within the bounds of order.

Chapter XXIV

CAUSES WHICH RENDER DEMOCRATIC ARMIES WEAKER THAN OTHER ARMIES AT THE OUTSET OF A CAMPAIGN, AND MORE FORMIDABLE IN PROTRACTED WARFARE

ANY ARMY is in danger of being conquered at the outset of a campaign, after a long peace; any army that has long been engaged in warfare has strong chances of victory: this truth is peculiarly applicable to democratic armies. In aristocracies the military profession, being a privileged career, is held in honor even in time of peace. Men of great talents, great attainments, and great ambition embrace it; the army is in all respects on a level with the nation, and frequently above it.

We have seen, on the contrary, that among a democratic people the choicer minds of the nation are gradually drawn away from the military profession, to seek by other paths distinction, power, and especially wealth. After a long peace, and in democratic times the periods of peace are long, the army is always inferior to the country itself. In this state it is called into active service, and until war has altered it, there is danger for the country as well as for the army.

I have shown that in democratic armies and in time of peace the rule of seniority is the supreme and inflexible law of promotion. This is a consequence, as I have before observed, not only of the constitution of these armies, but of the constitution of the people, and it will always occur.

Again, as among these nations the officer derives his position in the country solely from his position in the army, and as he draws all the distinction and the competency he enjoys from the same source, he does not retire from his profession, or is not superannuated, till very near the close of life. The consequence of these two causes is that when a democratic people goes to war after a long interval of peace, all the leading officers of the army are old men. I speak not only of the generals, but of the non-commissioned officers, who have most of them been stationary or have advanced only step by step. It may be remarked with surprise that in a democratic army after a long peace all the soldiers are mere boys, and all the superior officers in declining years, so that the former are wanting in experience, the latter in vigor. This is a leading cause of defeat, for the first condition of successful generalship is youth. I should not have ventured to say so if the greatest captain of modern times had not made the observation.

These two causes do not act in the same manner upon aristocratic armies: as men are promoted in them by right of birth much more than by right of seniority, there are in all ranks a certain number of young men who bring to their profession all the early vigor of body and mind. Again, as the men who seek for military honors among an aristocratic people enjoy a settled position in civil society, they seldom continue in the army until old age overtakes them. After having devoted the most vigorous years of youth to the career of arms, they voluntarily retire, and spend the remainder of their maturer years at home.

A long peace not only fills democratic armies with elderly officers, but also gives to all the officers habits of both body and mind which render them unfit for actual service. The man who has long lived amid the calm and lukewarm atmosphere of democratic conditions can at first ill adapt himself to the harder toils and sterner duties of warfare; and if he has not absolutely lost the taste for arms, at least he has assumed a mode of life that unfits him for conquest.

Among aristocratic nations the enjoyments of civil life exercise less influence on the manners of the army, because among those nations the aristocracy commands the army, and an aristocracy, however plunged in luxurious pleasures, has always many other passions besides that of its own well-being, and to satisfy those passions more thoroughly its well-being will be readily sacrificed.[1]

I have shown that in democratic armies in time of peace promotion is extremely slow. The officers at first support this state of things with impatience; they grow excited, restless, exasperated, but in the end most of them make up their

[1] See Appendix X.

minds to it. Those who have the largest share of ambition and of resources quit the army; others, adapting their tastes and their desires to their scanty fortunes, ultimately look upon the military profession in a civil point of view. The quality they value most in it is the competency and security that attend it; their whole notion of the future rests upon the certainty of this little provision, and all they require is peaceably to enjoy it. Thus not only does a long peace fill an army with old men, but it frequently imparts the views of old men to those who are still in the prime of life.

I have also shown that among democratic nations in time of peace the military profession is held in little honor and practiced with little spirit. This want of public favor is a heavy discouragement to the army; it weighs down the minds of the troops, and when war breaks out at last, they cannot immediately resume their spring and vigor. No similar cause of moral weakness exists in aristocratic armies: there the officers are never lowered, either in their own eyes or in those of their countrymen; because, independently of their military greatness, they are personally great. But even if the influence of peace operated on the two kinds of armies in the same manner, the results would still be different.

When the officers of an aristocratic army have lost their warlike spirit and the desire of raising themselves by service, they still retain a certain respect for the honor of their class and an old habit of being foremost to set an example. But when the officers of a democratic army have no longer the love of war and the ambition of arms, nothing whatever remains to them.

I am therefore of the opinion that when a democratic people engages in a war after a long peace, it incurs much more risk of defeat than any other nation; but it ought not easily to be cast down by its reverses, for the chances of success for such an army are increased by the duration of the war. When a war has at length, by its long continuance, roused the whole community from their peaceful occupations and ruined their minor undertakings, the same passions that made them attach so much importance to the maintenance of peace will be turned to arms. War, after it has destroyed all modes of speculation, becomes itself the great and sole speculation, to which all the ardent and ambitious desires that equality engenders are exclusively directed.

Hence it is that the selfsame democratic nations that are so reluctant to engage in hostilities sometimes perform prodigious achievements when once they have taken the field.

As the war attracts more and more of public attention and is seen to create high reputations and great fortunes in a short space of time, the choicest spirits of the nation enter the military profession; all the enterprising, proud, and martial minds, no longer solely of the aristocracy, but of the whole country, are drawn in this direction. As the number of competitors for military honors is immense, and war drives every man to his proper level, great generals are always sure to spring up. A long war produces upon a democratic army the same effects that a revolution produces upon a people; it breaks through regulations and allows extraordinary men to rise above the common level. Those officers whose bodies and minds have grown old in peace are removed or superannuated, or they die. In their stead a host of young men is pressing on, whose frames are already hardened, whose desires are extended and inflamed by active service. They are bent on advancement at all hazards, and perpetual advancement; they are followed by others with the same passions and desires, and after these are others, yet unlimited by aught but the size of the army. The principle of equality opens the door of ambition to all, and death provides chances for ambition. Death is constantly thinning the ranks, making vacancies, closing and opening the career of arms.

Moreover, there is a secret connection between the military character and the character of democracies, which war brings to light. The men of democracies naturally are passionately eager to acquire what they covet and to enjoy it on easy conditions. They for the most part worship chance and are much less afraid of death than of difficulty. This is the spirit that they bring to commerce and manufactures; and this same spirit, carried with them to the field of battle, induces them willingly to expose their lives in order to secure in a moment the rewards of victory. No kind of greatness is more pleasing to the imagination of a democratic people than military greatness, a greatness of vivid and sudden luster, obtained without toil, by nothing but the risk of life.

Thus while the interest and the tastes of the members of

a democratic community divert them from war, their habits of mind fit them for carrying on war well: they soon make good soldiers when they are aroused from their business and their enjoyments.

If peace is peculiarly hurtful to democratic armies, war secures to them advantages that no other armies ever possess; and these advantages, however little felt at first, cannot fail in the end to give them the victory. An aristocratic nation that in a contest with a democratic people does not succeed in ruining the latter at the outset of the war always runs a great risk of being conquered by it.

Chapter XXV

OF DISCIPLINE IN DEMOCRATIC ARMIES

IT IS a very common opinion, especially in aristocratic countries, that the great social equality which prevails in democracies ultimately renders the private soldier independent of the officer and thus destroys the bond of discipline. This is a mistake, for there are two kinds of discipline, which it is important not to confuse.

When the officer is noble and the soldier a serf, one rich, the other poor, the one educated and strong, the other ignorant and weak, the strictest bond of obedience may easily be established between the two men. The soldier is broken in to military discipline, as it were, before he enters the army; or rather military discipline is nothing but an enhancement of social servitude. In aristocratic armies the soldier will soon become insensible to everything but the orders of his superior officers; he acts without reflection, triumphs without enthusiasm, and dies without complaint. In this state, he is no longer a man, but he is still a most formidable animal trained for war.

A democratic people must despair of ever obtaining from soldiers that blind, minute, submissive, and invariable obedience which an aristocratic people may impose on them without difficulty. The state of society does not prepare them for it, and the nation might be in danger of losing its natural advantages if it sought artificially to acquire advantages of this particular kind. Among democratic communities military discipline ought not to attempt to annihilate the free action of the faculties; all that can be done by discipline is to direct it. The obedience thus inculcated is less exact, but it is more eager and more intelligent. It has its root in the will of him who obeys; it rests not only on his instinct, but on his reason; and consequently it will often spontaneously become more strict as danger requires. The discipline of an aristocratic army is apt to be relaxed in war, because that discipline is founded upon habits, and war disturbs those habits. The discipline of a democratic army, on the contrary, is strengthened in sight of the enemy, because every soldier then clearly perceives that he must be silent and obedient in order to conquer.

The nations that have performed the greatest warlike achievements knew no other discipline than that which I speak of. Among the ancients none were admitted into the armies but freemen and citizens, who differed but little from one another and were accustomed to treat each other as equals. In this respect it may be said that the armies of antiquity were democratic, although they came out of the bosom of aristocracy; the consequence was that in those armies a sort of fraternal familiarity prevailed between the officers and the men. Plutarch's lives of great commanders furnish convincing instances of the fact: the soldiers were in the constant habit of freely addressing their general, and the general listened to and answered whatever the soldiers had to say; they were kept in order by language and by example far more than by constraint or punishment; the general was as much their companion as their chief. I do not know whether the soldiers of Greece and Rome ever carried the minutiæ of military discipline to the same degree of perfection as the Russians have done, but this did not prevent Alexander from conquering Asia, and Rome the world.

Chapter XXVI

SOME CONSIDERATIONS ON WAR IN DEMOCRATIC COMMUNITIES

WHEN the principle of equality is spreading, not only among a single nation, but among several neighboring nations at the same time, as is now the case in Europe, the inhabitants of these different countries, notwithstanding the dissimilarity of language, of customs, and of laws, still resemble each other in their equal dread of war and their common love of peace.[1] It is in vain that ambition or anger puts arms in the hands of princes; they are appeased in spite of themselves by a species of general apathy and goodwill which makes the sword drop from their grasp, and wars become more rare.

As the spread of equality, taking place in several countries at once, simultaneously impels their various inhabitants to follow manufactures and commerce, not only do their tastes become similar, but their interests are so mixed and entangled with one another that no nation can inflict evils on other nations without those evils falling back upon itself; and all nations ultimately regard war as a calamity almost as severe to the conqueror as to the conquered.

Thus, on the one hand, it is extremely difficult in democratic times to draw nations into hostilities; but, on the other, it is almost impossible that any two of them should go to war without embroiling the rest. The interests of all are so interlaced, their opinions and their wants so much alike, that none can remain quiet when the others stir. Wars therefore become more rare, but when they break out, they spread over a larger field.

[1] It is scarcely necessary for me to observe that the dread of war displayed by the nations of Europe is not attributable solely to the progress made by the principle of equality among them. Independently of this permanent cause, several other accidental causes of great weight might be pointed out, and I may mention, before all the rest, the extreme lassitude that the wars of the Revolution and the Empire have left behind them.

Neighboring democratic nations not only become alike in some respects, but eventually grow to resemble each other in almost all.[2] This similitude of nations has consequences of great importance in relation to war.

If I inquire why it is that the Helvetic Confederacy made the greatest and most powerful nations of Europe tremble in the fifteenth century, while at the present day the power of that country is exactly proportioned to its population, I perceive that the Swiss have become like all the surrounding communities, and those surrounding communities like the Swiss; so that as numerical strength now forms the only difference between them, victory necessarily attends the largest army. Thus one of the consequences of the democratic revolution that is going on in Europe is to make nu-

[2] This is not only because these nations have the same social condition, but it arises from the very nature of that social condition, which leads men to imitate and identify themselves with each other.

When the members of a community are divided into castes and classes, they not only differ from one another, but have no taste and no desire to be alike; on the contrary, everyone endeavors, more and more, to keep his own opinions undisturbed, to retain his own peculiar habits, and to remain himself. The characteristics of individuals are very strongly marked.

When the state of society among a people is democratic—that is to say, when there are no longer any castes or classes in the community, and all its members are nearly equal in education and in property—the human mind follows the opposite direction. Men are much alike, and they are annoyed, as it were, by any deviation from that likeness; far from seeking to preserve their own distinguishing singularities, they endeavor to shake them off in order to identify themselves with the general mass of the people, which is the sole representative of right and of might to their eyes. The characteristics of individuals are nearly obliterated.

In the ages of aristocracy even those who are naturally alike strive to create imaginary differences between themselves; in the ages of democracy even those who are not alike seek nothing more than to become so and to copy each other, so strongly is the mind of every man always carried away by the general impulse of mankind.

Something of the same kind may be observed between nations: two nations having the same aristocratic social condition remain thoroughly distinct and extremely different, because the spirit of aristocracy is to retain strong individual characteristics; but if two neighboring nations have the same democratic social condition, they cannot fail to adopt similar opinions and manners, because the spirit of democracy tends to assimilate men to each other.

merical strength preponderate on all fields of battle and to constrain all small nations to incorporate themselves with large states, or at least to adopt the policy of the latter.

As numbers are the determining cause of victory, each people ought of course to strive by all the means in its power to bring the greatest possible number of men into the field. When it was possible to enlist a kind of troops superior to all others, such as the Swiss infantry or the French horse of the sixteenth century, it was not thought necessary to raise very large armies; but the case is altered when one soldier is as efficient as another.

The same cause that begets this new want also supplies means of satisfying it; for, as I have already observed, when men are all alike they are all weak, and the supreme power of the state is naturally much stronger among democratic nations than elsewhere. Hence, while these nations are desirous of enrolling the whole male population in the ranks of the army, they have the power of effecting this object; the consequence is that in democratic ages armies seem to grow larger in proportion as the love of war declines.

In the same ages, too, the manner of carrying on war is likewise altered by the same causes. Machiavelli observes, in *The Prince,* "that it is much more difficult to subdue a people who have a prince and his barons for their leaders than a nation that is commanded by a prince and his slaves." To avoid offense, let us read "public officials" for "slaves," and this important truth will be strictly applicable to our own time.

A great aristocratic people cannot either conquer its neighbors or be conquered by them without great difficulty. It cannot conquer them because all its forces can never be collected and held together for a considerable period; it cannot be conquered because an enemy meets at every step small centers of resistance, by which invasion is arrested. War against an aristocracy may be compared to war in a mountainous country; the defeated party has constant opportunities of rallying its forces to make a stand in a new position.

Exactly the reverse occurs among democratic nations: they easily bring their whole disposable force into the field, and when the nation is wealthy and populous it soon becomes victorious; but if it is ever conquered and its territory invaded, it has few resources at command; and if the enemy takes the capital, the nation is lost. This may very well be explained: as each member of the community is individually isolated and extremely powerless, no one of the whole body can either defend himself or present a rallying-point to others. Nothing is strong in a democratic country except the state; as the military strength of the state is destroyed by the destruction of the army, and its civil power paralyzed by the capture of the chief city, all that remains is only a multitude without strength or government, unable to resist the organized power by which it is assailed. I am aware that this danger may be lessened by the creation of local liberties, and consequently of local powers; but this remedy will always be insufficient. For after such a catastrophe not only is the population unable to carry on hostilities, but it may be apprehended that they will not be inclined to attempt it.

According to the law of nations adopted in civilized countries, the object of war is not to seize the property of private individuals, but simply to get possession of political power. The destruction of private property is only occasionally resorted to, for the purpose of attaining the latter object.

When an aristocratic country is invaded after the defeat of its army, the nobles, although they are at the same time the wealthiest members of the community, will continue to defend themselves individually rather than submit; for if the conqueror remained master of the country he would deprive them of their political power, to which they cling even more closely than to their property. They therefore prefer fighting to submission, which is to them the greatest of all misfortunes; and they readily carry the people along with them, because the people have long been used to follow and obey them, and besides have but little to risk in the war.

Among a nation in which equality of condition prevails, on the contrary, each citizen has but a slender share of political power, and often has no share at all. On the other hand, all are independent, and all have something to lose; so that they are much less afraid of being conquered and much more afraid of war than an aristocratic people. It will always be very difficult to convince a democratic people to take up arms when hostilities have reached its own territory. Hence the necessity of giving to such a people the rights and the political character which may impart to every citizen some of those interests that cause the nobles to act for the public welfare in aristocratic countries.

It should never be forgotten by the princes and other leaders of democratic nations that nothing but the love and the habit of freedom can maintain an advantageous contest with the love and the habit of physical well-being. I can conceive nothing better prepared for subjection, in case of defeat, than a democratic people without free institutions.

Formerly it was customary to take the field with a small body of troops, to fight in small engagements, and to make long regular sieges. Modern tactics consist in fighting decisive battles and, as soon as a line of march is open before the army, in rushing upon the capital city in order to terminate the war at a single blow. Napoleon, it is said, was the inventor of this new system; but the invention of such a system did not depend on any individual man, whoever he might be. The mode in which Napoleon carried on war was suggested to him by the state of society in his time; that mode was successful because it was eminently adapted to that state of society and because he was the first to employ it. Napoleon was the first commander who marched at the head of an army from capital to capital; but the road was opened for him by the ruin of feudal society. It may fairly be believed that if that extraordinary man had been born three hundred years ago, he would not have derived the same results from his method of warfare, or rather that he would have had a different method.

I shall add but a few words on civil wars, for fear of exhausting the patience of the reader. Most of the remarks that I have made respecting foreign wars was applicable *a fortiori* to civil wars. Men living in democracies have not naturally the military spirit; they sometimes acquire it when they have been dragged by compulsion to the field, but to rise in a body and voluntarily to expose themselves to the horrors of war, and especially of civil war, is a course that the men of democracies are not apt to adopt. None but the most adventurous members of the community consent to run into such risks; the bulk of the population remain motionless.

But even if the population were inclined to act, considerable obstacles would stand in their way; for they can resort to no old and well-established influence that they are willing to obey, no well-known leaders to rally the discontented, as well as to discipline and to lead them, no political powers subordinate to the supreme power of the nation which afford an effectual support to the resistance directed against the government.

In democratic countries the moral power of the majority is immense, and the physical resources that it has at its command are out of all proportion to the physical resources that may be combined against it. Therefore the party which occupies the seat of the majority, which speaks in its name and wields its power, triumphs instantaneously and irresistibly over all private resistance; it does not even give such opposition time to exist, but nips it in the bud.

Those who in such nations seek to effect a revolution by force of arms have no other resource than suddenly to seize upon the whole machinery of government as it stands, which can better be done by a single blow than by a war; for as soon as there is a regular war, the party that represents the state is always certain to conquer.

The only case in which a civil war could arise is if the army should divide itself into two factions, the one raising the standard of rebellion, the other remaining true to its allegiance. An army constitutes a small community, very closely knit together, endowed with great powers of vitality, and able to supply its own wants for some time. Such a war might be bloody, but it could not be long; for either the rebellious army would gain over the government by the sole display of its resources or by its first victory, and then the war would be over; or the struggle would take place, and then that portion of the army which was not supported by the organized powers of the state would speedily either disband itself or be destroyed. It may therefore be admitted as a general truth that in ages of equality civil wars will become much less frequent and less protracted.[3]

[3] It should be borne in mind that I speak here of sovereign and independent democratic nations, not of confederate democracies; in confederacies, as the preponderating power always resides, in spite of all political fictions, in the state governments and not in the federal government, civil wars are in fact nothing but foreign wars in disguise.

FOURTH BOOK

INFLUENCE OF DEMOCRATIC IDEAS AND FEELINGS ON POLITICAL SOCIETY

I SHOULD imperfectly fulfill the purpose of this book if, after having shown what ideas and feelings are suggested by the principle of equality, I did not point out, before I conclude, the general influence that these same ideas and feelings may exercise upon the government of human societies. To succeed in this object I shall frequently have to retrace my steps, but I trust the reader will not refuse to follow me through paths already known to him, which may lead to some new truth

Chapter I

EQUALITY NATURALLY GIVES MEN A TASTE FOR FREE INSTITUTIONS

THE PRINCIPLE of equality, which makes men independent of each other, gives them a habit and a taste for following in their private actions no other guide than their own will. This complete independence, which they constantly enjoy in regard to their equals and in the intercourse of private life, tends to make them look upon all authority with a jealous eye and speedily suggests to them the notion and the love of political freedom. Men living at such times have a natural bias towards free institutions. Take any one of them at a venture and search if you can his most deep-seated instincts, and you will find that, of all governments, he will soonest conceive and most highly value that government whose head he has himself elected and whose administration he may control.

Of all the political effects produced by the equality of conditions, this love of independence is the first to strike the observing and to alarm the timid; nor can it be said that their alarm is wholly misplaced, for anarchy has a more formidable aspect in democratic countries than elsewhere. As the citizens have no direct influence on each other, as soon as the supreme power of the nation fails, which kept them all in their several stations, it would seem that disorder must instantly reach its utmost pitch and that, every man drawing aside in a different direction, the fabric of society must at once crumble away.

I am convinced, however, that anarchy is not the principal evil that democratic ages have to fear, but the least. For the principle of equality begets two tendencies: the one leads men straight to independence and may suddenly drive them into anarchy; the other conducts them by a longer, more secret, but more certain road to servitude. Nations readily discern the former tendency and are prepared to resist it;

they are led away by the latter, without perceiving its drift; hence it is peculiarly important to point it out.

Personally, far from finding fault with equality because it inspires a spirit of independence, I praise it primarily for that every reason. I admire it because it lodges in the very depths of each man's mind and heart that indefinable feeling, the instinctive inclination for political independence, and thus prepares the remedy for the ill which it engenders. It is precisely for this reason that I cling to it.

Chapter II

THAT THE OPINIONS OF DEMOCRATIC NATIONS ABOUT GOVERNMENT ARE NATURALLY FAVORABLE TO THE CONCENTRATION OF POWER

THE NOTION of secondary powers placed between the sovereign and his subjects occurred naturally to the imagination of aristocratic nations, because those communities contained individuals or families raised above the common level and apparently destined to command by their birth, their education, and their wealth. This same notion is naturally wanting in the minds of men in democratic ages, for converse reasons; it can only be introduced artificially, it can only be kept there with difficulty, whereas they conceive, as it were without thinking about the subject, the notion of a single and central power which governs the whole community by its direct influence. Moreover, in politics as well as in philosophy and in religion the intellect of democratic nations is peculiarly open to simple and general notions. Complicated systems are repugnant to it, and its favorite conception is that of a great nation composed of citizens all formed upon one pattern and all governed by a single power.

The very next notion to that of a single and central power which presents itself to the minds of men in the ages of equality is the notion of uniformity of legislation. As every man sees that he differs but little from those about him, he cannot understand why a rule that is applicable to one man should not be equally applicable to all others. Hence the slightest privileges are repugnant to his reason; the faintest dissimilarities in the political institutions of the same people offend him, and uniformity of legislation appears to him to be the first condition of good government.

I find, on the contrary, that this notion of a uniform rule equally binding on all the members of the community was almost unknown to the human mind in aristocratic ages; either it was never broached, or it was rejected.

These contrary tendencies of opinion ultimately turn on both sides to such blind instincts and ungovernable habits that they still direct the actions of men, in spite of particular exceptions. Notwithstanding the immense variety of conditions in the Middle Ages, a certain number of persons existed at that period in precisely similar circumstances; but this did not prevent the laws then in force from assigning to each of them distinct duties and different rights. On the contrary, at the present time all the powers of government are exerted to impose the same customs and the same laws on populations which have as yet but few points of resemblance.

As the conditions of men become equal among a people, individuals seem of less and society of greater importance; or rather every citizen, being assimilated to all the rest, is lost in the crowd, and nothing stands conspicuous but the great and imposing image of the people at large. This naturally gives the men of democratic periods a lofty opinion of the privileges of society and a very humble notion of the rights of individuals; they are ready to admit that the interests of the former are everything and those of the latter nothing. They are willing to acknowledge that the power which represents the community has far more information and wisdom than any of the members of that community; and that it is the duty, as well as the right, of that power to guide as well as govern each private citizen.

If we closely scrutinize our contemporaries and penetrate to the root of their political opinions, we shall detect some of the notions that I have just pointed out, and we shall perhaps be surprised to find so much accordance between men who are so often at variance.

The Americans hold that in every state the supreme power ought to emanate from the people; but when once that power is constituted, they can conceive, as it were, no limits to it, and they are ready to admit that it has the right to do whatever it pleases. They have not the slightest notion of peculiar privileges granted to cities, families, or persons; their minds appear never to have foreseen that it might be possible not to apply with strict uniformity the same laws to every part of the state and to all its inhabitants.

These same opinions are more and more diffused in Europe; they even insinuate themselves among those nations that most vehemently reject the principle of the sovereignty of the people. Such nations assign a different origin to the supreme power, but they ascribe to that power the same characteristics. Among them all the idea of intermediate powers is weakened and obliterated; the idea of rights inherent in certain individuals is rapidly disappearing from the minds of men; the idea of the omnipotence and sole authority of society at large rises to fill its place. These ideas take root and spread in proportion as social conditions become more equal and men more alike. They are produced by equality, and in turn they hasten the progress of equality.

In France, where the revolution of which I am speaking has gone further than in any other European country, these opinions have got complete hold of the public mind. If we listen attentively to the language of the various parties in France, we find that there is not one which has not adopted them. Most of these parties censure the conduct of the government, but they all hold that the government ought perpetually to act and interfere in everything that is done. Even those which are most at variance are nevertheless agreed on this head. The unity, the ubiquity, the omnipotence of the supreme power, and the uniformity of its rules constitute the principal characteristics of all the political systems that have been put forward in our age. They recur even in the wildest visions of political regeneration; the human mind pursues them in its dreams.

If these notions spontaneously arise in the minds of private individuals, they suggest themselves still more forcibly to the minds of princes. While the ancient fabric of European society is altered and dissolved, sovereigns acquire new conceptions of their opportunities and their duties; they learn for the first time that the central power which they represent may and ought to administer, by its own agency and on a uniform plan, all the concerns of the whole community. This opinion, which, I will venture to say, was never conceived before our time by the monarchs of Europe, now sinks deeply into the minds of kings and abides there amid all the agitation of more unsettled thoughts.

Our contemporaries are therefore much less divided than is commonly supposed; they are constantly disputing as to the hands in which supremacy is to be vested, but they readily agree upon the duties and the rights of that supremacy. The notion they all form of government is that of a sole, simple, providential, and creative power.

All secondary opinions in politics are unsettled; this one remains fixed, invariable, and consistent. It is adopted by statesmen and political philosophers; it is eagerly laid hold of by the multitude; those who govern and those who are governed agree to pursue it with equal ardor; it is the earliest notion of their minds, it seems innate. It originates, therefore, in no caprice of the human intellect, but it is a necessary condition of the present state of mankind.[1]

[1] See Appendix Y.

Chapter III

THAT THE SENTIMENTS OF DEMOCRATIC NATIONS ACCORD WITH THEIR OPINIONS IN LEADING THEM TO CONCENTRATE POLITICAL POWER

IF IT IS true that in ages of equality men readily adopt the notion of a great central power, it cannot be doubted, on the other hand, that their habits and sentiments predispose them to recognize such a power and to give it their support. This may be demonstrated in a few words, as the greater part of the reasons to which the fact may be attributed have been previously stated.

As the men who inhabit democratic countries have no superiors, no inferiors, and no habitual or necessary partners in their undertakings, they readily fall back upon themselves and consider themselves as beings apart. I had occasion to point this out at considerable length in treating of individualism. Hence such men can never, without an effort, tear themselves from their private affairs to engage in public business; their natural bias leads them to abandon the latter to the sole visible and permanent representative of the interests of the community; that is to say, to the state. Not only are they naturally wanting in a taste for public business, but they have frequently no time to attend to it. Private life in democratic times is so busy, so excited, so full of wishes and of work, that hardly any energy or leisure remains to each individual for public life. I am the last man to contend that these propensities are unconquerable, since my chief object in writing this book has been to combat them. I maintain only that at the present day a secret power is fostering them in the human heart, and that if they are not checked, they will wholly overgrow it.

I have also had occasion to show how the increasing love of well-being and the fluctuating character of property cause democratic nations to dread all violent disturbances. The love of public tranquillity is frequently the only passion which these nations retain, and it becomes more active and powerful among them in proportion as all other passions droop and die. This naturally disposes the members of the community constantly to give or to surrender additional rights to the central power, which alone seems to be interested in defending them by the same means that it uses to defend itself.

As in periods of equality no man is compelled to lend his assistance to his fellow men, and none has any right to expect much support from them, everyone is at once independent and powerless. These two conditions, which must never be either separately considered or confounded together, inspire the citizen of a democratic country with very contrary propensities. His independence fills him with self-reliance and pride among his equals; his debility makes him feel from time to time the want of some outward assistance, which he cannot expect from any of them, because they are all impotent and unsympathizing. In this predicament he naturally turns his eyes to that imposing power which alone rises above the level of universal depression. Of that power his wants and especially his desires continually remind him, until he ultimately views it as the sole and necessary support of his own weakness.[1]

[1] In democratic communities nothing but the central power has any stability in its position or any permanence in its undertakings. All the citizens are in ceaseless stir and transformation. Now, it is in the nature of all governments to seek constantly to enlarge their sphere of action; hence it is almost impossible that such a government should not ultimately succeed, because it acts with a fixed principle and a constant will upon men whose position, ideas, and desires are constantly changing.

It frequently happens that the members of the community promote the influence of the central power without intending to. Democratic eras are periods of experiment, innovation, and adventure. There is always a multitude of men engaged in difficult or novel undertakings, which they follow by themselves without shackling themselves to their fellows. Such persons will admit, as a general principle, that the public authority ought not to interfere in private concerns; but, by an exception to that rule, each of them craves its assistance in the particular concern on which he is engaged and seeks to draw upon the influence of the government for his own benefit, although he would restrict it on all other occasions. If a large number of men applies this particular exception to a great variety of different purposes, the sphere of the central power extends

This may more completely explain what frequently takes place in democratic countries, where the very men who are so impatient of superiors patiently submit to a master, exhibiting at once their pride and their servility.

The hatred that men bear to privilege increases in proportion as privileges become fewer and less considerable, so that democratic passions would seem to burn most fiercely just when they have least fuel. I have already given the reason for this phenomenon. When all conditions are unequal, no inequality is so great as to offend the eye, whereas the slightest dissimilarity is odious in the midst of general uniformity; the more complete this uniformity is, the more insupportable the sight of such a difference becomes. Hence it is natural that the love of equality should constantly increase together with equality itself, and that it should grow by what it feeds on.

This never dying, ever kindling hatred which sets a democratic people against the smallest privileges is peculiarly favorable to the gradual concentration of all political rights in the hands of the representative of the state alone. The sovereign, being necessarily and incontestably above all the citizens, does not excite their envy, and each of them thinks that he strips his equals of the prerogative that he concedes to the crown. The man of a democratic age is extremely reluctant to obey his neighbor, who is his equal; he refuses to acknowledge superior ability in such a person; he mistrusts his justice and is jealous of his power; he fears and he despises him; and he loves continually to remind him of the common dependence in which both of them stand to the same master.

Every central power, which follows its natural tendencies, courts and encourages the principle of equality; for equality singularly facilitates, extends, and secures the influence of a central power.

In like manner it may be said that every central government worships uniformity; uniformity relieves it from inquiry

---

itself imperceptibly in all directions, although everyone wishes it to be circumscribed.

Thus a democratic government increases its power simply by the fact of its permanence. Time is on its side; every incident befriends it; the passions of individuals unconsciously promote it; and it may be asserted that the older a democratic community is, the more centralized will its government become.

into an infinity of details, which must be attended to if rules have to be adapted to different men, instead of indiscriminately subjecting all men to the same rule. Thus the government likes what the citizens like and naturally hates what they hate. These common sentiments, which in democratic nations constantly unite the sovereign and every member of the community in one and the same conviction, establish a secret and lasting sympathy between them. The faults of the government are pardoned for the sake of its inclinations; public confidence is only reluctantly withdrawn in the midst even of its excesses and its errors, and it is restored at the first call. Democratic nations often hate those in whose hands the central power is vested, but they always love that power itself.

Thus by two separate paths I have reached the same conclusion. I have shown that the principle of equality suggests to men the notion of a sole, uniform, and strong government; I have now shown that the principle of equality imparts to them a taste for it. To governments of this kind the nations of our age are therefore tending. They are drawn thither by the natural inclination of mind and heart; and in order to reach that result, it is enough that they do not check themselves in their course.

I am of the opinion that, in the democratic ages which are opening upon us, individual independence and local liberties will ever be the products of art; that centralization will be the natural government.[2]

[2] See Appendix Z.

Chapter IV

OF CERTAIN PECULIAR AND ACCIDENTAL CAUSES WHICH EITHER LEAD A PEOPLE TO COMPLETE THE CENTRALIZATION OF GOVERNMENT OR DIVERT THEM FROM IT

If all democratic nations are instinctively led to the centralization of government, they tend to this result in an unequal manner. This depends on the particular circumstances which may promote or prevent the natural consequences of that state of society, circumstances which are exceedingly numerous, but of which I shall mention only a few.

Among men who have lived free long before they became equal, the tendencies derived from free institutions combat, to a certain extent, the propensities superinduced by the principle of equality; and although the central power may increase its privileges among such a people, the private members of such a community will never entirely forfeit their independence. But when equality of conditions grows up among a people who have never known or have long ceased to know what freedom is (and such is the case on the continent of Europe), as the former habits of the nation are suddenly combined, by some sort of natural attraction, with the new habits and principles engendered by the state of society, all powers seem spontaneously to rush to the center. These powers accumulate there with astonishing rapidity, and the state instantly attains the utmost limits of its strength, while private persons allow themselves to sink as suddenly to the lowest degree of weakness.

The English who emigrated three hundred years ago to found a democratic commonwealth on the shores of the New World had all learned to take a part in public affairs in their mother country; they were conversant with trial by jury; they were accustomed to liberty of speech and of the press, to personal freedom, to the notion of rights and the practice of asserting them. They carried with them to America these free institutions and manly customs, and these institutions preserved them against the encroachments of the state. Thus among the Americans it is freedom that is old; equality is of comparatively modern date. The reverse is occurring in Europe, where equality, introduced by absolute power and under the rule of kings, was already infused into the habits of nations long before freedom had entered into their thoughts.

I have said that, among democratic nations the notion of government naturally presents itself to the mind under the form of a sole and central power, and that the notion of intermediate powers is not familiar to them. This is peculiarly applicable to the democratic nations which have witnessed the triumph of the principle of equality by means of a violent revolution. As the classes that managed local affairs have been suddenly swept away by the storm, and as the confused mass that remains has as yet neither the organization nor the habits which fit it to assume the administration of these affairs, the state alone seems capable of taking upon itself all the details of government, and centralization becomes, as it were, the unavoidable state of the country.

Napoleon deserves neither praise nor censure for having centered in his own hands almost all the administrative power of France; for after the abrupt disappearance of the nobility and the higher rank of the middle classes, these powers devolved on him of course: it would have been almost as difficult for him to reject as to assume them. But a similar necessity has never been felt by the Americans, who, having passed through no revolution, and having governed themselves from the first, never had to call upon the state to act for a time as their guardian. Thus the progress of centralization among a democratic people depends not only on the progress of equality, but on the manner in which this equality has been established.

At the commencement of a great democratic revolution, when hostilities have but just broken out between the different classes of society, the people endeavor to centralize the public administration in the hands of the government, in order to wrest the management of local affairs from the aristocracy. Towards the close of such a revolution, on the contrary, it is usually the conquered aristocracy that endeavors to make over the management of all affairs to the state, because such an aristocracy dreads the tyranny of a people that has become its equal and not infrequently its master. Thus it is not always the same class of the community that strives to increase the prerogative of the government; but as long as the democratic revolution lasts, there is always one class in the nation, powerful in numbers or in wealth, which is induced, by peculiar passions or interests, to centralize the public administration, independently of that hatred of being governed by one's neighbor which is a general and permanent feeling among democratic nations.

It may be remarked that at the present day the lower orders in England are striving with all their might to destroy local independence and to transfer the administration from all the points of the circumference to the center; whereas the higher classes are endeavoring to retain this administration within its ancient boundaries. I venture to predict that a time will come when the very reverse will happen.

These observations explain why the supreme power is always stronger, and private individuals weaker, among a democratic people that has passed through a long and arduous struggle to reach a state of equality than among a democratic community in which the citizens have been equal from the first. The example of the Americans completely demonstrates the fact. The inhabitants of the United States were never divided by any privileges; they have never known the mutual relation of master and inferior; and as they neither dread nor hate each other, they have never known the necessity of calling in the supreme power to manage their affairs. The lot of the Americans is singular: they have derived from the aristocracy of England the notion of private rights and the taste for local freedom; and they have been able to retain both because they have had no aristocracy to combat.

If education enables men at all times to defend their independence, this is most especially true in democratic times. When all men are alike, it is easy to found a sole and all-powerful government by the aid of mere instinct. But men require much intelligence, knowledge, and art to organize and to maintain secondary powers under similar circumstances and to create, amid the independence and individual weakness of the citizens, such free associations as may be able to struggle against tyranny without destroying public order.

Hence the concentration of power and the subjection of individuals will increase among democratic nations, not only in the same proportion as their equality, but in the same proportion as their ignorance. It is true that in ages of imperfect civilization the government is frequently as wanting in the knowledge required to impose a despotism upon the people as the people are wanting in the knowledge required to shake it off; but the effect is not the same on both sides. However rude a democratic people may be, the central power that rules them is never completely devoid of cultivation, because it readily draws to its own uses what little cultivation is to be found in the country, and, if necessary, may seek assistance elsewhere. Hence among a nation which is ignorant as well as democratic an amazing difference cannot fail speedily to arise between the intellectual capacity of the ruler and that of each of his subjects. This completes the easy concentration of all power in his hands: the administrative function of the state is perpetually extended because the state alone is competent to administer the affairs of the country.

Aristocratic nations, however unenlightened they may be, never afford the same spectacle, because in them instruction is nearly equally diffused between the monarch and the leading members of the community.

The Pasha who now rules in Egypt found the population of that country composed of men exceedingly ignorant and equal, and he has borrowed the science and ability of Europe to govern that people. As the personal attainments of the sovereign are thus combined with the ignorance and democratic weakness of his subjects, the utmost centralization has been established without impediment, and the Pasha has made the country his factory, and the inhabitants his workmen.

I think that extreme centralization of government ultimately enervates society and thus, after a length of time, weakens the government itself; but I do not deny that a centralized social power may be able to execute great undertakings with facility in a given time and on a particular point. This is more especially true of war, in which success depends much more on the means of transferring all the resources of a nation to one single point than on the extent of those resources. Hence it is chiefly in war that nations desire, and frequently need, to increase the powers of the central government. All men of military genius are fond of centralization, which increases their strength; and all men of centralizing genius are fond of war, which compels nations to combine all their powers in the hands of the government. Thus the democratic tendency that leads men unceasingly to multiply the privileges of the state and to circumscribe the rights of private persons is much more rapid and constant among those democratic nations that are exposed by their position to great and frequent wars than among all others.

I have shown how the dread of disturbance and the love of well-being insensibly lead democratic nations to increase the functions of central government as the only power which appears to be intrinsically sufficiently strong, enlightened, and secure to protect them from anarchy. I would now add that all the particular circumstances which tend to make the state of a democratic community agitated and precarious enhance this general propensity and lead private persons more and more to sacrifice their rights to their tranquillity.

A people is therefore never so disposed to increase the functions of central government as at the close of a long and bloody revolution, which, after having wrested property from the hands of its former possessors, has shaken all belief and filled the nation with fierce hatreds, conflicting interests, and contending factions. The love of public tranquillity becomes at such times an indiscriminate passion, and the members of the community are apt to conceive a most inordinate devotion to order.

I have already examined several of the incidents that may concur to promote the centralization of power, but the principal cause still remains to be noticed. The foremost of the incidental causes which may draw the management of all affairs into the hands of the ruler in democratic countries is the origin of that ruler himself and his own propensities. Men who live in the ages of equality are naturally fond of central power and are willing to extend its privileges; but if it happens that this same power faithfully represents their own interests and exactly copies their own inclinations, the confidence they place in it knows no bounds, and they think that whatever they bestow upon it is bestowed upon themselves.

The attraction of administrative powers to the center will always be less easy and less rapid under the reign of kings who are still in some way connected with the old aristocratic order than under new princes, the children of their own achievements, whose birth, prejudices, propensities, and habits appear to bind them indissolubly to the cause of equality. I do not mean that princes of aristocratic origin who live in democratic ages do not attempt to centralize; I believe they apply themselves as diligently as any others to that object. For them the sole advantages of equality lie in that direction; but their opportunities are less great, because the community, instead of volunteering compliance with their desires, frequently obey them with reluctance. In democratic communities the rule is that centralization must increase in proportion as the sovereign is less aristocratic.

When an ancient race of kings stands at the head of an aristocracy, as the natural prejudices of the sovereign perfectly accord with the natural prejudices of the nobility, the vices inherent in aristocratic communities have a free course and meet with no corrective. The reverse is the case when the scion of a feudal stock is placed at the head of a democratic people. The sovereign is constantly led, by his education, his habits, and his associations, to adopt sentiments suggested by the inequality of conditions, and the people tend as constantly, by their social condition, to those manners which are engendered by equality. At such times it often happens that the citizens seek to control the central power far less as a tyrannical than as an aristocratic power, and that they persist in the firm defense of their independence, not only because they would remain free, but especially because they are determined to remain equal.

A revolution that overthrows an ancient regal family in order to place new men at the head of a democratic people may temporarily weaken the central power; but however anarchical such a revolution may appear at first, we need not hesitate to predict that its final and certain consequence will be to extend and to secure the prerogatives of that power.

The foremost or indeed the sole condition required in

order to succeed in centralizing the supreme power in a democratic community is to love equality, or to get men to believe you love it. Thus the science of despotism, which was once so complex, is simplified, and reduced, as it were, to a single principle.

Chapter V

THAT AMONG THE EUROPEAN NATIONS OF OUR TIME THE SOVEREIGN POWER IS INCREASING, ALTHOUGH THE SOVEREIGNS ARE LESS STABLE

ON REFLECTING upon what has already been said, the reader will be startled and alarmed to find that in Europe everything seems to conduce to the indefinite extension of the prerogatives of government and to render every day private independence more weak, more subordinate, and more precarious.

The democratic nations of Europe have all the general and permanent tendencies which urge the Americans to the centralization of government, and they are moreover exposed to a number of secondary and incidental causes with which the Americans are unacquainted. It would seem as if every step they make towards equality brings them nearer to despotism.

And, indeed, if we only look around, we shall be convinced that such is the fact. During the aristocratic ages that preceded the present time, the sovereigns of Europe had been deprived of, or had relinquished, many of the rights inherent in their power. Not a hundred years ago, among the greater part of European nations, numerous private persons and corporations were sufficiently independent to administer justice, to raise and maintain troops, to levy taxes, and frequently even to make or interpret the law. The state has everywhere resumed to itself alone these natural attributes of sovereign power; in all matters of government the state tolerates no intermediate agent between itself and the people, and it directs them by itself in general affairs. I am far from blaming this concentration of power, I simply point it out.

At the same period a great number of secondary powers existed in Europe, which represented local interests and administered local affairs. Most of these local authorities have already disappeared; all are speedily tending to disappear or to fall into the most complete dependence. From one end of Europe to the other the privileges of the nobility, the liberties of cities, and the powers of provincial bodies are either destroyed or are upon the verge of destruction.

In the course of the last half-century Europe has endured many revolutions and counter-revolutions, which have agitated it in opposite directions; but all these perturbations resemble each other in one respect: they have all shaken or destroyed the secondary powers of government. The local privileges which the French did not abolish in the countries they conquered have finally succumbed to the policy of the princes who conquered the French. Those princes rejected all the innovations of the French Revolution except centralization; that is the only principle they consented to receive from such a source.

My object is to remark that all these various rights which have been successively wrested, in our time, from classes, guilds, and individuals have not served to raise new secondary powers on a more democratic basis, but have uniformly been concentrated in the hands of the sovereign. Everywhere the state acquires more and more direct control over the humblest members of the community and a more exclusive power of governing each of them in his smallest concerns.[1]

Almost all the charitable establishments of Europe were

[1] This gradual weakening of the individual in relation to society at large may be traced in a thousand things. I shall select from among these examples one derived from the law of wills.

In aristocracies it is common to profess the greatest reverence for the last wishes of a dying man. This feeling sometimes even became superstitious among the elder nations of Europe: the power of the state, far from interfering with the caprices of a dying man, gave full force to the very least of them and ensured to him a perpetual power.

When all the living men are weak, the will of the dead is less respected; it is circumscribed within a narrow range, beyond which it is annulled or checked by the supreme power of the laws. In the Middle Ages testamentary power had, so to speak, no limits; among the French at the present day a man cannot distribute his fortune among his children without the interference of the state; after having domineered over a man's whole life, the law insists upon regulating even his very last act.

formerly in the hands of private persons or of guilds; they are now almost all dependent on the supreme government, and in many countries are actually administered by that power. The state almost exclusively undertakes to supply bread to the hungry, assistance and shelter to the sick, work to the idle, and to act as the sole reliever of all kinds of misery.

Education, as well as charity, has become in most countries at the present day a national concern. The state receives, and often takes, the child from the arms of the mother to hand it over to official agents; the state undertakes to train the heart and to instruct the mind of each generation. Uniformity prevails in the courses of public instruction as in everything else; diversity as well as freedom is disappearing day by day.

Nor do I hesitate to affirm that among almost all the Christian nations of our days, Catholic as well as Protestant, religion is in danger of falling into the hands of the government. Not that rulers are over-jealous of the right of settling points of doctrine, but they get more and more hold upon the will of those by whom doctrines are expounded; they deprive the clergy of their property and pay them salaries; they divert to their own use the influence of the priesthood, they make them their own ministers, often their own servants, and by this alliance with religion they reach the inner depths of the soul of man.[2]

But this is as yet only one side of the picture. The authority of government has not only spread, as we have just seen, throughout the sphere of all existing powers, till that sphere can no longer contain it, but it goes further and invades the domain heretofore reserved to private independence. A multitude of actions which were formerly entirely beyond the control of the public administration have been subjected to that control in our time, and the number of them is constantly increasing.

[2] In proportion as the functions of the central power are augmented, the number of public officers by whom that power is represented must increase also. They form a nation within each nation; and as they share the stability of the government, they more and more fill up the place of an aristocracy.

In almost every part of Europe the government rules in two ways: it rules one portion of the citizens by the fear which they feel for its agents, and the other by the hope they have of becoming its agents.

Among aristocratic nations the supreme government usually contented itself with managing and superintending the community in whatever directly and ostensibly concerned the national honor, but in all other respects the people were left to work out their own free will. Among these nations the government often seemed to forget that there is a point at which the faults and the sufferings of private persons involved the general prosperity, and that to prevent the ruin of a private individual must sometimes be a matter of public importance.

The democratic nations of our time lean to the opposite extreme. It is evident that most of our rulers will not content themselves with governing the people collectively; it would seem as if they thought themselves responsible for the actions and private condition of their subjects, as if they had undertaken to guide and to instruct each of them in the various incidents of life and to secure their happiness quite independently of their own consent. On the other hand, private individuals grow more and more apt to look upon the supreme power in the same light; they invoke its assistance in all their necessities, and they fix their eyes upon the administration as their mentor or their guide.

I assert that there is no country in Europe in which the public administration has not become, not only more centralized, but more inquisitive and more minute; it everywhere interferes in private concerns more than it did; it regulates more undertakings, and undertakings of a lesser kind; and it gains a firmer footing every day about, above, and around all private persons, to assist, to advise, and to coerce them.

Formerly a sovereign lived upon the income of his lands or the revenue of his taxes; this is no longer the case now that his wants have increased as well as his power. Under the same circumstances that formerly compelled a prince to put on a new tax, he now has recourse to a loan. Thus the state gradually becomes the debtor of most of the wealthier members of the community and centralizes the largest amounts of capital in its own hands.

Small capital is drawn into its keeping by another method. As men are intermingled and conditions become more equal, the poor have more resources, more education, and more desires; they conceive the notion of bettering their condition, and this teaches them to save. These savings are daily producing an infinite number of small capitals, the slow and gradual produce of labor, which are always increasing. But the greater part of this money would be unproductive if it remained scattered in the hands of its owners. This circumstance has given rise to a philanthropic institution which will soon become, if I am not mistaken, one of our most important political institutions. Some charitable persons conceived the notion of collecting the savings of the poor and placing them out at interest. In some countries these benevolent associations are still completely distinct from the state; but in almost all they manifestly tend to identify themselves with the government; and in some of them, the government has superseded them, taking upon itself the enormous task of centralizing in one place, and putting out at interest, on its own responsibility, the daily savings of many millions of the working classes.

Thus the state draws to itself the wealth of the rich by loans and has the poor man's mite at its disposal in the savings banks. The wealth of the country is perpetually flowing around the government and passing through its hands; the accumulation increases in the same proportion as the equality of conditions; for in a democratic country the state alone inspires private individuals with confidence, because the state alone appears to be endowed with strength and durability.[3]

Thus the sovereign does not confine himself to the management of the public treasury; he interferes in private money matters; he is the superior, and often the master, of all the members of the community; and in addition to this he assumes the part of their steward and paymaster.

The central power not only fulfills of itself the whole of the duties formerly discharged by various authorities, extending those duties, and surpassing those authorities, but it performs them with more alertness, strength, and inde-

[3] On the one hand, the taste for worldly welfare is perpetually increasing; and, on the other, the government gets more and more complete possession of the sources of that welfare.

Thus men are following two separate roads to servitude; the taste for their own well-being withholds them from taking a part in the government, and their love of that well-being forces them to closer and closer dependence upon those who govern.

pendence than it displayed before. All the governments of Europe have, in our time, singularly improved the science of administration: they do more things, and they do everything with more order, more celerity, and at less expense; they seem to be constantly enriched by all the experience of which they have stripped private persons. From day to day, the princes of Europe hold their subordinate offices under stricter control and invent new methods for guiding them more closely and inspecting them with less trouble. Not content with managing everything by their agents, they undertake to manage the conduct of their agents in everything; so that the public administration not only depends upon one and the same power, but it is more and more confined to one spot and concentrated in the same hands. The government centralizes its agency while it increases its prerogative; hence a twofold increase of strength.

In examining the ancient constitution of the judicial power among most European nations, two things strike the mind: the independence of that power and the extent of its functions. Not only did the courts of justice decide almost all differences between private persons, but in very many cases they acted as arbiters between private persons and the state.

I do not here allude to the political and administrative functions that courts of judicature had usurped in some countries, but to the judicial duties common to them all. In most of the countries of Europe there were, and there still are, many private rights, connected for the most part with the general right of property, which stood under the protection of the courts of justice, and which the state could not violate without their sanction. It was this semi-political power that mainly distinguished the European courts of judicature from all others; for all nations have had judges, but all have not invested their judges with the same privileges.

Upon examining what is now occurring among the democratic nations of Europe that are called free, as well as among the others, it will be observed that new and more dependent courts are everywhere springing up by the side of the old ones, for the express purpose of deciding, by an extraordinary jurisdiction, such litigated matters as may rise between the government and private persons. The elder judicial power retains its independence, but its jurisdiction is narrowed; and there is a growing tendency to reduce it to be exclusively the arbiter between private interests.

The number of these special courts of justice is continually increasing, and their functions increase likewise. Thus the government is more and more absolved from the necessity of subjecting its policy and its rights to the sanction of another power. As judges cannot be dispensed with, at least the state is to select them and always to hold them under its control; so that between the government and private individuals they place the effigy of justice rather than justice itself. The state is not satisfied with drawing all concerns to itself, but it acquires an ever increasing power of deciding on them all, without restriction and without appeal.[4]

There exists among the modern nations of Europe one great cause, independent of all those which have already been pointed out, which perpetually contributes to extend the agency or to strengthen the prerogative of the supreme power, though it has not been sufficiently attended to: I mean the growth of manufactures, which is fostered by the progress of social equality. Manufacturers generally collect a multitude of men on the same spot, among whom new and complex relations spring up. These men are exposed by their calling to great and sudden alternations of plenty and want, during which public tranquillity is endangered. It may also happen that these employments sacrifice the health and even the life of those who gain by them or of those who live by them. Thus, the manufacturing classes require more regulation, superintendence, and restraint than the other classes of society, and it is natural that the powers of government should increase in the same proportion as those classes.

This is a truth of general application; what follows more especially concerns the nations of Europe. In the centuries which preceded that in which we live, the aristocracy was in possession of the soil, and was competent to defend it;

[4] A strange sophism has been uttered on this subject in France. When a suit arises between the government and a private person, it is not to be tried before an ordinary judge, in order, they say, not to mix the administrative and the judicial powers; as if it were not to confuse those powers and in the most dangerous and oppressive manner to invest the government with the office of judging and administering at the same time.

landed property was therefore surrounded by ample securities, and its possessors enjoyed great independence. This gave rise to laws and customs that have been perpetuated, notwithstanding the subdivision of lands and the ruin of the nobility; and at the present time landowners and agriculturists are still those among the community who most easily escape from the control of the supreme power.

In these same aristocratic ages, in which all the sources of our history are to be traced, personal property was of small importance and those who possessed it were despised and weak. The manufacturing class formed an exception in the midst of those aristocratic communities; as it had no certain patronage, it was not outwardly protected and was often unable to protect itself. Hence a habit sprang up of considering manufacturing property as something of a peculiar nature, not entitled to the same deference and not worthy of the same securities as property in general; and manufacturers were looked upon as a small class in the social hierarchy, whose independence was of small importance and who might with propriety be abandoned to the disciplinary passions of princes. On glancing over the codes of the Middle Ages, one is surprised to see, in those periods of personal independence, with what incessant royal regulations manufactures were hampered, even in their smallest details; on this point centralization was as active and as minute as it can ever be.

Since that time a great revolution has taken place in the world; manufacturing property, which was then only in the germ, has spread till it covers Europe: the manufacturing class has been multiplied and enriched by the remnants of all other ranks; it has grown and is still perpetually growing in number, in importance, in wealth. Almost all those who do not belong to it are connected with it at least on some one point; after having been an exception in society, it threatens to become the chief, if not the only class. Nevertheless, the notions and political habits created by it of old still continue. These notions and habits remain unchanged, because they are old, and also because they happen to be in perfect accordance with the new notions and general habits of our contemporaries.

Manufacturing property, then, does not extend its rights in the same ratio as its importance. The manufacturing classes do not become less dependent while they become more numerous, but, on the contrary, it would seem as if despotism lurked within them and naturally grew with their growth.[5]

As a nation becomes more engaged in manufactures, the lack of roads, canals, harbors, and other works of a semi-public nature, which facilitate the acquisition of wealth, is more strongly felt; and as a nation becomes more democratic, private individuals are less able, and the state more able, to execute works of such magnitude. I do not hesitate to assert that the manifest tendency of all governments at the present time is to take upon themselves alone the execution of these undertakings, by which means they daily hold in closer dependence the population which they govern.

On the other hand, in proportion as the power of a state increases and its necessities are augmented, the state consumption of manufactured produce is always growing larger; and these commodities are generally made in the arsenals or establishments of the government. Thus in every kingdom the ruler becomes the principal manufacturer: he collects and retains in his service a vast number of engineers, architects, mechanics, and handicraftsmen.

[5] I shall cite a few facts in support of this. Mines are the natural sources of manufacturing wealth; as manufactures have grown up in Europe, as the produce of mines has become of more general importance, and profitable mining more difficult because of the subdivision of property which is a consequence of the equality of conditions, most governments have asserted a right of owning the soil in which the mines lie, and of inspecting the works, which has never been the case with any other kind of property.

Thus mines, which were private property, subject to the same obligations and sheltered by the same guarantees as all other landed property, have fallen under the control of the state. The state either works them or leases them; their owners become mere tenants, deriving their rights from the state. Moreover, the state almost everywhere claims the power of directing their operations: it lays down rules, enforces the adoption of particular methods, subjects the miners to constant supervision, and, if refractory, they are ousted by a government court of justice, and the government transfers their contract to other hands; so that the government not only possesses the mines, but has all the men who work them in its power. Nevertheless, as industry increases, the working of old mines increases also; new ones are opened; the mining population expands and grows; day by day governments augment their subterranean dominions, and people them with their agents.

Not only is he the principal manufacturer, but he tends more and more to become the chief, or rather the master, of all other manufacturers. As private persons become powerless by becoming more equal, they can effect nothing in manufactures without combination; but the government naturally seeks to place these combinations under its own control.

It must be admitted that these collective beings, which are called companies, are stronger and more formidable than a private individual can ever be, and that they have less of the responsibility for their own actions; whence it seems reasonable that they should not be allowed to retain so great an independence of the supreme government as might be conceded to a private individual.

Rulers are the more apt to follow this line of policy as their own inclinations invite them to it. Among democratic nations it is only by association that the resistance of the people to the government can ever display itself; hence the latter always looks with ill favor on those associations which are not in its own power; and it is well worthy of remark that among democratic nations the people themselves often entertain against these very associations a secret feeling of fear and jealousy, which prevents the citizens from defending the institutions of which they stand so much in need. The power and the duration of these small private bodies in the midst of the weakness and instability of the whole community astonish and alarm the people, and the free use which each association makes of its natural powers is almost regarded as a dangerous privilege. All the associations that spring up in our age are, moreover, new corporate powers, whose rights have not been sanctioned by time; they come into existence at a time when the notion of private rights is weak and when the power of government is unbounded. Hence it is not surprising that they lose their freedom at their birth.

Among all European nations there are some kinds of associations or companies which cannot be formed until the state has examined their by-laws and authorized their existence. In several others attempts are made to extend this rule to all associations; the consequences of such a policy, if it were successful, may easily be foreseen.

If once the sovereign had a general right of authorizing

associations of all kinds upon certain conditions, he would not be long without claiming the right of superintending and managing them, in order to prevent them from departing from the rules laid down by himself. In this manner the state, after having reduced all who are desirous of forming associations into dependence, would proceed to reduce into the same condition all who belong to associations already formed; that is to say, almost all the men who are now in existence.

Governments thus appropriate to themselves and convert to their own purposes the greater part of this new power which manufacturing interests have in our time brought into the world. Manufactures govern us, they govern manufactures.

I attach so much importance to all that I have just been saying that I am tormented by the fear of having impaired my meaning in seeking to render it more clear. If the reader thinks that the examples I have adduced to support my observations are insufficient or ill-chosen, if he imagines that I have anywhere exaggerated the encroachments of the supreme power, and, on the other hand, that I have underrated the extent of the sphere which still remains open to the exertions of individual independence, I entreat him to lay down the book for a moment and to turn his mind to reflect upon the subjects I have attempted to explain. Let him attentively examine what is taking place in France and in other countries, let him inquire of those about him, let him search himself, and I am much mistaken if he does not arrive, without my guidance, and by other paths, at the point to which I have sought to lead him.

He will perceive that, for the last half-century, centralization has everywhere increased in a thousand different ways. Wars, revolutions, conquests, have served to promote it; all men have labored to increase it. In the course of the same period, during which men have succeeded one another with singular rapidity at the head of affairs, their notions, interests, and passions have been infinitely diversified; but all have, by some means or other, sought to centralize. This instinctive centralization has been the only settled point amid the extreme mutability of their lives and their thoughts.

If the reader, after having investigated these details of human affairs, will seek to survey the wide prospect as a whole, he will be struck by the result. On the one hand, the most settled dynasties shaken or overthrown; the people everywhere escaping by violence from the sway of their laws, abolishing or limiting the authority of their rulers or their princes; the nations which are not in open revolution restless at least, and excited, all of them animated by the same spirit of revolt; and, on the other hand, at this very period of anarchy, and among these untractable nations, the incessant increase of the prerogative of the supreme government, becoming more centralized, more adventurous, more absolute, more extensive, the people perpetually falling under the control of the public administration, led insensibly to surrender to it some further portion of their individual independence, till the very men who from time to time upset a throne and trample on a race of kings bend more and more obsequiously to the slightest dictate of a clerk. Thus in our days two contrary revolutions appear to be going on, the one continually weakening the supreme power, the other as continually strengthening it; at no other period in our history has it appeared so weak or so strong.

But upon a more attentive examination of the state of the world, it appears that these two revolutions are intimately connected together, that they originate in the same source, and that, after having followed a separate course, they lead men at last to the same result.

I may venture once more to repeat what I have already said or implied in several parts of this book: great care must be taken not to confound the principle of equality itself with the revolution which finally establishes that principle in the social condition and the laws of a nation. Here lies the reason for almost all the phenomena that occasion our astonishment.

All the old political powers of Europe, the greatest as well as the least, were founded in ages of aristocracy, and they more or less represented or defended the principles of inequality and of privilege. To make the novel wants and interests which the growing principle of equality introduced preponderate in government, our contemporaries had to overturn or to coerce the established powers. This led men to make revolutions and breathed into many of them that fierce love of disturbance and independence which all revolutions, whatever be their object, always engender.

I do not believe that there is a single country in Europe in which the progress of equality has not been preceded or followed by some violent changes in the state of property and persons; and almost all these changes have been attended with much anarchy and license, because they have been made by the least civilized portion of the nation against that which is most civilized.

Hence proceeded the twofold contrary tendencies that I have just pointed out. As long as the democratic revolution was glowing with heat, the men who were bent upon the destruction of old aristocratic powers hostile to that revolution displayed a strong spirit of independence; but as the victory of the principle of equality become more complete, they gradually surrendered themselves to the propensities natural to that condition of equality, and they strengthened and centralized their governments. They had sought to be free in order to make themselves equal; but in proportion as equality was more established by the aid of freedom, freedom itself was thereby rendered more difficult of attainment.

These two states of a nation have sometimes been contemporaneous: the last generation in France showed how a people might organize a stupendous tyranny in the community at the very time when they were baffling the authority of the nobility and braving the power of all kings, at once teaching the world the way to win freedom and the way to lose it.

In our days men see that constituted powers are crumbling down on every side; they see all ancient authority dying out, all ancient barriers tottering to their fall, and the judgment of the wisest is troubled at the sight: they attend only to the amazing revolution that is taking place before their eyes, and they imagine that mankind is about to fall into perpetual anarchy. If they looked to the final consequences of this revolution, their fears would perhaps assume a different shape. For myself, I confess that I put no trust in the spirit of freedom which appears to animate my contemporaries. I see well enough that the nations of this age are turbulent, but I do not clearly perceive that they are liberal; and I fear lest, at the close of those perturbations which rock the base of thrones, the dominion of sovereigns may prove more powerful than it ever was before.

Chapter VI

WHAT SORT OF DESPOTISM DEMOCRATIC NATIONS HAVE TO FEAR

I HAD remarked during my stay in the United States that a democratic state of society, similar to that of the Americans, might offer singular facilities for the establishment of despotism; and I perceived, upon my return to Europe, how much use had already been made, by most of our rulers, of the notions, the sentiments, and the wants created by this same social condition, for the purpose of extending the circle of their power. This led me to think that the nations of Christendom would perhaps eventually undergo some oppression like that which hung over several of the nations of the ancient world.

A more accurate examination of the subject, and five years of further meditation, have not diminished my fears, but have changed their object.

No sovereign ever lived in former ages so absolute or so powerful as to undertake to administer by his own agency, and without the assistance of intermediate powers, all the parts of a great empire; none ever attempted to subject all his subjects indiscriminately to strict uniformity of regulation and personally to tutor and direct every member of the community. The notion of such an undertaking never occurred to the human mind; and if any man had conceived it, the want of information, the imperfection of the administrative system, and, above all, the natural obstacles caused by the inequality of conditions would speedily have checked the execution of so vast a design.

When the Roman emperors were at the height of their power, the different nations of the empire still preserved usages and customs of great diversity; although they were subject to the same monarch, most of the provinces were separately administered; they abounded in powerful and active municipalities; and although the whole government of the empire was centered in the hands of the Emperor alone and he always remained, in case of need, the supreme arbiter in all matters, yet the details of social life and private occupations lay for the most part beyond his control. The emperors possessed, it is true, an immense and unchecked power, which allowed them to gratify all their whimsical tastes and to employ for that purpose the whole strength of the state. They frequently abused that power arbitrarily to deprive their subjects of property or of life; their tyranny was extremely onerous to the few, but it did not reach the many; it was confined to some few main objects and neglected the rest; it was violent, but its range was limited.

It would seem that if despotism were to be established among the democratic nations of our days, it might assume a different character; it would be more extensive and more mild; it would degrade men without tormenting them. I do not question that, in an age of instruction and equality like our own, sovereigns might more easily succeed in collecting all political power into their own hands and might interfere more habitually and decidedly with the circle of private interests than any sovereign of antiquity could ever do. But this same principle of equality which facilitates despotism tempers its rigor. We have seen how the customs of society become more humane and gentle in proportion as men become more equal and alike. When no member of the community has much power or much wealth, tyranny is, as it were, without opportunities and a field of action. As all fortunes are scanty, the passions of men are naturally circumscribed, their imagination limited, their pleasures simple. This universal moderation moderates the sovereign himself and checks within certain limits the inordinate stretch of his desires.

Independently of these reasons, drawn from the nature of the state of society itself, I might add many others arising from causes beyond my subject; but I shall keep within the limits I have laid down.

Democratic governments may become violent and even cruel at certain periods of extreme effervescence or of great danger, but these crises will be rare and brief. When I consider the petty passions of our contemporaries, the mildness of their manners, the extent of their education, the purity of their religion, the gentleness of their morality, their regular and industrious habits, and the restraint which they almost all observe in their vices no less than in their virtues, I have no fear that they will meet with tyranny in their rules, but rather with guardians.[1]

I think, then, that the species of oppression by which democratic nations are menaced is unlike anything that ever before existed in the world; our contemporaries will find no prototype of it in their memories. I seek in vain for an expression that will accurately convey the whole of the idea I have formed of it; the old words *despotism* and *tyranny* are inappropriate: the thing itself is new, and since I cannot name, I must attempt to define it.

I seek to trace the novel features under which despotism may appear in the world. The first thing that strikes the observation is an innumerable multitude of men, all equal and alike, incessantly endeavoring to procure the petty and paltry pleasures with which they glut their lives. Each of them, living apart, is as a stranger to the fate of all the rest; his children and his private friends constitute to him the whole of mankind. As for the rest of his fellow citizens, he is close to them, but does not see them; he touches them, but he does not feel them; he exists only in himself and for himself alone; and if his kindred still remain to him, he may be said at any rate to have lost his country.

Above this race of men stands an immense and tutelary power, which takes upon itself alone to secure their gratifications and to watch over their fate. That power is absolute, minute, regular, provident, and mild. It would be like the authority of a parent if, like that authority, its object was to prepare men for manhood; but it seeks, on the contrary, to keep them in perpetual childhood: it is well content that the people should rejoice, provided they think of nothing but rejoicing. For their happiness such a government willingly labors, but it chooses to be the sole agent and the only arbiter of that happiness; it provides for their security, foresees and supplies their necessities, facilitates their pleasures, manages their principal concerns, directs their industry, regulates the descent of property, and subdivides their inheritances: what remains, but to spare them all the care of thinking and all the trouble of living?

Thus it every day renders the exercise of the free agency

[1] See Appendix AA.

of man less useful and less frequent; it circumscribes the will within a narrower range and gradually robs a man of all the uses of himself. The principle of equality has prepared men for these things; it has predisposed men to endure them and often to look on them as benefits.

After having thus successively taken each member of the community in its powerful grasp and fashioned him at will, the supreme power then extends its arm over the whole community. It covers the surface of society with a network of small complicated rules, minute and uniform, through which the most original minds and the most energetic characters cannot penetrate, to rise above the crowd. The will of man is not shattered, but softened, bent, and guided; men are seldom forced by it to act, but they are constantly restrained from acting. Such a power does not destroy, but it prevents existence; it does not tyrannize, but it compresses, enervates, extinguishes, and stupefies a people, till each nation is reduced to nothing better than a flock of timid and industrious animals, of which the government is the shepherd.

I have always thought that servitude of the regular, quiet, and gentle kind which I have just described might be combined more easily than is commonly believed with some of the outward forms of freedom, and that it might even establish itself under the wing of the sovereignty of the people.

Our contemporaries are constantly excited by two conflicting passions: they want to be led, and they wish to remain free. As they cannot destroy either the one or the other of these contrary propensities, they strive to satisfy them both at once. They devise a sole, tutelary, and all-powerful form of government, but elected by the people. They combine the principle of centralization and that of popular sovereignty; this gives them a respite: they console themselves for being in tutelage by the reflection that they have chosen their own guardians. Every man allows himself to be put in leading-strings, because he sees that it is not a person or a class of persons, but the people at large who hold the end of his chain.

By this system the people shake off their state of dependence just long enough to select their master and then relapse into it again. A great many persons at the present day are quite contented with this sort of compromise between administrative despotism and the sovereignty of the people; and they think they have done enough for the protection of individual freedom when they have surrendered it to the power of the nation at large. This does not satisfy me: the nature of him I am to obey signifies less to me than the fact of extorted obedience.

I do not deny, however, that a constitution of this kind appears to me to be infinitely preferable to one which, after having concentrated all the powers of government, should vest them in the hands of an irresponsible person or body of persons. Of all the forms that democratic despotism could assume, the latter would assuredly be the worst.

When the sovereign is elective, or narrowly watched by a legislature which is really elective and independent, the oppression that he exercises over individuals is sometimes greater, but it is always less degrading; because every man, when he is oppressed and disarmed, may still imagine that, while he yields obedience, it is to himself he yields it, and that it is to one of his own inclinations that all the rest give way. In like manner, I can understand that when the sovereign represents the nation and is dependent upon the people, the rights and the power of which every citizen is deprived serve not only the head of the state, but the state itself; and that private persons derive some return from the sacrifice of their independence which they have made to the public. To create a representation of the people in every centralized country is, therefore, to diminish the evil that extreme centralization may produce, but not to get rid of it.

I admit that, by this means, room is left for the intervention of individuals in the more important affairs; but it is not the less supressed in the smaller and more privates ones. It must not be forgotten that it is especially dangerous to enslave men in the minor details of life. For my own part, I should be inclined to think freedom less necessary in great things than in little ones, if it were possible to be secure of the one without possessing the other.

Subjection in minor affairs breaks out every day and is felt by the whole community indiscriminately. It does not drive men to resistance, but it crosses them at every turn, till they are led to surrender the exercise of their own will. Thus their spirit is gradually broken and their character enervated; whereas that obedience which is exacted on a few important but rare occasions only exhibits servitude at certain intervals and throws the burden of it upon a small number of men. It is in vain to summon a people who have been rendered so dependent on the central power to choose from time to time the representatives of that power; this rare and brief exercise of their free choice, however important it may be, will not prevent them from gradually losing the faculties of thinking, feeling, and acting for themselves, and thus gradually falling below the level of humanity.

I add that they will soon become incapable of exercising the great and only privilege which remains to them. The democratic nations that have introduced freedom into their political constitution at the very time when they were augmenting the despotism of their administrative constitution have been led into strange paradoxes. To manage those minor affairs in which good sense is all that is wanted, the people are held to be unequal to the task; but when the government of the country is at stake, the people are invested with immense powers; they are alternately made the playthings of their ruler, and his masters, more than kings and less than men. After having exhausted all the different modes of election without finding one to suit their purpose, they are still amazed and still bent on seeking further; as if the evil they notice did not originate in the constitution of the country far more than in that of the electoral body.

It is indeed difficult to conceive how men who have entirely given up the habit of self-government should succeed in making a proper choice of those by whom they are to be governed; and no one will ever believe that a liberal, wise, and energetic government can spring from the suffrages of a subservient people.[2]

A constitution republican in its head and ultra-monarchical in all its other parts has always appeared to me to be a shortlived monster. The vices of rulers and the ineptitude of the people would speedily bring about its ruin; and the nation, weary of its representatives and of itself, would create freer institutions or soon return to stretch itself at the feet of a single master.

[2] See Appendix BB.

Chapter VII

CONTINUATION OF THE PRECEDING CHAPTERS

I BELIEVE that it is easier to establish an absolute and despotic government among a people in which the conditions of society are equal than among any other; and I think that if such a government were once established among such a people, it not only would oppress men, but would eventually strip each of them of several of the highest qualities of humanity. Despotism, therefore, appears to me peculiarly to be dreaded in democratic times. I should have loved freedom, I believe, at all times, but in the time in which we live I am ready to worship it.

On the other hand, I am persuaded that all who attempt, in the ages upon which we are entering, to base freedom upon aristocratic privilege will fail; that all who attempt to draw and to retain authority within a single class will fail. At the present day no ruler is skillful or strong enough to found a despotism by re-establishing permanent distinctions of rank among his subjects; no legislator is wise or powerful enough to preserve free institutions if he does not take equality for his first principle and his watchword. All of our contemporaries who would establish or secure the independence and the dignity of their fellow men must show themselves the friends of equality; and the only worthy means of showing themselves as such is to be so: upon this depends the success of their holy enterprise. Thus the question is not how to reconstruct aristocratic society, but how to make liberty proceed out of that democratic state of society in which God has placed us.

These two truths appear to me simple, clear, and fertile in consequences; and they naturally lead me to consider what kind of free government can be established among a people in which social conditions are equal.

It results from the very constitution of democratic nations

and from their necessities that the power of government among them must be more uniform, more centralized, more extensive, more searching, and more efficient than in other countries. Society at large is naturally stronger and more active, the individual more subordinate and weak; the former does more, the latter less; and this is inevitably the case.

It is not, therefore, to be expected that the range of private independence will ever be so extensive in democratic countries; nor is this to be desired; for among aristocratic nations the mass is often sacrificed to the individual, and the prosperity of the greater number to the greatness of the few. It is both necessary and desirable that the government of a democratic people should be active and powerful; and our object should not be to render it weak or indolent, but solely to prevent it from abusing its aptitude and its strength.

The circumstance which most contributed to secure the independence of private persons in aristocratic ages was that the supreme power did not affect to take upon itself alone the government and administration of the community. Those functions were necessarily partially left to the members of the aristocracy; so that, as the supreme power was always divided, it never weighed with its whole weight and in the same manner on each individual.

Not only did the government not perform everything by its immediate agency, but as most of the agents who discharged its duties derived their power, not from the state, but from the circumstance of their birth, they were not perpetually under its control. The government could not make or unmake them in an instant, at pleasure, or bend them in strict uniformity to its slightest caprice; this was an additional guarantee of private independence.

I readily admit that recourse cannot be had to the same means at the present time, but I discover certain democratic expedients that may be substituted for them. Instead of vesting in the government alone all the administrative powers of which guilds and nobles have been deprived, a portion of them may be entrusted to secondary public bodies temporarily composed of private citizens: thus the liberty of private persons will be more secure, and their equality will not be diminished.

The Americans, who care less for words than the French,

still designate by the name of County the largest of their administrative districts; but the duties of the count or lord-lieutenant are in part performed by a provincial assembly.

At a period of equality like our own, it would be unjust and unreasonable to institute hereditary officers; but there is nothing to prevent us from substituting elective public officers to a certain extent. Election is a democratic expedient, which ensures the independence of the public officer in relation to the government as much as hereditary rank can ensure it among aristocratic nations, and even more so.

Aristocratic countries abound in wealthy and influential persons who are competent to provide for themselves and who cannot be easily or secretly oppressed; such persons restrain a government within general habits of moderation and reserve. I am well aware that democratic countries contain no such persons naturally, but something analogous to them may be created by artificial means. I firmly believe that an aristocracy cannot again be founded in the world, but I think that private citizens, by combining together, may constitute bodies of great wealth, influence, and strength, corresponding to the persons of an aristocracy. By this means many of the greatest political advantages of aristocracy would be obtained without its injustice or its dangers. An association for political, commercial, or manufacturing purposes, or even for those of science and literature, is a powerful and enlightened member of the community, which cannot be disposed of at pleasure or oppressed without remonstrance, and which, by defending its own rights against the encroachments of the government, saves the common liberties of the country.

In periods of aristocracy every man is always bound so closely to many of his fellow citizens that he cannot be assailed without their coming to his assistance. In ages of equality every man naturally stands alone; he has no hereditary friends whose co-operation he may demand, no class upon whose sympathy he may rely; he is easily got rid of, and he is trampled on with impunity. At the present time an oppressed member of the community has therefore only one method of self-defense: he may appeal to the whole nation, and if the whole nation is deaf to his complaint, he may appeal to mankind. The only means he has of making this appeal is by the press. Thus the liberty of the press is infinitely more valuable among democratic nations than among all others; it is the only cure for the evils that equality may produce. Equality sets men apart and weakens them; but the press places a powerful weapon within every man's reach, which the weakest and loneliest of them all may use. Equality deprives a man of the support of his connections, but the press enables him to summon all his fellow countrymen and all his fellow men to his assistance. Printing has accelerated the progress of equality, and it is also one of its best correctives.

I think that men living in aristocracies may, strictly speaking, do without the liberty of the press; but such is not the case with those who live in democratic countries. To protect their personal independence I do not trust to great political assemblies, to parliamentary privilege, or to the assertion of popular sovereignty. All these things may, to a certain extent, be reconciled with personal servitude. But that servitude cannot be complete if the press is free; the press is the chief democratic instrument of freedom.

Something analogous may be said of the judicial power. It is a part of the essence of judicial power to attend to private interests and to fix itself with predilection on minute objects submitted to its observation. Another essential quality of judicial power is never to volunteer its assistance to the oppressed, but always to be at the disposal of the humblest of those who solicit it; their complaint, however feeble they may themselves be, will force itself upon the ear of justice and claim redress, for this is inherent in the very constitution of courts of justice.

A power of this kind is therefore peculiarly adapted to the wants of freedom, at a time when the eye and finger of the government are constantly intruding into the minutest details of human actions, and when private persons are at once too weak to protect themselves and too much isolated for them to reckon upon the assistance of their fellows. The strength of the courts of law has always been the greatest security that can be offered to personal independence; but this is more especially the case in democratic ages. Private rights and interests are in constant danger if the judicial power does not grow more extensive and stronger to keep pace with the growing equality of conditions.

Equality awakens in men several propensities extremely

dangerous to freedom, to which the attention of the legislator ought constantly be directed. I shall only remind the reader of the most important among them.

Men living in democratic ages do not readily comprehend the utility of forms: they feel an instinctive contempt for them, I have elsewhere shown for what reasons. Forms excite their contempt and often their hatred; as they commonly aspire to none but easy and present gratifications, they rush onwards to the object of their desires, and the slightest delay exasperates them. This same temper, carried with them into political life, renders them hostile to forms, which perpetually retard or arrest them in some of their projects.

Yet this objection which the men of democracies make to forms is the very thing which renders forms so useful to freedom; for their chief merit is to serve as a barrier between the strong and the weak, the ruler and the people, to retard the one and give the other time to look about him. Forms become more necessary in proportion as the government becomes more active and more powerful, while private persons are becoming more indolent and more feeble. Thus democratic nations naturally stand more in need of forms than other nations, and they naturally respect them less. This deserves most serious attention.

Nothing is more pitiful than the arrogant disdain of most of our contemporaries for questions of form, for the smallest questions of form have acquired in our time an importance which they never had before; many of the greatest interests of mankind depend upon them. I think that if the statesmen of aristocratic ages could sometimes despise forms with impunity and frequently rise above them, the statesmen to whom the government of nations is now confided ought to treat the very least among them with respect and not neglect them without imperious necessity. In aristocracies the observance of forms was superstitious; among us they ought to be kept up with a deliberate and enlightened deference.

Another tendency which is extremely natural to democratic nations and extremely dangerous is that which leads them to despise and undervalue the rights of private persons. The attachment that men feel to a right and the respect that they display for it are generally proportioned to its importance or to the length of time during which they have enjoyed it. The rights of private persons among democratic nations are commonly of small importance, of recent growth, and extremely precarious; the consequence is that they are often sacrificed without regret and almost always violated without remorse.

But it happens that, at the same period and among the same nations in which men conceive a natural contempt for the rights of private persons, the rights of society at large are naturally extended and consolidated; in other words, men become less attached to private rights just when it is most necessary to retain and defend what little remains of them. It is therefore most especially in the present democratic times, that the true friends of the liberty and the greatness of man ought constantly to be on the alert to prevent the power of government from lightly sacrificing the private rights of individuals to the general execution of its designs. At such times no citizen is so obscure that it is not very dangerous to allow him to be oppressed; no private rights are so unimportant that they can be surrendered with impunity to the caprices of a government. The reason is plain: if the private right of an individual is violated at a time when the human mind is fully impressed with the importance and the sanctity of such rights, the injury done is confined to the individual whose right is infringed; but to violate such a right at the present day is deeply to corrupt the manners of the nation and to put the whole community in jeopardy, because the very notion of this kind of right constantly tends among us to be impaired and lost.

There are certain habits, certain notions, and certain vices which are peculiar to a state of revolution and which a protracted revolution cannot fail to create and to propagate, whatever, in other respects, are its character, its purpose, and the scene on which it takes place. When any nation has, within a short space of time, repeatedly varied its rulers, its opinions, and its laws, the men of whom it is composed eventually contract a taste for change and grow accustomed to see all changes effected by sudden violence. Thus they naturally conceive a contempt for forms which daily prove ineffectual; and they do not support without impatience the dominion of rules which they have so often seen infringed.

As the ordinary notions of equity and morality no longer

suffice to explain and justify all the innovations daily begotten by a revolution, the principle of public utility is called in, the doctrine of political necessity is conjured up, and men accustom themselves to sacrifice private interests without scruple and to trample on the rights of individuals in order more speedily to accomplish any public purpose.

These habits and notions, which I shall call revolutionary because all revolutions produce them, occur in aristocracies just as much as among democratic nations; but among the former they are often less powerful and always less lasting, because there they meet with habits, notions, defects, and impediments that counteract them. They consequently disappear as soon as the revolution is terminated, and the nation reverts to its former political courses. This is not always the case in democratic countries, in which it is ever to be feared that revolutionary tendencies, becoming more gentle and more regular, without entirely disappearing from society, will be gradually transformed into habits of subjection to the administrative authority of the government. I know of no countries in which revolutions are more dangerous than in democratic countries, because, independently of the accidental and transient evils that must always attend them, they may always create some evils that are permanent and unending.

I believe that there are such things as justifiable resistance and legitimate rebellion; I do not therefore assert as an absolute proposition that the men of democratic ages ought never to make revolutions; but I think that they have especial reason to hesitate before they embark on them and that it is far better to endure many grievances in their present condition than to have recourse to so perilous a remedy.

I shall conclude with one general idea, which comprises not only all the particular ideas that have been expressed in the present chapter, but also most of those of which it is the object of this book to treat. In the ages of aristocracy which preceded our own, there were private persons of great power and a social authority of extreme weakness. The outline of society itself was not easily discernible and was constantly confounded with the different powers by which the community was ruled. The principal efforts of the men of those times were required to strengthen, aggrandize, and secure the supreme power; and, on the other hand, to circumscribe individual independence within narrower limits and to subject private interests to the interests of the public. Other perils and other cares await the men of our age. Among the greater part of modern nations the government, whatever may be its origin, its constitution, or its name, has become almost omnipotent, and private persons are falling more and more into the lowest stage of weakness and dependence.

In olden society everything was different; unity and uniformity were nowhere to be met with. In modern society everything threatens to become so much alike that the peculiar characteristics of each individual will soon be entirely lost in the general aspect of the world. Our forefathers were always prone to make an improper use of the notion that private rights ought to be respected; and we are naturally prone, on the other hand, to exaggerate the idea that the interest of a private individual ought always to bend to the interest of the many.

The political world is metamorphosed; new remedies must henceforth be sought for new disorders. To lay down extensive but distinct and settled limits to the action of the government; to confer certain rights on private persons, and to secure to them the undisputed enjoyment of those rights; to enable individual man to maintain whatever independence, strength, and original power he still possesses; to raise him by the side of society at large, and uphold him in that position; these appear to me the main objects of legislators in the ages upon which we are now entering.

It would seem as if the rulers of our time sought only to use men in order to make things great; I wish that they would try a little more to make great men; that they would set less value on the work and more upon the workman; that they would never forget that a nation cannot long remain strong when every man belonging to it is individually weak; and that no form or combination of social polity has yet been devised to make an energetic people out of a community of pusillanimous and enfeebled citizens.

I trace among our contemporaries two contrary notions which are equally injurious. One set of men can perceive nothing in the principle of equality but the anarchical tendencies that it engenders; they dread their own free agency, thev fear themselves. Other thinkers, less numerous but more enlightened, take a different view: beside that track which starts from the principle of equality to terminate in anarchy, they have at last discovered the road that seems to lead men to inevitable servitude. They shape their souls beforehand to this necessary condition; and, despairing of remaining free, they already do obeisance in their hearts to the master who is soon to appear. The former abandon freedom because they think it dangerous; the latter, because they hold it to be impossible.

If I had entertained the latter conviction, I should not have written this book, but I should have confined myself to deploring in secret the destiny of mankind. I have sought to point out the dangers to which the principle of equality exposes the independence of man, because I firmly believe that these dangers are the most formidable as well as the least foreseen of all those which futurity holds in store, but I do not think that they are insurmountable.

The men who live in the democratic ages upon which we are entering have naturally a taste for independence; they are naturally impatient of regulation, and they are wearied by the permanence even of the condition they themselves prefer. They are fond of power, but they are prone to despise and hate those who wield it, and they easily elude its grasp by their own mobility and insignificance.

These propensities will always manifest themselves, because they originate in the groundwork of society, which will undergo no change; for a long time they will prevent the establishment of any despotism, and they will furnish fresh weapons to each succeeding generation that struggles in favor of the liberty of mankind. Let us, then, look forward to the future with that salutary fear which makes men keep watch and ward for freedom, not with that faint and idle terror which depresses and enervates the heart.

Chapter VIII

GENERAL SURVEY OF THE SUBJECT

BEFORE finally closing the subject that I have now discussed, I should like to take a parting survey of all the different characteristics of modern society and appreciate at last the general influence to be exercised by the principle of equality upon the fate of mankind; but I am stopped by the difficulty of the task, and, in presence of so great a theme, my sight is troubled and my reason fails.

The society of the modern world, which I have sought to delineate and which I seek to judge, has but just come into existence. Time has not yet shaped it into perfect form; the great revolution by which it has been created is not yet over; and amid the occurrences of our time it is almost impossible to discern what will pass away with the revolution itself and what will survive its close. The world that is rising into existence is still half encumbered by the remains of the world that is waning into decay; and amid the vast perplexity of human affairs none can say how much of ancient institutions and former customs will remain or how much will completely disappear.

Although the revolution that is taking place in the social condition, the laws, the opinions, and the feelings of men is still very far from being terminated, yet its results already admit of no comparison with anything that the world has ever before witnessed. I go back from age to age up to the remotest antiquity, but I find no parallel to what is occurring before my eyes; as the past has ceased to throw its light upon the future, the mind of man wanders in obscurity.

Nevertheless, in the midst of a prospect so wide, so novel, and so confused, some of the more prominent characteristics may already be discerned and pointed out. The good things and the evils of life are more equally distributed in the world: great wealth tends to disappear, the number of small fortunes to increase; desires and gratifications are multiplied, but extraordinary prosperity and irremediable penury are alike unknown. The sentiment of ambition is universal, but the scope of ambition is seldom vast. Each individual stands apart in solitary weakness, but society at large is active, provident, and powerful; the performances of private persons are insignificant, those of the state immense.

There is little energy of character, but customs are mild and laws humane. If there are few instances of exalted heroism or of virtues of the highest, brightest, and purest temper, men's habits are regular, violence is rare, and cruelty almost unknown. Human existence becomes longer and property more secure; life is not adorned with brilliant trophies, but it is extremely easy and tranquil. Few pleasures are either very refined or very coarse, and highly polished manners are as uncommon as great brutality of tastes. Neither men of great learning nor extremely ignorant communities are to be met with; genius becomes more rare, information more diffused. The human mind is impelled by the small efforts of all mankind combined together, not by the strenuous activity of a few men. There is less perfection, but more abundance, in all the productions of the arts. The ties of race, of rank, and of country are relaxed; the great bond of humanity is strengthened.

If I endeavor to find out the most general and most prominent of all these different characteristics, I perceive that what is taking place in men's fortunes manifests itself under a thousand other forms. Almost all extremes are softened or blunted: all that was most prominent is superseded by some middle term, at once less lofty and less low, less brilliant and less obscure, than what before existed in the world.

When I survey this countless multitude of beings, shaped in each other's likeness, amid whom nothing rises and nothing falls, the sight of such universal uniformity saddens and chills me and I am tempted to regret that state of society which has ceased to be. When the world was full of men of great importance and extreme insignificance, of great wealth and extreme poverty, of great learning and extreme ignorance, I turned aside from the latter to fix my observation on the former alone, who gratified my sympathies. But I admit that this gratification arose from my own weakness; it is because I am unable to see at once all that is around me that I am allowed thus to select and separate the objects of my predilection from among so many others. Such is not the case with that Almighty and Eternal Being whose gaze necessarily includes the whole of created things and who surveys distinctly, though all at once, mankind and man.

We may naturally believe that it is not the singular prosperity of the few, but the greater well-being of all that is most pleasing in the sight of the Creator and Preserver of men. What appears to me to be man's decline is, to His eye, advancement; what afflicts me is acceptable to Him. A state of equality is perhaps less elevated, but it is more just: and its justice constitutes its greatness and its beauty. I would strive, then, to raise myself to this point of the divine contemplation and thence to view and to judge the concerns of men.

No man on the earth can as yet affirm, absolutely and generally, that the new state of the world is better than its former one; but it is already easy to perceive that this state is different. Some vices and some virtues were so inherent in the constitution of an aristocratic nation and are so opposite to the character of a modern people that they can never be infused into it; some good tendencies and some bad propensities which were unknown to the former are natural to the latter; some ideas suggest themselves spontaneously to the imagination of the one which are utterly repugnant to the mind of the other. They are like two distinct orders of human beings, each of which has its own merits and defects, its own advantages and its own evils. Care must therefore be taken not to judge the state of society that is now coming into existence by notions derived from a state of society that no longer exists; for as these states of society are exceedingly different in their structure, they cannot be submitted to a just or fair comparison. It would be scarcely more reasonable to require of our contemporaries the peculiar virtues which originated in the social condition of their forefathers, since that social condition is itself fallen and has drawn into one promiscuous ruin the good and evil that belonged to it.

But as yet these things are imperfectly understood. I find that a great number of my contemporaries undertake to make a selection from among the institutions, the opinions, and the ideas that originated in the aristocratic constitution of society as it was; a portion of these elements they would willingly relinquish, but they would keep the remainder and transplant them into their new world. I fear that such men are wasting their time and their strength in virtuous but unprofitable efforts. The object is, not to retain the peculiar advantages which the inequality of conditions bestows upon mankind, but to secure the new benefits which equality may supply. We have not to seek to make ourselves like our progenitors but to strive to work out that species of greatness and happiness which is our own.

For myself, who now look back from this extreme limit of my task and discover from afar, but at once, the various objects which have attracted my more attentive investigation upon my way, I am full of apprehensions and of hopes. I perceive mighty dangers which it is possible to ward off, mighty evils which may be avoided or alleviated; and I cling with a firmer hold to the belief that for democratic nations to be virtuous and prosperous, they require but to will it.

I am aware that many of my contemporaries maintain that nations are never their own masters here below, and that they necessarily obey some insurmountable and unintelligent power, arising from anterior events, from their race, or from the soil and climate of their country. Such principles are false and cowardly; such principles can never produce aught but feeble men and pusillanimous nations. Providence has not created mankind entirely independent or entirely free. It is true that around every man a fatal circle is traced beyond which he cannot pass; but within the wide verge of that circle he is powerful and free; as it is with man, so with communities. The nations of our time cannot prevent the conditions of men from becoming equal, but it depends upon themselves whether the principle of equality is to lead them to servitude or freedom, to knowledge or barbarism, to prosperity or wretchedness.

Appendix I

Appendix A.—Vol. I, p. 21

For information concerning all the countries of the West which have not yet been visited by Europeans, consult the account of two expeditions undertaken at the expense of Congress by Major Long. This traveler particularly mentions, on the subject of the great American desert, that a line may be drawn nearly parallel to the 20th degree of longitude (meridian of Washington),[1] beginning from the Red River and ending at the River Platte. From this imaginary line to the Rocky Mountains, which bound the valley of the Mississippi on the west, lie immense plains, which are generally covered with sand incapable of cultivation, or scattered over with masses of granite. In summer these plains are destitute of water, and nothing is to be seen on them but herds of buffaloes and wild horses. Some tribes of Indians are also found there, but in no great numbers.

Major Long was told that in traveling northwards from the River Platte you find the same desert lying constantly on the left; but he was unable to ascertain the truth of this report. (Long's *Expedition*, Vol. II, p. 361.)

However worthy of confidence may be the narrative of Major Long, it must be remembered that he passed through only the country of which he speaks, without deviating widely from the line which he had traced out for his journey.

Appendix B.—Vol. I, p. 22

South America, in the regions between the tropics, produces an incredible profusion of climbing plants, of which the flora of the Antilles alone furnishes forty different species.

Among the most graceful of these shrubs is the passion-flower which, according to Descourtiz, climbs trees by means

[1] The 20th degree of longitude, meridian of Washington, corresponds to about 99° of the meridian of Paris.

of the tendrils with which it is provided, and forms moving bowers of rich and elegant festoons, decorated with blue and purple flowers, and fragrant with perfume. (Vol. I, p. 265.)

The *Acacia à grandes gousses* is a creeper of enormous and rapid growth, which climbs from tree to tree and sometimes covers more than half a league. (Vol. III, p. 227.)

APPENDIX C.—Vol. I, p. 23

The languages that are spoken by the Indians of America, from the Pole to Cape Horn, are said to be all formed on the same model and subject to the same grammatical rules; whence it may fairly be concluded that all the Indian nations sprang from the same stock.

Each tribe of the American continent speaks a different dialect; but the number of languages, properly so called, is very small, a fact which tends to prove that the nations of the New World had not a very remote origin.

Moreover, the languages of America have a great degree of regularity, from which it seems probable that the tribes which employ them had not undergone any great revolutions or been incorporated, voluntarily or by constraint, into foreign nations; for it is generally the union of several languages into one that produces grammatical irregularities.

It is not long since the American languages, especially those of the North, first attracted the serious attention of philologists. When they were carefully studied, the discovery was made that this idiom of a barbarous people was the product of a very complicated system of ideas and of exceedingly well-conceived systems. These languages were found to be very rich, and great pains had been taken at their formation to render them agreeable to the ear.

The grammatical system of the Americans differs from all others in several points, but especially in the following:

Some nations of Europe, among others the Germans, have the power of combining at pleasure different expressions, and thus giving a complex sense to certain words. The Indians have given a most surprising extension to this power, so as to connect a great number of ideas with a single term. This will be easily understood with the help of an example quoted by Mr. Duponceau, in the *Memoirs of the American Philosophical Society.*

"A Delaware woman playing with a cat or a young dog," says this writer, "is heard to pronounce the word *kuligatschis,* which is composed thus: *k* is the sign of the second person, and signifies 'thou' or 'thy'; *uli* (pronounced *ouli*) is a part of the word *wulit,* which signifies 'beautiful,' 'pretty'; *gat* is another fragment of the word *wichgat,* which means 'paw'; and, lastly, *schis* (pronounced *chise*) is a diminutive giving the idea of smallness. Thus, in one word, the Indian woman has expressed 'Thy pretty little paw.' "

Take another example of the felicity with which the savages of America have composed their words. A young man, in the Delaware tongue, is called *pilapé.* This word is formed from *pilsit,* chaste, innocent; and *lenapé,* man; hence man in his purity and innocence.

This facility of combining words is most remarkable in the strange formation of their verbs. The most complex action is often expressed by a single verb, which serves to convey all the shades of an idea by the modification of its construction.

Those who may wish to examine more in detail this subject, which I have only glanced at superficially, should read:

1. "The Correspondence of Mr. Duponceau and the Rev. Mr. Heckewelder [*sic,* Bowen] relative to the Indian languages," found in Volume I of the *Memoirs of the American Philosophical Society,* published at Philadelphia, by Abraham Small, 1819, pp. 356–464.

2. The grammar of the Delaware or Lenape language by Geiberger, and its preface by Mr. Duponceau. All these are in the same collection, Vol. III.

3. An excellent account of these works, which is at the end of Volume VI of the *American Encyclopædia.*

APPENDIX D.—Vol. I, p. 25

See, in Charlevoix, Vol. I, p. 235, the history of the first war which the French inhabitants of Canada carried on, in 1610, against the Iroquois. The latter, armed with bows and arrows, offered a desperate resistance to the French and their allies. Charlevoix is not a great painter, yet he exhibits clearly enough in this narrative the contrast between the European manners and those of savages, as well as the different sense which the two races had of honor.

"When the French," says he, "seized upon the beaver-skins which covered the Indians who had fallen, the Hurons, their allies, were greatly offended at this proceeding; but they set to work in their usual manner, inflicting horrid cruelties upon the prisoners, and devouring one of those who had been killed, which made the Frenchmen shudder. Thus the barbarians prided themselves upon a disinterestedness which they were surprised at not finding in our nation, and could not understand that there was less to reprehend in stripping dead bodies than in devouring their flesh like wild beasts."

Charlevoix, in another place (Vol. I, p. 230), thus describes the first torture of which Champlain was an eyewitness, and the return of the Hurons into their own village.

"Having proceeded eight leagues," says he, "our allies halted; and having singled out one of their captives, they reproached him with all the cruelties that he had practised upon the warriors of their nation who had fallen into his hands, and told him that he might expect to be treated in like manner, adding that if he had any spirit, he would prove it by singing. He thereupon chanted his war-song, and all the songs he knew, but in a very mournful strain," says Champlain, who was not then aware that all savage music has a melancholy character. "The tortures which succeeded, accompanied by all the horrors which we shall mention hereafter, terrified the French, who made every effort to put a stop to them, but in vain. The following night, one of the Hurons having dreamt that they were pursued, the retreat was changed to a real flight, and the savages never stopped until they were out of the reach of danger.

"The moment they perceived the huts of their own village, they cut themselves long sticks, to which they fastened the scalps which had fallen to their share, and carried them in triumph. At this sight, the women swam to the canoes, where they took the bloody scalps from the hands of their husbands and tied them round their necks.

"The warriors offered one of these horrible trophies to Champlain; they also presented him with some bows and arrows, the only spoils of the Iroquois which they had ventured to seize, entreating him to show them to the King of France."

Champlain lived a whole winter quite alone among these barbarians, without being under any alarm for his person or property.

Appendix E.—Vol. I, p. 41

Although the puritanical strictness which presided over the establishment of the English colonies in America is now much relaxed, remarkable traces of it are still found in their habits and laws. In 1792, at the very time when the antichristian republic of France began its ephemeral existence, the legislative body of Massachusetts promulgated the following law, to compel the citizens to observe the Sabbath. I give the preamble and a few articles of this law, which is worthy of the reader's attention.

"Whereas," says the legislator, "the observation of the Sabbath is an affair of public interest; inasmuch as it produces a necessary suspension of labor, leads men to reflect upon the duties of life and the errors to which human nature is liable, and provides for the public and private worship of God, the Creator and Governor of the universe, and for the performance of such acts of charity as are the ornament and comfort of Christian societies;

"Whereas irreligious or light-minded persons, forgetting the duties which the Sabbath imposes, and the benefits which these duties confer on society, are known to profane its sanctity, by following their pleasures or their affairs; this way of acting being contrary to their own interest as Christians, and calculated to annoy those who do not follow their example; being also of great injury to society at large, by spreading a taste for dissipation and dissolute manners;

"Be it enacted and ordained by the Governor, Council, and Representatives convened in General Court of Assembly, that:

"1. No one will be permitted on Sunday to keep his store or workshop open. No one will be permitted on that day to look after any business, to go to a concert, dance, or show of any sort, or to engage in any kind of hunting, game, recreation, without penalty of fine. The fine will not be less than 10 nor exceed 20 shillings for each infraction.

"2. No traveller, conductor, or driver shall be allowed to travel on Sunday unless necessary, under the same penalty.

"3. Tavernkeepers, storekeepers, and innkeepers will prevent anyone living in their district from coming to pass the time there for pleasure or business. The innkeeper and his guest will pay a fine in case of disobedience. Furthermore, the innkeeper may lose his license.

"4. Those who, being in good health, without sufficient reason, fail to worship God publicly for three months, shall be fined 10 shillings.

"5. Those who behave improperly within the precincts of a church shall pay from 5 to 40 shillings fine.

"6. The tything men of the township are charged with the execution of the law.[1] They have the right to visit on Sunday all the rooms of hotels or public places. The innkeeper who refuses them admission will be fined 40 shillings.

"The tything men may stop travellers and ask their reasons for travelling on Sunday. Those who refuse to answer will be fined 5 pounds stirling.

"If the reason given by the traveller does not seem sufficient to the tything men, he may prosecute said traveller before the district justice of the peace." Law of March 8, 1792; *General Laws of Massachusetts,* Vol. I, p. 410.

On the 11th of March 1797 a new law increased the amount of fines, half of which was to be given to the informer (same collection, Vol. I, p. 525).

On the 16th of February 1816 a new law confirmed these same measures (same collection, Vol. II, p. 405).

Similar enactments exist in the laws of the state of New York, revised in 1827 and 1828 (see *Revised Statutes,* Part I, Chap. XX, p. 675). In these it is declared that no one is allowed on the Sabbath to hunt, to fish, to play at games, or to frequent houses where liquor is sold. No one can travel, except in case of necessity.

[1] These are officers, elected annually, who according to their functions resemble both the warden and the officer attached to the police magistrate in France.

And this is not the only trace which the religious strictness and austere manners of the first emigrants have left behind them in the American laws.

In the *Revised Statutes of the State of New York,* Vol. I, p. 662, is the following clause:

"Whoever shall win or lose in the space of twenty-four hours, by gaming or betting, the sum of twenty-five dollars (about 132 francs), shall be found guilty of a misdemeanor, and, upon conviction, shall be condemned to pay a fine equal to at least five times the value of the sum lost or won; which shall be paid to the inspector of the poor of the township. He that loses twenty-five dollars or more may bring an action to recover them; and if he neglects to do so, the inspector of the poor may prosecute the winner, and oblige him to pay into the poor's box both the sum he has gained and three times as much besides."

The laws I quote are of recent date, but they are unintelligible without going back to the very origin of the colonies. I have no doubt that in our days the penal part of these laws is very rarely applied. Laws preserve their inflexibility long after the customs of a nation have yielded to the influence of progress. It is still true, however, that nothing strikes a foreigner on his arrival in America more forcibly than the regard paid to the Sabbath.

There is one, in particular, of the large American cities in which all social movement begins to be suspended even on Saturday evening. You traverse its streets at the hour when you expect men in the middle of life to be engaged in business, and young people in pleasure; and you meet with solitude and silence. Not only have all ceased to work, but they appear to have ceased to exist. You can hear neither the movements of industry, nor the accents of joy, nor even the confused murmur that arises from the midst of a great city. Chains are hung across the streets in the neighborhood of the churches; the half-closed shutters of the houses scarcely admit a ray of sun into the dwellings of the citizens. Now and then you perceive a solitary individual, who glides silently along the deserted streets and lanes.

But on Monday at early dawn the rolling of carriages, the noise of hammers, the cries of the population, begin again to make themselves heard. The city is awake once more. An eager crowd hastens towards the resort of commerce and industry; everything around you bespeaks motion, bustle, hurry. A feverish activity succeeds to the lethargic stupor of yesterday; you might almost suppose that they had but one day to acquire wealth and to enjoy it.

Appendix F.—Vol. I, p. 46

It is unnecessary to say that in the chapter which has just been read I have not pretended to give a history of America. My only object has been to enable the reader to appreciate the influence that the opinions and manners of the first immigrants have exercised upon the fate of the different colonies and of the Union in general. I have therefore cited only a few detached fragments.

I do not know whether I am deceived, but it appears to me that by pursuing the path which I have merely pointed out, it would be easy to present such pictures of the American republics as would not be unworthy the attention of the public and could not fail to suggest to the statesmen matter for reflection. Not being able to devote myself to this labor, I am anxious at least to render it easy to others; and for this purpose I append a short catalogue and analysis of the works which seem to me the most important to consult.

At the head of the general documents which it would be advantageous to examine, I place the work entitled: *Historical Collection of State Papers and Other Authentic Documents, intended as materials for an hystory of the United States of America,* by Ebenezer Hazard. The first volume of this compilation, which was printed at Philadelphia in 1792, contains a literal copy of all the charters granted by the Crown of England to the emigrants, as well as the principal acts of the colonial governments, during the first period of their existence. One can find there, among other things, a great number of authentic documents on the affairs of New England and Virginia during this period. The second volume is almost entirely devoted to the acts of the Confederation of 1643. This federal compact, which was entered into by the colonies of New England with the view of resisting the Indians, was the first instance of union afforded by the Anglo-Americans. There were several other such compacts, up to the one of 1776, which led to the independence of the colonies.

The Philadelphia historical collection is in the Library of Congress.

Each colony has, besides, its own historic monuments, some of which are extremely curious, beginning with Virginia, the state that was first peopled. The earliest historian of Virginia was its founder, Captain John Smith. Captain Smith has left us a quarto volume, entitled *The general Historie of Virginia and New-England, by Captain John Smith, some time Governor in those Countries, and Admiral of New England;* printed at London in 1627. (This volume is to be found in the Bibliothèque royale.) Smith's work is illustrated with very curious maps and engravings which date from the period when it was printed. The historian's account extends from 1584 to 1626. Smith's book is well thought of and merits being so. The author is one of the most celebrated adventurers who has appeared in a century full of adventurers; he lived at its end. The book itself breathes that ardor of discovery, that spirit of enterprise, which characterizes such men; there one finds those chivalric manners which are often mingled with trade and made to serve the acquisition of riches.

But what is remarkable about Captain Smith is that he combined the virtues of his contemporaries with qualities which were alien to most of them; his style is simple and clear, his accounts have the mark of truth, his descriptions are not elaborated. This author throws valuable light on the state of the Indians at the time of the discovery of North America.

The second historian to consult is Beverley. Beverley's work, a volume in duodecimo, was translated into French, and published at Amsterdam, in 1707. The author begins his narrative in 1585 and ends it in 1700. The first part of his book contains historical documents, properly so called, relative to the infancy of the colony. The second affords a most curious picture of the state of the Indians at this remote period. The third conveys very clear ideas concerning the manners, social condition, laws, and political customs of the Virginians in the author's lifetime.

Beverley was a Virginian, which leads him to say, in opening, that he begs the reader "not to examine my work in too critical a spirit for, since I was born in the Indies, I cannot aspire to purity of language." Despite this colonist's modesty, the author shows throughout his book that he vigorously supports the supremacy of the mother country. Numerous instances of that spirit of civil liberty that has since then inspired the English colonies in America are also found in Beverley's work. Evidence of the divisions which so long existed among them and delayed their independence is likewise to be found. Beverley detests his Catholic neighbors in Maryland more than the English government. This author's style is simple; his descriptions are often full of interest and inspire confidence. The French translation of Beverley's history may be found in the Bibliothèque royale.

I saw in America, but was unable to find in France, another work which ought to be consulted entitled *The History of Virginia,* by William Stith. This book affords some curious details, but I thought it long and diffuse.

The oldest as well as the best document to be consulted on the history of Carolina is a work in small quarto, entitled *The History of Carolina,* by John Lawson, printed at London in 1718. This work contains, in the first part, a journey of discovery in the west of Carolina, the account of which, given in the form of a journal, is in general confused and superficial; but it contains a very striking description of the mortality caused among the savages of that time by both smallpox and the immoderate use of brandy; with a curious picture of the corruption of manners prevalent among them, which was increased by the presence of Europeans. The second part of Lawson's book is devoted to a description of the physical condition of Carolina and its products.

In the third part the author gives an interesting description of the customs, habits, and government of the Indians at that time. Wit and originality are often to be found in this part of the book. Lawson's history concludes with the Charter granted Carolina in the reign of Charles II. This work is light in tone, often licentious, and presents a complete contrast to the very serious style of works published at the same time in New England. Lawson's history is an extremely rare volume in America, and cannot be acquired in Europe. Nevertheless, there is a copy in the Bibliothèque royale.

From the southern I pass at once to the northern extremity of the United States, as the intermediate space was not peopled till a later period.

I would first mention a very curious compilation, entitled *Collections of the Massachusetts Historical Society,* printed for the first time at Boston in 1792, and reprinted in 1806. This work is not in the Bibliothèque royale, nor, I believe, in any other library. This collection, which is continued to the present day, contains a great number of very valuable documents relating to the history of the different states of New England. Among them are letters which have never been published, and authentic pieces which had been buried in provincial archives. The whole work of Gookin, concerning the Indians, is inserted there.

I have mentioned several times, in the chapter to which this note relates, the work of Nathaniel Morton, entitled *New England's Memorial;* sufficiently, perhaps, to prove that it deserves the attention of those who would be conversant with the history of New England. Nathaniel Morton's book is an octavo volume, reprinted at Boston in 1826. It is not in the Bibliothèque royale.

The most valuable and important authority that exists on the history of New England is the work of the Rev. Cotton Mather, entitled *Magnalia Christi Americana, or the Ecclesiastical History of New England, 1620–1698,* 2 vols., 8vo, reprinted at Hartford, in 1820. I do not believe it is in the Bibliothèque royale. The author divided his work into seven books. The first presents the history of the events which prepared and brought about the establishment of New England. The second contains the lives of the first governors and chief magistrates who presided over the country. The third is devoted to the lives and labors of the evangelical ministers who during the same period had the care of souls. In the fourth the author relates the institution and progress of the university at Cambridge (Massachusetts). In the fifth he describes the principles and the discipline of the Church of New England. The sixth is taken up in retracing certain facts which, in the opinion of Mather, prove the merciful interposition of Providence in behalf of the inhabitants of New England. Lastly, in the seventh, the author gives an account of the heresies and the troubles to which the Church of New England was exposed. Cotton Mather was an evangelical minister, who was born at Boston and passed his life there. His narratives are distinguished by the same ardor and religious zeal which led to the foundation of the colonies of New England. Traces of bad taste often occur in his manner of writing; but he interests because he is full of enthusiasm. He is often intolerant, still oftener credulous, but he never betrays an intention to deceive.

Sometimes there are even brilliant passages, and even true and profound reflections, such as these: "Before the arrival of the Puritans," he says (Vol. I, chap. iv, p. 61), "there were more than a few attempts of the *English*, to people and improve the parts of *New-England*, which were to the northward of *New-Plymouth;* but the designs of those attempts being aimed no higher than the advancement of some *worldly interests,* a constant series of disasters has confounded them, until there was a plantation erected upon the nobler designs of *christianity* [*sic*]; and that plantation, though it has had more adversaries than perhaps any one upon earth; yet, *having obtained help from God, it continues to this day.*"

Mather sometimes softens the severity of his story with touches of warmth and tenderness: after talking of an English woman who, with her husband, was brought to America by religious zeal, and shortly after died from fatigue and suffering of exile, he adds: "As to her virtuous spouse, Isaac Johnson, he tried to live without her, and being unable to, he died" (Vol. I, p. 71) [*sic*].

Mather's book admirably portrays the times and country he wishes to describe. Desiring to show us what motives led the Puritans to seek a refuge beyond the seas, he says:

"Briefly, the God of Heaven served as it were, a *summons* upon the *spirits* of his people in the English nation; stirring up the spirits of thousands which never saw the *faces* of each other, with a most unanimous inclination to leave all the pleasant accommodations of their native country, and go over a terrible *ocean,* into a more terrible *desart,* for the *pure enjoyment of all his ordinances.* It is now reasonable that before we pass any further, the *reasons* of this undertaking should be more exactly made known unto *posterity,* especially unto the *posterity* of those that were the *undertakers,* lest they come at length to forget and neglect *the true interest of* New-England. Wherefore I shall now transcribe some of *them* from a manuscript, wherein they were then tendred unto consideration.

" '*First,* It will be a service unto the Church of great consequence, to carry the *Gospel* into *those* parts of the world, and raise a *bulwark* against the kingdom of *antichrist,* which the *Jesuites* labour to rear up in *all* parts of the world.

" '*Secondly,* All other Churches of *Europe* have been brought under *desolations;* and it may be feared that the like judgments are coming upon *us;* and who knows but God hath provided this place to be a *refuge* for many, whom he means to save out of the *General Destruction.*

" '*Thirdly,* The land grows weary of her *inhabitants,* insomuch that *man,* which is the most precious of all creatures, is here more vile and base than the earth he treads upon: *children, neighbours* and *friends,* especially the *poor,* are counted the greatest *burdens,* which if things were right would be the chiefest earthly *blessings.*

" '*Fourthly,* We are grown to that intemperance in all *excess of riot,* as no mean estate almost will suffice a man to keep sail with his *equals,* and he that fails in it, must live in scorn and contempt: hence it comes to pass, that all *arts* and *trades* are carried in that deceitful manner, and unrighteous course, as it is almost impossible for a good upright man to maintain his constant charge, and live comfortably in them.

" '*Fifthly,* The *schools* of learning and religion are so corrupted, as (besides the unsupportable charge of education) most children, even the best, wittiest, and of the fairest hopes, are perverted, corrupted, and utterly overthrown, by the multitude of evil examples and licentious behaviours in these *seminaries.*

" '*Sixthly,* The *whole earth* is the *Lord's garden,* and he hath given it to the sons of *Adam,* to be tilled and improved by them: why then should we stand starving here for places of habitation, and in the mean time suffer whole countries, as profitable for the use of man, to lye waste without any improvement?

" '*Seventhly,* What can be a better or nobler work, and

more worthy of a *christian,* than to erect and support a *reformed particular Church* in its infancy, and unite our forces with such a company of faithful people, as by a timely assistance may grow stronger and prosper; but for want of it, may be put to great hazards, if not be wholly ruined.

" '*Eighthly,* If any such as are known to be godly, and live in wealth and prosperity here, shall forsake all this to join with this *reformed church,* and with it run the hazard of an hard and mean condition, it will be an example of great use, both for the removing of *scandal,* and to give more *life* unto the *faith* of God's people in their prayers for the plantation, and also to encourage others to join the more willingly in it.' "

Later, in stating the principles of the Church of New England with respect to morals, Mather inveighs with violence against the custom of drinking healths at table, which he denounces as a pagan and abominable practice. He proscribes with the same rigor all ornaments for the hair used by the female sex, as well as their custom of having the arms and neck uncovered. In another part of his work he relates several instances of witchcraft which had alarmed New England. It is plain that the visible action of the Devil in the affairs of this world appeared to him as incontestable and evident fact.

At many points this book reveals the spirit of civil liberty and political independence that characterized the author's contemporaries. Their principles in matters of government are in evidence throughout. Thus, for example, we find that in the year 1630 [*sic*], ten years after the settlement of Plymouth, the inhabitants of Massachusetts contributed 400 pounds sterling towards the establishment of the university at Cambridge.

In passing from the general documents relative to the history of New England to those which describe the several states comprised within its limits, I ought first to mention *The History of the Colony of Massachusetts,* by Thomas Hutchinson, Lieutenant-Governor of the Massachusetts Province, 2 vols., 8vo. There is a copy of this work at the Bibliothèque royale, a second edition printed at London in 1765. The history by Hutchinson, which I have several times quoted in the chapter to which this note relates, commences in the year 1628 and ends in 1750. Throughout the work there is a striking air of truth and the greatest simplicity of style; it is full of minute details.

The best history to consult concerning Connecticut is that of Benjamin Trumbull, entitled *A Complete History of Connecticut, Civil and Ecclesiastical, 1630–1764,* 2 vols., 8vo, printed in 1818, at New Haven. I do not believe that Trumbull's work is in the Bibliothèque royale. This history contains a clear and calm account of all the events which happened in Connecticut during the period given in the title. The author drew from the best sources, and his narrative bears the stamp of truth. His remarks on the early days of Connecticut are extremely interesting. See, especially, in his work, "The Constitution of 1639," Vol. I, chap. vi, p. 100, and also "The Penal Laws of Connecticut," Vol. I, chap. vii, p. 125.

The History of New Hampshire, by Jeremy Belknap, is a work held in merited esteem. It was printed at Boston in 1792, in 2 vols., 8vo. The third chapter of the first volume is particularly worthy of attention for the valuable details it affords on the political and religious principles of the Puritans, on the causes of their emigration, and on their laws. Here we may find a curious quotation from a sermon delivered in 1663: "New England must always remember that she was founded with a religious and not a commercial aim. Her visage shows that purity in doctrine and discipline is her vocation. Let tradesmen and all those who are engaged in heaping penny upon penny remember that religion and not profit was the aim in founding these colonies. If there is anyone among us who, in his valuation of the world and of religion, regards the former as thirteen and the latter as only twelve, he is not inspired by the feelings of a true son of New England." The reader of Belknap will find in his work more general ideas and more strength of thought than are to be met with in other American historians even to the present day. I do not know whether this book is in the Bibliothèque royale.

Among the central states which deserve our attention for their early origin, New York and Pennsylvania are the foremost. The best history we have of the former is entitled: *A History of New York,* by William Smith, printed at London in 1757. There is a French translation, also printed at London, in 1767, one vol., duodecimo. Smith gives us important details of the wars between the French and English in America. His is the best account of the famous confederation of the Iroquois.

With respect to Pennsylvania, I cannot do better than point out the work of Proud, entitled the *History of Pennsylvania, fiom the original Institution and Settlement of that Province, under the first Proprietor and Governor, William Penn, in 1681, till after the Year 1742,* by Robert Proud, 2 vols., 8vo, printed at Philadelphia in 1797. This work is deserving of the especial attention of the reader; it contains a mass of curious documents concerning Penn, the doctrine of the Quakers, and the character, manners, and customs of the first inhabitants of Pennsylvania. As far as I know, there is no copy at the Bibliothèque.

I need not add that among the most important documents relating to this state are the works of Penn himself and those of Franklin. These works are familiar to a great many readers.

I consulted most of the works just cited during my stay in America. Some were made available to me by the Bibliothèque royale, and others were lent me by M. Warden, author of an excellent book on America, former Consul General of the United States at Paris. I cannot close this note without expressing my gratitude to M. Warden.

Appendix G.—Vol. I, p. 53

We read in Jefferson's *Memoirs* as follows:

"At the time of the first settlement of the English in Virginia, when land was to be had for little or nothing, some provident persons having obtained large grants of it, and being desirous of maintaining the splendor of their families, entailed their property upon their descendants. The transmission of these estates from generation to generation, to men who bore the same name, had the effect of raising up a distinct class of families, who, possessing by law the privilege of perpetuating their wealth, formed by these means a sort of patrician order, distinguished by the grandeur and luxury of their establishments. From this order it was that the King usually chose his councillors of state."

In the United States the principal provisions of English

law respecting inheritance have been universally rejected. "The first rule that we follow," says Chancellor Kent, "touching inheritance, is the following: If a man dies intestate, his property goes to his heirs in a direct line. If he has but one heir or heiress, he or she succeeds to the whole. If there are several heirs of the same degree, they divide the inheritance equally among them, without distinction of sex."

This rule was prescribed for the first time in the state of New York, by a statute of the 23d of February 1786. (See *Revised Statutes,* Vol. III, Appendix, p. 48.) At the present day this law holds good throughout the whole of the United States, with the exception of the state of Vermont, where the male heir inherits a double portion. (Kent's *Commentaries,* Vol. IV, p. 370.) Chancellor Kent, in the same work (Vol. IV, pp. 1–22), gives a historical account of American legislation on the subject of entail; by this we learn that previous to the Revolution the colonies followed the English law of entail. Estates tail were abolished in Virginia in 1776, on motion of Mr. Jefferson. (See Jefferson's *Memoirs.*) They were suppressed in New York in 1786, and have since been abolished in North Carolina, Kentucky, Tennessee, Georgia, and Missouri. In Vermont, Indiana, Illinois, South Carolina, and Louisiana entail was never introduced. Those states which thought proper to preserve the English law of entail modified it in such a way as to deprive it of its most aristocratic tendencies. "Our general principles on the subject of government," says Kent, "tend to favor the free circulation of property."

It cannot fail to strike the French reader who studies the law of inheritance that on these questions French legislation is infinitely more democratic than even the American.

American law makes an equal division of the father's property, but only in the case of his will not being known; "for every man," says the law (*Revised Statutes,* Vol. III, Appendix, p. 51), "in the State of New York, has entire liberty, power, and authority to dispose of his property by will, to leave it entire, or divided in favor of any persons he chooses as his heirs, provided he does not leave it to a political body or any corporation." The French law obliges the testator to divide his property equally, or nearly so, among his heirs.

Most of the American republics still admit of entails, under certain restrictions; but the French law prohibits entail in all cases.

If the social condition of the Americans is more democratic than that of the French, the laws of the latter are the more democratic of the two. This may be explained more easily than at first appears to be possible. In France democracy is still occupied in the work of destruction; in America it reigns quietly over the ruins it has made.

APPENDIX H.—Vol. I, p. 60

SUMMARY OF THE QUALIFICATIONS OF VOTERS IN THE UNITED STATES

All the states agree in granting the right of voting at the age of twenty-one. In all of them it is necessary to have resided for a certain time in the district where the vote is cast. This period varies from three months to two years.

As to qualifications, in the state of Massachusetts it is necessary to have an income of three pounds sterling, or a capital of sixty pounds.

In Rhode Island a man must possess landed property to the amount of 133 dollars (704 francs).

In Connecticut he must have property which gives an income of seventeen dollars (about 90 francs). A year of service in the militia also gives the electoral privilege.

In New Jersey an elector must have a property of fifty pounds.

In South Carolina and Maryland the elector must possess fifty acres of land.

In Tennessee he must possess some property.

In the states of Mississippi, Ohio, Georgia, Virginia, Pennsylvania, Delaware, and New York the only necessary qualification for voting is that of paying the taxes; and in most of the states, service in the militia is equivalent to the payment of taxes.

In Maine and New Hampshire any man can vote who is not on the pauper list.

Lastly, in the states of Missouri, Alabama, Illinois, Louisiana, Indiana, Kentucky, and Vermont voting requirements have no reference to property of the elector.

I believe there is no other state beside that of North Carolina in which different requirements govern voting for the Senate and electing the House of Representatives. The electors of the former, in this case, must possess a property of fifty acres of land; to vote for the latter, nothing more is required than to pay taxes.

Appendix I.—Vol. I, p. 98

The United States has a prohibitive tariff. The small number of custom-house officers employed in the United States, and the great extent of the coast, render smuggling very easy; notwithstanding, it is less practiced than elsewhere because everybody endeavors to repress it. In America there is no fire-prevention service, and fires are more frequent than in Europe; but, in general, they are more speedily extinguished, because the surrounding population is prompt to lend assistance.

Appendix K.—Vol. I, p. 100

It is incorrect to say that centralization was produced by the French Revolution: the Revolution brought it to perfection, but did not create it. The mania for centralization and government regulation dates from the period when jurists began to take a share in the government, in the time of Philip the Fair; ever since this period they have been on the increase. In the year 1775 M. de Malesherbes, speaking in the name of the *Cour des Aides,* said to Louis XVI:[1]

"Every corporation and every community of citizens retained the right of administering its own affairs, a right which not only forms part of the primitive constitution of

* Toqueville did not include the letter J in numbering his appendices.

[1] See *Mémoires pour servir à l'histoire de la France en matière d'impôts,* Brussels, 1779, p. 654.

the kingdom, but has a still higher origin; for it is the right of nature and of reason. Nevertheless, your subjects, Sire, have been deprived of it; and we do not fear to say that, in this respect, your government has fallen into puerile extremes. From the time when powerful ministers made it a political principle to prevent the convocation of a national assembly, one consequence has succeeded another, until the deliberations of the inhabitants of a village are declared null if they have not been authorized by the Intendant. Of course, if the community has an expensive undertaking to carry through, it must remain under the control of the subdelegate of the Intendant, and, consequently, follow the plan he proposes, employ his favorite workmen, pay them according to his pleasure; and if an action at law is deemed necessary, the Intendant's permission must be obtained. The cause must be pleaded before this first tribunal previous to its being carried into a public court; and if the opinion of the Intendant is opposed to that of the inhabitants, or if their adversary enjoys his favor, the community is deprived of the power of defending its rights. Such are the means, Sire, which have been exerted to extinguish the municipal spirit in France and to stifle, if possible, the opinions of the citizens. The nation may be said to lie under an interdict, and to be in wardship under guardians."

What could be said more to the purpose at the present day, when the Revolution has achieved what are called *its victories* in centralization?

In 1789 Jefferson wrote from Paris to one of his friends: "There is no country where the mania for over-governing has taken deeper root than in France, or been the source of greater mischief." (*Letter to Madison,* August 28, 1789.)

The fact is that for several centuries the central power of France has done everything it could to extend central administration; it has acknowledged no other limits than its own strength. The central power to which the Revolution gave birth made more rapid advances than any of its predecessors, because it was stronger and wiser than they had been. Louis XVI committed the welfare of the municipal communities to the caprice of an Intendant; Napoleon left them to that of the Minister. The same principle governed both, though its consequences were more or less far-reaching.

APPENDIX L.—Vol. I, p. 104

This immutability of the Constitution in France is a necessary consequence of the laws.

To begin with the most important of all the laws, that which decides the order of succession to the throne, what can be more immutable in its principle than a political order founded upon the natural succession of father to son? In 1814 Louis XVIII established the perpetual law of hereditary succession in favor of his own family. Those who controlled the outcome of the Revolution of 1830 followed his example; they merely established the perpetuity of the law in favor of another family. In this respect they imitated Chancellor Maupeou, who, when he erected the new Parliament upon the ruins of the old, took care to declare in the same ordinance that the rights of the new magistrates should be as inalienable as those of their predecessors had been.

The laws of 1830, like those of 1814, point out no way of changing the Constitution, and it is evident that the ordinary means of legislation are insufficient for this purpose. As the King, the Peers, and the Deputies all derive their authority from the Constitution, these three powers united cannot alter a law by virtue of which alone they govern. Without the Constitution they are nothing; where, then, could they take their stand to effect a change in its provisions? The alternative is clear: either their efforts are powerless against the Charter, which continues to exist in spite of them, in which case they only reign in the name of the Charter; or they succeed in changing the Charter, and then, the law by which they existed being annulled, they themselves cease to exist. By destroying the Charter they destroy themselves.

This is much more evident in the laws of 1830 than in those of 1814. In 1814 the royal prerogative took its stand above and beyond the Constitution; but in 1830 it was avowedly created by and dependent on the Constitution.

A part, therefore, of the French Constitution is immutable, because it is united to the destiny of a family; and the body of the Constitution is equally immutable, because there appear to be no legal means of changing it.

These remarks are not applicable to England. That country having no written Constitution, who can tell when its Constitution is changed?

APPENDIX M.—Vol. I, p. 104

The most esteemed authors who have written upon the English Constitution agree with each other in establishing the omnipotence of Parliament.

Delolme says (Chap. X, p. 77): "It is a fundamental principle with the English lawyers, that Parliament can do everything except make a woman a man, or a man a woman."

Blackstone expresses himself more in detail, if not more energetically, than Delolme, in the following terms:

"The power and jurisdiction of Parliament, says Sir Edward Coke (4 Inst., 36), is so transcendant and absolute, that it cannot be confined, either for causes or persons, within any bounds. And of this high Court, he adds, may truly be said, '*Si antiquitatem spectes, est vetustissima; si dignitatem, est honoratissima; si jurisdictionem, est capacissima.*' It hath sovereign and uncontrollable authority in the making, confirming, enlarging, restraining, abrogating, repealing, reviving, and expounding of laws, concerning matters of all possible denominations; ecclesiastical or temporal; civil, military, maritime, or criminal; this being the place where that absolute despotic power which must, in all governments, reside somewhere, is intrusted by the Constitution of these kingdoms. All mischiefs and grievances, operations and remedies, that transcend the ordinary course of the laws, are within the reach of this extraordinary tribunal. It can regulate or new-model the succession to the Crown; as was done in the reign of Henry VIII and William III. It can alter the established religion of the land; as was done in a variety of instances in the reigns of King Henry VIII and his three children. It can *change and create afresh even the Constitution of the kingdom,* and of parliaments themselves; as was done by the Act of Union and the several statutes for triennial and septennial elections. It can, in short, do everything that is not naturally impossible to be done; and, therefore, some have not scrupled to call its power, by a figure rather too bold, the omnipotence of Parliament."

Appendix N.—Vol. I, p. 115

There is no question on which the American Constitutions agree more fully than on that of political jurisdiction. All the Constitutions which take cognizance of this matter give to the House of Representatives the exclusive right of impeachment; excepting only the Constitution of North Carolina, which grants the same privilege to grand juries. (Article 23.)

Almost all the Constitutions give to the Senate, or to the legislative body which occupies its place, the exclusive right of trying the impeachment and pronouncing judgment.

The only punishments which the political tribunals can inflict are removal from office, and exclusion from public functions for the future. The Constitution of Virginia alone enables them to inflict any kind of punishment.

The crimes which are subject to political jurisdiction are, in the Federal Constitution (Article I, Section 4), in that of Indiana (Art. 3, paragraphs 23 and 24), of New York (Art. 5), of Delaware (Art. 5): high treason, bribery, and other high crimes or misdemeanors.

In the Constitution of Massachusetts (Chap. I, Section 2), that of North Carolina (Art. 23), of Virginia (p. 252): misconduct and maladministration.

In the Constitution of New Hampshire (p. 105): corruption, intrigue, and maladministration.

In Vermont (Chap. 2, Art. 24): maladministration.

In South Carolina (Art. 5), Kentucky (Art. 5), Tennessee (Art. 4), Ohio (Art. 1, 23, 24), Louisiana (Art. 5), Mississippi (Art. 5), Alabama (Art. 6), Pennsylvania (Art. 4): crimes committed in the performance of official duties.

In the states of Illinois, Georgia, Maine, and Connecticut no particular offenses are specified.

Appendix O.—Vol. I, p. 178

It is true that the powers of Europe may carry on maritime wars against the Union; but it is always easier and less dangerous to undertake a maritime than a continental war.

Maritime warfare requires only one species of effort. A commercial people which consents to furnish its government with the necessary funds is sure to possess a fleet. And it is far easier to induce a nation to part with its money, almost unconsciously, than to reconcile it to sacrifices of men and personal efforts. Moreover, defeat by sea rarely compromises the existence or independence of the people which endures it.

As for continental wars, it is evident that the nations of Europe cannot threaten the American Union in this way. It would be very difficult to transport and maintain in America more than 25,000 soldiers, an army which may be considered to represent a nation of about 2,000,000 men. The most populous nation of Europe, contending in this way against the Union, is in the position of a nation of 2,000,000 inhabitants at war with one of 12,000,000. Add to this that America has all its resources within reach, while the European is 4,000 miles distant from his, and that the immensity of the American continent would of itself present an insurmountable obstacle to its conquest.

Appendix P.—Vol. I, p. 195

The first American newspaper appeared in April 1704, and was published at Boston. (See *Collections of the Historical Society of Massachusetts,* Vol. VI, p. 66.)

It would be a mistake to suppose that the press has always been entirely free in the American colonies: an attempt was made to establish something like censorship and posting of bonds. (Consult the *Legislative Documents of Massachusetts,* January 14, 1722.)

The Committee appointed by the General Court (the legislative body of the province) for the purpose of examining an affair to a paper entitled *The New England Courant* expresses its opinion that "the tendency of the said journal is to turn religion into derision, and bring it into contempt; that it mentions the sacred writers in a profane and irreligious manner; that it puts malicious interpretations upon the conduct of the ministers of the Gospel; and that the government of His Majesty is insulted, and the peace and tranquillity of the Province disturbed, by the said journal. The

Committee is consequently of opinion that the printer and publisher, James Franklin, should be forbidden to print and publish the said journal or any other work in future, without having previously submitted it to the Secretary of the Province; and that the justices of the peace for the county of Suffolk should be commissioned to require bail of the said James Franklin for good conduct during the ensuing year."

The suggestion of the Committee was adopted, and passed into a law; but the effect was null, for the journal eluded the prohibition by putting the name of Benjamin Franklin instead of James Franklin at the bottom of its columns, and this maneuver was supported by public opinion.

Appendix Q.—Vol. I, p. 293

To be a voter in the county (those who represent landed property) before the Reform Bill passed in 1832, it was necessary to have unencumbered, in one's own ownership or on lease for life, land bringing in at least 40 shillings' income. This law was enacted about 1450 under Henry VI. It has been reckoned that 40 shillings in the time of Henry VI might be the equivalent of £30 sterling of our time. The English, however, have allowed this qualification, adopted in the fifteenth century, to persist up to 1832, which proves how democratic the English Constitution became with the passage of time even while it appeared static. (See Delolme, Bk. I, ch. 4; see also Blackstone, Bk. I, ch. 4.)

English juries are chosen by the sheriff of the county (Delolme, Bk. I, ch. 12). The sheriff is generally an important man in the county; he discharges judicial and administrative duties; he represents the king and is named by him every year (Blackstone, Bk. I, ch. 9). His position places him above the suspicion of corruption on the part of any litigants; besides, if his impartiality is questioned, they can dismiss the entire jury which he has chosen, and then another officer is entrusted with the task of choosing new jurymen (see Blackstone, Bk. III, ch. 23).

In order to have the right to be a juryman, you have to be the owner of a piece of land yielding a minimum of 10 shillings' income (Blackstone, Bk. III, ch. 23). It will be noted that the qualification was required under the reign of William and Mary, that is to say about 1700, a period when the value of money was infinitely greater than it is today. It is obvious that the English have based their jury system not on ability but on landed property, as is the case with all their other political institutions.

They have finally admitted farmers to serve on juries, but they have required that their leases be very long and that they have a net income of 20 shillings, independent of rents (Blackstone, idem.).

Appendix R.—Vol. I, p. 294

The Federal Constitution has introduced the jury into the tribunals of the Union, just as the states had introduced it into their own several courts; but as it has not established any fixed rules for the choice of jurors, the Federal courts select them from the ordinary jury list which each state makes for itself. The laws of the states must therefore be examined for the theory of the formation of juries. See Story's *Commentaries on the Constitution,* Book III, Chap. xxxviii, pp. 654–9; Sergeant's *Constitutional Law,* p. 165. See also the Federal laws of 1789, 1800, and 1802 on this subject.

In order thoroughly to understand American principles with respect to the formation of juries, I examined the laws of widely separated states, and the following observations were the result of my inquiries:

In America all the citizens who exercise the elective franchise have the right of serving on a jury. The great state of New York, however, has made a slight difference between the two privileges, but in a spirit quite contrary to that of the laws of France; for in the state of New York there are fewer persons eligible as jurymen than there are electors. It may be said, in general, that the right of forming part of a jury, like the right of electing representatives, is open to all the citizens; the exercise of this right, however, is not put indiscriminately into any hands.

Every year a body of town or county magistrates (called *selectmen* in New England, *supervisors* in New York, *trustees* in Ohio, and *sheriffs of the parish* in Louisiana) chooses for each county a certain number of citizens who have the right of serving as jurymen, and who are supposed to be capable of doing so. These magistrates, being themselves elective, excite no distrust; their powers, like those of most republican magistrates, are very extensive and very arbitrary, and they frequently make use of them, especially in New England, to remove unworthy or incompetent jurymen.

The names of the jurymen thus chosen are transmitted to the county court; and the jury who have to decide any case are drawn by lot from the whole list of names.

The Americans have endeavored in every way to make the common people eligible for the jury and to render the service as little onerous as possible. The jurors being very numerous, each one's turn does not come round oftener than once in three years. The sessions are held in the chief town of every county. The county is roughly equivalent to our arrondissement. Thus the court comes to the jury, instead of bringing the jury to it, as in France. Finally, the jury are indemnified for their attendance either by the state or by the parties concerned. They receive in general a dollar per day (5.42 francs), besides their traveling-expenses. In America being placed upon the jury is looked upon as a burden, but it is a burden that is easily borne, and to which everyone readily submits.

See *Brevard's Digest of the Public Statute Law of South Carolina,* Vol. II, p. 338; idem., Vol. I, pp. 454, 456; idem., Vol. II, p. 218.

See *The General Laws of Massachusetts Revised and Published by Authority of the Legislature,* Vol. II, pp. 331, 187.

See *The Revised Statutes of the State of New York,* Vol. II, pp. 720, 411, 717, 643.

See *The Statute Law of the State of Tennessee,* Vol. I, p. 209.

See *Acts of the State of Ohio,* pp. 95, 210.

See *Digeste générale des actes de la législature de la Louisiane,* Vol. II, p. 55.

Appendix S.—Vol. I, p. 297

If we attentively examine the constitution of the jury in civil proceedings in England, we shall readily perceive that the jurors are under the immediate control of the judge. It is true that the verdict of the jury, in civil as well as in criminal cases, comprises the questions of fact and of law in the same reply. Thus a house is claimed by Peter as having been purchased by him; this is the fact to be decided. The defendant puts in a plea of incompetency on the part of the vendor; this is the legal question to be resolved. The jury simply says that the house shall be delivered to Peter, and thus decides both the questions of fact and of law.

But according to the practice of the English courts, the opinion of the jury is not held to be infallible in civil as it is in criminal cases, if the verdict is for acquittal. If the judge thinks that their verdict has made a wrong application of the law, he may refuse to receive it, and send back the jury to deliberate over again. Even if the judge allows the verdict to pass without observation, the case is not yet finally determined; there are still many modes of arresting judgment. The principal one consists in asking the court to set aside the verdict and order a new trial before another jury. It is true that such a request is seldom granted, and never more than twice; yet I have actually known this to happen. (See Blackstone, Book III, Chap. xxiv; idem., Book IV, Chap. xxv.)

Appendix T.—Vol. II, p. 164

Some aristocracies, however, have devoted themselves eagerly to commerce and have cultivated manufactures with success. The history of the world furnishes several conspicuous examples. But, generally speaking, the aristocratic principle is not favorable to the growth of trade and manufactures. Moneyed aristocracies are the only exception to the rule. Among such aristocracies there are hardly any desires that do not require wealth to satisfy them; the love of riches becomes, so to speak, the high road of human passions, which is crossed by or connected with all lesser tracks. The love of money and the thirst for that distinction which attaches to power are then so closely intermixed in the same souls that it becomes difficult to discover whether men grow covetous from ambition or whether they are ambitious from covetousness. This is the case in England, where men seek to get rich in order to arrive at distinction, and seek distinctions as a manifestation of their wealth. The mind is then seized by both ends, and hurried into trade and manufactures, which are the shortest roads that lead to opulence.

This, however, strikes me as an exceptional and transitory circumstance. When wealth has become the only symbol of aristocracy, it is very difficult for the wealthy to maintain sole possession of political power, to the exclusion of all other men. The aristocracy of birth and pure democracy are the two extremes of the social and political state of nations; between them moneyed aristocracy finds its place. The latter approximates the aristocracy of birth by conferring great privileges on a small number of persons; it so far belongs to the democratic element that these privileges may be successfully acquired by all. It frequently forms a natural transition between these two conditions of society, and it is difficult to say whether it closes the reign of aristocratic institutions or whether it even now ushers in the new era of democracy.

Appendix U.—Vol. II, p. 214

I find in my traveling-journal a passage that may serve to convey a more complete notion of the trials to which the women of America, who consent to follow their husbands into the wilds, are often subjected. This description has nothing to recommend it but its perfect truth.

"From time to time we come to fresh clearings; all these places are alike; I shall describe the one at which we halted tonight, since it will serve me for a picture of all the others.

"The bell which the pioneers hang around the necks of their cattle, in order to find them again in the woods, announced from afar our approach to a clearing; and we soon afterwards heard the stroke of the axe, hewing down the trees of the forest. As we came nearer, traces of destruction marked the presence of civilized man: the road was strewn with cut boughs; trunks of trees, half consumed by fire, or mutilated by the axe, were still standing in our way. We proceeded till we reached a wood in which all the trees seemed to have been suddenly struck dead; in the middle of summer their boughs were as leafless as in winter; and upon closer examination we found that a deep circle had been cut through the bark, which, by stopping the circulation of the sap, soon kills the tree. We were informed that this is commonly the first thing a pioneer does, as he cannot, in the first year, cut down all the trees that cover his new domain; he sows Indian corn under their branches, and puts the trees to death in order to prevent them from injuring his crop. Beyond this field, at present imperfectly traced out, the first work of civilization in the desert, we suddenly came upon the cabin of its owner, situated in the center of a plot of ground more carefully cultivated than the rest, but where man was still waging unequal warfare with the forest; there the trees were cut down, but not uprooted, and the trunks still encumbered the ground which they so recently shaded. Around these dry blocks, wheat, oak seedlings, and plants of every kind grow and intertwine in all the luxuriance of wild, untutored nature. Amid this vigorous and varied vegetation stands the house of the pioneer, or, as they call it, the *log house*. Like the ground about it, this rustic dwelling bore marks of recent and hasty labor: its length seemed not to exceed thirty feet, its height fifteen; the walls as well as the roof were formed of rough trunks of trees, between which a little moss and clay had been inserted to keep out the cold and rain.

"As night was coming on, we determined to ask the master of the log house for a lodging. At the sound of our footsteps the children who were playing among the scattered branches sprang up, and ran towards the house, as if they were frightened at the sight of man; while two large dogs, half wild, with ears erect and outstretched nose, came growling out of their hut to cover the retreat of their young masters. The pioneer himself appeared at the door of his dwelling; he looked at us with a rapid and inquisitive glance, made a sign to the dogs to go into the house, and set them the example, without betraying either curiosity or apprehension at our arrival.

"We entered the log house: the inside is quite unlike that of the cottages of the peasantry of Europe; it contains more that is superfluous, less that is necessary. A single window with a muslin curtain; on a hearth of trodden clay an immense fire, which lights the whole interior; above the hearth, a good rifle, a deerskin, and plumes of eagles' feathers; on the right hand of the chimney, a map of the United States, raised and shaken by the wind through the crannies in the wall; near the map, on a shelf formed of a roughly hewn plank, a few volumes of books: a Bible, the first six books of Milton, and two of Shakespeare's plays; along the wall, trunks instead of closets; in the center of the room, a rude table, with legs of green wood with the bark still on them, looking as if they grew out of the ground on which they stood; but on this table a teapot of British china, silver spoons, cracked teacups, and some newspapers.

"The master of this dwelling has the angular features and lank limbs peculiar to the native of New England. It is evident that this man was not born in the solitude in which we have found him: his physical constitution suffices to show that his earlier years were spent in the midst of civilized society and that he belongs to that restless, calculating, and adventurous race of men who do with the utmost coolness things only to be accounted for by the ardor of passion, and who endure the life of savages for a time in order to conquer and civilize the backwoods.

"When the pioneer perceived that we were crossing his threshold, he came to meet us and shake hands, as is their custom; but his face was quite unmoved. He opened the conversation by inquiring what was going on in the world; and when his curiosity was satisfied, he held his peace, as if he were tired of the noise and importunity of mankind. When we questioned him in our turn, he gave us all the information we asked; he then attended sedulously, but without eagerness, to our wants. While he was engaged in providing thus kindly for us, how did it happen that, in spite of ourselves, we felt our gratitude die on our lips? It is that our host, while he performs the duties of hospitality, seems to be obeying a painful obligation of his station; he treats it as a duty imposed upon him by his situation, not as a pleasure.

"By the side of the hearth sits a woman with a baby on her lap; she nods to us without disturbing herself. Like the pioneer, this woman is in the prime of life; her appearance seems superior to her condition, and her apparel even betrays a lingering taste for dress; but her delicate limbs appear shrunken, her features are drawn in, her eye is mild and melancholy; her whole physiognomy bears marks of religious resignation, a deep quiet of all passions, and some sort of natural and tranquil firmness, ready to meet all the ills of life without fearing and without braving them.

"Her children cluster about her, full of health, turbulence, and energy: they are true children of the wilderness. Their mother watches them from time to time with mingled melancholy and joy: to look at their strength and her languor, one might imagine that the life she has given them has exhausted her own, and still she does not regret what they have cost her.

"The house inhabited by these emigrants has no internal partition or loft. In the one chamber of which it consists the whole family is gathered for the night. The dwelling is itself a little world, an ark of civilization amid an ocean of foliage: a hundred steps beyond it the primeval forest spreads its shades, and solitude resumes its sway."

Appendix V.—Vol. II, p. 215

It is not the equality of condition that makes men immoral and irreligious; but when men, being equal, are also immoral and irreligious, the effects of immorality and irreligion more easily manifest themselves, because men have but little influence over each other, and no class exists which can undertake to keep society in order. Equality of condition never creates profligacy of morals, but it sometimes allows that profligacy to show itself.

Appendix W.—Vol. II, p. 236

Aside from all those who do not think at all and those who dare not say what they think, the immense majority of Americans will still be found to appear satisfied with their political institutions; and I believe they really are so. I look on this state of public opinion as an indication, but not as a proof, of the absolute excellence of American laws. National pride, the gratification, by legislation, of certain ruling passions, fortuitous circumstances, unperceived defects, and, more than all the rest, the influence of the majority which shuts the mouth of all opponents, may long perpetuate the delusions of a people as well as those of a man.

Look at England throughout the eighteenth century. No nation was ever more prodigal of self-applause, no people were ever better satisfied with themselves; then every part of their constitution was right, everything, even to its most obvious defects, was irreproachable. At the present day a vast number of Englishmen seem to be occupied only in proving that this constitution was faulty in a thousand respects. Which was right, the English people of the last century, or the English people of the present day?

The same thing occurred in France. It is certain that, during the reign of Louis XIV the great bulk of the nation was devotedly attached to the form of government which then governed the community. It is a vast error to suppose that there was anything degraded in the character of the French of that age. There might have been some instances of servitude in France at that time, but assuredly there was no servile spirit among the people. The writers of that age felt a species of genuine enthusiasm in raising the power of their King over all other authority; and there was no peasant so obscure in his hovel as not to take a pride in the glory of his sovereign, or who would not die cheerfully with the cry "*Vive le Roi!*" upon his lips. These same forms of loyalty have now become odious to the French people. Which were wrong, the French of the age of Louis XIV or their descendants of the present day?

Our judgment of the laws of a people, then, must not be founded exclusively upon its inclinations, since those inclinations change from age to age; but upon more elevated principles and a more general experience. The love which a people may show for its laws proves only this: that we should not be in a hurry to change them.

Appendix X.—Vol. II, p. 291

In the chapter to which this note relates I have pointed out one source of danger; I am now about to point out another, more rare indeed, but more formidable if it were ever to appear.

If the love of physical gratification and the taste for well-being, which are naturally suggested to men by a state of equality, were to possess the mind of a democratic people and to fill it completely, the manners of the nation would become so totally opposed to military pursuits that perhaps even the army would eventually acquire a love of peace, in spite of the peculiar interest which leads it to desire war. Living amid a state of general relaxation, the troops would ultimately think it better to rise without efforts, by the slow but commodious advancement of a period of peace, than to purchase more rapid promotion at the cost of all the toils and privations of the field. With these feelings, they would take up arms without enthusiasm and use them without energy; they would allow themselves to be led to meet the foe, instead of marching to attack him.

It must not be supposed that this pacific state of the army would render it adverse to revolutions; for revolutions, and especially military revolutions, which are generally very rapid, are attended indeed with great dangers, but not with protracted toil; they gratify ambition at less cost than war; life only is at stake, and the men of democracies care less for their lives than for their comfort.

Nothing is more dangerous for the freedom and the tranquillity of a people than an army afraid of war, because as such an army no longer seeks to maintain its importance and its influence on the field of battle, it seeks to assert them elsewhere. Thus it might happen that the men of whom a democratic army consists would lose the interests of citizens without acquiring the virtues of soldiers; and that the army would cease to be fit for war without ceasing to be turbulent. I shall here repeat what I have said in the text: the remedy for these dangers is not to be found in the army, but in the country; a democratic people which has preserved the manliness of its character will never be at a loss for military prowess in its soldiers.

Appendix Y.—Vol. II, p. 309

Men place the greatness of their idea of unity in the means, God in the ends; hence this idea of greatness, as men conceive it, leads us to infinite littleness. To compel all men to follow the same course towards the same object is a human conception; to introduce infinite variety of action, but so combined that all these acts lead in a thousand different ways to the accomplishment of one great design, is a divine conception.

The human idea of unity is almost always barren; the divine idea is infinitely fruitful. Men think they manifest their greatness by simplifying the means they use; but it is the purpose of God which is simple; his means are infinitely varied.

Appendix Z.—Vol. II, p. 313

Not only is a democratic people led by its own taste to centralize its government, but the passions of all the men by whom it is governed constantly urge it in the same direction. It may easily be foreseen that almost all the able and ambitious members of a democratic community will labor unceasingly to extend the powers of government, because they all hope at some time or other to wield those powers themselves. It would be a waste of time to attempt to prove to them that extreme centralization may be injurious to the state, since they are centralizing it for their own benefit. Among the public men of democracies, there are hardly any but men of great disinterestedness or extreme mediocrity who seek to oppose the centralization of government; the former are scarce, the latter powerless.

Appendix AA.—Vol. II, p. 336

I have often asked myself what would happen if, amid the laxity of democratic customs, and as a consequence of the restless spirit of the army, a military government were ever to be established among any of the nations of our times. I think that such a government would not differ much from the outline I have drawn in the chapter to which this note refers, and that it would retain none of the fierce characteristics of a military oligarchy. I am persuaded that in such a case a sort of fusion would take place between the practices of civil officials and those of the military service. The administration would assume something of a military character, and the army some of the practices of the civil administration. The result would be a regular, clear, exact, and absolute system of government; the people would become the reflection of the army, and the community be regimented like a garrison.

Appendix BB.—Vol. II, p. 339

It cannot be absolutely or generally affirmed that the greatest danger of the present age is license or tyranny, anarchy or despotism. Both are equally to be feared; and the one may proceed as easily as the other from one and the same cause: namely, that *general apathy* which is the consequence of individualism. It is because this apathy exists that the executive government, having mustered a few troops, is able to commit acts of oppression one day; and the next day a party which has mustered some thirty men in its ranks can also commit acts of oppression. Neither the one nor the other can establish anything which will last; and the causes which enable them to succeed easily prevent them from succeeding for long; they rise because nothing opposes them, and they sink because nothing supports them. The proper object, therefore, of our most strenuous resistance is far less either anarchy or despotism than that apathy which may almost indifferently beget either the one or the other.

Appendix II

A HISTORICAL ESSAY

ON THE morning of May 11, 1831 two young men walked down the gangplank of the steamer *President* from Providence, just berthed at Cortlandt Street at the foot of Manhattan. They were remarkable young men but not many of their fellow passengers had remarked upon their landing in America. Thirty-eight days by sailing vessel from Havre to Newport, Rhode Island, and by steamer the rest of the way, they had come on an official mission for their government. At the moment they were tired; they had been so eager to see America that they had hardly slept since first sighting the shores of Long Island, and landing in Newport on May 9. After a brief look around the town on lower Manhattan, they went to bed at four in the afternoon. "The morrow at 8," they were still asleep.

Not for long, however, for they were soon up and out. Picking up the morning's *Mercantile Advertiser,* they found that their arrival was already "news." The item announced that "two young magistrates . . . have arrived . . . sent here by order of the Minister of the Interior, to examine the various prisons in our country, and make a report on their return to France." It was reprinted that day in the *New York Evening Post,* and within a week in papers all the way from Boston to Annapolis.

From New York, Tocqueville and Beaumont traveled as far east as Boston, as far west as Green Bay, as far north as Sault Ste. Marie and Quebec, as far south as New Orleans. By steamer and stagecoach where possible, on horseback through the wilderness regions of the northern, western, and southern frontiers, they traversed over seven thousand miles of this country and Canada before they sailed for France on February 20, 1832. During those nine months they had touched every (present) state east of the Mississippi except Maine, New Hampshire, Vermont, Florida, Illinois, and Indiana. From Buffalo they had traveled to Quebec and back again to New England and New York. They had stayed long enough in most of them to learn a good deal about the land and the people; the one they found as varied as the other.

Who were these young men and what was their mission? Did it compel their travels? Or were they, like other Europeans of the time, simply curious about a country and a nation strange in all aspects—physical, cultural, and political —to the peoples of the older civilizations?

THE AUTHOR AND HIS PURPOSE

Alexis Charles Henri Clerel de Tocqueville was not quite twenty-six when he landed in America; he had been born in Paris on July 29, 1805. The Tocquevilles were a Norman family counting themselves among the *petite noblesse*. Alexis's maternal grandfather, a marquis of the *ancien régime,* and an aunt had been guillotined by the Revolution; his parents had been imprisoned. Only after the fall of Napoleon did his father return to public life; Hervé de Tocqueville served the Bourbon government as a prefect in several departments, was promoted to the court at Versailles and finally elevated to the peerage.

The young Tocqueville was first educated at home under the tutorship of an old family friend and parish priest, the Abbé Lesueur, who had also instructed his father. When he was fifteen, he went to the Lycée at Metz, where his father was stationed as prefect; at eighteen he returned to Paris to take up the study of law. When he was eligible, at twenty-one, he began a career in the magistracy; his father secured him an appointment as *juge auditeur* in the court at Versailles. There he met his fellow-traveler-to-be to America, Gustave de Beaumont, like himself a young French nobleman with liberal interests. The two young officials instantly took to each other. Their first acquaintance ripened into a friendship that lasted throughout their lives and survived Tocqueville's death. Beaumont's devotion to Tocqueville was evidenced in his editing posthumously the *Œuvres Complètes*.

Although Tocqueville never entirely deserted the values

of the aristocratic tradition, he was early imbued with liberal ideas. When he was only fifteen, he discovered some of the eighteenth-century French philosophers in his father's library. Already an eager reader, he found among them new ideas which helped to shape his lifelong interest in and support of freedom of inquiry and free trade in ideas. The Catholic faith in which he had been reared under the Abbé Lesueur's tutelage was never completely restored; he remained devoutly religious, but not so much as a practitioner as a believer. From this time on, Tocqueville's mind moved steadily away from the political ideas of the *ancien régime* and towards those of his contemporaries in the French liberal movement.

Much as he was influenced by the writings and lectures of such men as Royer-Collard and Guizot, he began to explore even wider frontiers of speculation than those they had opened to him on the nature and conditions of stability in society. More and more he turned from the narrow path of the law to the broader field of politics, both in his studies and in his search for a satisfying career. With Beaumont he embarked on a thorough course of independent inquiry into problems of political organization and motivation. Liberalism in its new manifestations in England, where he had already visited, and in America in the midst of the Jacksonian revolution, inevitably enlisted an increasing intellectual interest—and attachment—from two young Frenchmen troubled by the continuing political unrest at home. The Revolution had not yet taken root in firmly established institutions; a balance between the aristocratic and the democratic traditions had not been worked out in practice. France was torn between the two; Tocqueville saw clearly enough that the democratic impulse, if it was to triumph, must create a stable political order to give France the vitality it so much needed at the time.

When the Bourbon dynasty fell in the July Revolution of 1830, Tocqueville and Beaumont found themselves in a quandary. They took the oath of allegiance to the government of Louis Philippe only reluctantly and with many doubts. As judicial officers they remained loyal to their duties, but they felt themselves out of sympathy with the new government.

It was then that the decision to make the voyage to America crystallized into action. Tocqueville had already conceived the purpose of writing about democracy—as the specific for Europe's (and especially France's) travails in bringing to birth a new order to supplant the old, outworn, aristocratic order. He now saw the opportunity to avoid the misgiving felt in his position as an official of a government with which he was not in sympathy and to fulfill his hope of observing democracy in action in America. He would thus at once both escape his moral scruples and equip himself to complete the grand design of examining the nature and working of democracy as it might be applicable in Europe. Beaumont, whose sympathies lay in the same direction, eagerly agreed to accompany Tocqueville.

Their only question was how to accomplish their purpose. Tocqueville, already thought by his superiors to be indifferent to the new government, had been demoted to *juge suppléant* and required to take the oath a second time. Both were already suspect, but they hit on a proposal that succeeded. They petitioned the Minister of Justice for an eighteen months' leave of absence and a commission from the government to study the prison system in America. Prison reform was then in the air in France; the Americans had developed some interesting ideas and practices in their new prisons; it would be useful to the French government to have first-hand information about American procedures.

They were given their commissions, but only after many delays and after overcoming much obstruction and red tape. All the outside pressure that could be mustered by their families and friends had to be exerted before they received official permission to undertake the mission. They had offered, in their original petition, to defray their own expenses; the government now took them quite literally and refused to underwrite the trip to America. Their families came to their rescue and supplied the money.

So at last they were on their way. The record of their preparations, their official and unofficial introductions, their voyage, their experiences in America from their first landing at Newport to their departure from New York City, how *Democracy in America* came to be written, the character of its author, his day-to-day itinerary and experiences, have all been brilliantly portrayed by the foremost American Tocqueville scholar, George Wilson Pierson, in his *Tocque-*

ville and Beaumont in America.[1] Professor Pierson has not only given us a detailed biography of a book and its author, but an exhaustive study of the voyage of those two young Frenchmen to America. He has placed the romance and the importance of *Democracy in America* in the perspective of its permanent values. Many admirers of the *Democracy* have received new insights into its significance for our time no less than into its design in the mind and the spirit of a young man of twenty-five. For many others who will discover the *Democracy* for the first time, Professor Pierson's account of its origins will be read foı its own sake, as well as for an adequate appreciation of the author and the book.

Tocqueville and Beaumont visited all the important prisons in this country. Tocqueville especially sought to dig below the surface of new prison practices, such as solitary confinement, in order to discover their effects on the reformation of prisoners. He spent many hours interviewing the inmates in all the prisons he visited and kept meticulous notes on these conversations. He talked with prison officials and others in public and private life to determine what Americans of all types thought about their prisons. On the basis of these official contacts, Tocqueville and Beaumont drafted a comprehensive report[2] for their government; it

[1] G. W. Pierson: *Tocqueville and Beaumont in America* (New York: Oxford; 1938). Reference should be made to Professor Pierson's study not only for the details of Tocqueville's and Beaumont's experiences in America, but for the major events in the former's life in France after his return.

References to bibliographical sources will be indicated as follows. The particular item as numbered in the Bibliography (Appendix V at end of Vol. II) will be followed by the relevant page reference, separated by a colon, thus (e.g., for page 1 of Pierson's volume indicated in this note): 68:1.

[2] *Du Système pénitentiaire aux États-Unis et son application en France* (Paris: H. Fournier; 1833). It appeared in the United States in the same year, with notes by Francis Liebler (11 *D. A. B.* 236), under the title, *The Penitentiary System in the United States and Its Application in France* (Philadelphia, Carey, Lea and Blanchard, 1833). The second and subsequent French editions appeared in two volumes with additional notes by the authors. The Académie Française awarded the work the Prix Monthyon. It was quickly translated into "German, English, Portuguese, etc., etc." (2nd Paris edition, 1836, I, 1), and was widely reviewed in this country and abroad (ibid., II, 358 ff.). On the influence of the *Penitentiary System,* see 68:54. For American reviews, see 14 *American Quarterly Review* (September 1883) 228; 20 *Christian Examiner and General Review*

was a joint work, but Tocqueville contributed a major share of the research involved. Not only was this report by far the most complete study yet made of American prisons, but it became a major source of French prison-reform activities for many years thereafter.

Tocqueville and Beaumont, having completed their official mission, were now ready to follow their principal purpose in coming to America, the analysis of democracy as a working principle of society and of government. The search for the essence of democracy was undertaken and prosecuted with zeal; Tocqueville had come to America primarily to discover the inner meaning and the actual functioning of democracy in action, in a country which had never known aristocracy. What he found tempered some of his original enthusiasm for the universal applicability of American democratic ideas and practices. If he went home to write the *Democracy* with a more sober view of our institutions than he had had before his visit to America, he did not allow his experiences here to distort his perspective, or to make him less careful in his observations, analyses, and judgments. He found much that was missed altogether or entirely ignored by others of his contemporaries who visited America with the same curiosity about democracy, but often with very different motives in studying it. Even though his criticisms and appraisals, which cumulative observation and wide travel inspired, were not always favorable, Tocqueville never lost sight of his original purpose or deviated from his objective approach.

Tocqueville's intellectual standards and methods of research were stricter than those of most of his contemporaries. His references and citations, complete in the footnotes presented in this edition,[3] are evidence of his wide search in

---

(July 1836) 376 (by Samuel Atkins Eliot); 37 *North American Review* (July 1833) 117 (by Edward Everett.)

[3] Many notes, references, or citations were altogether suppressed in the first Bowen edition and in subsequent issues of this text. The editions using the Reeve text contained more, but not all, of Tocqueville's citations.

Tocqueville noted in his *Introduction* one reason why he himself did not cite sources for some materials provided him by his American friends (I, 15–16). The following excerpt from a letter by Joseph Story suggests that Tocqueville's frequent failure to cite Story specifically had much to do with the latter's

original sources. The range and variety of the printed sources which he used indicate how much care he took to obtain the most authentic books and documents.[4] The extent of his travels suggests that he was not satisfied with second-hand information about the places, the conditions, or the institutions of which he wrote. On his various expeditions he wrote extensive daily notes, and included many details of his experiences in letters to his family and friends at home, which would be available to him on his return. After each interview with a prominent American he drew up a précis for future reference.[5] From others he requested and received memoranda on particular aspects of our institutions about which he desired more detailed data than were available in printed sources. Altogether, Tocqueville adhered to far more scholarly standards than many of his successors, to say

---

irritation at Tocqueville's apparent neglect of his aid. The same may have been the feeling of other of Tocqueville's American friends, for the same reason.

"I do not wonder that you are struck with the barrenness of foreign treatises on Constitutional Law; and especially as applied to forms of government like ours. Europeans know little on the subject. It is surprising how little they read of what has been written here. The work of de Tocqueville has had great reputation abroad, partly founded on their ignorance that he has borrowed the greater part of his reflections from American works, and little from his own observations. The main body of his materials will be found in the *Federalist*, and in Story's *Commentaries on the Constitution; sic vos non vobis*. You know ten times as much as he does of the actual workings of our system and of its true theory." Letter to Francis Lieber, May 9, 1840. Quoted in W. W. Story: *Life and Letters of Joseph Story*, 329 (Boston: Little, Brown; 1851). See also 68:730; 44:(II) 351.

In recently discovered worksheets for the *Democracy*, Tocqueville specifically noted his indebtedness to Story and others. "I have consulted the three most highly esteemed commentaries, that is to say, the *Federalist*, the work of the three principal drafters of the federal Constitution, the commentaries of Chancellor Kent, and those of Judge Story." See 54:7.

[4] See 68:727 n. for a list of sources utilized by Tocqueville. See ch. 59 as a whole as to "the materials for Tocqueville's work." His footnote references indicate that he had many materials forwarded to him in France after his return; e.g., I, 392, n. 48. Several American friends sent Tocqueville, at his request, notes and memoranda on particular aspects of American institutions.

[5] See 68: Appendix B, for a list of Beaumont's and Tocqueville's American acquaintances.

nothing of those who were writing of America or of political, social, and economic institutions a century ago.[6]

On returning to France—earlier than they had anticipated, because their leaves had been curtailed by the government—Tocqueville and Beaumont viewed the changing political scene and found it little to their liking. They were not received by the Minister of Justice, despite repeated requests for an opportunity to submit their report. Less than two months after their return Beaumont was dismissed from his judicial post for refusing to argue a case without merit but with scandalous political implications; he was deliberately required to support the government's position by a regime bent on embarrassing him. On the day his dismissal was announced, Tocqueville resigned his office in a letter of restrained but bitter criticism of the government.

Both were relieved by the end of their official careers. They could now devote themselves to their real interest—reflection and writing. Politics as a career attracted Tocqueville, but never absorbed his entire energies in the years following his return to France.[7] In the immediate context of

[6] No extended comparison of the *Democracy* with contemporary works of other foreign observers can be made here. Bibliographies and some critical materials will be found in: T. W. Evans: *European Impressions of America from early time to the present* (unpublished MS., Madison, Library School of the University of Wisconsin, 1930); H. Meyer: *Nord Amerika in Urteil des deutscher Shrift bis zu Mitte des 19 Jahrhunderts* (Hamburg: Friedrichsen de Guyter; 1929); F. Monaghan: *French Travellers in the United States, 1765–1932* (New York: New York Public Library; 1933); A. W. Nevins: *American Social History as recorded by British travellers* (New York: Holt; 1923); C. W. Plympton: *Select Bibliography on Travel in North America* (Albany: New York State Library; 1897); H. T. Tuckerman: *America and Her Commentators; with a critical sketch of travel in the United States* (New York: Scribner's; 1864); P. W. Wheeler: *America through British Eyes; a study of the attitude of the Edinburgh Review toward the United States of America from 1802 to 1861* (Rock Hill, S.C.: the author; 1935).

[7] Tocqueville turned to politics soon after his return to France—as a means perhaps, of putting his ideas to the test of French experience. He ran for the Chamber of Deputies in 1837, but lost; he won in 1839. He sat for nearly a decade (till the Revolution of 1848), holding office briefly after 1848 as Minister for Foreign Affairs. Politics, however, did not become for Tocqueville a primary concern; he never gave it an undivided interest. As Pierson has pointed out (68:777), he "belonged to the race of thinkers, not of actors." See also 59: ch. 5.

their political disgrace, Tocqueville and Beaumont threw themselves into their first task, the completion of their prison report. When that was out of the way, each began to draft the broader work which he had brought home from America in his observations and his notebooks.

Before leaving for America it had apparently been decided by the two young friends to write a joint book on political democracy. It is not known when or why they decided to write individually of their experiences in America. Their friendship had that pure and untrammeled quality which is all too rare among those who can easily become literary competitors. Beaumont's interest seems to have centered more and more on the conditions of the Indians and Negroes in this country. At some point in their travels they agreed to write of different aspects of American life and institutions. Their pact made no rift in their friendship, literary or personal. Each found in the other's work a unique satisfaction; each maintained his separate way in perfect accord.[8]

Beaumont's reflections on America appeared in *Marie, ou l'esclavage aux États-Unis,*[9] with a subtitle *Tableau des mœurs Américaines.* Never translated into English, it has remained relatively unknown. It contains many acute and penetrating observations on race relations, North and South, in the 1830's, lightly concealed in the framework of a novel. Like Tocqueville, Beaumont included many notes, references, and citations. These were buried in appendixes, in

[8] See 68: Index, especially under Beaumont, G., *Marie, Quinze Jours au Désert,* Tocqueville, A. In carrying out their agreement, Tocqueville never published his *Quinze Jours au Désert;* it appeared only posthumously under Beaumont's editorship. This delightful account of frontier life, as observed by Tocqueville on his expedition west from Buffalo, described some of the scenes and the conditions treated by Beaumont in his *Marie.* Tocqueville would not allow it to be published because he considered the portrayal of this aspect of American life belonged to his friend (68:231 n.). The translated text of *Quinze Jours au Désert,* with Tocqueville's notes, is to be found in 68: chs. 20–1.

Beaumont undertook, in his *L'Irlande sociale, politique, et religieuse* (2 vols.; Paris: Ch. Gosselin; 1839), a survey of Irish political institutions very much like the *Democracy* in conception if not altogether in execution. The work gained considerable recognition in France and some notice abroad. See 4 *Journal des Savants* (ser. 3, 1839) 705 (J. B. Biot).

[9] 2 vols.; Paris: Ch. Gosselin; 1835.

obedience to the literary form in which Beaumont chose to clothe his observations. He also included three long essays on "The Social and Political Condition of Negro Slaves and Freedmen," "Religious Movements in the United States," and "The Early State and Present Condition of the Indian Tribes of North America." [10]

The plot of *Marie* is simple. A young Frenchman falls in love with a beautiful girl in Baltimore who, her father informs her lover secretly, is of mixed blood, although she does not appear to be. He refuses to let the young man marry his daughter, despite the latter's protest, until he has seen with his own eyes the true position of Negroes in America. With her brother he sets out on a tour of city and country, only to witness race riots and all the other forms of discrimination then—and now—present in America. The young Frenchman returns and renews his proposal; the father consents. They are almost mobbed at the wedding ceremony and flee to the wilderness to live an idyllic life of solitude and companionship. The girl soon dies; the idyll is shattered. The sources and character of race discrimination are pitilessly portrayed as they affect the thought of a youth untouched before coming to America by the attitudes he finds here.

It is natural that *Marie,* designedly a work slighter than the *Democracy* in scope and in materials, should not have received as wide notice or acclaim.[11] Its quality as a novel is

[10] For a summary of the plot of *Marie* and of Beaumont's ideas and observations paralleling Tocqueville's, see 68: ch. 38; p. 718 n. *Marie* contains, in addition to a prologue and epilogue, 15 chapters entitled, respectively: "Women"; "Ludovic or Departure from Europe"; "Inside an American Family"; "Marie"; "The Alms House at Baltimore"; "The Mystery"; "The Revelation"; "The Test" (four Chapters, the last two of which carry added subtitles: "Episode at Oneida," "Literature and the Fine Arts"); "A (Slave) Uprising"; "Departure from Civilized America"; "The Virgin Forest and the Wilderness"; "The Conclusion."

[11] An unsigned review appeared in 53 *Quarterly Review* (1835) 289. The review was highly favorable: "The French book now before us is the most interesting that has ever yet been published on the subject of American society and manners by a native of the European continent." He compared *Marie* with the recently published accounts of America by such English travelers as Hall, Hamilton, and Mrs. Trollope—in favor of Beaumont. See also, *Atkinson's Casket,* No. 8 (August 1835), 474; 27 *Museum of Foreign Literature* (July 1835) 33 (reprinting the

entirely secondary to the searching character of its insights into a problem which was then, as it is today, one of the major tests of democracy in action. Beaumont observed the the position of Negroes, and Indians also, in all sections of the America of the 1830's—observed it with a shrewd and critical eye. What he saw burned into his memory—deep lines of conscientious revolt which he etched as deeply in his tragic romance of a mixed marriage. As a novel of protest *Marie* drives home the basic issues in race relations in our time as for Beaumont's readers a century ago, with an emotional force perhaps more inexorable than the more intellectual analysis of the *Democracy*.

Tocqueville's grand design was rapidly completed, once the prison report was out of the way. Working with the aid

---

[London] *Quarterly Review*); I *National Enquirer* (December 10, 1836) 56 ("Amalgamation in New Orleans," an excerpt from *Marie*); 5 *Western Monthly Magazine* (August 1836) 471 (translation of passages from *Marie*).

Beaumont delivered a paper before L'Académie des Sciences Morales et Politiques on his American observations. See 1 *Mémoires de L'Académie* . . . (2nd series, 1837), 125 ff. A paper by Tocqueville follows immediately.

A comparison of individual topics discussed by both Beaumont and Tocqueville is interesting; the following table indicates some of the more important:

Topic	*Marie*		*Democracy in America*		
	Vol.	*Pages*	*Vol.*	*Part*	*Chapters*
Women	I	22–3	II	3	ix. Education of Women
					x. Woman as wife
					xii. Equality of sexes
Family	I	53–65		3	viii. Democracy and the family
					xi. Equality and morals
					xii. Family circles
Conversation	I	68–72		3	xiv. Manners
					xv. Gravity of Americans
					xvii. Society in America
Religion	I II	96–9 181–255		1	v. Religion and democracy
					vi. Catholicism
					vii. Democracy and pantheism
				2	xv. Religion and immaterial interests

of the documents and memoranda he had brought home or sent for after his return, the notes and diaries he had collected on his trip to America, he devoted himself to the task of writing the *Democracy* under a rigid daily schedule. He employed two young Americans resident in Paris, Theodore Sedgwick III and Francis J. Lippitt,[12] to aid him in translating documents and abstracting materials. In the summer of 1834 Part I of *Democracy in America* was ready for the press; it was published in the following January. Part II was written at a more leisurely pace; it appeared in 1840, to complete a project conceived by Tocqueville a decade earlier.

The purpose of the trip to America was achieved. The *Democracy* presented the whole panorama of politics, observed in detail in one country, to be sure, but projected on a universal canvas. The first part treated specific aspects of government and politics in America: the Federal Constitution and the working of the Federal government; less of the state governments, but even more of local government (where Tocqueville found the taproot of democracy in self-government). Behind these formal or structural elements of democratic government, Tocqueville explored such questions as the advantages and defects of universal suffrage, the idea and the practice of the rule of law in America, the nature

Topic	*Marie*		*Democracy in America*		
	Vol.	*Pages*	*Vol.*	*Part*	*Chapters*
Literature, Arts, and Sciences	I	242–66		1	ix. Science, literature, arts
					x. Practical work
					xi. Spirit in art
					xii. American monuments
					xiii–xiv. Literature
					xvi. English language
					xvii. Poetry
					xviii. Oratory
					xix. Drama
					xx. Historians
					xxi. Parliamentary eloquence
Negroes	I	167–76	I		xviii. Situation of the Blacks
	I	191–8			
	II	226–311			
Indians	I	182–91			xviii. (343–70)
	II	226–311			

[12] 68:731 ff. and notes.

of majority rule and the likelihood of a "tyranny of the majority," the effects of centralized administration on the citizen's interest in his government, the relations of religion and democracy, and the future of the three principal races in America. The first part as a whole is as comprehensively descriptive as it is critically analytical. There are frequent references to statutes, legislative reports, statistical data, and commentaries on their own institutions by Americans, as well as to many direct observations of his own. It is a treatise on government by the people—in America in the 1830's. There are, however, presages of the more general approach that Tocqueville was to adopt in the second part.

The second part is essentially a philosophical examination of social and economic as well as political change, traced more through the application of universal generalizations than of American data or experience. Although America is its focus and many references to American phenomena are utilized by Tocqueville, he is here less an observer than a prophet of change at home. Many of his particular forecasts of social, economic, and political change in America have been vindicated by events; others have not. His observations are not less interesting or significant to us today because not all have proved true for ourselves, or for other countries. We catch shrewd glimpses of life in America as it was a century ago from Tocqueville's observations of our society and economy as well as of our polity. Even more, we discover some of the permanent factors and conditions affecting the working of democracy as idea as well as practice.

The position of women, our aptitude for "association," the influence of the frontier on manners and morals, the diffusion of knowledge and culture (without the high attainment of the older European, aristocratic societies), the armed services in a democracy, the conditions likely to create an "aristocracy of manufactures"—these are only a few of the topics in the second part on which Tocqueville offers acute descriptions and judgments. One is impressed throughout by his search for the principles underlying action, principles susceptible of universal, not merely American, application. Here Tocqueville seems to be fulfilling the original purpose of his trip to America, to provide for every people a guide by which it can achieve the advantages of democracy without accepting its potential defects. The permanent—and perennial—quality of his observations and insights is evident even when the data on which they are based are no longer relevant. The second part ranks even among the greatest of social philosophies from Aristotle to Pareto; as a reasoned and objective appraisal of the democratic way of life it is unsurpassed.[13]

His original purpose in the trip to America and in the design for the *Democracy* was constantly in his thoughts during this period and continuously animated his writing. He expressed that purpose in a letter to one of his closest friends scarcely a month after the first part of his work appeared. Tocqueville's words give us a clear impression of his faith in his ultimate objective.

This is the political object of the work:

I wished to show what a democratic people really was in our day; and by a rigorously accurate picture to produce a double effect on the men of my day. To those who have fancied an ideal democracy, a brilliant and easily realized dream, I endeavored to show that they had clothed the picture in false colors; that the republican government which they extol, even though it may bestow substantial benefits on a people that can bear it, has none of the elevated features with which their imagination would endow it, and moreover that such a government cannot be maintained without certain conditions of intelligence, of private morality, and of religious belief that we, as a nation, have not reached, and that we must labor to attain before grasping their political results.

To those for whom the word *democracy* is synonymous with destruction, anarchy, spoliation, and murder, I have tried to show that under a democratic government the fortunes and the rights of society may be respected, liberty preserved, and religion honored; that though a republic may develop less than other governments some of the noblest powers of the human mind, it yet has a nobility of its own; and that after all it may be God's will to spread a moderate amount of happiness over all men, instead of heaping a large sum upon a few by allowing only a small minority to approach perfection. I attempted to prove to them that whatever their opinions might be, deliberation was no longer in their power; that society was tending every day more and more towards equality, and dragging them and everyone else along with it; that the only choice lay between two inevitable evils; that the question had ceased to be whether they would have an aristocracy or a democracy, and now lay between a democracy without poetry

[13] For a more complete analysis of the contents and significance of the two parts, see, especially, 68: chs. 56–8; 15 and 16, *passim*.

or elevation indeed, but with order and morality; and an undisciplined and depraved democracy, subject to sudden frenzies, or to a yoke heavier than any that has galled mankind since the fall of the Roman Empire.

I wish to diminish the ardor of the republican party and, without disheartening them, to point out their only wise course. I have endeavored to abate the claims of the aristocrats and to make them bend to an irresistible future; so that the impulse in one quarter and resistance in the other being less violent, society may march on peaceably towards the fulfillment of its destiny. This is the dominant idea in the book—an idea which embraces all the others, and which you ought to have made out more clearly. Hitherto, however, few have discovered it. I please many persons of opposite opinions, not because they penetrate my meaning, but because, looking at only one side of my work, they think that they can find in it arguments in favor of their own convictions. But I have faith in the future, and I hope that the day will come when all will see clearly what now only a few suspect. . . .[14]

HOW "DEMOCRACY IN AMERICA" WAS RECEIVED

From the first, *Democracy in America* was recognized as a political treatise of the first order. It served the intellectual leaders of the day as a litmus paper by which to test the process of change from aristocratic to democratic institutions. Wherever thoughtful men weighed the prospect of revolutionary change, then as now the concern of every European capital, the *Democracy* won instant recognition if not universal acclaim. Here was a book that went to the heart of the profound issues confronting the Continent. It was at once eagerly read and widely reviewed.

[14] Letter to M. Stoffels (Paris, February 21, 1835), 90:I, 397. An interesting minor discussion arose in the 1860's regarding the true authorship of the *Democracy*. An article appeared in 1864, under the title: "The authorship of 'Democracy in America,'" (18:332). The writer records a conversation held several years previously with an Alexandre Vittemare of Paris, who asserted unequivocally that it was the work of John C. Spencer, not of Tocqueville. His proof was an examination of internal evidence of the *Democracy's* opinions on American institutions and of its style. In a review, attributed by Pierson to Heilprin, of the eighth volume of the *Œuvres Complètes,* in 45:247, the reviewer refers to "Spencer, whose philosophic views on various important topics, as expressed in his lucid answers to the traveler's queries, fully agree with, if they have not originated, the conclusions arrived at by the latter in his analysis of American institutions." See 97:VIII, 236 ff.

Before the second part had appeared, the first had been translated into English and Spanish; the second part was immediately translated into these languages. During the next few decades translations were made into at least five others: Danish, German, Italian, Russian, and Serbian. In America the *Democracy* ran through many early editions and was soon issued in various abridgments for school use. From the 1840's to the 1940's it has remained an enduring source of insight and inspiration for each new generation in search of the fundamental criteria of and conditions for economic, social, and political democracy.

The intellectual history of a book like the *Democracy* is itself an index of the character of the changes that have occurred in ideas and institutions and the validity of the new directions of public policy and private action that have been pursued. A review of contemporary and later opinions about *Democracy in America* will, therefore, help to suggest its original influence on Western thought as well as something of its continuing significance for our own time. We may well begin by noting its reception in France, and from there proceed to England and then to America. Finally we may compare some of these early appraisals with those of today.[15]

In France

Although even the publisher, Gosselin, remarked apropos of the reception accorded the *Democracy:* "Ah, but it seems that you have created a masterpiece!" and although Tocque-

[15] The appraisals and criticisms noted in this section bear upon the general character of the *Democracy* rather than upon Tocqueville's specific observations and judgments. Many reviews and comments were found to contain numerous accords with or dissents from particular elements of the book. To analyze them in detail would be interesting but minuscule in result. Many of the conditions underlying Tocqueville's commentary on democracy have changed so greatly as to make his minor errors seem, in the transit of time, major faults of analysis. It is more relevant to trace here the recurrent awareness of the *Democracy's* uniqueness and timeliness than to determine the exact correctness of either its contemporary descriptions and appraisals or the permanent validity of its prophecies. An effort has been made to analyze all the reviews of the *Democracy* that have appeared in American, English, and French journals. See note 86.

ville was ultimately elected to the Académie Française,[16] England and America at first gave the work as much attention as did his native country. Tocqueville had not written the *Democracy* only for the benefit of Americans, that they might better understand and appreciate the working of their institutions. He had studied those institutions—as indeed the second part of his work even more clearly demonstrated—in order to show how and to what extent democracy was applicable to Europe and especially to France. It was to his fellow countrymen living in a time of domestic crisis that the *Democracy* was primarily addressed.

Tocqueville's work received immediate acknowledgment from philosophers and politicians of his own country from the day of its first publication. The *Democracy* was widely reviewed in French journals and in the press, one review appearing even before the book was published. Almost without exception, these reviews were enthusiastic, few reserved or critical, in their praise.[17] Among the intellectual leaders, whose judgments were tempered by an informed sense of the quality of Tocqueville's thought and style, Sainte-Beuve's comment is typical. "There is not a chapter in the book which does not bespeak one of the best and most resolute minds, one of the most gifted in political observation in a field in which there have been few such brilliant and substantial contributions since the incomparable monument reared by Montesquieu." In summing up his opinion of the first part, he wrote:

> M. de Tocqueville's book, if read completely, would furnish material for the study of all great questions in modern politics; we have tried only to depict its general conclusions and the spirit that produced it. In praising this book so recently published we indeed merely confirm the already established judgment of serious and competent persons. The opinions of

[16] In 1841. He had been elected to the Académie des Sciences Morales et Politiques in 1838. See 55:887–90. See also A. de Tocqueville: *Discours de M. de Tocqueville prononcé dans la séance publique* [de l'Institut royale de France, Académie Française] *de 21 Avril, 1842* (Paris: Didot; 1842).

[17] See 68:3–6, 78–93 for a list of the more important early French reviews and appraisals. Another list appears in Beaumont's *Introduction* to the *Democracy* in *L'Œuvres Complètes de Alexis de Tocqueville* (published by Madame de Tocqueville, 9 vols., Paris, 1861–5) 97:I, vi. Pierson (68:4 n.) notes only one adverse appraisal among twenty-three contemporary French articles on the *Democracy*.

Chateaubriand, of Royer-Collard, of Lamartine, have been strongly enough stated for us to record them without fear of deception by pleasant appearances. It is necessary to go far into the past to find a work of scholarship and political observation that has attracted and rewarded the attention of serious thinkers to the same degree.[18]

Many of the early French reviewers were more enthusiastic than understanding; they sometimes utilized Tocqueville's ideas as a basis for expounding their own rather than evaluating his observations and theories. This was perhaps natural since Tocqueville was writing for his own countrymen about problems then deeply agitating the French nation. An exception was a review by Rossi, who said, especially of the second part of the *Democracy:*

To speak of democracy, of the power of this factor in society, of the difficulty of tracing it and studying it thoroughly amid the complexities of modern society, this is to speak of M. de Tocqueville's book; and especially, of the second part of his great study, two volumes he has just added to this splendid work which placed him, still so very young, among the ablest writers and most eminent thinkers of our times. . . .

Within the balance of his thoughtful, careful mind, M. de Tocqueville has let us glimpse his likes and his dislikes, his hopes and his fears. Although he preferred to speak of the facts and opinions he had observed, rather than the feelings he had experienced, M. de Tocqueville did not affect a detachment, an indifference, which would hardly be conceivable in the discoverer of a new mineral. He remained a man and a citizen before the facts he observed and never concealed his varied and successive impressions.

The sincerity of a writer who thus revealed himself in his book, not only the working of his mind but the emotions of his soul, this sincerity led some persons to say of his first work that he had changed his opinion of democracy as he went along; that he had begun and completed his book with two contrary points of view. We cannot possibly accept this opinion; the author had not changed, but democracy, which, like all things human, is far from uniform in all its manifestations and all its effects. . . .

We seek in vain, in the second part, for the precise and well-defined contours, the positive conclusions and irrefutable proofs which characterized the first part. M. de Tocqueville could not do the impossible and change the nature of things. . . .

Among the great variety of topics, opinions, and judgments, a reader will without doubt disagree with the author on more

[18] 26:42.

than one point; but no objective reader will fail to admire on every page the clarity of presentation, the keenness of observation, the wise judgment, the ingenious strokes, the simple and lively, yet firm and graceful style that characterize the writing of M. de Tocqueville. His book is an exquisite work of a perfection that leaves nothing to be desired, unless, perhaps, some carelessness. . . .

M. de Tocqueville has, then, written the book he wished to write, and we are grateful to him for having written a work on higher political philosophy of the first order, a profound and conscientious analysis of a most complex social condition, but therefore all the more worthy of study in that it harbors within its depths the future of the world.[19]

Writing the same year, also of the second part, Villemain said:

The success of the first two volumes is established; many people considered them not only excellent, but comprehensive, and then recognized in general that no subject had for a long tine been treated with so much force and wisdom, better method, a more natural and vigorous style. . . .

This second work is, in truth, more difficult and less effective than the first; the author is not equally sustained by a foundation of actual laws and historic events; he had only the details to portray, anecdotes to assemble, moral inferences to grasp or sometimes even to conjecture. . . .[20]

Laboulaye, in assessing the reasons for the failure of the second part to attain the success of the first, attributed it to the varying approaches to the problem of democracy which Tocqueville had adopted. In a review (written about twenty years after the first) he said:

The same error of M. de Tocqueville is not to have perceived that the name of democracy covers the most diverse societies; there are in play a thousand influences that intermingle and combine with political life: that is why any general conclusions seem to me hazardous and almost always, upon reflection, contradictory.[21]

[19] 78:890–9 (*passim*).

[20] 98:257–9.

[21] 50:173. The point made by Laboulaye should be borne in mind by the reader of the *Democracy*. The word "democracy" is used by Tocqueville in at least half a dozen senses in relation to various questions he discusses. These senses will appear to the thoughtful reader who seeks to penetrate below the surface of Tocqueville's language to his thought. One of the most careful modern students of Tocqueville, Salomon, has suggested to me that, in fact, Tocqueville more often analyzed what we would

In the same year Loménie wrote of the *Democracy:*

In studying American democracy on the scene, in seeing this kind of government, mankind's most recent creation, at work, he understood all the inherent force in the principle of equality which serves as its basis. While taking into serious account the differences that arise from the backgrounds and customs of each people, he recognized that the democratic principle whose most general results were everywhere about the same, after having established control in the New World, tended more and more to take possession of the Old World; and from then on he undertook to study it in all its manifestations on the very scene of its fullest realization, and to analyze at the same time the philosophic anatomy of American democracy in particular, and of the democratic principle in general. . . .

The first two volumes . . . caused a lively sensation. The profundity of its meaning, the beauty, at once elegant and severe, of its style, the elevation and newness of its opinions, the logic of its thoughts, the nobility and warmth of its sentiments, immediately placed this work among the masterpieces of our serious literature; and the author, practically unknown on the eve before, was, at his first attempt, placed among the greatest writers and most profound thinkers of our century: he was not yet thirty. In this kind of philosophic and political literature there are few examples of such precociousness. . . .

It is in these last two volumes that the eloquent publicist, departing from an exclusive study of American society, has offered, in our opinion, the most profound and newest ideas on the most varied subjects. . . .

The literally universal fame of so profound a work, its reputation already consecrated by the passing of time, is it not the most irrefutable sign of superiority, and does it not excuse us from defending the quiet and manly genius of Alexis de Tocqueville against those who might fail to recognize his power? Let us say only that if the author of *Democracy in America* could boldly disdain the pleasure of witty arguments, it was because he could grasp directly the most important, most general and pressing social phenomenon of the nineteenth century, see through it, and analyze it in all its parts, reduce it by a synthesis to its most essential elements, and impress its meaning upon the public both because of the elevation, the profundity, the clarity of his ideas, and the charm of an

---

today call "liberalism" than "democracy." Pierson discusses this point with great insight; see 68:158 n., 163, 165, 745, 746, 748, 757–8. He suggests that the title might well have been *Concerning Equality in America.*

austere style which betrayed emotion at the deep seriousness of the issues.[32]

Two years after Tocqueville's death, Paul Janet, more briefly than Loménie, discussed Tocqueville's purpose in writing the *Democracy*, and the relative success with which his purpose had been achieved:

> He believed that the democratic revolution was inevitable, or rather that it was already accomplished, and instead of debating a priori on the justice or injustice of that great fact, he thought that it would be better to observe it, and to leave to others the task of either exalting or condemning it; he limited himself to knowing it, and understanding it. It was this impartiality that both astonished and at the same time attracted in *Democracy in America*. People admire without understanding it.[33]

Janet also noted that the major issue which Tocqueville set himself to analyze and to answer was still unresolved:

> A major fault already noted in the *Democracy* is that the viewpoint of the author is constantly divided between two different subjects, which in spite of several essential similarities, cannot be brought into the same system, namely democracy. It is certain, it is evident that the problem that disturbed M. de Tocqueville and that brought him to the United States is the problem of European democracy. It is this very fact which gives to this book its grandeur, I might almost say its emotional quality, but which at the same time introduces a certain obscurity. Tocqueville describes America, but he thinks of Europe; hence those contradictory observations that cannot be applied at the same time to both.[34]

As the years passed, the *Democracy* was less read in France; the writer and the work were less discussed. The death of Tocqueville in 1859 produced a series of notable eulogies, both French and English; of the former, those of Guizot and Lacordaire, his successor at the Académie Française, were laudatory and appreciative of his greatness. Not until the centennial of the *Democracy* was Tocqueville again widely discussed in France. A few isolated writers, however,

[32] 55:401–7 ff.
[33] 47:105.
[34] Ibid.:116.

such as Emile Faguet, near the close of the century, took notice of the work. Faguet thought that:

> . . . This book, which gave cause for so much thought and which is so worthy of its reputation, had only the fault of being too full and too comprehensive. Tocqueville is so preoccupied and obsessed with the idea of democracy that he records all that he saw in the United States, and attributes to the existence of democracy on American soil all that which is characteristic and striking, and even ordinary, from Boston to New Orleans. . . .
>
> There were the makings of two works in his notes, one on American life, the other on American democracy. He should have written each one separately.[25]

Pierre Marcel was equally critical:

> . . . Tocqueville often let himself indulge in developing to no end the effects of non-decisive causes; and he did not stop until he had raised his observations to a high degree of abstraction. . . .
>
> Spontaneously, he then admits proceeding by preconceived ideas. Whatever he may say to the contrary, veering toward a different direction, he warns us himself that his works have one aim: to demonstrate a thesis. An observer thus always in danger of being partial, he runs the risk of imposing on history and on the study of reality certain arbitrary personal notions; he does not disguise facts, but he tends toward choosing them; selecting those most favorable for his thesis, he ends up by dealing with fine points and exaggerated subtleties in a vacuum.
>
> He was convinced that moral forces alone had a significant value. Tocqueville thus deprived himself of a precious resource to his disadvantage, especially in the treatment of "democracy."
>
> If he bases his inquiry on strict documentation and much significant evidence, in his very exposition he seeks too much to discard all particular proof, to which he attributes only the value of brief illustrative examples which could give only an inconclusive point to the picture. . . .
>
> Tocqueville overdid his approach; he committed the great mistake of not realizing that the name "democracy" covers the most diverse societies. . . . His views are debatable when he presents them as laws of democracy itself.[26]

Most French writers who commented on Tocqueville during this period continued to discuss points of individual difference of opinion with Tocqueville's ideas, especially on particular aspects of his analysis of democracy (or equal-

[25] 32:656.
[26] 57:90–101.

ity). Recognition of the *Democracy's* qualities of insight and perspective was often somewhat tempered; criticism of errors of prophecy or of observation, no longer applicable to changed conditions, was not infrequent.

A century after the publication of the first part of the *Democracy* the event was celebrated on both sides of the Atlantic. Tocqueville again came into his own; appreciation of the enduring greatness of his work was more general. Modern appraisals were frequently, however, less critical analyses of the work than discussions of the validity of Tocqueville's prophecies. With the advantage of a century of change against which to project the altered conditions of American democracy, some of these appraisals now acknowledged the remarkable accuracy with which Tocqueville had foreseen future trends in democratic institutions.

In England

Although Tocqueville wrote about American democracy primarily for the benefit of his fellow countrymen, the book received its fullest and most critical consideration in England, which Tocqueville considered to be intellectually his "second country." [27] Upon the publication of the first part in France, Tocqueville sent copies to several British journals, hoping they would give it notice. The slowness with which they complied was explained to the author by his friend the British economist Nassau William Senior, in a letter of March 24, 1834:

> My dear Sir,—Pray accept my best thanks for your excellent work "De la Démocratie en Amérique," which I have read with great interest, delight, and I hope instruction. It appears to me one of the most remarkable books of the age. I am anxious that it should be reviewed and translated here; but there is great difficulty in getting a review of any book requiring much thought. Those who are competent for such a work seldom like to write anonymously.[28]

The *Democracy* was, however, reviewed in the latter part of 1835. The first and perhaps the most notable English review was that by John Stuart Mill, the leader of English

[27] 89:I, 5.
[28] Ibid.:2.

liberalism, in the *London and Westminster Review*. *De la démocratie en Amérique* had by this time been translated into English; the translator, Henry Reeve, was at first skeptical of the book's success, because of the unfavorable light in which he thought Tocqueville had presented democratic government.[29] In his preface to the third English edition Reeve, who had become an enthusiastic admirer of the work, attempted to extenuate his earlier views by stating:

> It is presumed that the lesson will not be less worthy of our attention because it is given us by a writer whose national experience and whose standard of comparison is more democratic than anything which we are acquainted with in England.[30]

Mill, who was from the first deeply impressed by the *Democracy*, said in the same vein:

> But though we would soften the colors of the picture we would not alter them; M. de Tocqueville's is in our eyes, the true view of the position in which mankind now stand: and on the timely recognition of it as such, by the influential classes of our own and other countries, we believe the most important interests of our race to be greatly dependent.

Mill went on to comment upon the lack of bias which so struck all readers, and which provided both liberals and conservatives of the time with material for substantiating their views:

> Not a trace of prejudice, or so much as a previous leaning either to the side of democracy or aristocracy, shows itself in his work. He is indeed anything but indifferent to the ends to which all forms of government profess to be the means. He manifests the deepest concern for all the great interests, material and spiritual of the human race.[31]

He also noted the ambivalent quality of the *Democracy* in a review of the second part, in commenting on its use to justify such conservative ideas as Sir Robert Peel's.[32] After examining and criticizing several of Tocqueville's ideas, Mill summed up the work as follows:

> The book of which we have now described the plan and purpose, has been executed in a manner worthy of so noble a

[29] See J. K. Laughton: *Memoirs of the Life and Correspondence of Henry Reeve* (2 vols.; London: Macmillan; 1898).
[30] 74:vii.
[31] 62:91–3.
[32] 63:II, 80.

scheme. It has at once taken its rank among the most remarkable productions of our time; and is a book with which, both for its facts and its speculations, all who would understand, or who are called upon to exercise influence over their age, are bound to be familiar. It will contribute to give to the political speculations of our time a new character.

M. de Tocqueville, among the first, has set the example of analysing democracy. . . . He does this with so noble a field as a great nation to demonstrate upon; which field he has commenced by minutely examining; selecting, with a discernment of which we have had no previous example, the material facts, and surveying these by the light of principles, drawn from no ordinary knowledge of human nature. We do not think his conclusions always just, but we think them always entitled to the most respectful attention, and never destitute of at least a large foundation of truth. The author's mind, except that it is of a soberer character, seems to us to resemble Montesquieu most among the French writers.

. . . We feel how impossible it is, in the space of an article to exemplify all the features of a work, every page of which has nearly as great a claim to citation as any other. For M. de Tocqueville's ideas do not float upon a sea of words, none of his propositions are unmeaning, none of his meanings superfluous; not a paragraph could have been omitted without diminishing the value of the work.[83]

Following the first Mill article, other reviews of varying degrees of enthusiasm appeared in England; none pleased the author as much as that of Mill. In a letter to Mill of December 3, 1835, Tocqueville wrote:

. . . Of all my reviewers, you are perhaps, the only one who has thoroughly understood me; who has taken a general bird's-eye-view of my ideas; who sees their ulterior aim, and yet has preserved a clear perception of the details. The profession of an author would be too delightful if one met with many such readers! Your article, therefore, gave me intense pleasure. I keep it carefully, to prove to myself that it really is possible to understand me. I wanted this testimony to console me for all the false conclusions that are drawn from my book. I am constantly meeting people who want to persuade me of opinions that I proclaim, or who pretend to share with me opinions that I do not hold.[84]

Many English reviewers seemed, however, to catch the challenge of the *Democracy* to their own conservative ideas

[83] Ibid.:94–5. See also J. S. Mill: *Autobiography* (J. J. Cross, ed. New York: Columbia University Press: 1924), 134–6, 141.
[84] 90:II. 18.

and institutions at home. They were more than ready to criticize, perhaps because they also realized that the works of English (and other) travelers were responsible for the misconceptions about America that existed prior to, and even after, the publication of the *Democracy*. Apparently they did not wish to grant too much credit to a Frenchman. A review in *Blackwood's Edinburgh Magazine* in 1835 suggests the general tone of the English reviews. The review, although recognizing the general ignorance concerning American institutions, went on to claim credit for the English for all that was commendable in American democracy. It emphasized the divergencies from English, and the least favorable aspects of American, institutions. It noted particularly their instability without adding Tocqueville's qualifications as to the causes for this instability. The review, as did many of its successors, praised the impartiality as well as the design of the work, recommending it "as the very best plan on the subject of America that we have ever met with." [35]

The *Quarterly Review* of 1836 discussed the dubious reliability of previous European and American works on American democracy. Here much of the credit is given to Tocqueville's nationality. Lacking the greater familiarity with American institutions that the English possessed, he was all the more careful in his analysis and observation, thus avoiding important omissions that might have resulted from this familiarity. The reviewer summarized his opinion in the following words:

> Heretofore, almost every writer has confined himself, generally without any consciousness of the fact, to a description of the results; or if he has indulged in speculations thereupon it is mostly with a view to advance some favorable dogma of his own—to sustain those political views to which he is attached in his own country—or to amuse himself and his readers with the expansion of some philosophical principles which he considers of practical importance in the science of political economy. We speak just now of the foreigners who have undertaken to describe the United States.
>
> The effect of all this had been, to introduce an extremely loose and incorrect notion of the true condition of the United States in Europe, and in no country are these vague and false impressions more generally diffused than in England. . . .

[35] 107:766.

It is our opinion that M. de Tocqueville has approached the working of the American institutions in a better temper, and treated it in a far more philosophical manner than any preceding writer.[86]

Continuing as did Mill to praise Tocqueville's absence of bias, so unique at the time in a work of the sort, the reviewer recognized its importance to the English public as a source of information and enlightenment on a faith which would inevitably lead to a way of life.

Persons, indeed, who seek in these pages for materials to advance any merely party, or other selfish purposes, will certainly be disappointed, for they are entirely free from "envy, hatred, and malice, and all uncharitableness." Neither is there any satire contained in them, expressed or understood; all is grave and plain, and aboveboard, and withal so temperate that even where we do not agree with his deductions, our confidence in his good faith and singleness of purpose remains unbroken. This is a great charm. We cannot, indeed, recall to memory another work at all similar to this, in which there is no narrative, nor any other enlivening circumstance to give it animation, and yet in which the interest is sustained from beginning to end without ever once flagging. . . .

It is due to Mr. Reeve, the translator of M. de Tocqueville's very nice and delicate language to bear our testimony to the fidelity with which he has executed a task of considerable difficulty. We strongly recommend him to use his influence with his publisher, to bring out the book in a cheaper shape, in order that the interesting information and practical wisdom with which it abounds may be placed within the reach of those classes where prejudice and error take their firmest stand. In conclusion we once more congratulate the public on their having at last obtained a popular account of America, written in the very purest spirit of philosophy, and with rare temperance, and that persons of all parties, and of all shades of parties, may read it not only with profit, but without their patience being ruffled.[87]

The reviewer for the *British and Foreign Review* of the same year came even closer to Tocqueville's true intent. Tocqueville, he thought, had carefully examined democratic institutions as he saw them operate in America and had tried to point out those principles that were best suited to being transplanted from the United States to Europe. This was evidenced by the generalizations that Tocqueville was

[86] 43:137. The reviewer was Captain Basil Hall.
[87] Ibid.:133–4.

able to draw from his observations in explaining the strengths and weaknesses of the principles he discussed. He did not attempt to force any set of principles upon the French, for whom he was writing. Recognizing the variety of conditions existing in the two countries, Tocqueville indicated similarities in these conditions, but offered no program of action for France. Although the reviewer thought there was little of value for the English reader, he felt that Tocqueville had performed an invaluable service for those to whom democracy was still new and strange. In discussing "the accurate and instructive account of the government of the United States which is here for the first time presented to the European public," he said:

> Whatever may be the ends of government, his first object has been to describe the means by which democracy has been established in America; whilst he approves the skillful adaptation of a new political system to that new people, he leaves the reader to adapt such conclusions as to the value and fitness of the democratic principle in itself, as may result from a knowledge of what it is able, and what it is unable to effect.[89]

Despite individual differences of opinion and criticisms of portions of the first part, especially from the conservatives, there was common appreciation of its general excellence of observation and analysis. The eagerness with which the second part was awaited, as well as the widespread acclaim received by the first, made its appearance in 1840 almost anticlimactic. A five-year period had elapsed; it was impossible to maintain public interest for so long a time (as Tocqueville, indeed, was well aware). The increasing prestige of the first part served to place the new and more philosophically speculative section of his work at some disadvantage in British opinion.

The continuing praise of the first part created wide divergence of critical opinion when the two were compared. Tocqueville, in another letter to John Stuart Mill (December 18, 1840), with regard to a review by Mill of the second part, which had occupied so much more of his time than the more popular first part, voiced his concern over its reception:

> The success of the second part of the *Democracy* has been less general in France than that of the first part. In our day,

[89] 112:305.

I seldom think the public mistaken; I, therefore, am applying myself industriously to discover the fault that I have committed, probably a considerable one. I think that it belongs to the purpose for which the book was written, which is too abstract and raises too many questions to please the public. When I wrote only upon the democratic society in the United States I was understood directly. If I had written upon democratic society in France as it exists at the present day, that again would have been easily understood. But using the ideas derived from American and French democracy only as data, I endeavoured to paint the general features of democratic societies; no complete specimen of which can yet be said to exist. This is what an ordinary reader fails to appreciate. Only those who are much accustomed to searching for abstract and speculative truths care to follow me in such an inquiry. I believe that the comparatively little effect produced by my book is to be attributed to the original sin of the subject itself, rather than to the manner in which I have treated my particular portion.[39]

It was, indeed, this new approach that was largely responsible for some unfavorable comments. The first part had been criticized for its tendency to reduce all facts to generalizations. In the second, Tocqueville seemed to be speculating on the basis of generalizations, to be trying to make them factual. More closely reasoned and less concrete than the first part, the second required greater concentration from the reader, an effort that many were not disposed to make.

One English reviewer said of the second part of the work that Tocqueville's thesis was "more within the compass of his natural ability and acquired knowledge than that with which he attempted to grapple in his former publication." The review continued:

The want of logical sequence is so great, that we nowhere find in the whole book one example of a general principle evolved from a collection of facts. He rambles on, saying, in every sentence, something striking or instructive; but never approximating to a result; leaving the mind of the reader completely at sea. . . . We retain an agreeable impression of many brilliant and touching passages: but we have been taught nothing like a practical truth. . . . The mode of thought, the feelings which he attributes, is, in many instances essentially French.[40]

[39] 90:II, 62.
[40] 146:507–8.

Another attempted to explain the difficulty by comparing the two parts. According to this reviewer, the first part was a

> . . . Solid body of facts . . . whether they [the readers] liked or disliked the inferences to which his remarks seemed to point, they acknowledged, either promptly or reluctantly, that his statements, and his comments upon them,. were fair, luminous, and most eminently instructive.
>
> His treatment of the second part of his subject . . . is not . . . likely to meet with the same universal approbation and applause. These volumes are purely reflective. . . . To give to generalizations the preciseness and applicability of practical deduction is quite impossible.[47]

It was not so much the content of the second part that the reviewer complained of as what seemed to him the absence of facts to substantiate the disputable conclusions Tocqueville advocated. The presentation of universal theories evolved from generalizations on conditions observed only under democratic institutions in the United States seemed to him unjustified. Part of the difficulty was ascribed to the varying attitudes on equality that were held in France and America. Tocqueville was well aware of this weakness, and would perhaps have agreed with the reviewer that:

> In France he [Tocqueville] seems to fancy he has discovered the passion of all nations; and this notion, which forms the very base of the whole argument of his two volumes, falsifies radically all the dubious and frightened deductions he has drawn from it.[48]

A review in the *British and Foreign Review* recognized the reasons for the English reception of the second part in the very situation the previous critic disparaged. Tocqueville was writing for France with America in mind; it would be only natural that the work would be better understood and appreciated in those two countries than in a nation that had not advanced as far as democratically as had America. Not only did Tocqueville face the universal difficulty of repeating a success, but the lack of facts, which had substantiated and made the generalizations of the first part so valuable, made controversy over the second almost inevitable. The style in which these volumes were written was even more precise and concentrated, and Tocqueville's attitude was not

[47] 108:463.
[48] Ibid.:470.

quite so impartial. He had had time to reflect on what he had seen and to speculate on how far American institutions would be applicable to France, as well as on the practical difficulties that would inevitably arise in their application. This resulted at times in an almost fatalistic note, which was absent in the earlier part. The reviewer admitted, however, that:

> No brief critical sketch can give a complete notion of the coherence of the ideas to be traced in the thoughtful perusal, which hardly any man who thinks at all on such subjects, can fail to bestow on these volumes. . . .
>
> The design of these volumes is far more extensive and profound than that of a mere disquisition on existing social phenomena, intended simply to excite the understanding, or beget an opinion. There is a spirit in the book of a more living and practical nature,—a spirit of expostulation and exhortation, a constant vindication of the higher elements of social existence, and an eminent attachment to those great spiritual and moral truths upon which the life of nations does in reality depend. Its principal object is to educate men for the condition which it foretells, to warn them of its dangers, and to teach them how to apply its principles.[43]

The review of the second part in the *Dublin University Magazine* was far less favorable. Commenting on the general success of the first part and admitting originality and insight inherent in the materials of the second, the reviewer summed up Tocqueville's thesis of the necessity of equality by saying that:

> Of all social conditions, equality is, previous to inquiry, the most attractive; but our parting impression is, that every candid person who forms his estimate of democracy from these volumes, when the subject is fully considered, and in no hostile spirit, must arrive at the one conclusion,—that it is unfavorable to the happiness of man, that its influences on his highest interests are so often malignant that it may be fairly regarded as nothing less than the greatest misery principle, and that, reversing the proposition of the Benthamites, it is calculated to effect the greatest misery of the greatest number.[44]

But the same magazine also said some years later:

> Its appearance, if greeted generally with less warmth than the first two volumes, drew forth the quiet approval of all

[43] 113:551–7.
[44] 114:563.

who could follow the author in his pursuit of abstract and speculative truths.[45]

And of the work as a whole it stated:

> The high-toned purpose audible in every line, the tacit reference throughout to French affairs, the mixture, so rare in France, of patient research, and sound judgment, with great force of rhetorical handling and a very quick eye for large results; all these combined to insure it a welcome more or less hearty from readers of very different kinds.[46]

In *Blackwood's Edinburgh Review* several years later Tocqueville was hailed as the greatest political philosopher of his day. Noting the fact that his book was no longer widely quoted, the reviewer remarked correctly that it would have a greater permanent than popular fame. He commended the capacity and judgment of the author:

> Alone of all the moderns, he has fixed the public attention upon the real danger of purely republican institutions; he first has discerned in their working in America, where it is that the lasting peril is to be apprehended. . . .

The reviewer concurred, however, in the general opinion that Tocqueville had somewhat impaired his reputation by the publication of the second part because of its "more questionable opinions."

> . . . His opinions do not equally as in the first two volumes bear the slight mark of truth stamped upon them. They are more speculative and fanciful; founded rather on contemplation of future than observation of present effects.[47]

John Stuart Mill's criticism of the second part noted the unusual interest of the British public in the work. Of the *Democracy* in general, he said:

> Its reputation was as sudden and is as extensive in this country as in France, and in that large part of Europe which receives its opinions from France. . . .
>
> [It is] the first philosophical book ever written on Democracy as it manifests itself in modern society; a book, the essential doctrines of which it is not likely that any future speculations will subvert, to whatever degree they may modify them; while

[45] 115:50.
[46] Ibid.:48.
[47] 109:526.

its spirit, and the general mode in which it treats its subject, constitute it the beginning of a new era in the science of politics.

M. de Tocqueville has endeavoured to ascertain and discriminate the various properties and tendencies of the Democracy; the separate relations which it stands towards, the different interests of society and the different moral and social requisites of human nature . . . he has earned the double honor of being the first to make the attempt, and of having done more towards the success of it than probably will ever be done again by any one individual.

Even Mill noted, however, that:

It is perhaps the greatest secret of M. de Tocqueville's book, that, from the scarcity of examples, his propositions even when derived from observation, have the air of being mere abstract speculations.[48]

Mill did not agree with those critics who emphasized the divergencies in order to explain Anglo-American reluctance to accept the second part. He thought that many similarities in English and American institutions did exist, and that the differences discussed in the second part were not unique to American democracy.

The *Democracy* received wide attention outside intellectual circles in England. The first Reform Bill had been enacted in 1832; its results were still being debated. Those who feared or hoped for the progress of democratic ideas and institutions in England discovered in Tocqueville arguments to buttress their opinions. Two or three examples will suggest the wide variety of the uses to which the *Democracy* was put.

Sir Robert Peel was elected Lord Rector of the University of Glasgow in 1836. The election was recognized as a victory for conservative opinion in a period when liberalism was still struggling for representation in all segments of English life, not least the educational. A public dinner was tendered to Peel at Glasgow on January 13, 1837, two days after his inauguration, from which some of his opponents for the Lord Rectorship deliberately absented themselves. Peel utilized the occasion to justify the superiority of conservative principles and institutions; he drew several of his

[48] 63:II, 80, 81, 82–3.

arguments from Tocqueville's fear of the tyranny of the majority.[49]

Thirty years later, electoral reform was again in the air; the merits of the Reform Bill of 1868 were already being debated on the hustings. Every level of English society was involved in the argument. It was a period when workingmen listened to classical scholars. On January 3, 1867 Professor J. S. Blackie of Edinburgh University delivered a lecture "On Democracy" to the Working Men's Institute, in which he utilized many of Tocqueville's observations on American democracy to prove the undesirability of its further extension in England. On the following evening, with only a single day's preparation, Ernest Jones replied—again finding in the *Democracy* many of his arguments for broadening the basis of English suffrage.[50]

Were nineteenth-century debates on democracy in England followed through the fugitive literature, the journals, and the works of the philosophers and political commentators, Tocqueville's continuing influence on English thought would be evident. Democracy took on new meanings and became more insistent during the last third of the century. The spirit of equality in politics spread to new areas of English life—education, industry, welfare, colonial government. Both liberals and conservatives drew, as we have seen, support for their economic, social, and political viewpoints and policies from the pages of the *Democracy*. Tocqueville's fear of the tyranny of the majority and his observations on its operation in America provided the conservatives with an arsenal of arguments against modifying the existing structure of English society. His optimism about the possibility of improving the conditions of life for all the people under democracy equipped the liberals with the factual as well as moral reasons for hastening the change. In his

[49] See letter to Peel from Edward Everett of March 29, 1837, commenting on his speech with approval, in C. S. Parker: *Sir Robert Peel from His Private Papers* (3 vols.; London: John Murray; 1899), II, 233; *A Correct Report of the speeches delivered by the right honourable Sir Robert Peel . . . on his inauguration into the office of lord rector of the University of Glasgow, January 11, 1837, and at the public dinner at Glasgow, January 13, 1837* (6th ed.; London: John Murray; 1837), 81 ff.

[50] J. S. Blackie: *On Democracy* (Edinburgh: Edmonston and Douglas; 1867), 32 ff.; E. Jones: *Democracy Vindicated* (Manchester: John Heywood; 1867), 12.

"second country" Tocqueville influenced popular as well as intellectual thought even more deeply than in his native France.

In the United States

In America the *Democracy* was, of course, eagerly read and its merits were warmly debated; it was our own democracy that was the major concern of the work, and Americans were already sensitive about foreign comments on domestic institutions. Despite its subject and the excellence of its manner of treatment, there were conflicting currents in its reception on this side of the Atlantic. On the whole, American reviews were favorable, even enthusiastic. The Americans were in a position to appreciate the truths Tocqueville presented; his lack of bias and his amazing degree of accuracy made the *Democracy* an unprecedented event in the annals of foreign writings on the American scene.

Nevertheless, the first American editions did not meet with the expected recognition. Some of the reasons were set forth by Jared Sparks in a letter to Tocqueville, of June 6, 1837. The date, as compared with those of the first French and English editions of the *Democracy*, evidences the delay in the appearance of an American edition. It should also be recalled that anti-French feeling was running high at the time in America; the Spoliation Claims had not been adjusted and Americans were not very sympathetic towards Frenchmen or French ideas.

I am vexed and mortified that an edition of your "Democratie" has not yet been published in America. The causes might be explained, but I can only hint at them in this letter. The work came out just at the time of the unfortunate "Indemnity Controversy," and then General Jackson's war spirit began to stir up in the people a hostile feeling towards France. Hence little interest was felt for a book by a French writer. Again, our newspapers have been filled with extracts from the English reviews, containing the parts of your work most objectionable to American readers; that is your remarks on the defects of Democratic institutions. But you may be assured that all the intelligent persons among us who have read your treatise have applauded its ability and candor. I have pressed several publishing houses to republish the English translation. Three months ago I had really completed all arrangements with a house in Boston, and almost consented to write a preface and notes suited to American readers, but at that moment an advertisement appeared in the newspapers by a publisher in New York, announcing that he should immediately put it to press. I have heard nothing about it since, and I presume the terrible commercial disasters, which have prostrated all enterprise, have suspended if not defeated the execution of his design.[51]

A number of the less favorable foreign reviews, especially those appearing in England, which had stressed the most critical aspects of the first part while omitting reference to its more favorable sections, were almost immediately reprinted in this country. Their publication merely underlined Tocqueville's own observations on the sensitiveness of Americans to what they considered to be unfriendly criticism, of which they had more than enough. Many undoubtedly felt that here was still another of those casual and vitriolic travelogues ridiculing Americans and their institutions. To counteract this impression, the 1835 review by John Stuart Mill was reprinted in New York a year later by Theodore Foster, with the following introduction:

> The work of M. de Tocqueville upon American democracy has been read with so intense an interest throughout all political as well as social circles of Europe; its character is held to be so philosophical, and so utterly devoid of prejudice, whether of party, nation, or form of government; it is so universally lauded by all who have perused it with attention, and the praise has been so generally re-echoed on this side of the water by such as have examined it here, that it has been thought advisable to give a reprint of the most elaborate criticism of the book, in order to show the estimation in which the American form of government is held by those who have taken due pains to examine it, and have talent enough to appreciate it.[52]

American sensitivity to foreign criticism did, however, affect some of the earlier reviewers here. Too many adverse opinions had been expressed by too many previous travelers; the *Democracy* was subjected to a preliminary analysis from this point of view before its broader perspectives and deeper insights were recognized and acclaimed.

In a series of articles in the *United States Magazine and Democratic Review* the works of other travelers were dis-

[51] 1:38–9. See also 44:I, 203.
[52] 36:ii.

cussed in reviewing the *Democracy*. Their effect upon European ideas about, and interest in, American democratic institutions was emphasized; for it was this interest, in many cases little more than curiosity, that had gained for them an American as well as a European audience.

That such is the case is amply shown by the number of books upon our manners, institutions, and history, that are constantly appearing in Europe, and are received with the greatest avidity. We have before us several which have come out within the last year or two, including those of de Tocqueville . . . decidedly the most remarkable and really valuable work that has yet appeared upon this country from the hand of a foreigner. As this comparative distinction may not, however, convey any very enviable praise, we will add, in evidence of its high appreciation in Europe, as a work of genius and philosophical observation, the testimony of M. Thiers, well known as a man of the highest political eminence . . . that he thought himself happy to have lived in the same age that produced this book. . . . Sir Robert Peel, also, and other high English authorities have expressed themselves with equal emphasis. In this country, on the other hand it may well be a subject of surprise that it has received little public notice. . . . There is nothing, however, more important to us, in the way of political information, than the observations of a truly intelligent foreigner, upon the structure and operation of our government; and we have thought that we should render an acceptable service to our readers in bringing this work under their notice, although it has been already for some time before the public. . . .

As to an announcement of a future work . . . we look forward with particular interest to the appearance of another work on this country. . . . In point of style alone, this is a work of uncommon merit . . . tone of dignity, seriousness and good faith. . . . In this, as in most other respects, it contrasts advantageously with that of the great majority of foreign works on this country, in which the greatest interests of society are habitually discussed with the flippancy of the worst newspapers. M. de Tocqueville has been led into errors, in part by the prejudices of the circles of society into which he naturally fell—in part by the mere effect of the imperfect generalizations, which, to a certain extent, are almost unavoidable in this kind of writing. But there are no faults in this book which are not entirely consistent with great powers of thought and language, the most upright intentions, and an uncommon freedom from the class of prejudice to which the race of travellers are more particularly liable. . . .

The difference between M. de Tocqueville and our common herd of travellers, is, that when he speaks of the principles of government he knows what he is talking of.[58]

[58] 147:I, 91–2, 94.

Treating more specifically of the chapters on the tyranny of the majority, as well as the American reaction to some of the British reviews, the reviewer stated that these chapters had been received with

Great approbation by the foreign critics who have spoken of the book, especially in England. The London *Quarterly Review,* though somewhat at a loss how to treat a work of undoubted talent, and at the same time of democratic tone, and highly favorable to our country, has contrived, by the help of these chapters, to draw from it the materials for an article written in the usual tone of that journal.[54]

Summing up Tocqueville's observations in general, the critic believed that:

They are the first observations of the kind which our institutions have yet elicited from any foreign mind; and are far more valuable, even in their errors, than the commonplace truisms and boarding-school rhetoric of the every-day tourist.[55]

Having the character of the earlier travelers' reports on America in mind, another American reviewer remarked:

The reciprocal influence of manners and political institutions upon each other,—in other words, the connection between their civil and social habits, is the first object with which an intelligent traveller should make himself acquainted. By most it is neglected altogether.[56]

The reviewer further noted that it was the "fate of all countries to be misrepresented." America, like many other nations, had been the victim of her institutions. Their strangeness to the foreign observer, his lack of acquaintance with their origins or their value, rendered them inferior in his eyes, and so they were believed to be by his reading public. Consequently, "the sensitiveness at which Europeans affect to wonder, is not the result of their disdain, but of our own self-respect." With the publication of the new work, the day of these travelers' tales was ended. Here at last was a book about America worthy of its subject.

M. de Tocqueville, the author of *Democracy in America,* is an unobtrusive and enlightened person who visited the United States a few years since in pursuance of an important commission, en-

[54] Ibid.: 102.
[55] Ibid.: II, 337.
[56] 105: 124.

trusted to him by the French Government. He brought with him an enquiring spirit, a liberal and instructed mind, and a discriminating judgment. To such a man, in our country every source of information is accessible. That he availed himself of his means of ascertaining truth, is evident from the accuracy of his local knowledge and his correct views of the theory of our somewhat complicated institutions. He has produced an original and philosophical disquisition upon the rise, progress, and present condition of the North American republics; enquired into their history, and discussed their manners, religion and laws with a candour and propriety, a regard for truth and decency, and at the same time, with a degree of research and intelligence, to which we have hitherto been strangers.[57]

Edward Everett, in the *North American Review*, emphasized the interaction of the democratic processes between America and England, and the lack of comprehension of this fact shown by previous writers. Calling Tocqueville "an original thinker, an acute observer, an eloquent writer," Everett praised the truth and profundity of the work, which was by far the best philosophical work on American democracy yet written.[58]

The *American Monthly Magazine* remarked that no foreigner, nor any American, had shown such insight in describing the Federal government and the causes of American liberty.

In tracing these causes, in examining how far they continue to influence our conduct, manners and opinions, and in searching for means to prevent their decay or destruction, the intelligent American reader can find no better guide.[59]

Though American opinions might differ from those of the author, none could criticize his motives or the forthrightness of his observations. The excellence of the Reeve translation was further praised as having caught the spirit of the original. Commenting on the attention the book had received from writers, reviewers, and statesmen throughout Europe, and noting that the book was so little known in America, the reviewer urged a second printing in order to inform the American people of the greatness of their democratic principles.

The *Knickerbocker Magazine* of the same year expanded

[57] Ibid.: 129–30.
[58] 31: 179.
[59] 103: 379–80.

happily upon this new understanding of American institutions which Tocqueville had inaugurated. Stating that "we have hitherto been an enigma to all the world; our author has at last partly solved it," the reviewer went on to say:

> He has analyzed our history, from the beginning and from the bottom, and attempted to show the effect and drift of the whole. But the latter task was too mighty even for him. For notwithstanding all his skill in combination and composition, he has left the field and the scene a chaos; a world in existence but not reduced to order.

Whether the reviewer was reluctant to praise the book too strongly because he was not quite sure that America had indeed received the treatment she deserved, or whether he deliberately refused to overpraise the *Democracy*, he continued:

> M. de Tocqueville has certainly bestowed on us some compliments—we may say, many. For all that he has done we may respect ourselves, and shall be respected. Comparing all the faults he has found in us, with the excellencies he has awarded to us, we are still a great, and may be a proud people.[60]

Having established himself with the American people by the first part, Tocqueville experienced little delay in the publication in this country of the second part of the *Democracy*. Because of their closer acquaintance with the institutions and customs he described, American reviewers were inclined to be more lenient in their criticism than were the Europeans. As the reviewer in the *New York Review* put it:

> The first part of M. de Tocqueville's *Democracy in America*, presented the ablest view, by a foreigner, of our government, and political and administrative systems, that has ever appeared. It fixed the eyes of all upon the practicability of self-government; and gained for its author a distinguished reputation, which has been more than sustained in his second and concluding part of his work. . . .
>
> M. de Tocqueville is the first writer who has attempted to point out the origin and tendency of American democratic institutions, or estimate their value and to contrast them fairly and impartially with those effects which are produced under the aristocratic forms of government in Europe. No author of our age has looked deeper, or with more prophetic eye into the destinies of mankind, and the mighty causes which are now in progress to change the future political and social conditions of

[60] 120:257.

our race. . . . Perhaps his method of generalizing facts is occasionally pushed too far, but it is a mode of writing now commonly practised in France, and even by ourselves; and appears to us well-adapted to subjects which would otherwise become tedious and impertinent by frequent citation of specialties. M. de Tocqueville does not name any individual, nor is there a single personal allusion, or reference throughout his volumes. We speak of this to his credit, for nothing can be more offensive to good taste and good breeding than the common practice of writers in revealing the name of those of whose hospitality and civility they have partaken.[61]

In contrasting the second part of the *Democracy* with similar works by British travelers, the *United States Magazine and Democratic Review,* after making several uncomplimentary references to the review that appeared in *Blackwood's Edinburgh Review,* remarked that the reason for the inferiority and inaccuracy of British writers on America was their narrow-minded, self-confident attitude of superiority. The Americans know this to be true; no matter what is shown these travelers in America, the result, as reflected in their writings, is the same. Americans, therefore, have tended to mislead them purposely! Of Tocqueville's work the review said:

[It] is of the nature of a philosophical inquiry for political and moral truth, independent of all idea of praise or censure. It is, therefore, not to be condemned because its conclusions are not always such as to gratify our national vanity.[62]

The reviewer for *Hunt's Merchant's Magazine* said that:

In our deliberate judgment it is the most original, comprehensive, and profound treatise that has ever appeared regarding our republic;—a treatise which is destined to live and take rank with the master-works of foreign ages.[63]

The more critical *New York Review* of the same year remarked that although Tocqueville had made mistakes and "had sometimes drawn false deductions from his facts," these were "generally upon incidental or comparatively trifling topics, while the whole spirit of his work is as just as it is philosophical." [64]

[61] 132:233, 234.
[62] 148:123.
[63] 119:443.
[64] 131:142.

Also in that year two articles attributed to Horace Greeley appeared praising the author of the *Democracy* and his book:

It is by far the most important book that has been written on the nature and influence of Democracy, and it should be studied by everyone who aims at exerting an influence on the direction of public affairs in the United States. Although it contains some isolated passages that will not much gratify our national vanity, it is written with the utmost candor. The author advances no proposition which he does not support with reasons, and he arrives at no conclusions in haste or prejudice.

He was as desirous that the peculiar causes which controlled these results, and often gave them a new direction, quite different from what would occur in Europe, should be well understood. Hence the minuteness and care with which he analyzes our history, and examines our institutions, to discover the agencies that counteract the ordinary influences of democracy. This will account for the severity of some of the opinions of the work expressed in France and thoughtlessly promulgated in this country. The English, at first, were lavish in their praise of the "great commentator" on our government and institutions, but when a close examination of the work convinced them that it was not a censure of democracy in general and on American democracy in particular, they denied the correctness of their first judgment and denounced the book as visionary, dull, obscure; and we have regretted to see some of these deprecating criticisms republished in this country in advance of the appearance of the essay itself, which will by no means occasion such estimates in the minds of intelligent and candid men.[65]

In his Preface to the American edition of the *Democracy*, John C. Spencer, who had been a personal friend of the author, said of the first part:

The following work of M. de Tocqueville has attracted great attention throughout Europe, where it is universally regarded as a sound philosophical, impartial, and remarkably clear and distinct view of our political institutions, and of our manners, opinions and habits as influencing or influenced by those institutions. Writers, reviewers and statesmen of all parties, have united in the highest commendations of its ability and integrity. The people, described by a work of such character, should not be the only one in Christendom unacquainted with its content. . . .

He has discussed many subjects on which very different opinions are entertained in the United States; but with an ability, a

[65] 133:I, 146.

candor, and an evident devotion to the cause of truth, which will commend his views to those who most radically dissent from them. . . .

He has exhibited with admirable skill, the causes and circumstances which prepared our forefathers, gradually, for the enjoyment of free institutions, and which enable them to sustain, without abusing, the utmost liberty that was ever enjoyed by any people. In tracing these causes, in examining how they continue to influence our conduct, manners, and opinions, and in searching for the means of preventing their decay or destruction, the intelligent American reader will find no better guide than M. de Tocqueville.[66]

In an appraisal of the work as a whole, written some twenty years after it had first appeared, another American critic commented:

These volumes not only supplied a vast amount of new material for thought, in the mass of facts and observations they contained, but they were also imminently suggestive of new trains of thought to European statesmen, to men of all classes indeed, who concerned themselves with political affairs. They formed an era anywhere abroad, as regards the knowledge of American institutions.[67]

Of the second part the same reviewer continued:

Even in the last two volumes of his work on the United States, in which his refinement of thought is greatest, and his generalizations most subtle and far-reaching, he never loses sight of the

[66] See any edition of the Reeve-Spencer *Democracy in America, passim.* Spencer's Preface to the second part is also interesting; his appraisal is not less enthusiastic: "Upon the whole, it is believed that this part of the continuation of the author's views, will be found as interesting, and more interesting, to the American reader, than its predecessor."

[67] 67:669. A comparison of "De Tocqueville and Lieber as writers on political science" appeared anonymously in 95:621. The author was Samuel Taylor. Although this review dealt principally with *L'Ancien Régime,* the *Democracy* is mentioned; many of the ideas in the former in fact originated in the latter. "In the mere literary art of luminous and animated expression, and of symmetrical form composing a treatise, we give a decided preference to De Tocqueville before Lieber." As to ideas, information, and analysis, Taylor thought Tocqueville a poor second. "There is not a political idea, much less a principle of political science propounded by De Tocqueville which Lieber had not before announced in his 'Civil Liberty.'" This comment is another example of American intellectual nationalism, already indicated in some of the reviews. The first edition of Lieber's *Civil Liberty* appeared in 1853.

facts with which he is dealing, nor ceases to advance with a firm and steady step.[68]

Shortly after Tocqueville's death several articles appeared reviewing the whole of his works. Of the *Democracy* in particular one critic, who knew this country well, said:

> Not merely his own countrymen, but England and the civilized world, were satisfied with the depth and originality of this masterly production. The style was clear, the reasoning cogent, the illustrations striking; but chiefly remarkable was its spirit of sagacity and forecast indicating profound thought and deep reflection.[69]

Summing up the view of the three nations concerned, a reviewer in the *North American Review* the following year stated:

> Frenchmen were proud that their young countryman should distance in one of the most difficult sciences, the ancient authorities of other nations. Englishmen were glad to see a work appear which tended to confirm a constitution sustained by an equipoise between crown and people. Americans venerated the man who alone of all foreigners that had crossed the Atlantic, fully understood a system so much reviled in the old world, and faults of a republican government.[70]

The reviewer continued to cite Tocqueville's qualifications as justification of the praise. To Tocqueville, democracy had been a living thing; he had seen it in action and was thus able to draw sound and profound conclusions based upon actual experience.

The same magazine, however, if not the same reviewer, with the experience of civil war on which to reflect, was not so ready to admit Tocqueville's prophetic insight on all points. "Much as he studied and well as he understood our institutions,—and he studied them deeply and with great fairness,—he signally failed, as late events have shown, to discover the real secret of their nature, or to fathom the character of our people." [71] Here criticism of particular points in the judgments expressed in the *Democracy*—in this case, the durability of the Union and the relations of the races—outweighs recognition of the broader aspects of

[68] Ibid.:679.
[69] 122:707.
[70] 138:146.
[71] 139:321.

Tocqueville's analysis. It is one of the few American reviews in which so negative an appraisal of Tocqueville's insight was expressed. The Civil War was hardly over and the racial problem was more acute than it had ever been. More recent trends have served to suggest the long-run validity of his analysis.

One of the most laudatory appraisals of the *Democracy*, written at the end of the last century, was that of another traveler, Lord Bryce, who himself wrote a classic work on American government. With Tocqueville's work as guide, he avoided the errors and omissions of many earlier visitors. Bryce, almost as much a citizen of this country as of his native England, called the *Democracy* "one of the treatises on the philosophy of politics which has risen to the rank of a classic." He went on to say:

It is a classic, and because it is a classic one may venture to canvass it fully, without the fear of seeming to detract from the fame of its author. The more one reads de Tocqueville, the more admiration does one feel for his acuteness, for the delicacy of his analysis, for the elegant precision of his reasonings, for the limpid purity of his style; above all for his love of truth and the elevation of his views. He is not only urbane, but judicial; not only noble, but edifying. There is perhaps no book of the generation to which he belonged which contains more solid wisdom in a more attractive dress. . . .

The first observation is that not only are its descriptions of democracy as displayed in America no longer true in many points, but that in certain points they were never true. That is to say, some were true of America, but not of democracy in general, while others were true of democracy in general but not true of America. . . . De Tocqueville is not much read in the United States, where the scientific, historical and philosophical study of the institutions of the country, apart from the legal study of the Constitution, is of quite recent growth. He is less read now than formerly in England and even in France. But his views of the American government and people have so passed into the texture of our thoughts that we cannot shake off his influence, and in order to profit by it are bound to submit his conclusions and predictions to a searching though respectful examination.

The defects of the book are due to three causes. He had a strong and penetrating intellect, but it moved by preference in the a priori or deductive path, and his power of observation, quick and active as it was, did not lead but followed the march of his reasonings.[73]

[73] 15:22–3.

Bryce noted two other causes. He thought Tocqueville's knowledge of England, "while remarkable in a foreigner, was not sufficient to show him how much in American institutions is really English, and explainable only from English sources." Tocqueville's French background, so evident throughout the *Democracy,* "made him think things abnormal which are merely un-French, it made him attach undue importance to phenomena which seemed to explain French events or supply a warning against French dangers." [73] These criticisms by Bryce are interesting in the light of the comments in the same vein noted previously. Although applied to England rather than to France, they suggest the survival of the opinion of his less acute English predecessors in appraising the *Democracy*. He qualified his remarks somewhat by saying that Tocqueville was writing primarily for his countrymen:

> The constant great reference to France goes deeper than the political philosophy of the book. It determines its scope and aim. The *Democracy in America* is not so much a political study as a work of edification. It is a warning to France of the need to adjust her political institutions to her social condition, and above all to improve the tone of her politics to create a moral and religious basis for her national life.

Bryce was aware, however, that the aim of the book was not so narrow:

> His book is permanently valuable, because its reflections and exhortations are applicable, not merely to the Frenchman of fifty years ago, but to mankind generally, since they touch upon failings and dangers permanently inherent to political society. . . .
>
> Had history falsified far more of de Tocqueville's predictions than she has done, his work would still remain eminently suggestive and stimulating. And it is edificatory not merely because it contains precepts instinct with the loftiest morality. It is a model of that spirit of fairness and justice, that love of pure truth which is conspicuously necessary and not less conspicuously difficult in the discussion, even the abstract discussion of the problems of political philosophy.[74]

An American political scientist, later to be Governor and President, compared the work of the two men, each without a peer in his presentation of America and her democracy at

[73] Ibid.:23 ff.
[74] Ibid.:27, 28, 30.

different stages of their development. He found Tocqueville superior in philosophic insight. Woodrow Wilson noted that:

> It will hardly be a disparagement of Mr. Bryce's style to say that it is inferior to de Tocqueville's; the thoughts it has to convey, the meanings it has to suggest, belong to quite another class than that to which de Tocqueville's judgments must be assigned; it is not meant to carry the illumination of the philosophical conceptions into the regions of fact which it explores; its task is rather exposition than judgment. Mr. Bryce does not feel called upon to compete with de Tocqueville in the field in which de Tocqueville is possibly beyond rivalry.[76]

This brief sampling of American opinions on the *Democracy* could be greatly expanded by tracing the uncounted references to it, some incidental, others extended, in American journals and books of the nineteenth and twentieth centuries. Such an exploration would reveal how widespread was Tocqueville's authority, in how many directions he influenced American thought. Citations of the *Democracy* would run into the thousands were a thorough search made of all types of American sources, literary, philosophical, economic, sociological, educational, and political.

Nineteenth-century writers of all shades of opinion gave to *Democracy in America* a high rank in the annals of human thought and aspiration. Even those who opposed the democratic impulse that Tocqueville did so much to strengthen recognized the penetrating quality of his diagnosis and prognosis. To those who wished to see democracy advanced in dominion and in achievement, the *Democracy* spoke with a compelling and prophetic power.

Three major streams of judgment and appraisal, French, English, and American, have been traced in their separate flow during the nineteenth century by soundings among typical reviews and comments on Tocqueville's work. The twentieth century has witnessed no decline in the attention given to the *Democracy* both here and abroad. There has, in fact, been a widespread revival of interest in and respect for its permanent—its timeless—contribution to our understanding of the character and conditions of economic, social, and political democratic organization. How Tocqueville and his work have been viewed by the moderns will therefore

[76] 101:154. For another comparison of Tocqueville and Bryce (by Lingelbach), see 54:14 ff.

be considered as a whole without seeking to chart the various courses of opinion in different countries.

After a Century

Recent evaluations of the *Democracy* have tended to place less emphasis on its individual sections, as, for instance, the influence of Catholicism or the importance of local institutions or the significance of English antecedents. Liberals and conservatives no longer peruse its pages seeking support for their arguments. Rather, the emphasis has been on Tocqueville as a moral and political philosopher and a sociologist—a prophet of democracy's future trends and potentialities. The comment that Tocqueville saw "more of the latent possibilities in democracy than most other men of his time," [76] as well as many of its dangers and limitations, has been validated by more than one event since he wrote the *Democracy*.

At the turn of the century it was still "the best philosophical discussion of democracy, using the United States as an example, that can be found in any language." It was said of Tocqueville that he "was, perhaps, the first to see clearly that the doctrines of political equality and of the sovereignty of the people were destined to run the world; and the interpretation he gave to his discovery placed him among the master minds of the century. No book of modern times has done more to influence the minds and thoughts of men. . . ." [77]

As a political treatise relevant to a particular period and applicable to a special set of circumstances, the *Democracy* suffered, for a time before the turn of the century, the fate such works often do. It was less frequently read and discussed, and the volumes were allowed to go out of print. Its vitality as a source of political ideas and insights was evidenced, however, by three separate editions that were prepared in this country between 1898 and 1904. All ran through a number of printings.

Again, one hundred years after the publication of the first part, the *Democracy* and its author received widespread rec-

[76] 34:39.
[77] 100:595, 597.

ognition on both sides of the Atlantic. Dinners were given in their honor in France and America; a number of books and articles appeared discussing different aspects of the work. Leading economists, philosophers, political scientists, and sociologists analyzed afresh Tocqueville's prophecies. His views on administrative bureaucracy, on the "mass-state," and on many other questions, as well as his emphasis on the character and functioning of society, were reappraised for their contemporary values. Tocqueville once more became, as he had been a century before, a source of new democratic ardor, a seminal influence in a reviving concern with the conditions and the hazards of democratic action.

The commentators of the 1930's, like those of the 1830's, found that the world needed Tocqueville; more especially, the democracies needed him. Equality had been realized under fascism, the kind of equality under despotism of which Tocqueville had forewarned. It might, so it seemed a decade ago, all too easily overwhelm the principle and practice of liberty, the equality of opportunity which he had championed as the essence of democracy, and which he thought attainable only within a democratic framework. The conclusions of the *Democracy* became more than mere records of outdated observations on a simpler society, applicable only to the transient era of its immaturity. They emerged anew as the very warp and woof of a working pattern of democratic faith and conduct in a world torn asunder again by an irreconcilable conflict of ideas.

Pierson clearly expressed these uncertainties of the period and Tocqueville's relation to them when he said: ". . . not only the celebration of the centenary of his great commentary in 1935, but a revived anxiety over democracy, a reopening of all the questions of government once thought so happily settled, have drawn scholar and statesman back to a serious restudy of nineteenth century thought." [78]

The general appraisals of the *Democracy* that appeared at the time of the centennial emphasized its intrinsic relevance to our time. Laski wrote of Tocqueville:

> Who does not know Tocqueville cannot understand liberalism . . . it implies a passion for liberty; and that the passion may be compelling it requires a power to be tolerant, even skeptical,

[78] 68:798.

about opinions and tendencies you hold to be dangerous, which is one of the rarest of human qualities.

The real lesson of his book is the argument that once a people had set its foot on the path of equality in the realm of material well-being there is no logical end to its journey until it has abolished significant differences with that realm.[79]

Another English appraisal indicated what is perhaps the heart of Tocqueville's contribution to our present concept of the meaning of democracy:

> Tocqueville is a dogmatist, but a dogmatist who had the sense of the evolution of his ideas and institutions. He had that sense clearly enough to believe that this evolution ought to be understood and studied as an experience, and not accepted as a sort of necessary and transcending revolution.[80]

Tocqueville's primary interest in writing the *Democracy* was, as we have seen, to provide his countrymen and Europeans generally with a key to economic, social, and political changes that he considered inevitable. Despite—perhaps because of—the profound cleavages in French life in the 1830's, the centennial aroused individual but limited interest in the *Democracy* as a guide to the solution of current domestic issues. A century later, Tocqueville's prescriptions for their solution seemed to be significant to only a few French leaders of politics or thought, when events were hastening his nation to the very doom he foretold for every irresolute democracy.[81]

In America the centennial evoked a more widespread reappraisal of the *Democracy's* relevance to our present circumstances as a nation still seeking to make democracy an effective instrument for achieving the social ends that Tocqueville envisaged. As in the earlier appraisals, there were numerous references to particular prophecies and criticism of them. An almost universal appreciation of the

[79] 52:110, 112.

[80] 53:393.

[81] It is ironic because Mayer remarks (59:172) that "the history of de Tocqueville's influence in France has, in fact, been subject to continuous misunderstanding." See, however, the sympathetic appreciations in France, especially 23; 79; 59: ch. 9. A committee of French notables was formed to commemorate the centennial of the *Democracy*. The committee held at least one conference (23) and the French government presented the President of the United States with a bust of Tocqueville (70).

perennial validity of Tocqueville's analysis of the conditions and potentialities of democracy animated these modern American criticisms. A few examples will illustrate the general attitude of those who reviewed the *Democracy* again, from whatever band of the ideological spectrum.

A political scientist emphasized the *Democracy's* objective and critical quality:

Among the intellectuals of that day democracy appeared to some as a lovely dream; to others, a promise of anarchy and ruin. De Tocqueville, in a single treatise, took democracy out of the realm of enigma and speculation and presented it simply as a fact. . . . A portrait of democracy in 1839 was necessarily a youthful one, but so skillfully was it drawn that it foreshadowed clearly the qualities of form and character which maturity brought. . . . No one has ever probed more deeply the inner nature of American society.[89]

A sociologist discovered the relevance of Tocqueville's analysis to our time:

The extraordinary success of the book, which brought praise and honors to the young writer and prepared the way for his political career, was due to its concentration upon the realities of the times. The theoretical and practical formation of modern democratic and liberal society was the burning problem of his epoch. . . . Although he sought to effect a compromise between the divergent political groups of his time, his intellectual endeavor essentially transcends any immediate purpose. . . .

The second part of his book is far from being an analysis of American democracy, and it presents only a few and fairly unimportant American illustrations . . . yet this volume reveals Tocqueville at his profoundest.[90]

A thoughtful commentator on the American scene offered a sober yet unqualified appraisal of its utility to the modern citizen as a "yardstick" by which to measure the meaning of contemporary events:

It is just a century since Alexis de Tocqueville's celebrated treatise, *Democracy in America*, was published in Boston. Reading this lucid and brilliant work, both as a compte rendu of the young republic of the 1830's and as a piece of reasoned philosophy, one finds it an excellent yardstick to measure or interpret the newspapers of today.

Democracy in America when it arrived was one of the most

[89] 94:14.
[90] 85:405–6, 409. See also 86: *passim*.

influential books of the whole nineteenth century, and served more than perhaps any other work to crystallize liberal convictions concerning the inevitability of political equality and democratic self-government. The author's reservations or prejudices against certain aspects of democracy made his work seem all the more objective; and if it resembled Montesquieu's writings in its formalism and its highly deductive approach, it also rivaled the work of the earlier philosopher in its depth and brilliance of formulation. Today Tocqueville's book is most valid (in a retrospective sense) for tracing the orientation of our democracy, and much of its judgment still seems to apply. . . .[84]

Over the century the *Democracy* has received many interpretations; they have varied not only in time but in the premises on which they have been based. The premises have been rooted in different cultural soils.

France, Tocqueville's homeland, has never completely adopted one of her most fertile minds, certainly one of her most perfect flowerings of the democratic spirit. He was received in his own time by a small but powerful coterie of those intellectuals who appreciated the true nature of his purpose and the fine energy of his performance. Despite the favorable reviews, the deep running fire of Tocqueville's devotion to democracy as a way of life—with all its shortcomings, which he portrayed with equal insight and candor —never lighted a tinder at home which continued to glow in the popular heart of France. He has ever since been recognized, but not often followed as a guide to action; his own political career was a symbol of the practical impress of his book.

The *Democracy* arrived in England while Reform was still struggling to achieve political mastery. Most of the leading intellectuals were liberals; for them Tocqueville became both preceptor and prophet. Here was the essence of democracy as it might be in England, given the necessary modifications to fit the different conditions of an old society. Small wonder that the *Democracy* became for them a manual of principle and practice. For the conservatives, Tocqueville presented a portent of the doom of English institutions and became the oracle of chaos. As the victory of evolution over revolution finally became evident and secure, Tocqueville's contributions to that victory were widely recognized. Even the conservatives accepted him as an impartial expo-

[84] 49:582.

nent of dangers of democracy—and, grudgingly, of its possibilities.

In America the *Democracy* represented a unique and welcome phenomenon in the plethora of contemporary foreign criticisms of our institutions. We were more sensitive then than we are today to the opinions held about us by the world. Here was almost the first appreciative appraisal from abroad; that it was penetrating as well as urbane raised its value in our eyes. Since it was so accurate and impartial in observation, so friendly in disposition, it became a popular as well as a literary favorite. Its many editions in the early decades, its frequent condensations for popular and school use, attested a wide appreciation here of Tocqueville's purpose and of the quality of his judgments about our institutions. When we compare his attitude towards us with those of other foreign commentators of the period, his objective but friendly appraisals, his unequivocal loyalty to the spirit of our institutions, his capacity to look below the surface evidences to catch the inner meaning of our beliefs and practices make the American response to the *Democracy* —then and ever since—seem inevitable. For us, as for all those who have come to know Tocqueville at first hand, he was "not only without true predecessors; he was without true successors." [85, 86]

THE PRESENT RELEVANCE OF THE "DEMOCRACY"

If these have been some of the appraisals of the *Democracy* over a century, what can we say of its message to us today—and tomorrow? What are some of Tocqueville's comments about the America of the 1830's from which the nation of the 1940's can draw a broader perspective, fresh insights, new hopes for the future?

[85] 57:46.

[86] The reviews and appraisals quoted here do not, of course, exhaust the list. From the many reviews and appraisals available, selection has been made of those which may be considered typical. Those noted in the Bibliography (Appendix V) and many other references, have been consulted. Duplications of the estimates presented here, by reproducing them all in detail, would serve no useful purpose. Variations in the major themes of those quoted are so infrequent as to be negligible so far as general, as distinct from particular, criticisms are concerned.

In drafting his project for the *Democracy*, Tocqueville's primary interest was in the political aspects of the American scene as they applied to the changes he foresaw for his native country. He completed his political analysis soon after his return to France. It was, in part, the impact of his travels upon his fertile mind that focused his attention more and more on the economic and social aspects of democracy.[87] The unfolding of new experiences during those travels—in the different conditions he encountered, the various types of Americans he met—served to broaden his concept of democracy, to enlarge the range of its connotations for him. That five years intervened between the publication of his political and his economic-social commentaries reflects the maturing of his judgment of what democracy means in the light of his observations in America.

There is more, however, to this extension of Tocqueville's examination of democracy from its political to its economic and social aspects. As a pioneer social scientist, he was exploring new frontiers of thought and of analysis. From one point of view, he merely utilized his American experience as a backdrop for his general analytical and methodological portrayal of the general problem of change in society. This is especially true of the second part of the *Democracy*.

In extending his definition of democracy to include these other aspects, Tocqueville was a pioneer of the first importance. What has become a commonplace for us, that democracy means more than a certain catalogue of political principles and practices, was in his day a new if not an unprecedented idea. There had been, of course, in Montesquieu and other of Tocqueville's predecessors in a long line back to Aristotle, a recognition that there is more to life than politics. Many of the seventeenth- and eighteenth-century political reformers, in seeking changes in the structure of the authoritarian governments of their time, had not been motivated only by abstract ideas about justice. The desire to

[87] It is worth while to recall that Tocqueville used the word "democracy" with more than one connotation. It would, perhaps, define his general attitude more accurately to speak of "liberalism" rather than of "democracy." I have retained "democracy" as a general term, with the connotation of liberalism as we understand it and as Tocqueville often thought of democracy. Tocqueville himself thought of using "*égalité*" in the title of the second part of the *Democracy*. See 97:VI, 67, 94.

achieve economic and social reforms, often with precise democratic—even equalitarian—implications, was in the air of Tocqueville's intellectual inheritance and contemporary experience.

None before him, however, had so clearly presented or so cogently demonstrated the interrelations of the political, the economic, and the social aspects of democracy. None had so thoroughly understood their connection or drawn into a single pattern of ideas their manifold and often conflicting phases. The writings of practically all of his contemporaries, whether European travelers to America or publicists, polemic and academic, when compared with the *Democracy*, are narrow in scope, biased in judgment, steeped in immediate comments and controversies. Beside them the *Democracy* stands out as a landmark in our progress towards an emergent liberal spirit and democratic thought, at once catholic in range, balanced in interpretation, and detached in the examination of every issue.

A landmark in the progress of liberal and democratic thought, it provides us also with a benchmark by which to measure our advance. Not alone on one front, the political, but on the economic and the social fronts as well, Tocqueville bequeathed us a unique and permanent record of our national evolution in the 1830's. In a period when we were on the threshold of great changes on all these fronts, he wove the strands of divergent trends into a clear and consistent design. From the details of that earlier design we can compute the distance we have traveled, appraise the character of the changes through which we have lived, and are living today.

Tocqueville gave to the world of his day a new conception of the meaning and the nature of democracy. That conception has been and remains an inescapable challenge to the aspiration and the effort of each succeeding generation. Were this all, the *Democracy* would still speak to our time and condition. It contains, however, many specific elements—descriptions, appraisals, analyses, prophecies—of great practical import for us today. What are some of these elements?

We may remind ourselves at the outset that no recording of a particular period in the nation's life will always remain accurate in all its generalizations. Changes in our material position over a century have, of course, altered the working of many institutions and the relevance of more than one idea. The rounding-out of the continental domain, the acquisition of colonies, the growth of world contacts, have affected our outlook on domestic as well as foreign relations. The technological revolution—which, in its social implications, Tocqueville in fact foresaw—has shifted the balance in economics and politics from the rural and the agrarian to the urban and the industrial. The growth of cities has altered the character of political as well as of economic and social organization as Tocqueville saw and described them. The catalogue of change can be extended in many other directions by the contemporary reader. That these changes should have required modification of some of Tocqueville's descriptions, appraisals, and prophecies is not remarkable. That so much of the *Democracy* remains still pertinent and timely suggests rather that it is to be cherished not merely as a brilliant record of the past but also as a more certain guide for the future.

LACUNÆ IN TOCQUEVILLE'S ANALYSIS

Before examining the *Democracy's* reservoir of insight for us today, we may note some of Tocqueville's comments and interpretations, as well as omissions, which are of only historical or transitory interest. For instance, he discussed in considerable detail the New England township and found its structure and administration a major source of democratic practice and so vitality. A century of increasing urbanization, of expanding functional responsibilities, and of multiplying political controls has transformed town government into something quite different from his enthusiastic account of its outlines and operation. In some of the smaller and more isolated towns of the New England frontier, and in similar regions where the New England pattern or its counterpart has been reproduced, the early vitality survives. The disappearance of institutions he described has done much, however, to weaken the democratic impulse in local government which he believed these institutions promoted. More recent developments, such as the representative town-meeting governments in New England and the city-manager plan, have done much to revitalize local government within our urban framework.

Again Tocqueville's description of the nature and operation of judicial review has been altered by time. He could hardly have envisaged the effects of the immense political power that Americans have entrusted to their courts when the major questions before the Supreme Court shifted from the political to the economic-social arena. Indeed, he was even then clearly wrong in stating that a single decision of unconstitutionality did not "abolish" a law, that "its final destruction [could] only be accomplished by reiterated attacks of judicial functionaries." He believed that legislation would be protected from "wanton assault" by linking the private interests of individuals with the attack upon its constitutionality. That assault he looked for in "the daily aggressions of party spirit . . . the tyranny of political assemblies." If it has come from sources quite different from those he foresaw, it is because of forces in our national life that were not yet strong—some not yet born. He did, none the less, underrate the influence of the judiciary as a Third Estate in the legislative process.

A third matter on which Tocqueville's description and appraisal would seem anachronistic today is the "political institution" of the jury. He believed the jury, especially the civil jury, to be "the most energetic means of making the people rule, the most efficacious means of teaching it to rule well." He rejected the idea that, because many jurors may be ignorant, the jury system is not a most efficient means of educating all ranks in society in a respect for law. Experience has not borne out his enthusiasm in this respect. Few would hold today that a judge "continues to influence the habits of thought, and even the characters, of those who acted with him in his official capacity"—at least, of any broad cross-section of the community. The widespread desire to avoid jury duty and the development of blue-ribbon juries suggest the decline of the jury as a political institution with a permeating civic influence.

Tocqueville discusses the future of the federal system in considerable detail. He makes some shrewd observations on its operation, but does not altogether foresee the shifting balance of power between the states and the Federal government which was even then impending. He anticipated that the strength of the Federal government was likely to decrease, that of the state governments to increase. His analysis of their relative magnetism for the citizen's allegiance is reminiscent of Madison's argument in Number 45 of the *Federalist*. The interests of the citizen have not, over the last century, proved to be more closely allied to his state than to the national government. This shift, perhaps already nascent but not yet clearly evident in the 1830's, has resulted from economic and social forces that were then only emergent in our national life.

On the other hand, Tocqueville has proved fundamentally correct in his forecast of the primary forces holding the Union together. One, he thought, was the common commercial interest among the people of all the states—the advantages of a continental free-trade area. The other was their fundamental identity in political principle—the democratic faith of the people. That these influences have increased rather than decreased the relative strength of the Federal government, despite, perhaps because of, armed conflict between the states, suggests that Tocqueville's analysis was essentially correct. Whatever differences in detail may have eventuated from the impact of new forces, economic and social, the enhancement of Federal power has continued to rest on these foundations.

Among the few omissions from Tocqueville's searching analysis of the American scene, perhaps the most curious is his lack of attention to the structure and operation of state government. He devotes a scant four pages to a detailed discussion of the state and only scattered and incidental descriptions and appraisals elsewhere to its political or administrative aspects. Compared with his analyses of local government and of various aspects of the character and working of the Federal government, his inattention to state government is almost startling. Although he utilized the states tangentially in many of his generalizations, he nowhere provides a comprehensive account or a critical scrutiny of their origins or organization.

Why does so conspicuous a lacuna occur in Tocqueville's otherwise comprehensive survey of our constitutions? The explanation lies, perhaps, in the interests and political attachments of those whom Tocqueville knew most intimately in this country. Although he visited a number of state capitals, he did not have much contact with many state officials or with citizens active in state politics. In one of the most important capitals, Albany, he met a Governor who, at best, was an unimpressive executive and he found no substantial public buildings that might symbolize the importance of state government. His associations were with intellectuals or with those whose political interests were primarily in their local rather than in the national government. As he moved from one town to the next, he carried new letters of introduction; they were, for the most part, to people with similar interests. His American acquaintances did not include many who would, from their own experience, direct his attention to or give him much enlightenment on the details of state government. The omission is all the more curious, moreover, because his official contacts in investigating our prison system were generally with state officials. He was, in fact, officially concerned with studying the operation of a state activity. Perhaps it was these very contacts that obscured for him the importance of state government in other fields.[88]

It would be possible to extend the list of items about American institutions and ideas that do not appear in the *Democracy*. Their contemporary aspects, economic and social as well as political, are, in many cases, different from those which Tocqueville described. To complete such a list is of little more than pedantic importance; the inquiring reader may make his own, and add his gloss to the observations of the author of the *Democracy*. What is more pertinent is to extract the essence of Tocqueville's observations which are of immediate and instructive relevance. The *Democracy's* seedbed is so fertile in contemporary insights, in confirmed perceptions, that even a gleaning of the whole yields an abundant harvest of counsel and caution for our time.

THE POLITICAL PERSPECTIVE

If we look first at Tocqueville's political observations, several strike the reader at once as if they came from the

[88] I am indebted to Professor Pierson for some of these comments on Tocqueville's neglect of state government. See also 139:321.

best of today's editorial or political commentary. It is easy, for instance, to select such items as his discussion of the re-election of the president as having a direct bearing on the 1940's. Written long before the third-term issue was raised as a matter of practical politics, it has a very modern ring. "When the chief magistrate enters the lists [for re-election], he borrows the strength of the government for his purposes. . . . The cares of government dwindle for him into second-rate importance, and the success of his election is his first concern. All public negotiations, as well as all laws, are to him nothing more than electioneering schemes; places become the reward of services rendered, not to the nation but to its chief; and the influence of the government, if not injurious to the country, is at least no longer beneficial to the community for which it was created." By not making the President ineligible for re-election, the framers "partly destroyed" one great merit of the Constitution, an executive enjoying a degree of independence in its sphere. That independence is important as a means of making the executive "able to resist [the] caprices, and refuse [the] most dangerous demands," of the majority, while its permanent determinations "must be complied with." Similarly, the executive, by its independence, would be able "to resist the encroachments of the legislature. If re-eligible, and this is particularly true at the present day, when political morality is relaxed and great men are rare, the President . . . becomes an easy tool in the hands of the majority. He adopts its likings and its animosities, he anticipates its wishes, he forestalls its complaints, he yields to its idlest cravings, and instead of guiding it . . . he merely follows its bidding. Thus, in order not to deprive the state of the talents of an individual, those talents have been rendered almost useless; and to keep an expedient for extraordinary perils, the country has been exposed to continual dangers."

Or take the current attitudes in America as to the quality of our office-holders under our present system of elections inherited from the 1830's. Tocqueville discusses the question incidentally at many points. "It is a constant fact that, at the present day, the ablest men . . . are rarely placed at the head of the affairs. . . . The democracy [people] not only lack that soundness of judgment which is necessary to select men really deserving of their confidence, but often have not the desire or the inclination to find them out. . . . An instinct not less strong induces able men to retire from the political arena, in which it is so difficult to retain their independence, or to advance without becoming servile. . . . Those who engage in the perplexities of political life are persons of very moderate pretensions. The pursuit of wealth generally diverts men of great talents and strong passions from the pursuit of power; and it frequently happens that a man does not undertake to direct the fortunes of the state until he has shown himself incompetent to conduct his own."

These comments might have been written yesterday. They are among the most aristocratic in temper and outlook in the *Democracy*. Tocqueville goes so far as to advocate the extension of the system of indirect selection then in use for the choice of senators, "or run the risk of perishing miserably among the shoals of democracy." The complaint Tocqueville voices here has been perennial in writings on American political life. Every generation, or certainly every other, is inclined to look upon the politics of a generation or two ago as, if not the Golden Age, at least infinitely better than that of today. Each comments on the relative degradation of its own political standards in men and morality.

Two or three considerations are worth recalling here. First, it is not altogether true that first-rate talent had not, before Tocqueville's day, entered politics, or does not today. It may be true that there have been fewer classically educated politicians at any time since the days of and after the Philadelphia Convention of 1787. Certainly the great political writers of the past, whether in the original or in translation, are not cited in legislative halls or in administrative documents, in debate or correspondence, as often as they once were. The real "governors" of our political system are not, however, always the office-holders. There have been and still are many examples of men of first-rate ability in actual control of our political machines, openly or behind the scenes. They may not be scholars and may even murder the King's English. They are by no means men who have proved themselves incompetent to conduct their own affairs —often identified by them with the efficient operation of the machines they control. The politician, as a specialist in a difficult and ruthless game, has been too often underrated intellectually as well as morally. A Hanna as the manager of a national party organization, as well as many a state and local boss, is generally an individual of superior intelligence, acumen, and initiative.

There is, however, a qualitative difference between the politicians of the constitutional era or even those of the Jacksonian period and those of more recent decades. The growth in size and the decline in homogeneity of the nation have brought into political life not merely new names but different ideas of the ends of political power—and of the legitimate means of achieving it. The technological changes that have modified the older economic and social patterns have altered the perquisites of that power and so the character of the rules in the "great game of politics." The moral standards, the vision ot ends and means, the personal uses to which political power is put by those who acquire it, today seem—although, in fact, they may not be—narrower, more personal. Tocqueville foresaw very clearly the effects of the idea of equality on moral standards in politics. He warned us no less clearly of the possible effects of the idea in practice—on the character and the purposes of political leaders.

Another aspect of this question, closely related to Tocqueville's comments on the caliber of politicians, is the nature and degree of corruption in American political life. He devotes relatively little attention to the matter. He did not hear of vote-purchasing, but often heard "the probity of public officers questioned; still more frequently have I heard their successes attributed to low intrigues and immoral practices. If, then, the men who conduct an aristocracy sometimes endeavor to corrupt the people, the heads of a democracy are themselves corrupt." Here, again, although the comment is as fresh as it was in the 1830's, its focus is blurred. Most of those who write about the corruption of American politics forget that it takes two to make a bargain. They ignore the fact that a politician who promotes a private interest in a political "deal" is merely following current business practices and ethics. Indeed, it is generally true that the initiative for corruption in this sense comes to, not from, the politician; the interests seek his favors, not he theirs. An objective comparison between current standards and practices among business men and politicians—as to, for instance, nepotism, or the word as good as the bond—might today yield the higher rating for the politicians. At whatever level of the hierarchy of politics or business such a comparison was made, the conduct of the former would not be so very different from that of the latter.

It is moreover, possible to raise the question whether our political leadership, except, perhaps, in the literary sense, does not measure up today to that of our classic past. The great game of politics still seems to attract men, and now women, of first-rate ability into public life. Does not our political talent, both legislative and executive, measure up today to the standards to which Tocqueville referred? Was not, indeed, that political talent high at the very time Tocqueville was writing, as we look back on the Jacksonian period? Over the past quarter-century, certainly, in more than one of our cities, in a number of our states, as well as in the national political arena, there have emerged young, able, and progressive legislators, executives, and administrators. These new leaders may use different vehicles for the expression of their ideas—the national magazines and the radio rather than longhand letters and learned treatises. They may display, as some certainly have displayed, the same ability and courage in meeting the challenges of our day as did the Framers of theirs. These new leaders, it may be noted in passing, have not infrequently captured the political machines and made the older brand of bosses their henchmen. If they have had to, they have built new machines of their own, and beaten the old timers at their own game.

The problem of political leadership in a democracy, and of its selection, which Tocqueville raises here is still critical in our time. If we have survived without an aristocracy of intellect (or letters) in our politics, it is no sign of peculiar genius. If the ability that has been attracted to the control of our political machines has adapted the standards of private business to the conduct of public affairs, it provides no special satisfaction. Few will gainsay that the caliber of some of those who are today active in party organization, as well as of those who have stood for office in state and national politics, has improved. If we have had in recent years, however, a perennial stream of able and informed participants in the game of politics, it is no guarantee of their sufficient number or of their efficient quality for the future. We must, as Tocqueville did, look deeper to discover the contradictions in democratic politics, the sources of its strength and weaknesses. Tocqueville devoted more attention to this than to any other political question. It remains the central question for us, in a world in which a total war is being waged beween rival and irreconcilable political ideals and the institutions that embody them.

Tyranny of the Majority

Tocqueville focuses his analysis upon the "possible tyranny of the majority." He examines the reasons why the majority in America is "omnipotent," the factors that may mitigate its potential tyranny, and the "causes" that will maintain democracy despite the dangers of this tyranny. Throughout both parts of the *Democracy* this inquiry runs as a continuous thread in the design, a recurrent element in the whole pattern. It is not too much to say that it is the real *raison d'être* for the writing of the Democracy.

The omnipotence, "the absolute sovereignty," of the majority Tocqueville believed is buttressed by a number of peculiar American institutions as well as by several popular and prevalent ideas. Among the institutions, he placed first the practice of universal suffrage; among ideas, the sentiment of equality. Universal suffrage makes the majority omnipotent, as it can impose its will upon the minority. The sentiment of equality arises from the practical material equality achieved by us in a new and little populated country, where everyone can hope to improve his economic position. A count of heads is believed, therefore, to offer a sure index of political wisdom. "The moral authority of the majority is partly based upon the notion that there is more intelligence and wisdom in a number of men united than in a single individual." Since the material circumstances, the everyday experiences, the educational and moral background of nearly all the people are essentially similar, the majority must be right. Tocqueville observed that this omnipotence expresses itself in several ways, of none of which he approved.

First, direct and frequent elections make for lack of independence on the part of legislators, a tendency exaggerated by the practice of instructing representatives on how to vote for specific measures. The result is a marked instability in legislative policy. Second, the executive, which might, as we have seen, become a stabilizing influence in government through its independence of popular whim, is subordinated to many legislative checks. Third, the trend towards the election of judges (which Tocqueville strongly disapproved) marks the same insistence of the majority on its complete domination of the government.

Were Tocqueville writing today, what would he observe of these indications of the omnipotence of the majority in America? Certainly we have made some changes in the relations of the people to their representatives, changes which cut both ways. The trend away from frequent elections has been marked in our states since the early constitutions in the old and the new states alike. Today only one state (New Jersey) holds annual elections of its legislature (and of the lower house only; the senate is elected for three years). Only four (New Jersey, New York, Rhode Island, South Carolina) convene their legislatures annually.

On the other hand, it can be argued that we trust our legislatures less than we used to. The new democratic upsurge of the late nineteenth and twentieth centuries, a reaction to the political manipulations of Big Business, expressed itself in the initiative, referendum, and recall. Today twenty states have adopted the legislative initiative, twenty-two the legislative referendum, and twelve the recall of elected public officials. A few states, moreover, have implemented the traditional custom of instructing representatives on prospective legislative measures by laws that establish a regular election procedure for so doing. It cannot be said that experience has led us to reduce the ease of direct action on legislative policy by the people.

Their direct influence on legislators, moreover, has been enhanced by the pressure-politics devices that the rise of new types of "political associations" since Tocqueville's day have introduced in popular political action. Tocqueville devoted considerable attention to these associations and remarked on the difference in their organization and purposes from those in Europe. While he was here, he had an opportunity to note the creation and activities of one of the earliest examples of a national pressure group, the anti-tariff convention of 1831. He thought spontaneous and untrammeled political associations, as he found them here, were a safety valve against revolution. "In countries where associations are free, secret societies are unknown. In America there are factions, but no conspiracies."

What Tocqueville called political associations have proliferated in number and variety since his day, have taken on new purposes as well as new forms. It is the change in their objectives that has made them so significant a factor in weighing the present omnipotence of the majority. As they have increased in number, they have penetrated every aspect of our life, every facet of governmental action, economic and social as well as political. From the loosely organized and popularly based national, state, or local propaganda "association" to the tightly controlled and specifically directed (and financed) lobby is a long step away from majority rule as Tocqueville envisaged it. The "tyranny" we have to fear today, especially as to our legislatures, is not the defeat of majority demands, however transitory. It is rather the distortion of the majority concern—the promotion of the general welfare—by the organized and concentrated pressures of specific minorities pursuing special interests. Tocqueville certainly was not unaware of the economic basis of politics. He did not, however, foresee the impact on popular sovereignty of the new forces in the American economy just then beginning to become politically active. Minority-influenced legislation has resulted more from the manipulative control of legislatures by these special interests than from the use of the regular machinery of elections. Although these pressure groups have ignored it when it suited their purposes, they have often preferred to operate within legislative chambers rather than on the hustings. In the long run, therefore, it may turn out that direct and frequent elections are one of the surest ways of returning government to the majority. Perhaps its "tyranny" in the framing of legislative policy is less to be feared than the omnipotence of special interests.

When we turn to the executive branch, we also find substantial changes in its dependence on the popular majority since Tocqueville's day. The terms of governors have been lengthened, their veto power extended, their control of finance and personnel enhanced, their administrative authority co-ordinated and enlarged. Today twenty-four governors are elected for four-year terms, one for three years, twenty-three for two years. This trend in state government is even more marked in local government; the strong mayor or city-manager type of charter is typical rather than exceptional. At the national level, too, the President is increasingly a legislative as well as an administrative leader. He is more a people's representative and less an amanuensis of congressional dictates.

It would be interesting to examine the reasons for this broadening executive independence over the past century. It is one of the most significant phenomena in our political evolution. The reader can explore for himself the nuances of its development from many sources—the commentaries, legislative debates, the activities of our executives, often portrayed in the daily press. What is important to note here is that the American executive has not remained the slave of the will of the omnipotent majority, exercised through legislative domination. Rather he has emerged as the most identifiable spokesman of that long-run majority opinion on which Tocqueville rested his chief reliance for the survival of a liberal democracy. As the executive has become more independent of legislative control, he has acquired the capacity, from the nature of his office, to speak for the community, the state, the nation. In becoming so, he is in a position to recall the majority to the long-run interests, the permanent values, which it also shares with minorities. Perhaps no other institutional development since 1830 has created so effective a barrier to hasty or ill-considered action by a transitory and tyrannical majority.

Tocqueville's fear of the effects of election on the independence of the judiciary—the third institutional bulwark against the tyranny of the majority—have not been confirmed by experience. Today only seven states have completely appointive benches; in three others some of the lower-court judges are elected, others appointed. In thirty-eight states all judges are elected.

There is a vast literature on the relative merits of the two systems of selection. Little evidence exists, however, to indicate that the electorates in states where judges are elected wish to change to an appointive bench. Nor is there an observable difference in the respect with which the decisions of elective and appointive supreme courts are received by their colleagues of the bench and bar. The decisions of several elective courts are cited, for instance, about as frequently by the Supreme Court of the United States as are those of the most respected appointive courts.

The record is different in many lower courts, of which it is often asserted in more than one state that certain decisions are motivated by political considerations. Many lawyers as well as laymen remark that the caliber of judges in some courts of lower jurisdiction is inferior, even dangerously low. This is especially true of municipal courts in great metropolitan areas where long-entrenched political machines have been able to extend their control to the selection of judges. These charges are too often true. It also frequently happens that lower courts, realizing that their decisions can be appealed, are less careful to maintain high standards, including that of political independence, in making their decisions.

If the influence of judges as a counterpoise to popular impetuosity is a stabilizing element in a nation in which the majority rule (as Tocqueville and other liberals conceived it) has declined, it is for other reasons. Respect for the law as an institutional bulwark is not, perhaps, so strong as it once was. Large immigrant groups have come from countries where their contacts were with legal systems utilized by the ruling class, so they felt, as tools of repression rather than as instruments of justice. Avoidance rather than use of the courts in seeking redress of grievances was for many of them a natural result of their European experience with political justice. The disappearance of a common English background, with its deep-rooted tradition of respect for the rule of law among the people as a whole, is in part, then, an explanation of the declining influence of our lower courts as a stabilizing political force.

There has been, furthermore, a decline over a century in the predominant place of the law in popular thought and activity. Lack of respect, even disrespect, for the law has grown as other pursuits, chiefly economic, have engrossed a large share of the individual's energies. His major concern has been to avoid court action in his business and other commitments made under the more general aspects of the law, as it has been for the immigrant in his contacts with personal and property law. Certainly the most lucrative segment of legal practice in private offices and even in the courts has had to do with attacks upon regulatory legislation, or with advice to clients on how to avoid its terms. New branches of the law, dealing with economic and social questions, have been developed over the past half-century in such fields as taxation, labor relations, corporate organization. As regulation has increased in intensity and widened in scope, the desire to escape its application has reached into all levels of the community. The apogee was reached in the popular response to prohibition.

This new attitude towards the rule of law is present in practically every relationship on which the popular majority has exerted its will through legislation. As regulatory legislation has increased, moreover, the judge must more and more apply economic and social rather than purely legal criteria in arriving at his decision. The law moves from its position of abstract isolation and detachment into a more debatable arena where the layman feels himself as expert as the judge. Judicial decisions increasingly affect everyday affairs and deal with questions where logic is less a guide than experience and technical knowledge.

The past century has not, however, on the whole resulted in any lowering of the respect in which the judge is held by the people. The center of interest in our national life has shifted since the *Democracy* was written. If, in individual instances, regard for particular laws has declined, deference to the rule of law in society seems hardly less pervasive. The reaction, popular as well as professional, to the Supreme Court Reorganization Bill of 1936 suggests that veneration for the law and for the courts as symbols of its rule is still deeply rooted in America. The high regard in which a Mr. Justice Holmes or a Mr. Justice Cardozo is held by the nation is evidence that the law commands the allegiance of both the majority and the minority. That the independence of the judiciary is secure, and remains a durable force making for continuity in democratic action, seems as true today as when Tocqueville emphasized its importance.

Administration

Another aspect of the American political scene to which Tocqueville devoted particular attention, and on which his observations have peculiar relevance for our own time, was that of administration. Accustomed to the Napoleonic inheritance of a highly centralized administrative system, he was struck by the absence of administration (in the French sense) in America and by the political effects of our decentralized governmental structure on democracy. The basis of his argument for the superiority of a decentralized administrative structure, from the point of view of preserving popular interest in active participation in government, is suggested in the following passages. Tocqueville's analysis is so pertinent to our time, so contemporary in its bearing on issues being debated afresh, that I give the essence of his argument as he outlined it in the first part of the *Democracy*. He returned to the issue frequently and developed the same theme, with new notes of concern over the effects of centralization on the interest of a democratic people in self-government, in the second part.

"Centralization" is a word in general and daily use, without any precise meaning being attached to it. Nevertheless, there exist two distinct kinds of centralization, which it is necessary to distinguish with accuracy.

Certain interests are common to all parts of a nation, such as the enactment of its general laws. . . . Other interests are peculiar to certain parts of the nation, such, for instance, as the business of the several townships. When the power that directs the former or general interests is concentrated in one place or in the same persons, it constitutes a centralized government. To concentrate in like manner in one place the direction of the latter or local interests, constitutes what may be termea a centralized administration. . . .

Indeed, I cannot conceive that a nation can live and prosper without a powerful centralization of government. But I am of the opinion that a centralized administration is fit only to enervate the nation in which it exists, by incessantly diminishing their local spirit. Although such an administration can bring together at a given moment, on a given point, all the disposable resources of a people, it injures the renewal of these resources. It may ensure a victory in the hour of strife, but it gradually relaxes the sinews of strength. It may help admirably the transient greatness of a man, but not the durable prosperity of a nation. . . .

The partisans of centralization . . . are wont to maintain that the government can administer the affairs of each locality better than the citizens could do it for themselves; this may be true when the central power is enlightened and the local authorities are ignorant; when it is alert and they are slow; when it is accustomed to act and they to obey. Indeed, it is evident that this double tendency must augment with the increase of centralization, and that the readiness of the one and the incapacity of the others must become more and more prominent. But I deny that it is so when the people are as enlightened, as awake to their interests, and as accustomed to reflect on them as the Americans are. I am persuaded, on the contrary, that in this case the collective strength of the citizens will always conduce more efficaciously to the public welfare than the authority of the government. . . . Whenever a central administration affects completely to supersede the persons most interested, I believe that it is either misled or desirous to mislead. . . . These are not the conditions on which the alliance of the human will is to be obtained; it must be free in its gait and responsible for its acts, or (such is the constitution of man) the citizen had rather remain a passive spectator than a dependent actor in schemes with which he is unacquainted. . . . It is not the *administrative,* but the *political* effects of the decentralization that I most admire in America.

Tocqueville's comments on the effects of centralization, only outlined here, are among the most incisive, indeed prophetic, ever written. If we apply them to the present scene, they have a ring of contemporaneity almost as clear as today's newspaper editorial or Congressional debate on "bureaucracy." Their validity as indices of present trends and future developments in American administration deserves our particular attention at a time when this has become again a major element of political debate.

The *Democracy* treats, as we have seen, of two consequences of centralized administration. The first is concerned with the relations of the different levels of government to each other, the second with the consequences of centralization on government itself. These consequences affect both the theory of the separation of powers and the extension of governmental controls into the sphere of the citizen's so-called private affairs. In each of these aspects of centralization great changes have occurred since Tocqueville wrote; the changes have only sharpened his appraisals of the underlying issues.

Intergovernmental Relations

Federal-state relations had been a major question in the Convention of 1787 and had very nearly proved a stumbling-block to a more perfect union. The driving force of Mr. Chief Justice Marshall's nationalism had, in the early years of the Republic, woven a strongly Federal pattern of doctrine and of practice out of the vague definitions of the Constitution. But the issue of Federal-state relations was not settled by the opinions of the Supreme Court. Before Tocqueville arrived in this country, Jackson had been elected President on, among other planks, the restriction of Federal powers. While here, he had observed a rising tide of states'-rights feeling, which culminated in South Carolina's Nullification Resolutions.

Nor was a final political balance of Federal-state relations struck by the Civil War. Although a formal relationship of Federal superiority was established by the victory of the North, the interstitial conflicts of competitive economic "interests" (as Madison used the term in Number 10 of *The Federalist*) have gone on ever since within the loose framework of constitutional prescriptions. They have frequently been reflected in party platforms and Congressional debates, often intensified in sectional votes on bills and even in decisions of the Supreme Court.

Since Tocqueville's day conflicts over centralization have also been extended from the field of Federal-state to those of Federal-local and state-local relations. In many states and over various issues the contest as to which level of government should regulate a particular activity has been as intense as on the higher plane of dual sovereignty. The lack of persuasive constitutional arguments available to the advocates of states' rights in their debates with the federalists has not encumbered the partisans of the extension of state as against local control. Nor have they been deterred by the fact that they have sometimes argued on opposite sides of the issue of centralization. With one breath, they have opposed Federal encroachments on the states; with the next, favored state assumption of local functions. State-local relations have, indeed, produced almost as many dynamic discords as have Federal-state relations.

Why has this political abstraction of federalism possessed so great a vitality over so long a period? What are the prospects of its continuing to be a magnet of controversy in the future? How far can the major demand on government by the people—to promote the general welfare—be satisfied within the Federal pattern?

One clue to an answer to the first question has already been suggested. The arguments have been used, on one side or the other, by those interests which had a stake in the degree and effectiveness of governmental regulation. The stakes have most frequently been economic and social changes desired by the people. Those who wished maximum freedom from regulation have been advocates of states' rights. Those who desired more, and more effective, controls of the economy and of social conditions have argued in favor of Federal powers. The century since the *Democracy* was written has been filled with issues in which the stakes have been high, the interests involved powerful—and seemingly irreconcilable. From Calhoun's ingenious elaboration of the doctrine of minority consent to the more mundane disquisitions of today, the lineaments of the interests behind the mask of the states'-rights argument have generally been apparent.

Underlying the argument, the changes in our economy have created new alignments of interests, new social forces in the nation. When the economy was predominantly local in organization and control, when markets were still hardly regional, the issue of regulation was not a paramount concern beyond the community or at most the state. As industry and commerce have become national in structure and ownership and international in their trading activities, they have pretty largely escaped the legal—and the political—control of a single state. Regulation by the states of labor relations, management mechanisms, or fiscal policies has become increasingly fictional. For those, therefore, who desired that the people, acting through government, should define standards of corporate or individual conduct, Federal control of the economy seemed the surest, perhaps the only guarantee.

This mutation in the structure of the economy has also

generated changes in social relations, in the concept of American individualism on which Tocqueville laid so much stress. An economy nation-wide in scope and control creates nation-wide repercussions on the conditions of individual security. Depressions are no longer local in scale or effect. Many people whose chance for a job is regulated by the economic cycle can no longer depend on their own resources or initiative. They can neither avoid the impacts of economic forces originating a thousand miles away nor, by their own decisions, control them. Insurance or relief against the attrition of personal security by the corporations is no longer within the fiscal capacity of local or state governments. Only the nation seems capable of meeting the psychological as well as the pecuniary need of the individual for security and status within a nation-wide economy. The differentials in the rate and degree of economic integration in the various sections of the country have only enhanced the problem of security. They have also made the responses of competing sectional interests to the doctrines of Federal authority or states' rights the more articulate and diverse.

The shift in the scale of the economy from local to national has, then, inevitably modified the natural parochialism of popular opinion. When people buy in chain stores most of the things they need—that is, products advertised nationally and manufactured by a company with plants in a dozen states—localism does not flourish. When the individual's job depends on decisions taken in distant offices and as the result of considerations that have little or no relation to the community where he lives, he does not look homeward for his security. Strong as the pull of community feeling still is, even in economic matters, the integration of our present-day economy has done much to temper if not to obliterate it. As the economy has become national in scope, so have the attitudes of the people towards its control by government.

The trend towards increasing and broadening Federal powers was noted by Tocqueville; it has continued ever since with undiminished debate upon the merits. That the issue will continue as a focus of controversy seems clear. That it will survive as long as we adhere to our traditional ideas of the efficacy of free enterprise is equally clear. The interests that seek to expand or to avoid governmental regulation of the economy will alike base their political strategy on the abstraction of federalism. Both the extent and the degree of economic and social control by government will be subjected to debate. New theories of the balance of Federal and state (or state and local) powers will be developed to meet the changing conditions of our future. So long as that future remains relatively fluid in its economic organization and social practices, the abstraction of federalism will provide a fulcrum of argument and action.

With the emergence of new and the decline of old interests, votes in state legislatures and in Congress on issues often apparently only remotely related to the abstraction itself will measure the forces on either side. Their influence will also be reflected in the character of administrative action, Federal or state. Whether it will be vigorous, efficient, and pervasive or hesitant, vacillating, and limited in operation will, more often than not, depend on the weight of the pressures on either side of the issue. The advocates of Federal power or of states' rights may carry the front-line trenches of public opinion, of legislative policy, or of administrative action. Their opponents, however, as in the past, will retire to the ultimate bulwark of judicial review, where the issue of the proper balance between nationalism and localism has been traditionally determined. The Supreme Court will almost inevitably again become the battleground of competing interests. The debate on states' rights, often a political mask for basic economic or social objectives, is as old as the Constitution itself.

There seems little likelihood, then, that the debate over Federal-state relations will decrease in range or in intensity while we maintain our free-enterprise ideas. Are any arrangements possible, within the federal pattern, to meet the people's changing concepts of the general welfare and of the proper measures for promoting it? Is the current trend towards Federal centralization of authority the proper answer?

The evolution of working formulas for integrating Federal action with that of the states (or state with local), to promote particular aspects of the general welfare, is an interesting one. Its main outlines are known. From grants-in-aid and other stimuli to state (or local) action, the Federal government, through both Congressional and administrative initiative, has developed other co-operative devices. Joint use of personnel and facilities has occurred in more than one field—for instance, in health and welfare. Rebate of Federal taxation has been utilized by Congress to induce states to develop programs of their own—for instance, in inheritance taxation and unemployment insurance. Many Federal administrative agencies have co-operated with their state and local counterparts to improve standards and to develop more adequate services—for instance, in the fields of agriculture and social security.

It might seem to one who looked only at the formalized arrangements that the problem of balancing Federal-state relations was on the way to satisfactory adjustment. It is often, however, behind the shadow of these very formulas and arrangements that the most violent conflicts over Federal power and states' rights are waged. The number of conflicts has increased as the extent and degree of Federal or state control of economic and social relations has been expanded by new popular redefinitions of the general welfare.

The scene of conflict has broadened also; to the interests that Madison described has been added a new party in interest—the administration itself. Whether in a Federal or a state office, the "bureaucrat" appears to many to have marked out for himself an almost independent role in the regulatory process. Accretion of authority is the breath of his existence, the objective of his activity. The struggle between Federal and state (or state and local) administrative agencies has, indeed, become the most critical factor in the balancing of interests within federalism. That struggle between different levels of centralized administration has taken on almost a separate significance. The reconciliation of administrative rivalries has developed into a matter of major public concern both in and out of Congress and of the state legislatures.

Legislative-Executive Relations: The Role of the Administrator

This brings us to the second aspect of Tocqueville's analysis of the dual effects of centralized administration on government itself. First, he scrutinized its results upon the working, in theory and practice, of the principle of the separation of powers. Second, he examined its tendency to expand the range of governmental control across increasingly wider areas of so-called private affairs. What changes would Tocqueville find in this trend towards centralized administration were he to observe our institutions today? How far do his comments of the 1830's apply to the conditions of the 1940's?

The most remarkable alteration in the structure and working of American government since the *Democracy* was written has been the expansion, already noted, of its administrative responsibilities and activities. When Tocqueville wrote, he found the "omnipotent majority," the power of which he emphasized so strongly, exercising its pervasive influence on both the legislature and the executive. The emergence of a "fourth power" in government administration has profoundly modified not only that omnipotence but the very relations of the legislative and executive powers.

The functional expansion of government has made it less possible for the people to exercise their influence directly on the executive. Tocqueville found that because the majority considered itself omnipotent, it allowed its appointive officials a wide discretion. The bureaucracy (if there was one then in the modern sense) was "always at work in the majority's sight," and could be "directed or reprimanded [by it] at any time."

That condition is no longer true at any level of government, from the city to the nation. As governmental functions have grown in number, they have become more autonomous in their administration, especially from the point of view of popular control. A larger personnel, a more complex organization, a necessarily greater use of techniques and procedures known to the professionally trained administrator but not to the layman, typify modern administration. The "master" majority can no longer treat the administration system as its "servant"; the relationship is rather the reverse. Omnicompetence, if it exists at all in our present-day polity, resides not in the people but in the bureaucracy.

This evolution towards administrative governance has had no less significant an influence on the relations of the legislature and the executive, again at all levels of government. Mill and Bagehot noted it respecting English government a generation after Tocqueville wrote. Bryce remarked on its beginnings in this country a half-century after the *Democracy;* thirty-five years later he treated it as a major phenomenon of modern democracies. Recent commentators on the American Presidency have without exception emphasized the steady accretion of political prestige and influence in the executive, generally at the expense of the legislature. That war enhances executive powers in a democracy is a commonplace; that administrative governance is no less a hallmark of legislative-executive relations in peacetime is less generally recognized. The reasons for this shift in the balance of power between the legislature and the executive since Tocqueville's day are to be found in the conditions that have made for increased governmental intervention in economic and social affairs.

As our economy and our society have become more integrated and intricate, the "omnipotent majority" has looked to government to provide not merely the broad policies essential, as it believed, to the promotion of the general welfare. The people also demanded that government implement the policies with effective tools for their enforcement. The people might still be able to instruct its servants, the legislators, on what the policies should be. But they could not, nor could the legislators themselves, provide the detailed blueprints for the most effective ways and means for executing the policies they desired. The very complexity of the problems that the policies were designed to resolve required the technical advice, as well as the administrative independence, and even the wide discretion, of those charged with their execution. Thus the executive with his assistants, in a widening circle of governmental responsibilities and functions, has played an increasingly indispensable role in the framing as well as the application of public policy.

The formal evidences of this change in legislative-executive relations are many. Executive control of budget-making is now virtually complete and exclusive in our local, state, and national governments. Half a century after the *Democracy* was written, Wilson observed that practical power over the purse as well as over policy lay in Congressional committees. Within the next half-century the trend towards executive control of the budget had risen to full tide. Most city charters of the strong-mayor or city-manager type placed budget-making in the hands of the executive. State constitutional changes, especially after 1910, were in the same direction. The Budget and Accounting Act of 1921 created a Bureau of the Budget, which has come directly under the jurisdiction of the President. During the past twenty years the Bureau has provided the strongest single impetus in Washington towards centralizing control in the President's office, not merely over expenditures but over all aspects of administrative activity. True, the Act of 1921 resulted in the creation by the House of Representatives of a new Committee on Appropriations, but its practical powers are limited more to the scrutiny than the determination of expenditures. The House can no longer be said, except in a purely formal sense, to initiate money bills or even fiscal policy.

Again, the executive in Washington and in half the states and in most of our larger cities has predominant influence on the selection of personnel and in its allocation to various administrative duties. In the national government alone there were, on December 31, 1943, 3,002,453 civilian public servants. The President, with his advisers, including the Civil Service Commission, forecasts the personnel needs to carry out the manifold activities with which the executive is charged by Congressional statute. He determines the requirements for special technical and professional skills essential to their efficient administration, and defines most of the rules of selection and the conditions of employment. He proposes to Congress the budgetary amounts necessary to marshal this army for the public services and directs their activities after they have been appointed. Congress must accede to his proposals, as to both finance and personnel, or run the risk of executive challenge that the very policies it has outlined cannot be effectively performed.

In the framing of general legislation, moreover, the executive exerts an expanding influence. However broad the policy, the legislature must rely on expert advice if it is to choose between alternative programs for its achievement. Congress and state and local legislatures are even more dependent on administrative experience for defining powers and procedures adequate to implement any policy. The formal separation of powers established by our constitutions is today impossible of strict application if the effective conduct of the legislative process is to be achieved. The very extension of policy-framing to the great issues of contemporary economic and social regulation gives an inevitable influence to administrative opinion and advice. The executive, fortified by the expertise of the administrative agencies, is often the initiator of policy. It is always the analyst and critic of policy while it is still in the legislative stage.

Another factor in our political evolution has enhanced the position of the executive in his relations with the legislature. Four years before he was to become President, Wilson noted the fact that the Chief Executive had become a sort of prime minister, a spokesman for the people. In the cross-currents of sectional and group interest represented in Congress, no clear or "omnipotent" majority will find expression. So the President's role is to voice the nation's will, to advance those policies on which he believes there is a popular consensus. He has, in fact, by virtue of his office, a peculiar responsibility to promote a program of legislation that will reflect the people's interest, the majority demand, irrespective of party alignments.

Without analyzing the validity of Wilson's analogy between the American Presidency and the English Premiership, it is enough to note that our "strong" Presidents have acted on the theory he suggested. They have sought to impose their program of policy on Congress, and have often succeeded. In this century the two Roosevelts and Wilson did not hesitate to accept the responsibility of leadership in the framing of legislation as well as in its execution.

The potential leadership of the President, and only to a less dramatic degree of the governor and the mayor, in the practical making of legislative policy is well established. New tools have been fashioned to and by his hand with which he can exert great influence over large areas of legislative policy and governmental action. As to finance and personnel, that influence is predominant and is not likely to decline in the future. In other fields the very expansion of economic and social regulation has made his authority in the legislative process increasingly paramount. Without formal prerogatives beyond those assigned to him in the Constitution, he can enjoy a preponderant legislative position, because he commands the activity of the administration.

The Legislature's Declining Powers

What of the other side of the balance, the legislative? As executive influence has increased, how have our legislatures sought to redress the balance? What devices have they at their command or have they invented in order to maintain at least the formal semblance of legislative supremacy in policy-making?

There is, of course, the residual power to override a Presidential veto. It provides a check, if a tenuous and uncertain one, on executive interposition in policy determinations. There is, second, the power to reduce, or to initiate, appropriations, to alter tax proposals. The budget system, as we have seen, makes this a hazardous undertaking on the part of the legislature. Without time to appraise the facts, often not easily accessible to it, on which the executive budget and tax proposals rest, the legislature is placed at a disadvantage in revising them. It must either accept them or run the risk of frustrating the administrative implementation of policies it has itself approved. About all it can hope to do is to cut here and there, wherever it thinks it will most irritate or embarrass the executive, to indicate its own dissent from his program.

There is, third, the power to approve his appointments. Here, too, the legislature acts hesitantly; the executive naturally demands and receives wide discretion in selecting his executive assistants. The range of the legislature's approving power is, moreover, constantly shrinking. As the administration grows in range and so increases in size, the number of those who make what are, in effect, policy decisions rises, and reaches into new areas of policy.

There is, finally, the legislature's power of investigation of executive and administrative activities. In recent decades this has become an increasingly effective weapon in the hands of the legislature in its struggle against executive domination. It is likely to remain a major reserve in the arsenal of legislative influence over the executive. Scrutiny of the administration provides not only a check on its tendency towards independence of legislative prescription but a guide to future legislative restrictions upon that tendency.

Despite these tools for controlling the executive and the administration, our legislatures are aware of their declining influence even in the area of their own prerogative, the framing of policy. To an increasing extent, formulas are being sought by legislators to bridge the gap between the legislative and the executive branches created by the dogma of the separation of powers. Some are purely political in motivation, designed to restore the legislature's superiority over the executive, in the name of the "omnipotent" branch of government if not of the "omnipotent majority" of the people. Others have a broader objective, to establish co-operative relationships which will ensure an effective working partnership between the two branches for sound policy-making based on the expertise of the administrative services.

A Dies, a Kerr, or a Smith Committee to investigate individual administrators or administrative practices, often by star-chamber methods, originates in the fear of Congress that some executive appointees may not conform to standards of opinion or conduct that it approves. The standards may not be enlightened; the use of the investigatory power may be irresponsible, even biased. Congress may itself insufficiently scrutinize the activities of its own agencies for executive discipline. However inept the procedure or irrelevant the result, such committees do, none the less, reflect the deep dissatisfaction of our legislatures with their present position towards all relations with the executive. Congress's inability to control the over-all activities of the administrative machine it has itself created makes it all the more eager to dominate those who manage its operations.

Similarly, a MacKellar bill to subject administrators receiving $4,500 a year or more to Senatorial confirmation is only another evidence of the same frustration. It cuts, however, somewhat closer to the heart of the problem. If administration is now the real source of policy-making influence, even of power, it is not unnatural that the Senate should desire to apply its prior scrutiny to those who are, in fact, the draftsmen of policies on which it must later pass. As the actual advisers of the executive often hold positions far below cabinet rank or that of the heads of the "independent establishments" (the regulatory boards and commissions), their political position becomes increasingly anomalous. The Senate recognizes the anomaly. Its capacity to resolve it is limited both by constitutional prescriptions and by the growth of a civil-service tradition covering posts essentially policy-making in character. The MacKellar formula may be resisted by the executive as improper; it may even prove an ineffective instrument for restoring Senatorial control of the real policy-makers. It is none the less an illustration of current legislative frustration.

There are signs of a broader perspective in Congress and in some state legislatures on the problem of co-operative legislative-executive relations. The use by Congressional committees of administrative personnel in the preparation of policy and the review of its application is one indication of an emerging understanding between Capitol Hill and the White House. Another is the development of joint meetings between these committees and particular administrative agencies, as, for instance, between the Senate Committee on Foreign Relations and the Department of State on postwar foreign policies. In the states the growth of legislative councils, and of other agencies, similar in fact if not in name, suggests that the formal gap between the legislature and the executive implicit in the separation of powers is being closed in practice.

Were Tocqueville to review these varied and often conflicting contemporary trends in legislative-executive relations, what might be some of his observations? He would note first, no doubt, the increasing centralization of both government and administration. The Federal government, chiefly under interpretations of the taxing and interstate-commerce clauses of the Constitution, has greatly expanded the range of its activities. National policies now regulate many segments of the American economy and many aspects of society undreamed of in Jackson's day as being the proper concern of government at any level. Nationalism, in the sense of uniformity of policy, has been progressively accepted by the "omnipotent majority" as the proper and most effective means for promoting the general welfare in numerous new areas of governmental action. In the perspective of a century this trend towards centralization of government appears cumulative and continuous; temporary reversals of the trend have not substantially altered its course or for long stayed its progress.

As with centralization of government, the trend towards centralization of administration has been cumulative and continuous. The brief record of this process noted here indicates that many and often conflicting formulas have been proposed for resolving the dilemma of the separation of powers. What Tocqueville prophesied about "the transient greatness of a man" as a result of the centralization of administration has since Jackson's day been more than once charged in political campaigns and debates. Whether the index of administrative centralization in America has risen over the past century is no longer debatable. Whether the formulas we have devised will be effective in avoiding the consequences of this centralization, in an increasingly integrated economic and social order, is still debatable.

Executive dictatorship is, in the sphere of action of the modern democratic state, inevitably a focal point of controversy. There is no simple or certain answer to the question of how popular control of a complex administrative system, required by the people's needs in a technological era, can be achieved.

Tocqueville's belief in the ultimate capacity of the "omnipotent majority" to govern, tempered though it was, is not without profound value for us today. His belief rested not on a conviction of the positive capacity of the majority, but on the lack of any alternative system which would so well ensure a democratic society, economy, or polity. His warning against the dangers inherent in centralization of administration is, therefore, all the more timely. Active popular participation by the people in the governmental process, by voting for their governors and by sharing in the making of policy or its implementation at the grassroots, is the only ultimate guarantee that centralization of administration will not lead finally to executive dictatorship.

Tocqueville would, perhaps, approve the specific formulas we have devised to retard the accretion of executive power. He would test them all by their conformity to the principle of popular sovereignty, despite its deficiencies as a vehicle of strong government. "It is difficult to make the people participate in the government, but it is still more difficult to supply them with experience and to inspire them with the feelings which they need in order to govern well.

I grant that the wishes of the democracy are capricious, its instruments rude, its laws imperfect. But if it were true that soon no just medium would exist between the rule of democracy and the dominion of a single man, should we not rather incline towards the former than submit voluntarily to the latter?"

Tocqueville recognized that a majority could be tyrannical as well as unstable. He expressed frequent doubts of the superiority of the majority's rule or of its decisions to those of an aristocratic or even a dictatorial government. None the less, he placed his faith in the educative value of the process of self-government rather than in the laws enacted, in "religion" and in "customs" more than in "legislation."

It would be interesting to trace many of the other political ideas in the *Democracy* from their pertinence in the 1830's to their relevance for the 1940's. Part I is full of insights and prophecies not less significant than those that have been indicated here. What of liberty of the press? Is American democracy effective in the conduct of foreign affairs? How are Indians and Negroes considered and treated in America? What are the chances of the duration of republican institutions in America? These and other questions are raised by Tocqueville; to their analysis he brings the same capacity for incisive observation, the same catholicity of outlook and of judgment. The reader will find his mind carried back to vivid panoramas of our political past and forward to new conceptions of our present and our future democratic potentialities. It is an exciting adventure in ideas to find refracted here the image of our contemporary political institutions in their earlier outlines and original patterns.

After "a more accurate examination of the subject, and five years of further meditation," Tocqueville published the second part of the *Democracy*. Here he uses his observations of American institutions as the platform for wider generalizations on human society rather than as the basis for analyzing the conditions of a particular community. His comments relate chiefly to the economic and social aspects of society, but he returns often to their political bearing, especially as to the relative merits of democratic and of aristocratic governments.

SOME OF TOCQUEVILLE'S ECONOMIC VIEWPOINTS

Among Tocqueville's observations on economic conditions in the America of the 1830's several are of unique interest. In a chapter entitled: "What Causes Almost All Americans to Follow Industrial Callings," he suggests that democracy "diverts [men] from agriculture, it encourages their taste for commerce and manufactures." He attributes this encouragement to the desire for "physical gratifications" which can be more quickly secured from industrial than from agricultural callings. He notes, however, a second desire (or "drive," we might call it), "the love of constant excitement occasioned by that pursuit." Since democracy obliterates ranks in society and throws all callings open to all men on a basis of complete equality, these universal human desires find their most frequent outlets in economic, not in political activity. Rich and poor alike are animated by the same desires. Since the rich can obtain no special place or honors in democratic politics, they find satisfaction in "the excitement occasioned by [the] pursuit" of industrial success. Since the poor do not now possess the means for satisfying their desire for "physical gratifications," they enter these callings to obtain them.

Had Tocqueville written half a century or more later than he did, his observations would have seemed an accurate reflection of nineteenth-century economic trends. Written before industry had become significant, before there were many cities, and while many of the people with whom he talked were frontiersmen or political rather than business leaders, Tocqueville's analysis was prophetic in its insight into the American character.

The next chapter deals with the question of "How an Aristocracy May be Created by Manufactures." Here Tocqueville gives an almost Marxian interpretation of industrial evolution—a decade before the *Communist Manifesto,* a quarter-century before *Das Kapital.* "The manufacturing aristocracy of our age first impoverishes and debases the men who serve it, and then abandons them to be supported by the charity of the public." His analysis of the relations of employers and workers in an industrial society is one of the most searching, even searing, ever written. The fact that it was written by one who had been himself an aristocrat, and before many of the most inhuman results of the Industrial Revolution had been exposed by public inquiry or private accusation, makes Tocqueville's clear and inexorable judgments all the more prescient.

Another of Tocqueville's most far-reaching economic insights, closely related to that just noted, concerns the relations of government and industry. "Will the administration of the country ultimately assume the management of all the manufactures which no single citizen is able to carry on? . . . And . . . will it be necessary that the head of the government should leave the helm of state to follow the plow?"

Tocqueville discussed the problem in terms of the capacity of the Americans he observed to form associations, including commercial and industrial firms, for every conceivable purpose. He thought this capacity an admirable one, but he wondered whether it would not be enervated by increasing governmental intervention in the economy. He noted that several states were already engaged in large-scale business enterprises; it was the period of canal- and railroad-building. He doubted whether government was suited to "carry on the vast multitude of lesser undertakings which the American citizen performs every day, with the assistance of the principle of association." He considered his countrymen mistaken when they thought the more "enfeebled and incompetent the citizens became, the more able and active the government ought to be rendered, in order that society at large may execute what individuals can no longer accomplish."

Tocqueville would be claimed by the "free enterprisers" of our own day. Here he justifies both the superiority of an economy animated by individual initiative rather than by government operation and the virtue of Small Business functioning through the enterprise of its owners.

As to the first question, a century of experience has vindicated Tocqueville's insight that the issue was to be a central one in Western capitalistic society. The argument over governmental intervention in the economy has not diminished; its focus has changed as the economy itself has been transformed by technology and management-organization. It is no longer merely a question of whether governmental or private enterprise is more efficient in enlisting the initiative and co-operation of individuals, although that debate has not been definitely settled by experience. It is also a problem in the balance of power between government and free enterprise in a society nationalized in outlook and motivated by forces inherent in the new factors of concentrated finance, mass production, and integrated communication facilities.

The free play of these factors in a privately organized and managed economy during the nineteenth and twentieth centuries made inevitable the recurrence of the debate—in terms very much like those which Tocqueville suggested. That he foresaw the issue a half-century before the results of free enterprise had made the struggle between government and a powerful private economy a continuing political problem is another indication of his prescience. The Agrarian Crusade, the Big Stick of Theodore Roosevelt, Progressivism, the New Freedom of Wilson, the New Deal of Franklin Roosevelt, were different expressions of the struggle. They differed only as the technological context made variant formulas of governmental control, or regulation, of the economy essential.

As to the second question, the virtue of Small Business, technological change has inexorably imposed new patterns within free enterprise. The debate is not less acute today than a century ago; the balance between small and large enterprise has greatly shifted, however, especially since the turn of the century. The forces that have transformed the American economy are well known. Technology has made mass production possible under an industrial discipline only less rigorous than a military one. The lower costs of mass production have translated the products of many industries from luxuries for the few into necessities for the many. Concentrated financial control has made possible regulation of competition and so of prices—for the benefit of producers rather than consumers—through a complex of monopoly practices. In the process, Small Business has for half a century steadily lost ground to Big Business in the basic industries, in communications, in distribution, even in some of the service trades and professions.

Were Tocqueville writing today, what would he say of

this development? What new trends would he discover in the America of the 1940's? Certainly he would find his reflections on "an aristocracy of manufactures" and its impact on American society buttressed in many ways by the evolution of business practices over a century. The struggle for power between government and private economy has in large part resulted from the shift from small to large enterprise. The survival of Jeffersonian ideas has created a vortex of opinion and policy within the economy—again around the competition between Small and Big Business. The position of the individual, whether entrepreneur or worker, in the economic pattern we have carved out of the continent has been continuously and profoundly modified by the trends that Tocqueville foresaw. The intervention of government in economic affairs, directly through its own enterprises or indirectly by regulation, has, moreover, steadily increased.

New trends seem to be emerging, trends that may mask a partial return to the earlier pattern of our economy, a reversal of the drift towards mere size as the criterion of industrial success. Contemporary panegyrics on the orthodoxy of free enterprises are less significant than the still small voices--and actions—of the pioneers of a superior economic efficiency achieved by active co-operation between management and labor.

The belief is widely held today that self-management of small enterprises within the span of a single individual's control is an economically sound pattern for American industry. Such enterprises, it is argued, can produce as efficiently as the giant corporation remotely controlled by those not in immediate touch with its myriad operations. What was twenty years ago an idea has become a reality in more than one of our largest economic complexes. In the manufacture of automobiles and electrical products and other highly integrated industries, decentralization of plant units has proceeded far enough to indicate a substantial trend towards the practical application of more independent managerial control within mass-productive industries. The small entrepreneur in the classic sense of Adam Smith's description of free enterprise is making good in the face of the competition of large-scale corporations under concentrated control.

This trend suggests that the span of effective control in management has its limits no less in the economy than in the government. If what Tocqueville said of centralized administration is true of our political system, it may well be so of our economic organization as well. The vaunted efficiency of Big Business may have already reached its marginal utility—as a fashion in ideas not less than as a universal technique of management. Its inefficiencies, known to the insiders even though they may be hidden in price schedules and balance sheets, may in the future not support its overhead costs when confronted by the active competition of the alert independent entrepreneur. If the channels of competition are kept open—a tradition deeply rooted in our experience—the validity of "association" in a "vast multitude of lesser undertakings" may again assert itself in our economy.

There are, of course, limits in both directions. If we ever base our productive initiative and effort on the promotion of the general welfare in terms of the social values Tocqueville espoused, the ultimate test of size in business will be actual efficiency. Artificial efficiency resulting from organized monopoly for the crushing of competition will not meet the test. The criterion of size alone will become irrelevant; the scale of operations will in all likelihood fall well within the present outer limits of size at either end. The scale, moreover, will vary between different types of enterprise; to be efficient, the manufacture of shoes must almost necessarily be carried on in a larger plant than is required for the making of watches.

There are also signs of a trend towards more active labor-management co-operation within our free-enterprise system. The period of exploitation of labor by management may not be over, but it is clearly no longer either profitable or condoned. Voluntary profit-sharing has not progressed beyond the experimental stage; there are some conspicuous examples of its positive effects on morale and so on efficiency in production. In more than one industry, of which the clothing industry is an outstanding example, unions are co-operating with management to improve industrial relations; both profits and stable employment at agreed wages have resulted. Incentive wages, guaranteed at minimum levels and increased on the basis of performance and profits, are in effect in a number of industries. Labor-management committees are proving in every segment of the economy that ideas about more efficient management do not all originate in the front office.

These indications of new trends within our free-enterprise economy provide some hope that the value Tocqueville saw in individual initiative will not be lost in the drift towards governmental intervention. That trend has accelerated rapidly during the twentieth century—not only here, but throughout the world. With the growth of governmental intervention in the economy has come an unparalleled increase in authoritarian politics. The influence of economic irresponsibility on the rise of political dictatorship is evidenced by the experience of the last quarter-century in many countries, although the dictatorship is veiled. The possibility that the pressure for more governmental intervention in the economy will invoke a more open tolerance of political absolutism in its application, even in this country, is considered by many today to be more than fictional.

Such regulatory measures as our labor-relations, social-security, and wages-and-hours laws reflect a rising popular demand for limiting the irresponsible operation of an integrated economy by an aristocracy of manufactures. Management's self-imposed limitations, its progressive efforts to construct a more co-operative economic order, have not been sufficiently general or well enough timed as yet to meet demand. That greater co-operation is achievable has been demonstrated many times. The test of its popular acceptance—as a working formula within our free-enterprise system—will come in the period of postwar reconstruction.

If the economic pattern of the America of the 1940's is confused, its future design cannot omit the dual threads of Tocqueville's analysis of the 1830's. An irresponsible manufacturing aristocracy must become responsible to a broader community than its own, a community that includes both workers and consumers in the active conduct of a free-enterprise system. The economy must provide sufficient incentives to enlist a maximum initiative from citizens who are not "enfeebled and incompetent" from too little opportunity to make their own pecuniary decisions. The issue between these alternatives will be determined in a future more critical for the maintenance of the nation's economic stability and for the survival of its political democracy than when Tocqueville wrote.

THE SOCIOLOGICAL INSIGHTS

From the economic aspects of Tocqueville's thought we may turn to another facet of his analysis. The second part of the *Democracy* is primarily a sociological inquiry into the implications of democracy. As has been frequently pointed out, Tocqueville is less concerned with an analytical description of American social institutions than with a search for those universal principles which govern equalitarian societies. Even the economic ideas already noted and such others as, for instance, the Principle of (Self-) Interest, the Taste for Well-Being, the Influence of Democracy on Wages, are treated primarily in terms of their bearing on society as the living expression of mutual interests among men. All other aspects of American culture that Tocqueville described—religion, science, literature and the arts, manners and morals, the position of women, the influence of the military in a democracy, among others—are related to this central objective of his search. The essence of the second part is, therefore, less a commentary on American institutions than an examination of the true foundations of a democratic social order, and of the forces that facilitate it.

Tocqueville's development of sociological principles was a pioneering intellectual enterprise. He was the first, as Salomon has pointed out, "to show the change in forms of human existence in and through the process of social development." Tocqueville charted not only new fields of inquiry but hitherto unexplored approaches to an understanding of the process. Many of his successors have developed more scientific techniques of analysis. None has provided us with more fertile insights into the conditions of social development or with a surer guide for their appraisal.

Pierson has indicated some defects in Tocqueville's methodology and the consequent limitations on the validity of his generalizations. Tocqueville proceeded logically from observation of the facts to inductive inferences from them and thence to speculative deductions of generally applicable laws of social development. These generalizations did not always, Pierson thinks, flow from the facts Tocqueville observed or the inductive inferences he drew from the facts. The facts utilized by Tocqueville were often highly selective. Numerous sources of relevant information were ignored, as, for instance, the influence of English on American institutions, the rising tide of industrialization, the impact of urbanization, even the writings of past and contemporary foreign observers of America. Thus, according to Pierson, the very factual basis of the *Democracy,* and consequently the inductive inferences from that basis, are inadequate to support the deductive generalizations of laws of social development.

The criticism is not without justification, in the perspective of a century of progress in sociological methodology and theory. Few intellectual pioneers, of whom Tocqueville assuredly was one, create full-blown a complete or permanently satisfactory procedure or a final framework of ideas. Tocqueville's careful intellectual processes marked a great advance in sociological inquiry. His thorough recording of his observations, his use of a wide variety of official and unofficial documents and memoranda, his advanced techniques of analysis (displayed also in *The Penitentiary System*), are evidence of his significant contribution to a new scientific outlook on the study of society.[89] As Salomon has indicated, Tocqueville's unique service was to combine the historical and the sociological approaches to an understanding of social evolution.

Tocqueville's primary interest in formulating general laws of democratic evolution from his American observations was to provide a guide to his European contemporaries for controlling and directing the changes in ideas and institutions he regarded as inevitable. Throughout the second part of the *Democracy,* but especially in his sociological reflections on American conditions, he referred constantly to contrasts and similarities between America and Europe. Many passages are devoted specifically to an examination of the applicability of American data and experience to the Europe of his day and particularly to France. There is, therefore, more of prophecy and generalization, less of recording and inductive analysis, here than elsewhere in

[89] For an earlier estimate of Tocqueville's methodology, see 88:366 f.

the *Democracy*. It is none the less a remarkable mirror of American society in transition from its colonial origins to its continental adventure.

The table of contents of the second part suggests Tocqueville's inclusive conception of the nature and conditions of social evolution, as well as his minute observation of items that at first sight seem incidental or even irrelevant. While he is noting the high place of women in American society and the character of our family life, he is speculating on the reasons for our flamboyant political oratory and for our many "insignificant [public] monuments." While he is analyzing the character of American education and tracing the effects of democracy on the study of the classics, the arts, and the sciences, he is exploring "the trade of literature" in America and the character of our historical writing. While he is examining the influence of democracy on religious ideas and practices and democracy's dependence for its effective functioning on a strongly religious sentiment widely held among the people, he is recording modifications of the English language in America. Even as he proceeds to his broader analyses of the nature and bases of equality in society, of the causes and course of revolutions, of the nature of democratic and aristocratic despotism, he pauses to observe many detailed aspects of the America through which he traveled so widely.

The heart of his inquiry relates to the problems posed by and resulting from social inequality and its effects on the practice of political democracy. Like Jefferson he saw clearly enough that social (and economic) inequality leads to the attrition of democratic politics. Various means of avoiding the rise or the perpetuation of inequality in society are suggested.

The chief economic basis of inequality has changed since Tocqueville wrote. He noted the absence here of a landed aristocracy similar to those in Europe; the frontier spirit, even more than the frontier itself, has until comparatively recently prevented its rise. The fact that we have, in our sharecroppers, tenant farmers, and migratory farm workers, an agrarian proletariat not so different in status and outlook from that of Europe has recently become alike a subject of literary criticism and a concern of public policy. The technological changes which have created the aristocracy of manufactures that Tocqueville foresaw have made for far greater disparities in wealth also in the field of agriculture. The results of inequalities in economic condition on the stability of democratic institutions in many other countries need no underlining here; we have not been altogether immune from the impact of inequality on our own society, agrarian as well as industrial.

Tocqueville found in relative economic equality a sound basis for promoting both stability and progress. "As wealth is subdivided and knowledge diffused, no one is entirely destitute of education or of property; the privileges and disqualifications of caste being abolished . . . the notion of advancement suggests itself to every mind, the desire to rise swells in every heart, and all men want to rise above their station." He thought that although equality would remove a fundamental cause of revolution by ensuring a reasonable security to all, it would spur the more ambitious and able members of the community to improve their economic situation. Tocqueville did not relate this idea to the results he foresaw would follow from the rise of an "aristocracy of manufactures." Nor did he offer a formula for limiting the cumulative disparity in wealth produced by the activities of business leaders, which he thought on the whole desirable because they improved the over-all efficiency of the economy. From the Agrarian Crusade to the New Deal we have been searching for solutions for the very conditions he wished to avoid by maintaining our nineteenth-century equalitarian economic pattern.

Actively revolutionary groups have not emerged here from these struggles except in isolated instances and on a lilliputian scale. The record is altogether different in many of the countries where a manufacturing aristocracy succeeded or became an accessory of a landed aristocracy. An intervening period of social equality makes possible a "stability of opinions," naturally consequent upon equality. Unless that stability becomes a rooted habit of popular thought and action, social revolution is a constant menace to stability. During the nineteenth century revolution more than once overflowed the banks of political restraint, broke the "cake of custom," among those European peoples which had never known the practical equality Tocqueville observed in America. In the twentieth century revolution has become almost endemic in character and global in extent. The search for the social security that Tocqueville thought was a concomitant of relative economic equality has created the instability he believed was the principal enemy of the permanence of democratic ideas and institutions.

He did not state his case for equality as the surest guarantee of democracy only in economic terms. He realized that men live by ideals as well as by work or from relief. He saw clearly enough the dangers of even an equalitarian materialism. "Democracy encourages a taste for physical gratification; this taste, if it becomes excessive, soon disposes men to believe all is matter only; and materialism in its turn hurries them on to these same delights; such is the fatal circle within which democratic nations are driven around." What answer to this dilemma did he offer?

Tocqueville recognized that faith is an integral element in human action and its most powerful dynamic. He commented at a number of points on the influence of religion on American society, but he was more concerned to analyze the relation between religious faith and democratic practice. "When the religion of a people is destroyed, doubt gets hold of the higher powers of the intellect and paralyzes all the others. . . . When there is no longer any principle of authority in religion any more than in politics, men are speedily frightened at the aspect of . . . unbounded independence. . . . For my own part, I doubt whether man can ever support at the same time complete religious independence and entire political freedom." Again, he notes the check to materialism that religion—not sectarianism or dogmatism—provides. "Most religions are only general, simple, and practical means of teaching men the doctrine of the immortality of the soul. That is the greatest benefit which a democratic nation derives from its belief, and hence belief is more necessary to such a people than all others. When, therefore, any[90] religion has struck its roots deep into a democracy beware that you do not disturb it; but

[90] Tocqueville was able to transcend sectarian or even Christian lines of religious demarcation. He believed strongly in the values of the Christian tradition as the basis of a democratic faith, but, speaking of Western society, "I should not hesitate to decide that the community would run less risk of being brutalized by believing that the soul of man will pass into the carcass of a hog than by believing that man is nothing at all."

rather watch it carefully, as the most precious bequest of aristocratic ages."

Have we not had ample—and tragic—evidence in our time of the validity of Tocqueville's insight into the ultimate foundation of a democratic society as religious? We can observe the recognition of this insight and its prostitution by those who deny human equality and erect Leviathan as the Baal of the masses. The techniques as well as the doctrines of the totalitarian societies are founded on worship of the State and ritualistic obeisance to the Leaders. The new religion may not be overtly materialistic; its uses, in the hands of those who repudiate equality in human or theological terms, are more frightening than even Tocqueville envisaged.

If democracy has lost something of this indispensable ingredient of its own vitality in its perhaps too easy successes, others have put on the garments of religion to cloak their anti-democratic purposes. Their success in evoking deep responses from great masses is both a warning and a challenge. Men do not live by bread alone. Democracy—in peace no less than in war—may well demand unstinted service from its citizens if it is to prove to be, as Tocqueville believed it was, the ultimate way of life for every people. It can hardly hope to command the popular loyalty requisite to this enterprise if its perspective is materialistic only. A religious view of man's reason for existence, which places him a little lower than the angels, may well be, as Tocqueville was not afraid to affirm, the one sure answer democracy has to give to totalitarian materialism.

This brief catalogue does not exhaust the wide range of Tocqueville's sociological analysis, the profound quality of his insights. His observations on two areas of paramount concern to us today deserve our thoughtful, and sober, consideration. The most immediate is his appraisal of the capacity of a democratic people to wage war, and of the relations between the military and the civilian hierarchy. His discussion of these questions has the clear ring of contemporaneity. As to the first, his incisive estimate of the inherent nature of problems seems almost a summary of our experience in the intervening century rather than a forecast of the ability of a democratic people to stick together and to fight. As to the second, the warnings he sounded on the effects of military influence on civilian life and public policy are not without relevance for the future. Here, too, our experience has validated much of Tocqueville's prophetic insight. If many of the details he portrayed are incorrect, the broad outlines he traced can be discovered in the record of a century.

The other area of contemporary concern which Tocqueville analyzed is that of race relations. What he had to say a hundred years ago about the psychological and the material factors implicit in these relations is as pertinent as when he wrote. Here again the specific data which he analyzed and the particular influences that he drew from them are no longer exact. But the broader implications he presented of the problems we confront in making democracy effective in the relations of the races in our great society are as profoundly true today as they were a century ago.

The *Democracy* stands as a challenge to the peoples of the democratic nations as they confront the reconstruction of their own societies and the construction of a stable world order. When Tocqueville was writing, the likelihood of the spread of democratic ideas and institutions in Europe must have seemed to him a doubtful one. Their adoption as a world-wide goal by all the peoples who have dreamed his dream and are today striving to effectuate it would have seemed almost illusory. Most of the hazards he foresaw; none of the risks appalled him. Like Tocqueville we have set our hands to a task not easy or quick of accomplishment. Like him we cannot be assured of the outcome before the trial.

If we succeed, it will be because, like him, we hold an unshakable faith in the ultimate worth of men as men. That faith imposes obligations more complex and subtle than were those of a century ago. We have in our hands, however, more effective instruments for undertaking those obligations if we will but use them. Tocqueville offers us not merely a challenge to undertake them. He provides us also with a principle of action for our continuing effort to discharge them:

> The first of the duties that are at this time imposed upon those who direct our affairs is to educate democracy; to reawaken, if possible, its religious beliefs; to purify its morals; to mold its actions; to substitute a knowledge of statecraft for its inexperience, and an awareness of its true interest for its blind instincts;

to adapt its government to time and place, and to modify it according to men and to conditions. A new science of politics is needed for a new world.

QUEENS COLLEGE
FLUSHING, NEW YORK
July 29, 1944

Phillips Bradley

Appendix III

A NOTE ON THIS EDITION

A few further notes on the preparation of this edition may be useful to the reader interested in tracing the evolution of the English text and the record of the various editions of *Democracy in America.* The first translation, by Henry Reeve,[1] has remained the only translation made in England. It was utilized in all American editions until the appearance of the retranslation by Francis Bowen[2] in 1862. The Reeve translation was reprinted in England in the same year; no substantial changes in the earlier translation were apparently made.

The first American editor, utilizing the Reeve text, was John C. Spencer.[3] His preface and notes to the first American edition were reprinted many times. Many abbreviated versions of the *Democracy,* published for use in schools, appeared from the 1840's on. After Bowen's retranslation appeared, both the Reeve and the Bowen texts were reprinted in this country.

A new edition of the Bowen text appeared in 1898, with a

[1] Henry Reeve (September 9, 1813–October 21, 1895), author, editor, public official. Appointed Clerk of the Judicial Committee of the Privy Council in 1837; Registrar in 1847; retired in 1887. Contributor to the *British and Foreign Quarterly Review* in 1836, *The Times* in 1840. Became editor of the *Edinburgh Review* in 1855. 16 *D. N. B.* 849. See also J. K. Laughton: *Memoirs of the Life and Correspondence of Henry Reeve* (2 vols., London, Macmillan, 1898).

[2] Francis Bowen (September 8, 1811–January 21, 1890), scholar and writer. Noted for independence in intellectual ideas and politics. Taught at Phillips Exeter Academy. Appointed Alvord Professor of Natural Religion, Moral Philosophy, and Civil Polity in Harvard University in 1853, a chair which he held for thirty-six years. 2 *D. A. B.* 503.

[3] John C. Spencer (January 8, 1788–May 17, 1855), lawyer, legislator, Cabinet officer. Served as District Attorney and Assistant Attorney General for five western counties of New York State in 1817. Served also in New York State Assembly and Senate. Appointed by President Tyler as Secretary of War in 1841, and as Secretary of the Treasury in 1843. 17 *D. A. B.* 449.

significant introduction and notes on Tocqueville's life by Daniel C. Gilman.[4] The following year the Reeve text was reprinted with brief introductory notes by J. J. Ingalls[5] and J. T. Morgan.[6] This edition appeared several times during the next decade. In 1904 an edition of the Reeve text appeared with a new introduction by John Bigelow.[7]

Bowen's object in retranslating large parts of the Reeve text was set forth in his Editor's Preface. The significant parts of his preface, indicating his reasons for retranslating the Reeve text and presenting some examples of his changes, follows.

In accepting an invitation to become the editor of this work, I supposed that it would be only necessary for me to translate the new matter that had been appended to the recent editions of the original, and to supply such brief annotations as a careful revision of the text might show to be necessary. It was intended to furnish an exact reprint of the English translation, which passed to a second edition in London, a year ago, under the respectable name of Mr. Harry Reeve. But a comparison of it with the original was hardly begun, before I found to my dismay that this translation was utterly inadequate and untrustworthy. As a pretty thorough exposure of its demerits has recently been made in an English periodical, where there can be no suspicion of an unfavorable bias, I can have no scruple in speaking of it as it deserves. It is generally feeble, inelegant, and verbose, and too often obscure and incorrect. On comparing every line of it with the original, the alterations which were found to be necessary were so numerous and sweeping, that perhaps the present edition, of the first volume at least, might more fitly be called a new translation than an

[4] Daniel C. Gilman (July 6, 1831–October 13, 1908), author and university president. Assisted in making the Sheffield Scientific School one of the first institutions in the country to receive Federal funds under the Morrill Act. Appointed President of Johns Hopkins University in 1875; also President of the American Political Science Association and of the National Civil Service Reform League. 7 *D. A. B.* 229.

[5] John J. Ingalls (December 29, 1833–August 16, 1900), legislator, U.S. Senator; Secretary of the first Kansas Senate in 1861; state Senator in 1862; U.S. Senator in 1873–91. Noted as an orator. 9 *D. A. B.* 462.

[6] John T. Morgan (June 20, 1824–June 11, 1907), U.S. Senator from Alabama, 1876–1907. A strong advocate of states' rights, who often supported Republican policies. 13 *D. A. B.* 180.

[7] John Bigelow (November 25, 1817–December 19, 1911), editor, diplomatist, author. Owned and edited the New York *Evening Post,* 1848–61, with William Cullen Bryant as partner. Served as Minister to France, 1865–6. 2 *D. A. B.* 258.

amended one. The second volume, I ought to say, is somewhat better done; as it was published several years after the appearance of the first, forming in fact a distinct work, the translator had found time to increase his familiarity with the French language, and even to make some progress in his knowledge of English.

This is plain speaking, and I feel bound to vindicate it, by offering some specimens of the translation, both in its primitive and its amended state. The following extracts are taken almost at random from the body of the book, and the original is prefixed to facilitate the labor of comparison. The citations are all from the first volume, and the references for Mr. Reeve's translation are to the second London edition, Longmans, 1862.

Des hommes sacrifient à une opinion religieuse leurs amis, leur famille et leur patrie; on peut les croire absorbés dans la poursuite de ce bien intellectuel qu'ils sont venus acheter à si haut prix. On les voit cependant rechercher d'une ardeur presque égale les richesses matérielles et les jouissances morales, le ciel dans l'autre monde, le bien-être et la liberté dans celui-ci. Sous leur main les principes politiques, les lois et les institutions humaines semblent choses malléables, qui peuvent se tourner et se combiner à volonté. Devant eux s'abaissent les barrières qui emprisonnaient le société au scin de laquelle ils sont nés; les vieilles opinions, qui depuis des siècles dirigeaient le monde, s'évanouissent; une carrière presque sans bornes, un champ sans horizon se découvre: l'esprit humain s'y précipite; il les parcourt en tous sens; mais, arrivé aux limites du monde politique, il s'arrête de lui-même; il dépose en tremblant l'usage de ses plus redoutables facultés; il abjure le doute; il renonce au besoin d'innover; il s'abstient même de soulever le voile du sanctuaire; il s'incline avec respect devant des vérités qu'il admet sans les discuter.—p. 52.

Reeve's Translation

It might be imagined that men who sacrificed their friends, their family, and their native land to a religious conviction, were absorbed in the pursuit of the intellectual advantages which they purchased at so dear a rate. The energy, however, with which they strove for the acquirement of wealth, moral enjoyment, and the comforts as well as liberties of the world, is scarcely inferior to that with which they devoted themselves to Heaven.

Political principles, and all human laws and institutions were moulded and altered at their pleasure; the barriers of the society in which they were born were broken down before them; the old principles which had governed the world for ages were no more; a path without a term, and a field without a horizon were opened to the exploring and ardent curiosity of man: but at the limits of the political world he checks his researches, he discreetly lays aside the use of his most formidable faculties, he no longer consents to doubt or to innovate, but carefully abstaining from raising the curtain of the sanctuary, he yields with submissive respect to truths which he will not discuss. —p. 33.

Revised Translation

One would think that men who had sacrificed their friends, their family, and their native land to a religious conviction would be wholly absorbed in the pursuit of the treasure which they had just purchased at so high a price. And yet we find them seeking with nearly equal zeal for material wealth and moral good,—for well-being and freedom on earth, and salvation in heaven. They moulded and altered at pleasure all political principles, and all human laws and institutions; they broke down the barriers of the society in which they were born; they disregarded the old principles which had governed the world for ages; a career without bounds, a field without a horizon, was opened before them: they precipitate themselves into it, and traverse it in every direction. But, having reached the limits of the political world, they stop of their own accord, and lay aside with awe the use of their most formidable faculties; they no longer doubt or innovate; they abstain from raising even the veil of the sanctuary, and bow with submissive respect before truths which they admit without discussion.—p. 54.

Chez les petites nations, l'œil de la société pénètre partout; l'esprit d'amélioration descend jusque dans les moindres détails: l'ambition du peuple étant fort tempéré par sa faiblesse, ses efforts et ses ressources se tournent presque entièrement vers son bien-être intérieur, et ne sont point sujets à se dissiper en vaine fumée de gloire. De plus, les facultés de chacun y étant généralement bornées, les désirs le sont également. La médiocrité des fortunes y rend les conditions à peu près égales; les mœurs y ont une allure simple et paisible. Ainsi, à tout prendre et en faisant état des divers degrés de moralité et de lumière, on rencontre ordinairement chez les petites nations plus d'aisance, de population et de tranquillité que chez les grandes.—p. 190.

Reeve's Translation

In small nations the scrutiny of society penetrates into every part, and the spirit of improvement enters into the most trifling details; as the ambition of the people is necessarily checked by its weakness, all the efforts and resources of the citizens are turned to the internal benefit of the community, and are not likely to evaporate in the fleeting breath of glory. The desires of every individual are limited, because extraordinary faculties are rarely to be met with. The gifts of an equal fortune render the various conditions of life uniform; and the manners of the inhabitants are orderly and simple. Thus, if one estimate the gradations of popular morality and enlightenment, we shall generally find that in small nations there are more persons in easy circumstances, a more numerous population, and a more tranquil state of society, than in great empires.—p. 176.

Revised Translation

In small states, the watchfulness of society penetrates into every part, and the spirit of improvement enters into the smallest details; the ambition of the people being necessarily checked by its weakness, all the efforts and resources of the citizens are turned to the internal well-being of the community, and are not likely to evaporate in the fleeting breath of glory. The powers of every individual being generally limited, his desires are proportionally small. Mediocrity of fortune makes the various conditions of life nearly equal, and the manners of the inhabitants are orderly and simple. Thus, all things considered, and allowance being made for the various degrees of morality and enlightenment, we shall generally find in small nations more ease, population, and tranquillity than in large ones.—p. 202.

On ne rencontrera jamais, quoi qu'on fasse, de véritable puissance parmi les hommes, que dans le concours libre des volontés. Or, il n'y a au monde que le patriotisme, ou la religion, qui puisse faire marcher pendant longtemps vers un même but l'universalité des citoyens.

Il ne dépend pas des lois de ranimer des croyances qui s'éteignent; mais il dépend des lois d'intéresser les hommes aux destinées de leur pays. Il dépend des lois de réveiller et de diriger cet instinct vague de la patrie qui n'abandonne jamais le cœur de l'homme, et, en le liant aux pensées, aux passions, aux habitudes de chaque jour, d'en faire un sentiment réfléchi et durable. Et qu'on ne dise point qu'il est trop tard pour le tenter; les nations ne vieillissent point de la même manière que les hommes. Chaque génération qui naît dans leur sein est comme un peuple nouveau qui vient s'offrir à la main du législateur.—pp. 113, 114.

Reeve's Translation

Whatever exertions may be made, no true power can be founded among men which does not depend upon the free union of their inclinations; and patriotism or religion are the only two motives in the world which can permanently direct the whole of a body politic to one end.

Laws cannot succeed in rekindling the ardor of an extinguished faith; but men may be interested in the fate of their country by the laws. By this influence, the vague impulse of patriotism, which never abandons the human heart, may be directed and revived; and if it be connected with the thoughts, the passions, and the daily habits of life, it may be consolidated into a durable and rational sentiment. Let it not be said that the time for the experiment is already past; for the old age of nations is not like the old age of men, and every fresh generation is a new people ready for the care of the legislator.—p. 95.

Revised Translation

Do what you may, there is no true power among men except in the free union of their will; and patriotism or religion are the only two motives in the world which can long urge all the people towards the same end.

Laws cannot rekindle an extinguished faith; but men may be interested by the laws in the fate of their country. It depends upon the laws to awaken and direct the vague impulse of patriotism, which never abandons the human heart; and if it be connected with the thoughts, the passions, and the daily habits of life, it may be consolidated into a durable and rational sentiment. Let it not be said that it is too late to make the experiment; for nations do not grow old as men do, and every fresh generation is a new people ready for the care of the legislator.—p. 118.

La commune, prise en masse et par rapport au gouvernement central, n'est qu'un individu comme un autre, auquel s'applique la théorie que je viens d'indiquer.

La liberté communale découle donc, aux États-Unis, du dogme même de la souveraineté du peuple; toutes les républiques américaines ont plus ou moins reconnu cette indépendance; mais chez les peuples de la Nouvelle-Angleterre, les circonstances en ont particulièrement favorisé le développement.

Dans cette partie de l'Union, la vie politique a pris naissance au sein même des communes; on pourrait presque dire qu'à son origine chacune d'elles était une nation indépendante. Lorsque ensuite les rois d'Angleterre réclamèrent leur part de la souveraineté, ils se bornèrent à prendre la puissance centrale. Ils laissèrent la commune dans l'état où ils la trouvèrent; maintenant les communes de la Nouvelle-Angleterre sont sujettes; mais dans le principe elles ne l'étaient point ou l'étaient à peine. Elles n'ont donc pas reçu leurs pouvoirs; ce sont elles au contraire qui semblent s'être dessaissies, en faveur de l'État, d'une portion de leur indépendance: distinction importance, et qui doit rester présente à l'esprit du lecteur.

Les communes ne sont en général soumises à l'État que quand il s'agit d'un intérêt que j'appellerai *social,* c'est à dire qu'elles partagent avec d'autres. Pour tout ce qui n'a rapport qu'à elles seules, les communes sont restées des corps indépendants; et parmi les habitants de la Nouvelle-Angleterre, il ne s'en rencontre aucun, je pense, qui reconnaisse au gouvernement de l'État le droit d'intervenir dans la direction des intérêts purement communaux.

On voit donc les communes de la Nouvelle-Angleterre vendre et acheter, attaquer et se défendre devant les tribunaux, charger leur budget ou le dégrever, sans qu'aucune autorité administrative quelconque songe à s'y opposer.

Quant aux devoirs sociaux, elles sont tenues d'y satisfaire. Ainsi, l'État a-t-il besoin d'argent, la commune n'est pas libre de lui accorder ou de lui refuser son concours. L'État veut-il ouvrir une route, la commune n'est pas maîtresse de lui fermer son territoire. Fait-il un réglement de police, la commune doit l'exécuter. Veut-il organiser l'instruction sur un plan uniforme dans toute l'étendue du pays, la commune est tenue de créer les écoles voulues par la loi.—pp. 77, 78.

Reeve's Translation

The township, taken as a whole, and in relation to the government of the country, may be looked upon as an individual to whom the theory I have just alluded to is applied. Municipal independence is therefore a natural consequence of the principle of the sovereignty of the people in the United States: all the American republics recognize it more or less; but circumstances have peculiarly favored its growth in New England.

In this part of the Union, the impulsion of political activity was given in the township; and it may almost be said that each of them originally formed an independent nation. When the kings of England asserted their supremacy, they were contented to assume the central power of the State. The townships of New England remained as they were before; and although they are now subject to the State, they were at first scarcely dependent upon it. It is important to remember that they have not been invested with privileges, but that they have, on the contrary, forfeited a portion of their independence to the State. The townships are only subordinate to the State in those interests which I shall term *social,* as they are common to all the citizens. They are independent in all that concerns themselves; and amongst the inhabitants of New England I believe that not a man is to be found who would acknowledge that the State has any right to interfere in their local interests. The towns of New England buy and sell, prosecute or are indicted, augment or diminish their rates, without the slightest opposition on the part of the administrative authority of the State.

They are bound, however, to comply with the demands of the community. If the State is in need of money, a town can neither give nor withhold the supplies. If the State projects a road, the township cannot refuse to let it cross its territory; if a police regulation is made by the State, it must be enforced by the town. A uniform system of instruction is organized all over the country, and every town is bound to establish the schools which the law ordains.—pp. 60, 61.

Revised Translation

The township, taken as a whole, and in relation to the central government, is only an individual like any other to whom the theory I have just described is applicable. Municipal independence in the United States is, therefore, a natural consequence of this very principle of the sovereignty of the people. All the American republics recognize it more or less; but circumstances have peculiarly favored its growth in New England.

In this part of the Union, political life has its origin in the townships; and it may almost be said that each of them originally formed an independent nation. When the kings of England afterwards asserted their supremacy, they were content to assume the central power of the State. They left the townships where they were before; and although they are now subject to the State, they were not at first, or were hardly so. They did not receive their powers from the central authority, but, on the contrary, they gave up a portion of their independence to the State. This is an important distinction, and one which the reader must constantly recollect. The townships are generally subordinate to the State only in those interests which I shall term *social,* as they are common to all the others. They are independent in all that concerns themselves alone; and amongst the inhabitants of New England I believe that not a man is to be found who would acknowledge that the State has any right to interfere in their town affairs. The towns of New

England buy and sell, prosecute or are indicted, augment or diminish their rates, and no administrative authority ever thinks of offering any opposition.

There are certain social duties, however, which they are bound to fulfil. If the State is in need of money, a town cannot withhold the supplies; if the State projects a road, the township cannot refuse to let it cross its territory; if a police regulation is made by the State, it must be enforced by the town; if a uniform system of public instruction is enacted, every town is bound to establish the schools which the law ordains.—pp. 80, 81.

D'une autre part, je doute fort qu'un vêtement particulier porte les hommes publics à se respecter eux-mêmes, quand ils ne sont pas naturellement disposés à le faire; car je ne saurais croire qu'ils aient plus d'égard pour leur habit que pour leur personne.

Quand je vois, parmi nous, certains magistrats brusquer les parties ou leur adresser des bons mots, lever les épaules aux moyens de la défense et sourire avec complaisance à l'énumération des charges, je voudrais qu'on essayât de leur ôter leur robe, afin de découvrir si, se trouvant vêtus comme les simples citoyens, cela ne les rapellerait pas à dignité naturelle de l'espèce humaine.

Aucun des fonctionnaires publics des États-Unis n'a de costume, mais tous reçoivent un salaire.

Ceci découle, plus naturellement encore que ce qui précède, des principes démocratiques. Une démocratie peut environner de pompe ses magistrats et les couvrir de soie et d'or sans attaquer directement le principe de son existence. De pareils privilèges sont passagers; ils tiennent à la place, et non à l'homme. Mais établir des fonctions gratuites, c'est créer une classe de fonctionnaires riches et indépendants, c'est former le noyau d'une aristocratie. Si le peuple conserve encore le droit du choix, l'exercice de ce droit a donc des bornes nécessaires.

Quand on voit une république démocratique rendre gratuites les fonctions rétribuées, je crois qu'on peut en conclure qu'elle marche vers la monarchie. Et quand une monarchie commence à rétribuer les fonctions gratuites, c'est la marque assurée qu'on s'avance vers un état despotique ou vers un état républicain.—pp. 245, 246.

Reeve's Translation

On the other hand, it is very doubtful whether a peculiar dress contributes to the respect which public characters ought to have for their own position, at least when they are not otherwise inclined to respect it. When a magistrate (and in

France such instances are not rare) indulges his trivial wit at the expense of the prisoner, or derides the predicament in which the culprit is placed, it would be well to deprive him of his robes of office, to see whether he would recall some portion of the natural dignity of mankind when he is reduced to the apparel of a private citizen.

A democracy may, however, allow a certain show of magisterial pomp, and clothe its officers in silks and gold, without seriously compromising its principles. Privileges of this kind are transitory; they belong to the place, and are distinct from the individual: but if public officers are not uniformly remunerated by the State, the public charges must be intrusted to men of opulence and independence, who constitute the basis of an aristocracy; and if the people still retains its right of election, that election can only be made from a certain class of citizens.

When a democratic republic renders offices which had formerly been remunerated, gratuitous, it may safely be believed that that state is advancing to monarchical institutions; and when a monarchy begins to remunerate such officers as had hitherto been unpaid, it is a sure sign that it is approaching towards a despotic or a republican form of government.—pp. 238, 239.

Revised Translation

On the other hand, it is very doubtful whether a peculiar dress induces public men to respect themselves, when they are not otherwise inclined to do so. When a magistrate (and in France such instances are not rare) snubs the parties before him, or indulges his wit at their expense, or shrugs his shoulders at their pleas of defence, or smiles complacently as the charges are enumerated, I should like to deprive him of his robes of office, to see whether, when he is reduced to the garb of a private citizen, he would not recall some portion of the natural dignity of mankind.

No public officer in the United States has an official costume, but every one of them receives a salary. And this, also, still more naturally than what precedes, results from democratic principles. A democracy may allow some magisterial pomp, and clothe its officers in silks and gold, without seriously compromising its principles. Privileges of this kind are transitory; they belong to the place, and not to the man: but if public officers are unpaid, a class of rich and independent public functionaries will be created, who will constitute the basis of an aristocracy; and if the people still retain their right of election, the choice can be made only from a certain class of citizens.

When a democratic republic renders gratuitous offices which had formerly been remunerated, it may safely be inferred that the state is advancing towards monarchy. And when a monarchy begins to remunerate such officers as had hitherto been unpaid, it is a sure sign that it is approaching a despotic or a republican form of government.—pp. 263, 264.

Ce qu'ils apercevaient d'abord, c'est que le conseil d'État, en France, étant un grand tribunal fixé au centre du royaume, il y avait une sorte de tyrannie à renvoyer préliminairement devant lui tous les plaignants.—p. 126.

REEVE'S TRANSLATION

They were at once led to conclude that the Conseil d'État in France was a great tribunal, established in the centre of the kingdom, which exercised a preliminary and somewhat tyrannical jurisdiction in all political causes.—p. 108.

REVISED TRANSLATION

They at once perceived that, the Council of State in France being a great tribunal established in the centre of the kingdom, it was a sort of tyranny to send all complainants before it as a preliminary step.—p. 131.

Les peuples entre eux ne sont que des individus. C'est surtout pour paraître avec avantage vis-à-vis des étrangers qu'une nation a besoin d'un gouvernement unique.—pp. 137, 138.

REEVE'S TRANSLATION

The external relations of a people may be compared to those of private individuals, and they cannot be advantageously maintained without the agency of the single head of a Government.—p. 121.

REVISED TRANSLATION

The people in themselves are only individuals; and the special reason why they need to be united under one government is, that they may appear to advantage before foreigners. —p. 144.

Il y a des gens en France qui considèrent les institutions républicaines comme l'instrument passager de leur grandeur. Ils mesurent des yeux l'espace immense qui sépare leurs vices et leurs misères de la puissance et des richesses, et ils voudraient entasser des ruines dans cet abîme pour essayer de le combler. Ceux-là sont à la liberté ce que les compagnies franches du moyen âge étaient aux rois; ils font la guerre pour leur propre compte, alors même qu'ils portent ses couleurs: la république vivra toujours assez longtemps pour les tirer de leur bassesse présente. Ce n'est pas à eux que je parle.—p. 356.

Reeve's Translation

There are persons in France who look upon republican institutions as a temporary means of power, of wealth, and distinction; men who are the *condottieri* of liberty, and who fight for their own advantage, whatever be the colors they wear: it is not to these that I address myself.—p. 364.

Revised Translation

There are persons in France who look upon republican institutions only as a means of obtaining grandeur; they measure the immense space which separates their vices and misery from power and riches, and they aim to fill up this gulf with ruins, that they may pass over it. These men are the *condottieri* of liberty, and fight for their own advantage, whatever be the colors they wear. The republic will stand long enough, they think, to draw them up out of their present degradation. It is not to these that I address myself.—p. 393.

Perhaps it is not too much to say of a work which has hitherto been before the English and American public only in such a translation as this, that it still remains to be perused by them for the first time in a form in which it can be understood and appreciated. I have bestowed a good deal of labor upon it, in the hope of aiding the circulation of a book of which it has been justly said by the highest living authority on the science of general politics, Mr. John Stuart Mill, that it is "such as Montesquieu might have written, if to his genius he had superadded good sense, and the lights which mankind have since gained from the experiences of a period in which they may be said to have lived centuries in fifty years." Especially ought it to be studied here in the United States, where no thinking man who exercises the privileges of a voter can fail to derive from it profitable information respecting the nature of the institutions under which he lives, together with friendly warnings and wise counsel to aid him in the proper discharge of his political duties. (Cambridge, August 5, 1862.) [8]

In preparing this edition, I have made some modifications in the Bowen text. Many grammatical and syntactical inaccuracies have been corrected. Bowen, moreover, followed Reeve in adopting many peculiar changes in punctuation from Tocqueville's original text. The use of the dash instead of the comma or semicolon was, for instance, almost a hobby with both translators. Finally, a great many archaisms were found, reflecting the change in usage over the past eighty years. The modifications of the Bowen text in these three respects, made for this edition, amount to more than 1,100.

Other more important textual errors have also been found. Many words and phrases in the Bowen text do not accurately reflect Tocqueville's meaning or the true quality of his style. In many passages Bowen adopted an almost slavishly literal translation without much consideration of the context. One example will illustrate the point; the verb *subsister* was everywhere translated as *subsist,* whether or not it fitted the meaning that Tocqueville sought to convey in the passage. More than 300 modifications of such words and phrases have been made in the present text.

Bowen took other and more substantial liberties with Tocqueville's style—and meaning. He altogether suppressed portions or the whole of sentences and paragraphs, especially in the footnotes and appendices. Some of these suppressions seem to reflect disagreement with Tocqueville, or omissions of references which he considered irrelevant. Further, in a few instances he placed footnote comments and references

[8] A note on the first Bowen edition appeared in 95 *North American Review* (1862) 138. The author commented on Bowen's translation (p. 163) as follows: "In closing, we are glad to announce that the American edition—we might almost say translation—of the 'Democracy in America' will shortly appear. Mr. Reeve's version is, indeed, the basis for this issue; but it needed so many corrections and improvements as to have made Professor Bowen's task hardly less arduous than a first-hand translation would have been. His fidelity and accuracy leave nothing to be desired. His notes, too, form an important and valuable feature of this edition, which bears, withal, in typography and mechanical execution, ample testimony to the liberal enterprise of the publisher." See also 91:382, 390.

in the body of the text and vice versa. In many of his translations, moreover, Bowen departed, often quite radically, from Tocqueville's thought; some of his departures amount almost to inaccuracies in presenting the true meaning of the passage.

An attempt has been made to restore the original Tocqueville text of *Democracy in America* (collated from the 13th, 14th, and 15th French editions) in all these respects. Many retranslations have been made, running from a single sentence to whole paragraphs. Where textual changes, in footnotes or appendices or where omissions from text or footnotes were made by Bowen, the original form in the 14th French edition has been restored.[9] In making the retrans-

[9] The last edition which Tocqueville himself corrected was the 12th French edition. This edition was unavailable to me; it is believed that the text of the 13th and 14th editions (Vols. I–III of the *Œuvres Complètes*) conforms to the 12th edition. Comparisons have been made with the 13th, 14th, and 15th French editions, especially as to footnotes.

A number of points of purely critical interest, primarily questions of reference, have not been exhaustively pursued here. Several may be mentioned:

(a) *toise:* a French linear measure no longer used = 1.484 meters.

(b) *lieue* (league): a French linear measure no longer in common use, but variable for different purposes, generally for land measurement = 4444.5 meters. (See 10 *Grand Dictionnaire Universel de xix*e *siècle* (ed. 1873) 500; 3 *Dictionnaire de la langue française* (ed. 1883) 305.) Tocqueville makes rough calculations in some notes, omits them in others, as to the ratio between French leagues and American miles. Some of his ratios are inaccurate. In other notes he gives references to American sources for measurements in miles or square miles and reconverts them into French leagues.

(c) *franc:* Tocqueville generally utilizes the ratio, 3 francs 64 centimes = $1. He also quotes 5.42 francs = $1.

(d) *Alleghanies:* Tocqueville uses this generic term to define what we today think of as the *Appalachians*. The latter term did not come into common use in American geographical descriptions till about 1850; it is not found on maps of the period.

Tocqueville's use of American sources is not always uniform. In some cases he translated from English to French; in others he utilized available French translations of American (or English) works. The result is often confusing (e.g., as to quotations from Jefferson). The opportunity for changes in the original texts—in translating into French and back again into English—is obviously great. Neither Reeve nor Bowen utilized

lations, an attempt has been made not only to present Tocqueville's true meaning, but to keep them in the same general style as the surrounding passages in the Bowen text. These changes amount, in the two volumes, to more than 275.

All of Reeve's, Spencer's, and Bowen's notes have been omitted from this edition. Bowen inserted later statistical data in many footnotes; these have been eliminated. Many of Bowen's notes are negatively critical of Tocqueville's opinions or judgments; Spencer's are more incisive and impartial. Most of Spencer's and some of Bowen's notes are still worth consulting for their critical as well as their contemporary interest.

A word of caution, however, should be added here. This edition is in no sense a retranslation of *Democracy in America*. The revisions here made are intended to eliminate only the most obvious difficulties in Tocqueville's meaning, as Bowen often rendered it in a partial or archaic manner, even for his own time. Many other words and phrases may well strike the reader as worthy of further refinement. I am well aware that nothing short of a complete rendering of Tocqueville's own precise and often vivid French into the language of the twentieth century can give a true sense of the relation between style and thought in this perennially creative book. It is not without regret that that task could not be undertaken for this edition. The line between the kind of emendation attempted here and a thoroughgoing retranslation had, however, to be drawn somewhere; here it has been drawn by the publisher's exigencies in making this edition available at this time. The present text reflects, therefore, no more than one individual's effort to make *Democracy in America* more comprehensible to the contemporary reader. Others may wish to rephrase passages left as Bowen

---

the original sources from which Tocqueville quoted; they retranslated into English directly from Tocqueville's text. See, however, 1 *Democracy in America* 53 (Bowen or Gilman edition) for the one example noted by Bowen of substituting an original American source for Tocqueville's French text. Several American texts omitted by Bowen in Tocqueville's appendices have been restored from their American originals. No attempt has been made to restore originals of other quotations. A list of the sources Tocqueville utilized will be found in 68:727 n.; the editions of many of these works are there noted.

translated them. Tocqueville himself can still be read in the original—with profit as well as delight.

Appendix IV contains a list of the editions of *Democracy in America* so far as they can be traced in sources available in this country. The list is suggestive of the wide interest in Tocqueville's observations and appraisals in many countries in which, in the nineteenth century, French was generally understood by what he would call the upper ranks of society. That it was then translated into a number of languages of the nations still under the yoke of authoritarian governments indicates that it was recognized as a work with a polemic as well as a literary value. That it is still available to nourish democratic ideals and practices in the minds and wills of these nations as, a century later, they are again struggling to abolish totalitarianism is a happy circumstance for our time.

Appendix IV *

EDITIONS OF *DEMOCRACY IN AMERICA* BY ALEXIS CHARLES DE TOCQUEVILLE

FRENCH (FRANCE)

De la démocratie en Amérique. Paris: Charles Gosselin; 1835. 2 v.
De la démocratie en Amérique. 2nd ed. 1835. 2 v.
De la démocratie en Amérique. 4th ed. 1836. 2 v.
De la démocratie en Amérique. 5th ed. 1836. 2 v.
De la démocratie en Amérique. 6th ed. Paris: Charles Gosselin et W. Coquebert; 1838. 2 v.
De la démocratie en Amérique. 7th ed. Paris: Charles Gosselin; 1839. 2 v.
De la démocratie en Amérique. Seconde Partie. Paris: Charles Gosselin; 1840. 2 v.
De la démocratie en Amérique. Paris: Pagnerre; 1835–40. 4 v.
De la démocratie en Amérique. 9th. ed. Paris: Charles Gosselin; 1842. 4 v.
De la démocratie en Amérique. 12th ed. Rev., cor., et augm. d'un avertissement et d'un examen comparatif de la Démocratie aux États-Unis et en Suisse. Paris: Pagnerre; 1848. 4 v. (Vols. III–IV are of the 5th edition.)
De la démocratie en Amérique. 13th ed. Rev., cor., et augm. d'un examen comparatif de la démocratie aux États-Unis et en Suisse, et d'un appendice. Paris: Pagnerre; 1850. 2 v.
De la démocratie en Amérique. 14th ed. Revue avec le plus grand soin et augmentée de la préface mise en tête des œuvres complètes. Paris: Michel Levy Fréres; 1864. 3 v. (Œuvres complètes d'Alexis de Tocqueville publiées par Madame de Tocqueville, I–III.)
De la démocratie en Amérique. 15th ed. 1868. 3 v.
De la démocratie en Amérique. 16th ed. 1874. 3 v.
De la démocratie en Amérique. 17th ed. 1888. 3 v.
De la démocratie en Amérique. 1888–1890. 4 v.
De la démocratie en Amérique. Paris: Hatier; 193–? (Classiques pour tous.)

* The following bibliography includes a list of all editions which have been found in American libraries or are traceable in European libraries through catalogues and correspondence

French (Belgium)

De la démocratie en Amérique. Bruxelles: Hauman; 1835. 2 v.
De la démocratie en Amérique. 4th ed. Bruxelles: Hauman, Cattoir et cie.; 1837. 3 v.
De la démocratie en Amérique. Bruxelles: Hauman; 1840. 3 v. Part II.
De la démocratie en Amérique. Bruxelles: Hauman, Cattoir; 1837–40. 6 v. Parts I and II. (Part I is 4th edition.)
De la démocratie en Amérique. Bruxelles: Meline, Cans et compagnie; 1840. 2 v.
De la démocratie en Amérique. Bruxelles: Meline, Cans et compagnie; 1840. 5 v.

French (United States)

De la démocratie en Amérique. Extraits. Avec une préface par Gilbert Chinard. Princeton: Princeton University Press; 1943.

Danish

Demokratiet i Amerika, efter A. T. af Hother Hage. (In: *Selskabet for Trykkefrihedens rette Brug. Gjengangeren indeholdende Bidrag til den nyeste Tids Historie*. Kjobenhavn, 1844. Pp. 141–447.)

English (Great Britain)

Democracy in America. Trans. by Henry Reeve. London: Saunders and Otley; 1835. 2 v.
Democracy in America. 2nd ed. 1836. 2 v.
Democracy in America. 3rd ed. 1838. 2 v.
Democracy in America. Part the second. Trans. by Henry Reeve. Vols. III–IV. London: Saunders and Otley; 1840. 2 v.
Democracy in America. Trans. by Henry Reeve. London: Saunders and Otley; 1835–40. 4 v.
Democracy in America. 1838–40. 4 v.
Democracy in America. Trans. by Henry Reeve. A new ed., with introductory notice by the translator. London: Longman, Green, Longman, and Roberts; 1862. 2 v.
Democracy in America. 1875. 2 v.
Democracy in America. Trans. by Henry Reeve. New ed., with a biographical notice by the trans. and a preface. London: Longmans; 1889. 2 v.

ENGLISH (UNITED STATES)

Democracy in America. Tr. by Henry Reeve, Esq. With an original preface and notes by John C. Spencer. New York: Dearborn; 1838.

Democracy in America. Tr. by Henry Reeve, Esq. With an original preface and notes by John C. Spencer. New York: Adlard and Saunders; 1838. 2 v.

Democracy in America. 2nd American ed. New York: George Adlard; 1838.

Democracy in America. 2nd American ed. 1838–40. 2 v.

Democracy in America. 3rd American ed., rev. and cor. 1839.

Democracy in America. 3rd American ed., rev. and cor. 1839. 2 v.

Democracy in America. Tr. by Henry Reeve, Esq. With an original preface and notes by John C. Spencer. New York: Langley; 1840. 2 v.

Democracy in America. Part II. Tr. by Henry Reeve, Esq. With an original preface by John C. Spencer. New York: Langley; 1840.

Democracy in America. 4th ed., rev. and cor. from the 8th Paris ed. Tr. by Henry Reeve, Esq. With an original preface and notes by John C. Spencer. New York: Langley; 1841. 2 v.

Democracy in America. Vol. I, 4th ed. Tr. by Henry Reeve. With an original preface and notes by John C. Spencer. New York: Langley; 1843.

Democracy in America. 4th ed., rev. and cor. from the 8th Paris ed. 1845.

Democracy in America [in relation to political institutions]. Tr. by Henry Reeve. Adapted for the use of schools . . . by John C. Spencer. New York: Langley; 1845. (Part I only.)

Democracy in America. 6th ed. Part II. 1845.

Democracy in America. 1847.

Democracy in America. 7th ed., rev. and cor. from the 8th Paris ed. Tr. by Henry Reeve, Esq. With an original preface and notes by John C. Spencer. New York: Walker; 1847.

Democracy in America. Tr. by Henry Reeve, Esq. With an original preface and notes by John C. Spencer. New York: Pratt, Woodford, & Co.; 1848.

The Republic of the United States of America, and Its Political Institutions reviewed and examined. Tr. by Henry Reeves [*sic*]. With an original preface and notes by John C. Spencer. New York: Walker; 1849. 2 v. in 1.

Democracy in America [in relation to political institutions]. Tr. by Henry Reeve, Esq. Adapted for the use of schools and district libraries by John C. Spencer. New York: Walker; 1850.

The Republic of the United States of America and Its Political

Institutions, Reviewed and Examined. With preface and notes by John C. Spencer. New York: Barnes; 1851. 2 v. in 1.

American Institutions and Their Influence. With notes by John C. Spencer. New York: Barnes; 1851.

The Republic of the United States of America, and Its Political Institutions, Reviewed and Examined. Tr. by Henry Reeves [*sic*], Esq. With an original preface and notes by John C. Spencer. New York: Barnes; 1854. 2 v. in 1.

American Institutions and Their Influence. With notes by John C. Spencer. New York: Barnes; 1855.

The Republic of the United States of America, and Its Political Institutions, Reviewed and Examined. Tr. by Henry Reeves [*sic*], Esq. With an original preface and notes by John C. Spencer. New York: Barnes; 1856. 2 v. in 1.

Democracy in America. Tr. by Henry Reeve, Esq. Ed., with notes, the translations revised and in great part rewritten, and the additions made to the recent Paris editions now first translated, by Francis Bowen. Cambridge: Sever and Francis; 1862. 2 v.

Democracy in America. 6th ed. Tr. by Henry Reeve. Edited with notes by Francis Bowen. Boston: Allyn; 1862.

Democracy in America. 2nd ed. Tr. by Henry Reeve, Esq. Ed., with notes, the translations revised and in great part rewritten, and the additions made to the recent Paris editions now first translated, by Francis Bowen. Cambridge: Sever and Francis; 1863. 2 v.

Democracy in America. 3rd ed. 1863. 2 v.

Democracy in America. 4th ed. 1864. 2 v.

American Institutions. 4th ed. Boston: Allyn; 1869.

American Institutions. Tr. by Henry Reeve. Edited by Francis Bowen. Boston: Sever and Francis; 1869.

American Institutions. Tr. by Henry Reeve. Revised and edited, with notes, by Francis Bowen. Boston: Sever and Francis; 1870.

Democracy in America. 5th ed. Tr. by Henry Reeve. Edited with notes, the translations revised and in great part rewritten, and the additions made to the recent Paris editions now first translated, by Francis Bowen. Boston: Allyn; 1873.

The Republic of the United States of America, and Its Political Institutions, Reviewed and Examined. With preface and notes by John Spencer. New York: Barnes; 1873.

Democracy in America. 6th ed. Tr. by Henry Reeve. Edited by Francis Bowen. Boston: Allyn; 1876.

Democracy in America. 7th ed. 1882.

The Republic of the United States of America, and Its Political Institutions, Reviewed and Examined. Tr. by Henry Reeves [*sic*]. With an original preface and notes by John C. Spencer. New York: Barnes [189–?]. 2 v. in 1.

Democracy in America. Tr. by Henry Reeve, as revised and

annotated from the author's last edition, by Francis Bowen. With an introduction by Daniel C. Gilman. New York: Century; 1898. 2 v.

Democracy in America. Tr. by Henry Reeve. With a critical biographical introduction by John Bigelow. New York: Appleton; 1899. 2 v. (World's Great Books.)

Democracy in America. Rev. ed. Tr. by Henry Reeve. With special introductions by Hon. John T. Morgan . . . and Hon. John J. Ingalls. New York: Colonial Press [*c.* 1899]. 2 v. (The World's Great Classics.)

Democracy in America. Rev. ed. Tr. by Henry Reeve. With special introductions by Hon. John T. Morgan . . . and Hon. John J. Ingalls. New York: Collier [*c.* 1900]. 2 v. (The World's Greatest Literature.)

Democracy in America. Tr. by Henry Reeve. With a critical and biographical introduction by John Bigelow. New York: Appleton; 1904. 2 v. (Library Classics.)

Democracy in America. 1904. 2 v. (Landmarks of Civilization.)

Democracy in America. New York: Appleton; 1905. 2 v. (Appleton's Classical Library.)

Democracy in America. Tr. by Henry Reeve. With introductions by Hon. J. T. Morgan and Hon. J. J. Ingalls. New York: Lamb; 1908. 2 v.

Democracy in America. Tr. by Henry Reeve. With a critical and biographical introduction by John Bigelow. New York: Appleton; 1912. 2 v.

Republic of the United States and Its Political Institutions. Tr. by Henry Reeves [*sic*]. With an original preface and notes by John C. Spencer. New York: Barnes [n. d.].

German

Über die Demokratie in Nordamerika. Aus d. Franz. Übersetzt von F. A. Rüder. Leipzig: Kummer; 1836. 2 v.

Hungarian

A demokratia Amerikában. A franczia eredetiböl fordította Fábián Gábor. Búdan; 1841–3. 4 v.

Italian

La Democrazia in America. Torino: Unione Tipografico-editrice; 1884. (Biblioteca di Scienze Politiche e Amministrative [ser. 1.], v. 12.)

La Democrazia in America. Trad. e pref. di Georgio Candeloro.

Bologna: Capelli; 1932. 3 v. (Classici del Pensiero Politico. No. 3.)

Russian

Демократія въ Америкѣ. Перевёл А. Якубовичъ. кіевъ, въ тип. Антона Гаммершмида; 1860. 4 томы.
[Transliterated: *Demokratiya v Amerike.* Pereviol A. Yakubovich, Kiev: v. tep. Antona Hammerschmidta; 1860. 4 tomi.]

Serbian

О Демократији у Америци. Прев. с франц. Настас Петровић. Награсћ из фонда Коларца. Београд, 1872.
[Transliterated: *O demokratiji u Americi.* Prev. s franc. Nastas Petrović. Nagrać iz fonda Kolarca. Beograd, 1872.]

О Демокрацији у Америци. С францускоr перевео. Настас Петровић. Београд, 1872. Свеска прва.
[Transliterated: *O demokratiji u Americi.* S francuskog preveo Nastas Petrović. Beograd, 1872. Sveska prva.]

Spanish

De la democracia en la América del Norte. Traducida de la cuarta edición por D. A. Sánchez de Bustamante. Paris: Rosa; 1836. 2 v.
De la democracia en la América del Norte. 1837. 2 v.
De la democracia en la América del Norte. Traducida al español por Leopoldo Borda. Paris: Librería de D. Vicente Salvá; 1842. 2 v.
De la democracia en América. Traducido al español por D. L. Roado Brandaris. Madrid: Monier; 1843. (Incomplete; Vol. 1 only.)
De la democracia en América, con un examen de la democracia en los Estados Unidos y en Suiza. Seguido de un estudio sobre el carácter democrático de la sociedad española por E. Chao Madrid: Trujillo; 1854.
De la democracia en América. Traducción de la 10a edición francesa. Buenos Aires, 1864.
La democracia en América. Trad. española por Carlos Cerillo Escobar. Madrid: D. Jorro; 1911. 2 v. (Biblioteca Científico-filosófica.)

Swedish

Om folkväldet i Amerika. Ofversättning. Stockholm: P. A. Norstedt & Söner; 1839–46. 6 v.

Appendix V

A BIBLIOGRAPHY OF ITEMS RELATING TO *DEMOCRACY IN AMERICA* AND ITS AUTHOR *

Books and Journals

1. Adams, H. B.: *Jared Sparks and Alexis de Tocqueville,* 16 *Johns Hopkins University Studies in Historical and Political Science,* No. 12 (Baltimore: Johns Hopkins; 1898).
2. Allen, J. H.: "Prospects of American Democracy," 57 *Christian Examiner* (September 1854) 220.
3. Allen, J. H.: "Memoirs, Letters, and Remains," 72 *Christian Examiner* (March 1863) 297.
4. Allen, W. R.: "Democracy on Trial," 74 *Christian Examiner* (March 1863) 262.
5. Ampère, J.: "Épître à de Tocqueville," 1 *Revue Parisienne* [Revue Belge de Librairie] (Nos. 1–3, 1840) 205.
6. Ampère, J.: "Alexis de Tocqueville," 47 *Le Correspondant* (1859) 312.
7. Batault, G.: "Tocqueville et la littérature américaine," 135 *Mercure de France* (1919) 248.
8. Beaumont, G. de: "Memoirs of Alexis de Tocqueville," in 97: I, xviii. See also "Préface" by Beaumont in 97: I, i, where a number of reviews of the *Democracy* and of Tocqueville's other writings, as well as a selection of obituary notices, are listed. *De la démocratie en Amérique* comprises Vols. I–III of this edition.
9. Biré, E.: "Alexis de Tocqueville," in 2 *Mémoires et souvenirs* (Paris: Retaux; 1896) 300.
10. Blanc, L.: ["*Démocratie en Amérique*"], 5 *Revue Républicaine* (May 10, 1835) 114.

* This bibliography does not represent a complete list of all items on Tocqueville. With a few exceptions, it is confined to those relating directly or indirectly to the *Democracy*. The bibliographies in Mayer (59) and Pierson (68), the most easily available in English, should also be consulted for more general references relative to Tocqueville. The first section of the bibliography contains items the authors of which could be identified. The names indicated in brackets do not so appear in the items themselves; some others, not in brackets, have been identified in other bibliographical sources, especially 68 and 96. The "anonymous section" also contains some items not hitherto recorded.

11. BLOSSEVILLE, VICOMTE DE: ["Démocratie en Amérique"], *L'Écho Français* (February 11, 1835).
12. BOH, F.: *Ein Untersuchung über des Wese der Demokratie in den Vereinigten Staaten, mit besonderer Berücksichtigung von Alexis de Tocqueville* (Rostock: Boldt; 1870).
13. BRADLEY, P.: "A Century of *Democracy in America*," 9 *Journal of Adult Education* (1937) 19.
14. BROOKS, J. C.: "Criticism in the United States," 49 *Chautauquan* (1908) 184.
15. BRYCE, J.: *The Predictions of Hamilton and Tocqueville*, 5 *Johns Hopkins University Studies in Historical and Political Science*, No. 9 (Baltimore: Johns Hopkins; 1887).
16. BRYCE, J.: "The United States Constitution as Seen in the Past"; (The *Democracy in America* of Alexis de Tocqueville), in 1 *Studies in History and Jurisprudence* (New York: Oxford; 1901) 301.
17. CALDERÓN, F. G.: "Un Libro sobre Tocqueville," in *La Herencia de Lenin* (Paris: Garnier Hermanos; 1929) 91.
18. CANOLL, T. H.: "Authorship of 'Democracy in America,'" 8 *Historical Magazine* (1864) 332.
19. CESTRE, C.: "Alexis de Tocqueville, témoin et juge de la civilisation américaine," 34 *Revue des Cours et Conferences* (1935) Nos. 1 and 2.
20. CHAMBRIEU, J. DE: *Nos Histoires, Guizot, Tocqueville, Thiers* (Paris: C. Lévy; 1888).
21. CHAMPIGNY, F. DE: ["Tocqueville"], *Revue Européenne* (April 1, 1835).
22. CHARDON, T.: "Tocqueville et Lenine," 220 (*Institut de France*) *Académie des Sciences Morales et Politiques, Comptes Rendus* (Part 2, 1929) 353.
23. CHEVRILLON, A.: "Tocqueville et l'Amérique," in *Alexis de Tocqueville et les États-Unis* (Paris: Les Éditions France-Amérique; 1936) 1. This centennial "conférence" also contains two other interesting addresses: Roz, F.: "L'Actualité de Tocqueville" (p. 25); STROWSKI, F.: "Portrait d'Alexis de Tocqueville" (p. 19).
24. CHICCHIARELLI, E.: "Note sul pensiero politico de secolo XIX; Alexis de Tocqueville," 12 *Annali de Scienze Politiche* (December 1939) 1.
25. CHINARD, G.: "Alexis de Tocqueville," 9 *French Review* (1935) 101.
26. CHINARD, G., ed.: *Sainte-Beuve, Thomas Jefferson et Tocqueville* (Princeton: Princeton; 1943).
27. CLAUSEN, H.: *Demokratie und Staat bei A. de Tocqueville* (Jena: Masch Schr.; 1923).
28. COURCELLE, F. DE, ed.: "De la démocratie américaine," *Revue des Deux Mondes* (1835).
29. DICEY, A. V.: "Alexis de Tocqueville," 20 *National Review* (1893) 771.

29A. DUDEN, G.: *Die nordamerikanische Demokratie und das v. Tocqueville'sche Werk . . .* (Bonn: E. Weber; 1837).
30. EICHTHAL, E. DE: *Alexis de Tocqueville et la démocratie liberale* (Paris: C. Lévy; 1897).
31. EVERETT, E.: "Democracy in America," 43 *North American Review* (July 1836) 178.
32. FAGUET, E.: "Alexis de Tocqueville," 12 *Revue des Deux Mondes* (February 1894) 640. Reprinted in *Politicians and Moralists of the Nineteenth Century* (London: Benn; 1928) 73.
33. FAUCHER, L.: "De la démocratie aux États-Unis," *Le Courier Français* (December 24, 1834).
33A. FAUCHER, L.: "De la démocratie en Amérique," *Le Courier Français* (January 20, 1841).
34. FENTON, H. J.: "Democracy in War According to Tocqueville," 118 *Outlook* (January 9, 1918) 39.
35. FORD, R. C., ed.: *De Tocqueville's Voyage en Amérique* (Boston: Heath; 1909).
36. FOSTER, T.: Introduction to reprint of MILL, J. S.: *Review of Democracy in America* (New York: T. Foster; 1836). See 62.
37. GEORGE, W. H.: "Montesquieu and Tocqueville and Corporative Individualism," 16 *American Political Science Review* (1922) 10.
38. GILDER, J. B.: "Personal Sketch of Tocqueville," 39 *Current Literature* (1905) 93.
39. GILMAN, D. C.: "Alexis de Tocqueville and His Book on America—Sixty Years After," 56 *Century* (1898) 703.
40. GÖRING, H.: *Tocqueville und die Demokratie* (Munich: Oldenburg; 1928).
41. GRIBBLE, F.: "The Literary Work of Tocqueville," 47 *Critic* (1905) 21.
42. GUIZOT, F.: *Discours en réponse . . . à l'académie française, January 24, 1861* (Paris: Didier; 1861).
43. [HALL, B.]: "Tocqueville on the State of America," 57 *Quarterly Review* (1836) 132.
This review has been attributed in the past to the editor of the *Quarterly Review,* J. G. Lockhart. See BRIGHTFIELD, M. F.: "Lockhart's *Quarterly* Reviewers," 59 *Publications Modern Language Association* (1944) 491, 500. See also CHINARD, G.: "Alexis de Tocqueville et le Capitaine Basil Hall," *Bulletin de l'Institut Français de Washington* (No. 15, December 1942) 9.
44. HAWKINS, R. H.: "Unpublished Letters of A. de Tocqueville" (I) 19 *Romanic Review* (1928) 195; (II) 20 ibid. (1928) 351.
45. HEILPRIN, M.: "De Tocqueville in the United States," 1 *Nation* (1865) 247.

46. JACQUES, H.: *Alexis de Tocqueville, ein Lebens und Geistesbild* (Vienna: C. Gerald's Sohn; 1876).

47. JANET, P.: "Alexis de Tocqueville et la science politique aux XIXe siècle," 34 *Revue des Deux Mondes* (1861) 101.

48. JOHNSON, A. H.: "Correspondence of Tocqueville and Reeve"; (I) 238 *Edinburgh Review* (1923) 287; (II) 239 ibid. (1924) 83.

49. JOSEPHSON, M.: "A Century after de Tocqueville," 14 *Virginia Quarterly* (1938) 579.

49A. LABORIE, DE LANZAC DE: "L'Amitié de Tocqueville et de Royer-Collard d'après une correspondance inédite," 58 *Revue des Deux Mondes* (7th period, 1930) 876.

50. LABOULAYE, E.: "Alexis de Tocqueville," *Journal des Débats* (September 30, October 4, 1859). Reprinted in *L'État et ses limites* (Paris: Charpentier; 1863) 138.

51. LACORDAIRE, J. DE: *Discours de réception . . . à l'Académie française, January 24, 1861* (Paris: Poussielque-Rusand; 1861.)

52. LASKI, H. J.: "Alexis de Tocqueville and Democracy," in HEARNSHAW, F. J. C., ed.: *The Social and Political Ideas of Some Representative Thinkers of the Victorian Age* (London: Harrap; 1935) 100.

53. LEROY, M.: "Alexis de Tocqueville," 1 *Political* (1935) 393.

54. LINGELBACH, W. E.: "American Democracy and European Interpreters," 41 *Pennsylvania Magazine of History and Biography* (1937) 1.

55. LOMÉNIE, L. DE: "Alexis de Tocqueville," 21 *Revue des Deux Mondes* (2nd period, 1859) 402. Reprinted in *Esquisses historiques et littéraires* (Paris: C. Lévy; 1879) 397.

56. LUTTEROTH, [H.]: ["Alexis de Tocqueville"], *Le Semeur* (February 25, 1835). See 97: I, vi.

57. MARCEL, R. P.: *Essai politique sur Alexis de Tocqueville* (Paris: Alcan; 1940).

58. MATHIEU, R. G.: *Les Enquêteurs français aux États-Unis, 1830–37* (Paris: H. Champion; 1934).

59. MAYER, J. P.: *Alexis de Tocqueville* (New York: Viking; 1940).

60. MICHEL, H.: "L'École démocratique," in *L'Idée de l'état* (Paris: Hachette; 1896) 317.

61. MIGNET, F. A. M.: *Notice historique sur la vie et les travaux de M. Alexis de Tocqueville* (Paris: Diderot Frères; 1866).

62. MILL, J. S.: "De Tocqueville on Democracy in America," 30 *London (and Westminster) Review* (No. 2, 1835) 85.

63. MILL, J. S.: "M. de Tocqueville on Democracy in America," 72 *Edinburgh Review* (1840) 1. Reprinted in 2 *Dissertations and Discussions* (Boston: Spencer; 1868) 79.

64. NORTON, C. E.: "Alexis de Tocqueville," 8 *Atlantic Monthly* (1861) 551.
65. OHAUS, W.: *Volk und Völker im Urteil von Alexis de Tocqueville* (Berlin: Ebering; 1938).
66. OSGOOD, S.: "Democracy in America," 29 *Christian Examiner and General Review* (September 1840) 105.
67. PALMER, R.: "Alexis de Tocqueville," 21 *The New Englander* (October 1862) 669. Reprinted at Albany, N.Y., n. p., n. d.
68. PIERSON, G. W.: *Tocqueville and Beaumont in America* (New York: Oxford; 1938).
69. PIERSON, G. W.: "Alexis de Tocqueville in New Orleans," 1 *Franco-American Review* (1936) 25.
70. PIERSON, G. W.: "On the Centenary of Tocqueville's *Democracy in America,*" 10 *Yale Library Gazette* (1935) 33.
70A. POUSSIN, G.-T.: *Considérations sur le principe démocratique qui régit l'union américaine, et de la possibilité de son application à d'autres états* (Paris: C. Gosselin; 1841).
70B. PREVOST-PARADOL, L. A.: "De Tocqueville," *Essais de politique et de littérature,* 2nd series (Paris: Lévy, 1863), 58.
71. REDIER, A.: "Tocqueville," 220 *Le Correspondant* (1905) 239.
72. REDIER, A.: *Comme disait M. de Tocqueville* (Paris: Perrin; 1925).
73. REEVE, H.: "Remains of A. de Tocqueville," 113 *Edinburgh Review* (1861) 427.
74. REEVE, H.: Preface to *Democracy in America* (Part I, any early edition, London: Sanders and Otley; 1836 . . .).
74A. REEVE, H.: "Alexis de Tocqueville," in *Royal and Republican France* (2 vols. London: Longmans, Green; 1872), II, 77.
75. RÉMUSAT, C. DE: "De l'esprit de réaction: Royer-Collard et Tocqueville," 35 *Revue des Deux Mondes* (2nd period, 1861) 777.
76. ROBINSON, W. C. "A. de Tocqueville," 32 *Catholic World* (1880) 157.
77. ROLLAND, R.: "Le Conflit de deux générations: Tocqueville et Gobineau," 3 *Europe* (1923) 68.
78. ROSSI, M.: "De la démocratie en Amérique," 23 *Revue des Deux Mondes* (4th series, 1840) 886.
79. ROZ, F.: "Cent ans après: A. de Tocqueville et la démocratie en Amérique," 28 *Revue des Deux Mondes* (8th period, 105th year, 1935) 152. See 23.
80. SAINTE-BEUVE: ["Tocqueville"], *Le Temps* (April 7, 1835). See 26.
81. SAINTE-BEUVE: "A. de Tocqueville," *Le Moniteur* (December 31, 1860; January 7, 1861).

82. SAINTE-BEUVE: "M. de Tocqueville," in *Galérie de portraits littéraires, écrivains politiques et philosophes* (Paris: Garnier Frères; 1893) 439.
83. SÈLLIERE, E.: "A. de Tocqueville et A. de Gobineau," 185 (*Institut de France*) *Académie des Sciences Morales et Politiques, Comptes Rendus* (1916) 198.
84. SALOMON, A., ed.: *A. de Tocqueville, Autorität und Freiheit: Schriften, Reden und Briefen* (Zurich: Praschau; 1935).
85. SALOMON, A.: "Tocqueville, Moralist and Sociologist," 2 *Social Research* (1935) 405.
86. SALOMON, A.: "Tocqueville's Philosophy of Freedom," 1 *Review of Politics* (1939) 400.
87. SALVANDY, N.-A. DE: ["Tocqueville"], *Journal des Débats* (March 25, May 2, December 6, 1835).
87A. SCHAPIRO, J. S.: "Alexis de Tocqueville: Pioneer of Democratic Liberalism in France," 57 *Political Science Quarterly* (1942) 545.
88. SIDGWICK, H.: "Alexis de Tocqueville," 5 *Macmillan's Magazine* (1861) 37. Reprinted in *Miscellaneous Essays and Addresses* (London: Macmillan; 1904) 361.
89. SIMPSON, M. C. M., ed.: *Correspondence and Conversations of Alexis de Tocqueville with Nassau William Senior from 1834 to 1859* (2 vols. London: King; 1872).
90. [SIMPSON, M. C. M., ed.]: *Memoirs, Letters, and Remains of Alexis de Tocqueville* (2 vols. London: Macmillan; 1861).

    This collection was issued anonymously; actually the editor of both 89 and 90 was the same person, the daughter of Nassau William Senior. See 97: I, xix, note.
91. SMITH, C. C.: "Alexis de Tocqueville," 73 *Christian Examiner* (1862) 381.
92. SMITH, L.: "Alexis de Tocqueville and Public Administration," 2 *Public Administration Review* (1942) 221.
93. SPENDER, H.: "America Now and in the Thirties: In the Steps of de Tocqueville," 110 *Fortnightly Review* (1921) 1.
94. STOKE, H. W.: "De Tocqueville's Appraisal of Democracy—Then and Now," 36 *South Atlantic Quarterly* (1937) 14.
95. [TAYLOR, S.]: "De Tocqueville and Lieber as Writers on Political Science," 30 *Princeton Review* (1858) 621.
96. TOCQUEVILLE, COMTE DE: *Souvenirs de Alexis de Tocqueville* (Paris: C. Lévy: 1893).
97. TOCQUEVILLE, MADAME DE: *Œuvres Complètes d'Alexis de Tocqueville* (9 vols. Paris: M. Lévy; 1864–7).

    The actual editor was Beaumont. See 68: Appendix C and other references therein for a full analysis of Tocqueville's writings in various editions.

98. VILLEMAIN, A.: "De la démocratie en Amérique," *Journal des Savants* (May 1, 1840) 257.
99. WHITE, P. L.: "American Manners in 1830: *Tocqueville's Letters and Diary,*" 12 *Yale Review* (n. s. 1922) 116.
100. WILSON, R. R.: "Foreign Authors in America," 12 *Bookman* (1901) 589.
101. WILSON, W.: "Bryce's *American Commonwealth,*" 4 *Political Science Quarterly* (1889) 153.
102. WOODRUFF, D.: "De Tocqueville in the United States," 182 *Dublin Review* (1928) 275.

ANONYMOUS ARTICLES

103. "Democracy in America," 12 *American Monthly Magazine* (1838) 377.
104. "Democracy in America," 1 *American Museum of Literature, Science, and the Arts* (November 1838) 385; (December 1838) 484.
105. "Democracy in America," 19 *American Quarterly Review* (1836) 124.
106. "American Institutions and Their Sequence," 8 *American Whig Review* (1851) 382.
107. "Democracy in America," 37 *Blackwood's Edinburgh Magazine* (1835) 758. (See also 40 ibid. (1836) 293.)
108. "Democracy in America," 48 *Blackwood's Edinburgh Magazine* (1840) 463.
109. "M. de Tocqueville," 61 *Blackwood's Edinburgh Magazine* (1847) 525.
110. "Alexis de Tocqueville," 2 *Boston Review* (No. 10, 1862) 32.
111. "Catholicism," 4 *Boston Quarterly Review* (July 1841) 320.
112. "De la démocratie en Amérique" (Part I), 2 *British and Foreign Review* (1836) 304.
113. "De la démocratie en Amérique" (Part II), 10 *British and Foreign Review* (1840) 541.
114. "Democracy in America," 16 *Dublin University Magazine* (1840) 544.
115. "A. de Tocqueville, Statesman and Patriot," 59 *Dublin University Magazine* (1862) 44.
116. "Democracy in America," 8 *Eclectic Review* (n. s. 4, 1840) 1.
117. "Alexis de Tocqueville in Memoriam," 47 *Eclectic Magazine* (1859) 458. (From 59 *Fraser's Magazine* 9 (1859) 610.)
118. "Posthumous Writings of Alexis de Tocqueville," 122 *Edinburgh Review* (1863) 456.

119. "De Tocqueville's Democracy in America" (Part II), 3 *Hunt's Merchant's Magazine* (1840) 443.
120. "Democracy in America," 12 *Knickerbocker Magazine* (1838) 256.
121. "Democracy in America," 14 *The Ladies Companion* (November 1840) 48.
122. "Alexis de Tocqueville—in Memoriam," 66 *Littell's Living Age* (1860) 707. (Same reprint as 117; attributed to A. V. Kirwan.)
123. "M. de Tocqueville," 69 *Littell's Living Age* (1861) 456. (Reprinted from the *National Review.*)
124. "Memoirs and Remains of de Tocqueville," 72 *Littell's Living Age* (1862) 253. Reprinted from *The Examiner.*
125. "Writings of Alexis de Tocqueville," 87 *Littell's Living Age* (1865) 337. Reprinted from 122 *Edinburgh Review* (1865) 456; see 118.
126. "Tocqueville's Democracy in America," 28 *Littell's Museum of Foreign Literature* (1836) 535. Reprinted from the *British and Foreign Review;* see 112.
127. "Democracy in America," 30 *Museum of Foreign Literature* (n. s. 2, 1836) 354. Reprinted from the *Quarterly Review.*
128. "De Tocqueville's Conversations," 15 *Nation* (1872) 350, 366.
129. "Tocqueville's Souvenirs," 56 *Nation* (1893) 270, 310.
130. "M. de Tocqueville," 12 *National Review* (1861) 275.
131. "English and French Travelers in America," 6 *New York Review* (January 1840) 142.
132. "Democracy in America" (Part II), 7 *New York Review* (July 1840) 233.
133. "Social Influence of Democracy," 9 *The New Yorker* (I) (May 23, 1840) 145; (II) (May 30, 1840) 161. (Attributed to Horace Greeley.)
134. "Democracy in America," 10 *The New Yorker* (September 26, 1840) 29.
135. "Democracy in America," 11 *The New Yorker* (May 8, 1841) 125.
136. "Considérations sur le principe démocratique qui régit l'Union Américaine (et de la possibilité de son application à d'autres états)," 52 *North American Review* (1841) 529.
137. "Noticeable Books: Tocqueville's Souvenirs," 33 *Nineteenth Century* (1893) 883.
138. "Alexis de Tocqueville," 95 *North American Review* (1862) 138.
139. "The Error of de Tocqueville," 102 *North American Review* (1866) 321.
140. "Alexis de Tocqueville," 34 *North British Review* (1861) 330.

141. "Alexis de Tocqueville," 34 *North British Review* (1861) 173. (American edition of 140.)
142. "Democracy in America," 1 *Oasis* (June 30, 1838) 168.
143. "American Institutions," 42 *Princeton Review* (n. s. 1870) 167.
144. "Alexis de Tocqueville," 110 *Quarterly Review* (1861) 517.
145. "Correspondance entre Alexis de Tocqueville et Arthur de Gobineau," 39 *Revue des Deux Mondes* (5th period, 77th year, 1907) 591; 40 ibid. (1907) 49, 522.
146. "Influence of Democracy on Society," 7 *Tait's Edinburgh Magazine* (1840) 506.
147. "European Views of American Democracy," (I) 1 *United States Magazine and Democratic Review* (1838) 91; (II) 2 ibid. (1838) 337.
148. "De Tocqueville," 21 *United States Magazine and Democratic Review* (1847) 115.

Index to Volume II

ALEXIS-HENRI-CHARLES-MAURICE CLEREL, Comte de Tocqueville (1805–59), was sent in 1831 as an assistant magistrate by the French Government on a mission to examine prisons and penitentiaries in America. On his return he wrote his classic Democracy in America, *published in 1835 and 1840, the first comprehensive study of the political and social institutions of the United States. He was elected a member of the Académie des Sciences Morales et Politiques, and sat in the Chamber of Deputies for a number of years, becoming at various times vice-president of the Assembly and Minister of Foreign Affairs.*

VINTAGE POLITICAL SCIENCE AND SOCIAL CRITICISM

V-428 ABDEL-MALEK, ANOUAR *Egypt: Military Society*
V-625 ACKLAND, LEN AND SAM BROWN *Why Are We Still in Vietnam?*
V-196 ADAMS, RICHARD N. *Social Change in Latin America Today*
V-568 ALINSKY, SAUL D. *Reveille for Radicals*
V-286 ARIES, PHILIPPE *Centuries of Childhood*
V-604 BAILYN, BERNARD *Origins of American Politics*
V-334 BALTZELL, E. DIGBY *The Protestant Establishment*
V-335 BANFIELD, E. G. AND J. Q. WILSON *City Politics*
V-674 BARBIANA, SCHOOL OF *Letter to a Teacher*
V-198 BARDOLPH, RICHARD *The Negro Vanguard*
V-60 BECKER, CARL L. *The Declaration of Independence*
V-199 BERMAN, H. J. (ed.) *Talks on American Law*
V-81 BLAUSTEIN, ARTHUR I. AND ROGER R. WOOCK (eds.) *Man Against Poverty*
V-513 BOORSTIN, DANIEL J. *The Americans: The Colonial Experience*
V-358 BOORSTIN, DANIEL J. *The Americans: The National Experience*
V-621 BOORSTIN, DANIEL J. *The Decline of Radicalism: Reflections on America Today*
V-414 BOTTOMORE, T. B. *Classes in Modern Society*
V-44 BRINTON, CRANE *The Anatomy of Revolution*
V-234 BRUNER, JEROME *The Process of Education*
V-590 BULLETIN OF ATOMIC SCIENTISTS *China after the Cultural Revolution*
V-684 CALVERT, GREG AND CAROL *The New Left and the New Capitalism*
V-30 CAMUS, ALBERT *The Rebel*
V-33 CARMICHAEL, STOKELY AND CHARLES HAMILTON *Black Power*
V-664 CARMICHAEL, STOKELY *Stokely Speaks*
V-98 CASH, W. J. *The Mind of the South*
V-272 CATER, DOUGLASS *The Fourth Branch of Government*
V-290 CATER, DOUGLASS *Power in Washington*
V-555 CHOMSKY, NOAM *American Power and the New Mandarins*
V-640 CHOMSKY, NOAM *At War With Asia*
V-538 COX COMMISSION *Crisis at Columbia*
V-311 CREMIN, LAWRENCE A. *The Genius of American Education*
V-638 DENNISON, GEORGE *The Lives of Children*
V-746 DEUTSCHER, ISAAC *The Prophet Armed*
V-747 DEUTSCHER, ISAAC *The Prophet Unarmed*
V-748 DEUTSCHER, ISAAC *The Prophet Outcast*
V-617 DEVLIN, BERNADETTE *The Price of My Soul*
V-671 DOMHOFF, G. WILLIAM *The Higher Circles*
V-603 DOUGLAS, WILLIAM O. *Points of Rebellion*
V-645 DOUGLAS, WILLIAM O. *International Dissent*
V-390 ELLUL, JACQUES *The Technological Society*
V-692 EPSTEIN, JASON *The Great Conspiracy Trial*
V-661 FALK, RICHARD A., GABRIEL KOLKO, AND ROBERT JAY LIFTON *Crimes of War: After Songmy*
V-442 FALL, BERNARD B. *Hell in a Very Small Place: The Siege of Dien Bien Phu*
V-667 FINN, JAMES *Conscience and Command*

V-413 FRANK, JEROME D. *Sanity and Survival*
V-382 FRANKLIN, JOHN HOPE AND ISIDORE STARR (eds.) *The Negro in 20th Century America*
V-368 FRIEDENBERG, EDGAR Z. *Coming of Age in America*
V-662 FRIEDMAN, EDWARD AND MARK SELDEN (eds.) *America's Asia: Dissenting Essays in Asian Studies*
V-378 FULBRIGHT, J. WILLIAM *The Arrogance of Power*
V-688 FULBRIGHT, J. WILLIAM *The Pentagon Propaganda Machine*
V-475 GAY, PETER *The Enlightenment: The Rise of Modern Paganism*
V-668 GERASSI, JOHN *Revolutionary Priest: The Complete Writings and Messages of Camillo Torres*
V-657 GETTLEMAN, MARVIN E. AND DAVID MERMELSTEIN (eds.) *The Failure of American Liberalism*
V-451 GETTLEMAN, MARVIN E. AND SUSAN, AND LAWRENCE AND CAROL KAPLAN *Conflict in Indochina: A Reader on the Widening War in Laos and Cambodia*
V-174 GOODMAN, PAUL AND PERCIVAL *Communitas*
V-325 GOODMAN, PAUL *Compulsory Mis-education and The Community of Scholars*
V-32 GOODMAN, PAUL *Growing Up Absurd*
V-417 GOODMAN, PAUL *People or Personnel* and *Like a Conquered Province*
V-606 GORO, HERB *The Block*
V-633 GREEN, PHILIP AND SANFORD LEVINSON (eds.) *Power and Community: Dissenting Essays in Political Science*
V-457 GREENE, FELIX *The Enemy: Some Notes on the Nature of Contemporary Imperialism*
V-618 GREENSTONE, J. DAVID *Labor in American Politics*
V-430 GUEVERA, CHE *Guerrilla Warfare*
V-685 HAMSIK, DUSAN *Writers Against Rulers*
V-427 HAYDEN, TOM *Rebellion in Newark*
V-453 HEALTH PAC *The American Health Empire*
V-635 HEILBRONER, ROBERT L. *Between Capitalism and Socialism*
V-450 HERSH, SEYMOUR M. *My Lai 4*
V-283 HENRY, JULES *Culture Against Man*
V-644 HESS, KARL AND THOMAS REEVES *The End of the Draft*
V-465 HINTON, WILLIAM *Fanshen: A Documentary of Revolution in a Chinese Village*
V-576 HOFFMAN, ABBIE *Woodstock Nation*
V-95 HOFSTADTER, RICHARD *The Age of Reform: From Bryan to F.D.R.*
V-9 HOFSTADTER, RICHARD *The American Political Tradition*
V-317 HOFSTADTER, RICHARD *Anti-Intellectualism in American Life*
V-385 HOFSTADTER, RICHARD *Paranoid Style in American Politics and other Essays*
V-686 HOFSTADTER, RICHARD AND MICHAEL WALLACE (eds.) *American Violence, A Documentary History*
V-429 HOROWITZ, DE CASTRO, AND GERASSI (eds.) *Latin American Radicalism*
V-666 HOWE, LOUISE KAPP (ed.) *The White Majority: Between Poverty and Affluence*
V-630 HOROWITZ, DAVID *Empire and Revolution*
V-201 HUGHES, H. STUART *Consciousness and Society*
V-241 JACOBS, JANE *Death & Life of Great American Cities*
V-584 JACOBS, JANE *The Economy of Cities*
V-433 JACOBS, PAUL *Prelude to Riot*

V-332 JACOBS, PAUL AND SAUL LANDAU (eds.) *The New Radicals*
V-459 JACOBS, PAUL AND SAUL LANDAU, WITH EVE PELL *To Serve the Devil: Natives & Slaves,* Vol. I
V-460 JACOBS, PAUL AND SAUL LANDAU, WITH EVE PELL *To Serve the Devil: Colonials & Sojourners,* Volume II
V-456 JONES, ITA *The Grubbag*
V-369 KAUFMANN, WALTER (trans.) *The Birth of Tragedy* and *The Case of Wagner*
V-401 KAUFMANN, WALTER (trans.) *On the Genealogy of Morals* and *Ecce Homo*
V-337 KAUFMANN, WALTER (trans.) *Beyond Good and Evil*
V-582 KIRSHBAUM, LAURENCE AND ROGER RAPOPORT *Is the Library Burning?*
V-631 KOLKO, GABRIEL *Politics of War*
V-361 KOMAROVSKY, MIRRA *Blue-Collar Marriage*
V-675 KOVEL, JOEL *White Racism*
V-215 LACOUTURE, JEAN *Ho Chi Minh*
V-367 LASCH, CHRISTOPHER *The New Radicalism in America*
V-560 LASCH, CHRISTOPHER *The Agony of the American Left*
V-280 LEWIS, OSCAR *The Children of Sánchez*
V-421 LEWIS, OSCAR *La Vida*
V-634 LEWIS, OSCAR *A Death in the Sánchez Family*
V-637 LIBARLE, MARC AND TOM SELIGSON (eds.) *The High School Revolutionaries*
V-474 LIFTON, ROBERT JAY *Revolutionary Immortality*
V-384 LINDESMITH, ALFRED *The Addict and The Law*
V-533 LOCKWOOD, LEE *Castro's Cuba, Cuba's Fidel*
V-469 LOWE, JEANNE R. *Cities in a Race with Time*
V-659 LURIE, ELLEN *How to Change the Schools*
V-193 MALRAUX, ANDRE *Temptation of the West*
V-480 MARCUSE, HERBERT *Soviet Marxism*
V-502 MATTHEWS, DONALD R. *U. S. Senators and Their World*
V-577 MAYER, ARNO J. *Political Origins of the New Diplomacy, 1917-1918*
V-575 MCCARTHY, RICHARD D. *The Ultimate Folly*
V-619 MCCONNELL, GRANT *Private Power and American Democracy*
V-386 MCPHERSON, JAMES *The Negro's Civil War*
V-615 MITFORD, JESSICA *The Trial of Dr. Spock*
V-539 MORGAN, ROBIN (ed.) *Sisterhood Is Powerful*
V-274 MYRDAL, GUNNAR *Challenge to Affluence*
V-573 MYRDAL, GUNNAR *An Approach to the Asian Drama*
V-687 NEVILE, RICHARD *Play Power*
V-377 NIETZSCHE, FRIEDRICH *Beyond Good and Evil*
V-369 NIETZSCHE, FRIEDRICH *The Birth of Tragedy* and *The Case of Wagner*
V-401 NIETZSCHE, FRIEDRICH *On the Genealogy of Morals* and *Ecce Homo*
V-642 O'GORMAN, NED *Prophetic Voices*
V-583 ORTIZ, FERNANDO *Cuban Counterpoint: Tobacco and Sugar*
V-128 PLATO *The Republic*
V-648 RADOSH, RONALD *American Labor and U.S. Foreign Policy*
V-309 RASKIN, MARCUS AND BERNARD FALL (eds.) *The Viet-nam Reader*
V-719 REED, JOHN *Ten Days That Shook the World*
V-644 REEVES, THOMAS AND KARL HESS *The End of the Draft*

V-192 REISCHAUER, EDWIN O. *Beyond Vietnam: The United States and Asia*
V-548 RESTON, JAMES *Sketches in the Sand*
V-622 ROAZEN, PAUL *Freud: Political and Social Thought*
V-534 ROGERS, DAVID *110 Livingston Street*
V-559 ROSE, TOM (ed.) *Violence in America*
V-212 ROSSITER, CLINTON *Conservatism in America*
V-472 ROSZAK, THEODORE (ed.) *The Dissenting Academy*
V-431 SCHELL, JONATHAN *The Village of Ben Suc*
V-375 SCHURMANN, F. AND O. SCHELL (eds.) *The China Reader: Imperial China, I*
V-376 SCHURMANN, F. AND O. SCHELL (eds.) *The China Reader: Republican China, II*
V-377 SCHURMANN, F. AND O. SCHELL (eds.) *The China Reader: Communist China, III*
V-649 SEALE, BOBBY *Seize the Time*
V-279 SILBERMAN, CHARLES E. *Crisis in Black and White*
V-681 SNOW, EDGAR *Red China Today*
V-222 SPENDER, STEPHEN *The Year of the Young Rebels*
V-388 STAMPP, KENNETH *The Era of Reconstruction 1865-1877*
V-253 STAMPP, KENNETH *The Peculiar Institution*
V-613 STERNGLASS, ERNEST J. *The Stillborn Future*
V-439 STONE, I. F. *In a Time of Torment*
V-231 TANNENBAUM, FRANK *Slave & Citizen: The Negro in the Americas*
V-312 TANNENBAUM, FRANK *Ten Keys to Latin America*
V-686 WALLACE, MICHAEL AND RICHARD HOFSTADTER (eds.) *American Violence: A Documentary History*
V-206 WALLERSTEIN, IMMANUEL *Africa: The Politics of Independence*
V-543 WALLERSTEIN, IMMANUEL *Africa: The Politics of Unity*
V-454 WALLERSTEIN, IMMANUEL AND PAUL STARR (eds.) *The University Crisis Reader: The Liberal University Under Attack,* Vol. I
V-455 WALLERSTEIN, IMMANUAL AND PAUL STARR (eds.) *The University Crisis Reader: Confrontation and Counterattack,* Vol. II
V-323 WARREN, ROBERT PENN *Who Speaks for the Negro?*
V-405 WASSERMAN AND SWITZER *The Random House Guide to Graduate Study in the Arts and Sciences*
V-249 WIEDNER, DONALD L. *A History of Africa: South of the Sahara*
V-557 WEINSTEIN, JAMES *Decline of Socialism in America 1912-1925*
V-585 WEINSTEIN, JAMES AND DAVID EAKINS (eds.) *For a New America*
V-605 WILLIAMS, JOHN A. AND CHARLES HARRIS (eds.) *Amistad 1*
V-660 WILLIAMS, JOHN A. AND CHARLES HARRIS (eds.) *Amistad 2*
V-651 WILLIAMS, WILLIAM APPLEMAN *The Roots of the Modern American Empire*
V-545 WOOLF., S. J. (ed.) *The Nature of Fascism*
V-495 YGLESIAS, JOSE *In the Fist of the Revolution*
V-483 ZINN, HOWARD *Disobedience and Democracy*